PATTERNS OF POWER

PATTERNS
OF POWER

RELIGION AND POLITICS
IN AMERICAN CULTURE

David Chidester

Prentice Hall, Englewood Cliffs, New Jersey 07632

LIBRARY OF CONGRESS
Library of Congress Cataloging-in-Publication Data

Chidester, David.
    Patterns of power : religion and politics in American culture /
David Chidester.
        p.   cm.
    Includes index.
    ISBN 0-13-654005-8 : $17.00
    1. Religion and politics--United States. 2. United States-
-Religion.   I. Title.
BL2525.C46 1988
322'.1'0973--dc19   87-27135
                                                                     CIP

Editorial/production supervision: Cyndy Lyle Rymer
Cover design: Allen Moore + Associates
Manufacturing buyer: Margaret Rizzi

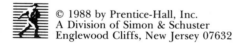
Printed in the United States of America

10 9 8 7 6 5 4 3 2 1

ISBN 0-13-654005-8 01

Prentice-Hall International (UK) Limited, *London*
Prentice-Hall of Australia Pty. Limited, *Sydney*
Prentice-Hall Canada Inc., *Toronto*
Prentice-Hall Hispanoamericana, S.A., *Mexico*
Prentice-Hall of India Private Limited, *New Delhi*
Prentice-Hall of Japan, Inc., *Tokyo*
Simon & Schuster Asia Pte. Ltd., *Singapore*
Editora Prentice-Hall do Brasil, Ltda., *Rio de Janeiro*

CONTENTS

v

PREFACE

I wrote this book while outside the United States, looking back and trying to make sense out of the American historical experience in conversation with people who had very different histories. The book emerged out of three years of graduate seminars involving students of different races, religious backgrounds, and political commitments. In those seminars, we tried to identify crucial religious and political issues in an unfamiliar American history and a foreign American society for purposes of comparison with the history and society of another place. That place was South Africa.

As I write this preface, the police are off the campus, the teargas has cleared, but things are not back to normal. Things were not normal to begin with. While protesting government action to break a transit worker strike, demonstrating against another attack on alleged terrorist bases in a neighboring country, and marching against the May 1987 whites-only election, students at the University of Cape Town campus were attacked and dispersed by police with whips, birdshot, and teargas. Just outside of the fifth floor window of the Religious Studies department office, police lined up in battle formation to fire rounds of teargas cannisters into the building. They looked mean, angry, vengeful, intending to teach protesting students a lesson. The next day the incident was reported in the *Cape Times*:

> Large parts of the University of Cape Town campus were at times uninhabitable yesterday afternoon and some lectures were disrupted as a result of actions by certain people which may not be reported in terms of state-of-emergency press censorship . . . . Sections of the campus became uninhabitable due to the spread of a chemical substance and the students retreated.[1]

With colleagues and students I also retreated. After a weekend interval the police returned to reassert their authority. Again, students were arrested, beaten, and dispersed as teargas filled the campus. Even the proverbial innocent bystander, such as myself, could experience what it was like to be fired upon by police as their teargas projectiles whizzed passed my head or landed at my feet. After closing for a day, the university returned to a kind of calm, but it was a tense calmness. Education proceeded in a state of siege.

Working in a university under siege certainly intensified questions about the role of academic institutions, disciplines, teaching, and research in their larger political environment. For a student of religion these questions required a re-examination of the linkages among religion, religious studies, and politics. I was compelled to refocus my academic attention away from a preoccupation with the *meaning* of religious studies categories—religion, symbol, myth, ritual, and tradition—toward their *power*. Religion, religions, and the academic analysis of religion and religions are necessarily implicated in the ceremonies of power in the network of social relations within which they operate. The violent repression of political protest at a university campus was merely a minor incident in the ongoing ceremonies of power in South African society. Political power has been controlled since 1948 by a white minority government committed to racial separation, military domination, and the political exclusion of the vast majority of the people of South Africa. Popular black political movements have been banned and exiled since 1960. Popular black nationalist leaders have been banned, detained without trial, or imprisoned for decades on charges of treason to a state that never even recognized them as citizens. The majority of the population has been excluded from full, equal participation in the South African ceremonies of power. Denial of civil rights to full participation in the ceremonies of power has denied the protection of human rights, such as those rights to life, liberty, and the pursuit of happiness enshrined in the American Declaration of Independence, and thereby has denied recognition of the full humanity of those excluded. In the face of that denial, alternative strategies for recovering the humanity of the excluded have been mobilized. But South Africa is a place, recalling the aphorism of John F. Kennedy, where violent revolution seems inevitable when peaceful revolution is made impossible. In that violent, highly charged context, everything, especially religion, has been immediately, unavoidably politicized.

Religion has been inextricably linked with both conquest and resistance, with repression and revolution, with empowerment, disempowerment, and reempowerment in the power struggles that have shaped South African history and society.[2] Religion has permeated politics. Religious and political power have been interwoven in many different ways—in the power of contending religiopolitical systems; in the power of civil religious ideologies; in the importance of land as a religious and political symbol; in the relations among religion, human rights, and civil rights; in the encounters with otherness, difference, and the potential for a dynamic pluralism in the public arena; in the relations between religion and military or revolutionary violence; in the agonies of a religious conscience when confronted with the demands of a military service it cannot morally support; in the tenuous freedom of religious belief, practice, and association; and in the various entanglements of religion with the state and the state with religion and religious institutions. All of these interpenetrations of religion and politics have appeared with a specific urgency in South African history and society. But they can also be located within the patterns of power that have animated American history and American society. The central purpose of this book, therefore, is to draw together the historical resources that would allow these issues to appear in as clear an outline as possible by means of a reconaissance of American religion and politics.

Comparative work in American and South African religion and politics allowed me to encounter the otherness of a different society in terms of religious and political categories that were familiar to me as an American. But it also provided a particular vantage point for reflecting back on the American experience in a new, strange, and unfamiliar light. This work became not only an exercise in comparison, but, for me, a work of recovery. It required a fresh engagement with the patterns of power in American society that have been simultaneously religious and political, and an attempt to recover the historical threads out of which those patterns have been woven in American religious and political life. I do not claim to have uncovered anything new in all this, but perhaps to have looked at some familiar facets of America in new ways. I have tried to recollect the historical, social, and ultimately symbolic dimensions of religious and political power in America in order to provide once again another point of departure for reflecting on those patterns of power. That reflection certainly may be critical, but it also may be profoundly appreciative of the potential for positive self-realization—as individuals, as communities, and as a nation—that is held by the particular distributions of religious and political power in America. The chapters that follow recall the historical grounds for both criticism and appreciation. But I also hope they will serve as mirrors for a certain self-recognition. This book recollects the basic patterns of American religious and political power in the hope that it might provide another opportunity for that often difficult recognition. These are the patterns of power within which Americans have appeared as Americans.

Both religion and politics are about being human and about the empowerment of human beings in society. Religion has been defined for purposes of analysis in two basic ways—as a particular type of cultural institution or as a particular type of cultural system. Religion has been defined as a cultural institution that deals with supernatural beings, supernatural forces, or supernatural powers.[3] Religious institutions mediate ultimate meaning and transcendent power in relation to economic, political, and other social institutions in its environment. A religious institution may be in tension or in harmony with society, it may reject or accept its prevailing social *milieu*, but as a particular cultural institution religion is in dynamic interaction with society. On the other hand, religion has been defined as a cultural system of symbolic discourse, practice, and forms of association imbued with a sense of the sacred.[4] Collective symbols, myths, and rituals that mediate ultimate meaning and transcendent power may be regarded as a religious system animating a society. These collective representations are central both to social cohesion and to social conflict. They are the terms and conditions within which a human identity may be negotiated.

In 1955 Will Herberg, the sociologist of religion, was able to assert that all Americans found their most basic human identities in terms of one of three religio-cultural institutions. Americans were either Protestants, Catholics, or Jews. Defined in terms of specific cultural institutions, these religious identities were also permeated with a religio-cultural system of beliefs, practices, and forms of association that Herberg called the "American way of life."[5] In 1967 the sociologist Robert Bellah would invoke the term "civil religion" for this complex religious system that seemed to pervade American social life.[6] Bellah, however, wrote his controversial and influential article on civil religion during a time when its worldview and ethos were being seriously tested by America's involvement in the Vietnam War, by a variety of countercultural interests, and by the assertion of alternative human identities that seemed to have been factored out of the mainstream religiopolitical mix of American civil religion. The center of American religiopolitical life was being contested. This book is written with particular attention to that type of contest as it has appeared throughout American history from a vantage point—if this is possible to imagine—that stands outside of the contest and allows for the possibility that there have been many different centers in American religion and politics.

For the sake of clarity, I should mention some things that this book is not about. The text is not concerned with assessing the effect of religious beliefs and institutions in American electoral politics. In other words, it is not about religion *in* politics.[7] I do not concentrate on the effects of religion on American voting patterns;[8] nor on the effects of religion on political attitudes;[9] nor on the religious affiliations of public officials;[10] nor on the lobbying efforts of religious interest groups;[11] nor on statements of religious groups concerning foreign and domestic public policy issues.[12] Although many of these concerns do appear, they are subordinated to a more general, but I think more fundamental, analysis of the distributions of power in American history and society. In this regard, this book is an attempt at cultural analysis in which, to modify a phrase from Paul Tillich, religion appears as the inside of culture and culture appears as the outside of religion.[13] Religion, however, is not treated simply in terms of those institutions or systems of belief, practice, and association concerned with *meaning*; religion also is a vehicle of *power*. At that point, religion intersects with politics within the systematic distribution of power that constitutes any social network. Close attention to the dynamics of power may bring us to new ways of looking at familiar relations of religion and politics in American culture.

The book is divided into three major sections. The first section deals with *systems of power* that involve the systematic distribution of both religious and political power. Theocracy, democracy, and civil religion have been (at least) three systems of power in American history that have set the conditions within which the complex relations between religion and politics have been negotiated. Part One outlines and analyzes those systems.

The second section explores *zones of conflict* which have arisen out of the encounter with otherness in American history. The historical experience of Native Americans, black Americans, and immigrant Americans raises important issues about the nature of religious and political power in America. The tensions between forces of exclusion and forces of inclusion have revealed the potential of otherness for producing both conflict and pluralism in American social relations. Part Two examines those tensions of inclusion and exclusion in American religion and politics by looking through the experience of those historically excluded.

Finally, the third section explores the legal context of religion in America in terms of the constitutional provisions for the free exercise of religion and the prohibition of an establishment of religion. On a deeper level, however, the force of law in American religion and politics suggests the presence of a *force field* of legal and military power within which religion has been allowed to appear in American society in the ways that it has appeared. Part Three examines conscientious objection to military service, alternative and new religious movements, and the fundamentalist politics of the New Religious Right as points at which religion may come into conflict with the legal order, but also as episodes in American history through which that legal force field has been redefined.

An introductory chapter briefly reviews some theoretical issues relating to religion, politics, and power that may place the specific study of religion and politics in America within a broader context. By way of conclusion, a postscript returns to some brief observations on how human identities are negotiated through the dynamics of inclusion and exclusion within religiopolitical systems. The result of all this, I hope, will be an opportunity once again to imagine the patterns of power that have animated American religion and politics and, in this way, to re-imagine America.

I was grateful to teachers, colleagues, and students at home and abroad who provided encouragement, support, and the necessary instruction to make these explorations of American religion and politics possible. Catherine Albanese, Walter Capps, W. Richard Comstock, Phillip E. Hammond, Edward Tabor Linenthal, and Robert Michaelsen (at home); John Cumpsty, John de Gruchy, Itumelung Mosala, Gabriel Setiloane, and Charles Villa-Vicencio (abroad); and Ninian Smart (omnipresent) have all provided inspiration for this project even when they were not aware that it was even going on. Other debts are reflected in the notes that I hope will provide an invitation and a series of avenues for further exploration. Special thanks go to Kevin Garcia, another displaced American, who helped tremendously in the collection of and the reflection on the materials that appear in this book, to Tzipporah Hoffman, and to the Board of Directors. Valuable suggestions (not always taken) and even more valuable encouragement were supplied by those who read this book in manuscript. In this regard, I would like to thank Martin Marty, Robert Ellwood, and, again, Walter Capps, Robert Michaelsen, and Edward Tabor Linenthal for their kind attention and warm concern for this book and its author.

NOTES

1. *Cape Times* (April 25, 1987).
2. See Charles Villa-Vicencio, *Between Christ and Caesar: Classic and Contemporary Texts on Church and State* (Grand Rapid, MI: Eerdmans, 1986): 197-269.
3. E.B. Tylor, *Primitive Culture*, 2 vols. (London, 1876): I: 424ff.; Melford Spiro, "Religion: Problems of Definition and Explanation," in: Michael Banton (ed.), *Anthropological Approaches to the Study of Religion* (London: Tavistock, 1966): 96; Rodney Stark and William Sims Bainbridge, *The Future of Religion: Secularization, Revival, and Cult Formation* (Berkeley: University of California Press, 1985): 1-14.
4. Émile Durkheim, *The Elementary Forms of the Religious Life* (tr.) Joseph Ward Swain (New York: The Free Press, 1965): 62; Clifford Geertz, "Religion as a Cultural System," in: Geertz, *The Interpretation of Cultures* (New York: Basic Books, 1973): 90; David Chidester, *Patterns of Action: Religion and Ethics in a Comparative Perspective* (Belmont, CA: Wadsworth Publishing Company, 1986): 1-6.
5. Will Herberg, *Protestant, Catholic, Jew: An Essay in American Religious Sociology* (Garden City, New York: Doubleday, 1960).

6. Robert Bellah, "Civil Religion in America," in Russell F. Richey and Donald G. Jones (eds.), *American Civil Religion* (New York: Harper and Row, 1974): 21-44.

7. Recent books that survey the role of religion *in* politics include Robert Booth Fowler, *Religion and Politics in America* (Metuchen, NJ: Scarecrow Press, 1985) and Richard T. McBrien, *Caesar's Coin: Religion and Politics in America* (New York: Macmillan, 1987).

8. Albert Menendez, *Religion at the Polls* (Philadelphia: Westminster, 1977).

9. Kathleen A. Frankovic, *The Effect of Religion on Political Attitudes* (New Brunswick, NJ: Rutgers University Press, 1974).

10. Berton Dulce and Edward J. Richter, *Religion and the Presidency* (New York: Macmillan, 1962; and Peter I. Benson and Dorothy L. Williams, *Religion on Capitol Hill: Myths and Realities* (San Francisco: Harper and Row, 1982).

11. Luke Eugene Ebersole, *Church Lobbying in the Nation's Capitol* (New York: Macmillan, 1951); and James Adams, *The Growing Church Lobby in Washington* (Grand Rapids, MI: Eerdmans, 1970).

12. Alfred Hero, Jr., *American Religious Groups View Foreign Policy: Trends in Rank and File Opinion, 1937-1969* (Durham, NC: Duke University Press, 1973).

13. Paul Tillich, *The Theology of Culture* (New York: Oxford University Press, 1959): 42.

INTRODUCTION: RELIGIOUS AND POLITICAL POWER

Religion and politics are dimensions of human experience engaged in the meaningful exercise of power. They are patterns of power, dynamic processes of action and interaction, and systems of power relations that reinforce the general distribution of power within any society. The anthropologist Kenelm Burridge has defined religion in terms of power. "Religions," Burridge has written, "are concerned with the systematic ordering of different kinds of power, particularly those seen as significantly beneficial or dangerous."[1] Religion, in this sense, is the way human beings orient themselves to the multitude of powers that impinge upon their lives. Religion identifies the ultimate field of power within which people act and interact. Religions are concerned with the classification of power: some forces are classified as helpful, some harmful; some powers are classified as ordinary, others as extraordinary, supernatural, or mysterious; some powers are to be cultivated, others are to be avoided. Religion is that dimension of human experience particularly concerned with varieties of power that are felt to be sacred.

One way to distinguish between religion and politics is to say that religion is involved with sacred power, while politics is engaged with ordinary, mundane, or profane power. The historian George Armstrong Kelly made this kind of distinction when he noted that "politics is the ultimate control system of the profane and religion is the ultimate control system of the sacred."[2] This distinction, which has been theoretically supported in the study of religion by the seminal work of the sociologist Emile Durkheim, illustrates the difference between qualitatively different dimensions of power in personal and social experience. Durkheim insisted that the division between sacred and profane was so basic to the way societies operate that "the mind irresistibly refuses to allow the two corresponding things to be confused, or even to be merely in contact with each other."[3] Whatever may be held to be sacred within a society is set apart from the ordinary, mundane, and profane life of the community. Sacred objects, buildings, and persons; sacred spaces and sacred times; and the entire domain of sacred power are felt to be radically *other* than the ordinary, everyday, profane existence of the community. Social systems engaged in controlling this sacred domain of power constitute religion; social systems involved in exercising control over the profane world may be regarded as political systems.

However, the theoretical distinction between sacred and profane power may be regarded as useful only if one recognizes that they are never so neatly separated in actual experience. Since religion and politics are both strategic networks of power relations, they are necessarily interrelated in the systematic distribution of power within any society. Kenelm Burridge has provided important insights into this necessary relationship between religious and political power. Religion, he has reminded us, "points to that which permeates and informs a whole way of life, and, more crucially, it indicates sources or principles of power which are regarded as particularly creative or destructive."[4] Religion, in this sense, is not simply a domain of power that is separate from the ordinary, mundane, or profane arenas of human action; it is a dynamic force that pervades all aspects of human life within a society. It involves human beings in beliefs, practices, and forms of association that activate a particular distribution of power. The powers represented by religion spill over into ordinary social actions and interactions. Therefore, there is a political dimension to religion, and a religious dimension to politics. "Because politics, too, [is] concerned with power," Burridge has observed, "it becomes clear and explicit that no religious movement lacks a political ideology." Conversely, no political movement lacks a religious dimension, "for not only are religions concerned with the truth about power, but the reverse also holds: a concern with the truth about power is a religious activity."[5] Recognizing that religion and politics, the sacred and profane, represent different dimensions of power, it may be necessary to use a term like *religiopolitical power* to capture the inevitable interrelation between religious and political power within any social system. This book is devoted to exploring, examining, and clarifying the social relations, and interrelations, generated by religiopolitical power in American society. This may serve as a useful introduction to patterns of religious and political power in America.

RELIGIOUS POWER

The sociology of religion in the twentieth century has largely seen the role of religious power in human societies either as one of *interdependence* or as one of *interaction*. Religious power has been perceived as a unifying force upon which the solidarity of a social group depends, or it has been regarded as a distinctive social force that may at any given time be in harmony or in conflict with a variety of different political, economic, and social institutions. From these two perspectives, society has been regarded as a field of power relations unified by the cohesive force of religion; or society has been analyzed as a network of cooperating and conflicting social institutions within which religion plays an important interactive role. It may be important to reflect briefly on these theoretical approaches to the place of religious power in human societies before considering the relation between religion and politics.

Social theory, which can be traced back to the foundational work of the French sociologist Emile Durkheim, has postulated a basic interdependence between religion and society. This interdependence was considered so important that religion was defined as a system of shared beliefs, practices, and forms of association that organizes, sustains, and unifies any particular social group. Durkheim's classic definition of religion, which he proposed in his *Elementary Forms of the Religious Life* (1912), emphasized this unifying social function of religious power. Religion was defined as "a unified system of beliefs and practices relative to sacred things, that is to say, things set apart and forbidden—beliefs and practices which unite into one single moral community . . . all those who adhere to them."[6] Religions are shared systems of symbolic forms, meanings, and values—what Durkheim called *collective representations*—that serve to hold a social group together. This concern for identifying the primary social function of religious power has tended to minimize the importance of any specific content such symbolic representations might convey, even to the point where the focus of religion has been regarded as society itself. Religious beliefs, ritual practices, and ethical patterns of action have been regarded as simply a common, shared vocabulary for social consensus. They provide the means by which individuals, according to Durkheim, "represent to themselves the society of which they are members, and the obscure but intimate relations they have to it."[7] Religion, in this sense, has been regarded as the mechanism by which individuals internalize the collective consciousness of the group and, thereby, reinforce their collective social solidarity.

This preoccupation with the interdependence of religion and society, with the ways in which religious power sustains a social order, has often obscured the range of tensions, contradictions, and conflicts that may occur between religion and the network of social relations in which it appears. Collective representations—the vocabulary of religious symbols, myths, and rituals—may just as easily provide a common vocabulary for conflict as for consensus. The Durkheimian perspective on religion has had some difficulty in accounting for the role of religion as a force in social change. If the function of religion is to unify the social order, how do we interpret situations in which religion is a motivating force or powerful justification for changes in that order? The observation that religion often serves as a force for social change suggests that there are situations in which religion is in dynamic interaction with society.

The work of the sociologist Max Weber has provided a basis for analyzing processes of interaction between religion and society. Weber regarded religion as a separate human institution which is inevitably involved in an ongoing process of interaction with other social institutions. Religion is a force in interaction with other social forces. From this perspective, religion is a process by which human beings negotiate issues of ultimate authority, meaning, and value within specific social, economic, and political contexts. Max Weber placed far greater emphasis than Durkheim on the efforts of individuals, including those extraordinary, charismatic formulators of religion, who struggle to come to terms with the social conditions within which they live. In this sense, religion becomes a motivation and a source of legitimation for social change. The charismatic power of religious leaders, prophets, and reformers may be regarded as an alternative source of social authority which tends to break crystallized patterns of traditional and legal authority. The religious power which Weber called *charisma* is invested in extraordinary individuals who seem to be set apart from the ordinary community. This charismatic religious power, Weber suggested, is revealed by "a certain quality of an individual personality by virtue of which he is set apart from ordinary men and treated as endowed with supernatural, superhuman, or at least specifically exceptional powers or qualities. These are not accessible to the ordinary person, but are regarded as of divine origin or as exemplary, and on the basis of them the individual concerned is treated as a leader."[8] Such charismatic power tends to disrupt the two other types of authority which become institutionalized in societies: *traditional* authority, which is based on the continuation of inherited customs; and *legal* authority, which is based on an independent, systematic, and rationalized rule of law. In charismatic power, religion is in dynamic interaction with other forms of social authority and institutional power.

Charismatic power was identified by Max Weber with movements of social change. A charismatic eruption of power may serve to mobilize forces of rebellion, revolution, or reform against the established social order. This religious motivation, however, must receive support from corresponding social interests, from the felt needs of individuals in society, in order for significant change to occur. The notion of "elective affinity" in Weber's thought captured this idea that there must be a sympathetic correspondence between a particular complex of religious beliefs and specific social interests in order for religion to be effective as a motive for change. As the sociologist William H. Friedland put it, "in sum, while there are plenty of people with messages, these must be relevant to social groups before they begin to be received and become the basis for action."[9] This correspondence between religion and social interests also seems to lie beneath Max Weber's argument that there was a certain correlation between Calvinism and the rise of capitalism in western Europe and America. The complex of religious concepts and commitments which surrounded the idea of a divine calling or *vocation* for disciplined work in the world (which was a prominent feature in certain forms of Calvinist theology) corresponded to certain social interests in hard work, frugality, self-denial, and the exploitation of human and natural resources that took social form in the rise of capitalism.[10] In other historical settings, however, religious ideas seemed to function as limiting factors in the development of capitalist economies in India and China.[11] In this sense, religion may be regarded as an interactive, motivational, or limiting force in the production of social forms.

Religion therefore may function as an interactive force in processes of social change. But another aspect of the interaction between religion and society is the inevitable tendency of the spontaneity of charisma and the creative power of religious ideas to become institutionalized in more or less stable social forms. At this point in the interaction between religion and society, religion may serve the function of social legitimation for various patterns of political organization, economic exchange, or social order. Social groups with an interest in justifying what may be regarded as certain social, economic, or political interests, may utilize religion to lend an aura of sacred legitimacy to their position in the social order. Social groups, as Max Weber noted, may "assign to religion the primary function of legitimizing their own life pattern and situation in the world."[12] In this sense, religious power may be invoked to reinforce a particular distribution of power in society. In the interaction between religion and society, religious power has not only been a motivational force for social change; it has been a powerful force for legitimating established patterns of political power.

POLITICAL POWER

The widest definition of politics would identify it as the network of power relations in a society. Politics represents the lines of authority, the instruments of control, the strategies of domination, and the enforcement of order that all contribute to a certain pattern in the distribution of power within a set of social relations. Politics is the exercise of institutional control over a social field; it is comprised of the "institutions that control and maintain the widest corporate group, that is, the society."[13] This is a very general and preliminary attempt at defining political power. Some refinements of the notion of politics as the power relations within society are necessary before the idea of political power can come into a greater focus.

First, political power relations may be constituted within the context of a state. Political anthropologists have made the useful distinction between the organization, maintenance, and control of tribal societies that are based on the social status of *kinship*, and the power relations based on a certain degree of control over a *territory* with more or less clearly defined geographical boundaries. Some anthropologists have insisted, as Lucy Mair has noted, that "the sphere of politics begins where kinship ends."[14] The power relations that give order, stability, and continuity to family units—often involving complicated patterns of kinship with intricate interrelated obligations—become subordinated to the interests of a political apparatus that exercises its authority over a certain territory. In this transition from power relations based on kinship to power relations based on territory lies the origin of the state as the primary locus of political power. The state becomes the basic frame of reference for political power in human social relations.

Second, the state exercises two essential dimensions of political power: legal and military. The legal power of the state refers to power relations within a society that establish and maintain social order by insuring and reinforcing internal cooperation. Law is more than simply custom; it is custom backed up by force or the threat of force.[15] If the legal function of political power maintains the internal organization of society through the implicit exercise of force, military power extends the use of force outside the territorial boundaries of society in order to guarantee the security of the state. In both legal and military power, politics involves the use of force over a geographical territory. On a deeper level, the legal and military functions of political power suggest the central importance of violence in politics. The sociologist Randall Collins has observed that "what we mean by the state is the way in which violence is organized."[16] Political power may be regarded as the organized exercise of violence over a territory. "A general theory of politics," as Collins has noted, "is an explanation of how violence is organized, the structure of the state."[17] Force in both legal and military power is legitimated by the political interests of the state. But this exercise of force in political power is the implicit (or explicit) potential for violence directed toward those who occupy the social space within a state and toward those who reside outside its boundaries. This notion of the state as a force field is important in any theory of political power.

Third, and finally, an appreciation of the role of politics in maintaining social order (an appreciation certainly influenced by the Durkheimian analysis of social systems) may obscure the dynamics of political processes in societies. Such a preoccupation with the mechanisms of social order, equilibrium, and solidarity may neglect the importance of conflict in political power. Political power may be generated out of the competition between mutually exclusive social interests. It may be a configuration of power relations that arises out of conflicts, tensions, and confrontations between different social groups. A political order which enforces certain customs necessarily generates conflict. As Lucy Mair has reminded us, "there is no society where rules are automatically obeyed."[18] With order there is necessarily rebellion. Social expressions of rebellion often serve as dynamic infusions of energy into the political process and may revitalize social relations. Within any political system, order and disorder define each other. They appear within a larger pattern of power relations; and rebellion against an established political order may provide the occasion for a reinforcement, reformation, or fundamental change in that order. In any event, such infusions of energy into a social system are indications of dynamic tensions that exist in the formation of political power systems.[19]

To appreciate the dynamic tensions that are engaged in political power it may be necessary to regard politics as a system, a zone, or a force field of power relations. The anthropologist Georges Balandier suggested the beginnings of such a systems approach to politics when he indicated that "power may be defined, for every society, as resulting from the need to struggle against the entropy that threatens it with disorder."[20] Power, in this sense, is the general distribution of energy within a social system. Political power takes the form of ongoing struggles against the forces which would cause the system to dissolve. This systems approach, which might be called a unified field theory of power, moves beyond the more conventional interpretation of political power as *dominance*. It has been customary for political scientists to define power as the ability of one individual, or social unit, to dominate another. A one-dimensional definition of political power would simply regard power as a situation in which x has control over y. In this sense, it would be possible to say that x has power over y. A two-dimensional model of political power would recognize situations in which x not only controls y, but also sets the terms within which political decision making is controlled. X might set the agenda within which y tries to realize its own political interests. A three-dimensional model of political power might recognize those situations in which x not only controls y, and not only controls the situations within which y might struggle for power, but even creates y's own interests. The effectiveness of education, propaganda, and advertising in modern political systems suggests the resources that may be used by a state to extend its domain to shape the interests, aspirations, and goals of persons under its control.[21]

These three dimensions of political control indicate the complex network of social interrelations within which power may be exercised. Political power is generated out of a conflict of interests, and it may be exercised to enforce one set of social interests over another, to set the terms within which social interests might be realized, and even to instill certain interests in those who find themselves under the control of a particular domain of power. But what are the basic conditions of possibility within which the interests of all the contending parties in political conflict arise? A unified field theory of political power would give priority to the network of power relations within which interests arise as social interests. The actors within a given system of political power are simply playing roles that are already assigned in the prevailing network of power relations.

In such a systems approach, power would not be regarded as a commodity that can be acquired, possessed, or lost, but as a pervasive dynamism or tension existing in a particular network of social relations. Power would not be seen as simply the control, coercion, or influence that one individual or social unit might exercise over another, but rather as a complex network of forces, tensions, and energy that constitute a political system. In an important sense, the "powerful" are dominated by a network of power relations in order to keep the "powerless" in their places. A powerful individual or social unit within a network of power relations may be controlled by being a controller. In this respect, everyone is locked into a different interrelated position in a society's power system.

Political power, therefore, is more than simply a matter of control; it is a pervasive system, zone, or field of power relations which distributes power within a society. In this sense, power pervades social relations; it produces the very strategies through which individuals participate in society; and it generates powerful symbols, myths, and ideologies through which contending individuals and social groups are defined and define themselves. Power is the dynamic energy that infuses a social system.[22]

This way of analyzing political power holds the potential for a unified field theory of power. Religion and politics may, in fact, be two aspects of the same distribution of power within a network of social relations. Three basic categories of religiopolitical power are essential to any interpretation of the way religion and politics operate in social relations. First, a *system of power* is an organized network of power relations. In a religiopolitical system, religious and political power are organized in a particular way that supports the structure of the system as a whole. The theocratic system of the Puritans who colonized the Massachusetts Bay area in the seventeenth century established a distinctive distribution of religious and political power that may usefully be considered as a religiopolitical system. The democratic order initiated by the American Revolution, and instituted through the constitutional development of the early republic, may also be regarded as a systematic distribution of religious and political power. Identifying systems of power is the first step in analyzing the relation between religion and politics in American society.

Second, a *zone of conflict* is a situation of social tension between two or more power systems. Zones of conflict have appeared in American society when mutually exclusive religiopolitical systems have encountered each other in the same territory. The New World was initially a zone of conflict between intrusive European colonizers and Native American societies. These were not simply political conflicts—they involved violent tensions between religions, cultures, and different ways of life. The zone of conflict that emerged was a fundamental encounter with *otherness* in both religious and political terms. A zone of conflict opens at the encounter between two or more mutually exclusive systems. The zone of conflict closes when one of the mutually exclusive systems has established religious and political hegemony, when it has managed to integrate the *other* into its particular religiopolitical system.[23] Black Americans, immigrants, Catholics, Jews, and alternative religious movements in an America dominated by white, Anglo-Saxon, Protestant political interests have all entered into zones of conflict in American society. Identifying such zones of conflict is the second step in analyzing the relationship between religion and politics in America.

Third, a *force field* is the organized exercise of violence within a religiopolitical system. The government of a state reserves the only legitimate uses of violence to itself. As Robert H. Jackson has noted, "the Government can suffer no rivals in the field of coercion."[24] That coercion may be implicit in a code of legal regulations that govern society through the threat of force, or coercion may be explicit in systems of disciplinary actions, fines, and punishments that a state may exercise to enforce a certain network of controls over a society. Borrowing a set of terms from the physical sciences, it is possible to discern two types of force that operate within a power system: *centripetal* force and *centrifugal* force.

A *centripetal* force binds a community together. Legal power may operate as a centripetal force that centers, organizes, and unifies a state by focusing the implicit (or explicit) force of violence in upon the members of that community. With regard to religion, the centripetal force of law may establish a force field within a community in which only certain religious expressions are allowed to appear. The strong centripetal force of the Puritan community, for example, required strict conformity in matters of religious belief and practice. The more diffused centripetal force of the democratic order, however, allowed a variety of religions to exist within the same civil space, as long as they did not present a direct threat to public health or safety. The perception of danger, however, within a religiopolitical force field is highly relative. The Puritans, as we shall see, perceived any deviation in religious belief as a threat to the public order, and they attempted to exclude such dangers by force. Legal power, and the centripetal force of public order, create a force field within which religions appear within a religiopolitical system.

A *centrifugal* force extends the power of a community beyond its boundaries. Military power is precisely such a centrifugal force that is exercised to extend the power, influence, and control of one religiopolitical system in relation to other systems. Warfare in human societies has always been infused with an aura of the sacred.[25] America's wars have characteristically been regarded in the popular imagination as holy wars. They have been contests between the forces of good and evil for the purpose of extending the powerful dominion of good over the world. This centrifugal force invested in military power has been often justified, legitimated, and infused by religious power. But situations have arisen in which personal religious or moral conscience has conflicted with the demands that military power places on individual citizens to support, participate, and ultimately sacrifice their lives in the interests of this centrifugal force. At these points, the American legal system has served to support military power by defining the conditions under which American citizens are bound to lend it their support.

A religiopolitical system, therefore, generates a legal force field which defines the public order within which religion may legitimately emerge. Three issues have been crucial to the force field of law and public order in American religion: religious objection to military service, the legal guarantee of free exercise for religion, and the constitutional prohibition of any establishment of religion. It will become evident in the final section of this book that these three issues involve critical tensions in the force field that supports the religiopolitical system in American society.

RELIGIOPOLITICAL SYSTEMS

Religion and politics are two aspects of the configuration of power in a social system. Religious and political power are part of a larger pattern of power relations that defines the distinctive force field of any society. The political scientist Donald Eugene Smith expressed this point when he observed that "this vital connection between religion and polity, so widespread as to be almost universal, is rooted, psychologically and doctrinally, in fundamental assumptions about *power*. The exercise of power is at the center of the polity and in virtually all cultures power is an attribute of divinity."[26] That religion and politics appear to be interwoven in the distribution of power within human societies may be a perennial feature of religion and politics. But there also seems to be a significant difference between what might be referred to as traditional and modern religiopolitical systems.

In traditional systems, the religious community is closely identified with the political community. In many cases, they are identical. Religious power may be exercised by political rulers, and political power may be exercised by religious leaders. Religion and politics may be closely integrated in the workings of a relatively stable social order. In such traditional societies, as Donald Eugene Smith has noted, "the religiopolitical system was thus an integrated system in which ruler, clergy, religious ideology, religious norms of behavior, and coercive governmental power were combined in order to maximize the stability of society."[27] Religio-political systems of this traditional variety may be distinguished between those based on an *organic* model and those based on a *church* model in the distribution of religious and political power.

In organic systems, there is a fusion of religious and political functions, usually performed within a single, unitary, and all-encompassing social structure. The traditional Hindu sacred order of a hierarchical class (*varna*) system , with corresponding sacred obligations for each social class (*varnadharma*), was such an organic religiopolitical system. The system was simultaneously supported by the coordinated efforts of a ruling class and a priestly class. Political and religious functions were unified to sustain the system as a whole. Traditional Islamic religiopolitical systems have also been based on a fusion of religious and political power in the Prophet and his successors. Muhammad and the subsequent caliphs were often regarded as both religious and political leaders of the Islamic community. Although a relatively independent clerical class, the *ulama*, did emerge, it tended to be subsumed under the power of Islamic states to enforce sacred law upon the entire community. These are examples of the organic model of traditional religiopolitical systems.

The church model assumes a close alliance between two distinct social institutions—governmental and ecclesiastical orders—that nevertheless are closely interrelated. The traditional, medieval Catholic doctrine of the two swords, however often it may have been contested in practice, reflected a distribution of power between Pope and Emperor that separated ecclesiastical authority from both lay society and temporal rulers. Church and Empire were regarded as two domains of power, but the authorities that governed these domains were theoretically integrated in a common religiopolitical ideal of Christendom. The *sangha*, or monastic order, in the Theravadan Buddhist kingdoms of South and Southeast Asia performed a similar function in a church model of religiopolitical power. *Sangha* and *ecclesia* both literally mean "assembly." The *sangha* stood as a separate locus of religious power. To enter the Buddhist monastic order, a person had to leave ordinary society. But in practice the social order of these Buddhist kingdoms was sustained by ongoing reciprocal support between the temporal rulers and the *sangha*.

The church model in traditional religiopolitical systems allowed for a number of variations in the distribution of power. The church may hold a dominant place over government in the religiopolitical system; the government may dominate the church; or there may be some balance of power between the religious and political spheres in the traditional church model. But in this model, as in the organic model, religious and political exercises of power are more closely integrated than they are in modern religiopolitical systems. Modern systems involve two important features: (1) the differentiation of religion as a separate social institution; and (2) the elaboration of religious and political theories regarding the relationship between that separate institution and the state.

The concept of modernization is certainly problematic. The meaning of modernization has been obscured by linking certain developments in the modern world with an ideology of evolution, progress, and social development through modernization. The term *modern* may still be useful, however, if it is recognized that these social changes have not necessarily been the inevitable result of a process of human evolution, and that modern forms of social relations are not necessarily evidence of progress in any moral, cultural, or ultimately human sense. However the term is used it must include significant social transformations in the direction of greater urbanization, industrialization, rationalization, and social differentiation. This last element, the complex differentiation of social institutions in modern societies, has had a profound impact on religiopolitical systems. At the risk of oversimplifying a long process of massive historical change, it is possible to single out three basic themes of religiopolitical modernization.

First, religion appears as one social institution among many. Religion is differentiated from other social institutions. Most societies in history have not had a term for religion because what we might identify as religion is regarded as a shared way of life, a system of beliefs, practices, and associations, that is diffused throughout society. In modern religiopolitical systems, however, religion is isolated as a separate institution. And, although religion may be invoked (usually in rather general terms) to legitimize certain social policies, it tends to be circumscribed within a separate sphere of operation.

Second, religious functions become diffused through a wide range of different institutions in society. Functions that were traditionally ascribed to religion—maintenance of social order, educational instruction, health care and healing, and so on—are assumed by other specialized institutions. One of the ironies of the differentiation of modern religion as a separate institution is that while religion has become increasingly isolated from society, traditional religious functions have become increasingly diffused throughout a complex network of social institutions.

Third, the state retains its aura of the sacred, but without any necessary reference to the institutions that are designated as religion. As the autonomous status, disciplinary controls, and potential violence of the state have dramatically increased, the state has itself become enveloped within the aura of a quasi-religious power. In modern religiopolitical systems, the state has become the supreme locus of power. The state has come to represent that transcendent, supreme power for which individuals in the modern world would be willing (or at least expected) to make the ultimate sacrifice. The ideology, ritualized practices, and institutions of nationalism in the modern world assume the dimensions of religious power in the political arena.[28] These features of modern religiopolitical systems have raised problematic issues about the relations between religion and politics, church and state, within modern systems of power.

The distribution of power in modern religiopolitical systems has generated a proliferation of political theory to address the problematic relations between religious and political power. This is a body of critical, speculative, and systematic "political theology" which has appeared in response to new religiopolitical configurations in the modern world. Every political system has its symbolic, theoretical, or ideological dimension. What the political anthropologist Sidney Verba has called the political culture of a society is "the system of empirical beliefs, expressive symbols, and values which defines the situation in which political action takes place. It provides the subjective orientation to politics."[29] Political culture is the symbolic discourse and theoretical knowledge that corresponds to a particular configuration of power relations within a society. Modern changes in the pattern of religious and political power (initiated during the Protestant Reformation of the sixteenth century, accelerated by the Industrial Revolution, and crystallized in the rise of modern nationalisms) have generated theoretical formulas for the relation between religion and politics in the modern world. The political culture of religiopolitical systems in America has been shaped by three theoretical patterns of the distribution of power between religion as a separate institution and the political order of the state.[30]

First is the pattern of separation between religious and political power. In the religiopolitical system proposed by the philosopher John Locke (1632-1704), religion and politics were regarded as two separate, legitimate spheres of human endeavor. In his *Letter Concerning Toleration*, Locke declared that "Every man has an immortal soul, capable of eternal happiness or misery; whose happiness depends [upon] his believing and doing those things in life, which are necessary to the obtaining of God's favor, and are prescribed by God to that end." Locke acknowledged that this religious activity is of ultimate importance. But, at the same time, human beings are engaged in the political work of insuring their mutual security in their temporal lives. The necessity of living in the world, Locke suggested, "obliges men to enter into society with one another; that by mutual assistance and joint force, they may secure unto each other their properties, in the things that contribute to the comforts and happiness of life."[31] This public life of social relations was regarded by Locke as essentially separate from the private life of religion. They are both necessary components of human life, but they operate in parallel spheres that do not necessarily intersect with, involve, or affect each other. Religion, as a separate institution, was not regarded as playing a direct role in the social agreements which Locke felt formed the basis of the state.

Second is the pattern of coordination between religious and political power in producing good citizens. This theoretical arrangement between religion and politics was proposed by the French philosopher Charles

Louis Montesquieu (1689-1755). In his *Spirit of the Laws*, Montesquieu argued that both religion and politics should be designed to make good citizens. They should both contribute to this same end. "Both religion and the civil laws," Montesquieu held, "should principally contribute to making men good citizens." Carrying this analysis further, Montesquieu suggested that the more religion enters into the disciplinary production of good citizens, the less political control will need to be exercised. The reverse is also the case: "the less religion disciplines, the more the civil laws ought to." The result of this cooperation between religion and the state would be a pattern of coordinated power exercised by religious and political institutions to produce disciplined citizens. The particular alignment of power that would result from such a coordination of religion and the state may be regarded as a type of civil religion. Montesquieu observed that "we cannot escape membership in some civic faith even if we wished to, for the alternative to organizing belief is chaos."[32] This organizing civic faith may suggest a distinctive configuration of religiopolitical power in modern states, somewhat independent from both organized religions and the institutions of the state, which nevertheless organizes the collective beliefs, practices, and values of citizens in the interest of a civil religion.

A third religiopolitical theory which seriously considers the differentiation between religious and political institutions, proposes an arrangement in which religion provides a critique of politics, while politics provides protection for religion. In such a pattern, religion and politics would also be coordinated exercises of power; but they would be exercised in the interests of religion rather than of the state. The Protestant theologian Karl Barth (1886-1968) suggested that the morality represented by religious systems should temper the coercive force of political institutions, while the legitimate uses of force by the state should protect a social space within which religion may flourish. Barth had this arrangement of religiopolitical power in mind when he observed that "Political systems create and preserve a space for. . . the fulfillment of the purpose of world history, a space for faith, repentance, and knowledge." At the same time, religious communities should reciprocate by "reminding the state of those things of which it is unlikely to remind itself."[33] Religion and the state would remain separate, but they would cooperate in furthering the moral goals in human society represented by religion.

This notion of the church as guide to the state, and the state as guardian of the church, echoes the New England Puritans, and their ambitions for a *theocratic* religiopolitical system in America. The church was regarded as the powerful center of a covenant community protected by the coercive power of the state. The arrangements for religion and politics proposed by Locke and Montesquieu, and the theoretical distributions of religiopolitical power that radiated from their thought, affected the revolutionary experiment in a *democratic* religiopolitical system in the United States. The constitutional separation of church and state created a new distribution of religious and political power in the early republic. But in the space opened up by that separation, a type of civic faith and a variety of civil religious beliefs, practices, and values emerged which constituted what has been called *civil religion* in America. While this civil religion has drawn upon the symbolic resources of a theocratic covenant theology and has treated democracy as if it were a species of religion, it may represent a third religiopolitical system in American society. Civil religions have drawn support from organized religious institutions, and have been closely linked with national institutions, ideologies, and historical experience, but they suggest a religiopolitical system in American society that has been relatively independent of both church and state.

Theocracy, democracy, and civil religion are all distributions of religiopolitical power in America. The first phase in the exploration of religion and politics in America will seek to clarify the historical situations which engendered these three religiopolitical systems. The second phase will explore the zones of conflict that have arisen from encounters with otherness in American civil space. The religiopolitical experience of Native Americans, black Americans, immigrants, Jews, and Catholics suggest that American society has always wrestled with the challenge of converting zones of conflict into a dynamic pluralism where varieties of otherness can mutually coexist. The last phase in this survey will examine the legal force field within which religion has taken shape. The religiopolitical issues of conscientious objection to military service; the free exercise of alternative religious beliefs, practices, and forms of association; and the prohibition of any establishment of religion are points of tension between religion and the network of power relations defining the force field of law and public order. These issues are all engaged in the shifting patterns of power which have animated the relations between religion and politics in America.

NOTES

1. KENELM BURRIDGE, *New Heaven, New Earth: A Study of Millenarian Activities* (Oxford: Basil Blackwell, 1980): 5.
2. GEORGE ARMSTRONG KELLY. "Politics and the American Religious Consciousness," *Daedelus* 111 (1982): 128; reprinted in Mary Douglas and Steven M. Tipton, eds., *Religion in America: Spirituality in a Secular Age* (Boston: Beacon Press, 1983): 208.
3. EMILE DURKHEIM, *The Elementary Forms of the Religious Life*, trans. Joseph Ward Swain (New York: Free Press, 1965): 55.
4. BURRIDGE, *New Heaven, New Earth*: 5.
5. *Ibid.*:7.
6. DURKHEIM, *The Elementary Forms of the Religious Life*: 97.
7. *Ibid.*: 257.
8. MAX WEBER, *The Theory of Social and Economic Organization* (New York: Free Press, 1947): 358-9.
9. WILLIAM H. FRIEDLAND, "For a Sociological Concept of Charisma," *Social Forces* 43 (1964): 21.

10. MAX WEBER, *The Protestant Ethic and the Spirit of Capitalism*, trans. Talcott Parsons (New York: Scribners, 1958).

11. See James L. Peacock, *Consciousness and Change: Symbolic Anthropology in Evolutionary Perspective* (Oxford: Basil Blackwell, 1975): 78-82.

12. MAX WEBER, *Economy and Society*, eds. Guenther Roth and Claus Wiltich, 3 vols. (New York: Bedminster Press, 1968): 491.

13. S.F. NADEL, *The Foundation of Social Anthropology* (London: Cohen, 1961): 141.

14. LUCY P. MAIR, *Primitive Government* (Harmondsworth, Middlesex: Penguin, 1962): 10.

15. Law has been defined as "the systematic and formal application of force by the state in support of explicit rules of conduct," in Robert Redfield, "Primitive Law," in Paul Bohannan, ed., *Law and Warfare: Studies in the Anthropology of Conflict* (Garden City, New York: The Natural Press, 1967): 4-5; also, see E. Adamson Hiebel, *The Law of Primitive Man: A Study of Comparative Legal Dynamics* (Cambridge: Harvard University Press, 1954): 28.

16. RANDALL COLLINS, *Conflict Sociology* (New York: Academic Press, 1975): 351.

17. *Ibid.*: 353.

18. MAIR, *Primitive Government*: 18.

19. Theoretical approaches to political power along these lines have been developed by Max Gluckman, *Custom and Conflict in Africa* (Oxford: Basil Blackwell, 1955); *Order and Rebellion in Tribal Africa* (London: Cohen, 1963); *Politics, Law, and Ritual in Tribal Society* (London: Clarendon Press, 1965); and Edmund R. Leach, *Political Systems in Highland Burma* (London: G. Bell, 1964).

20. GEORGES BALANDIER, *Political Anthropology*, trans. A.M. Sheridan Smith (London: Allen Lane, 1970): 36.

21. For a discussion of these different dimensions of political control, see Steven Lukes, *Power: A Radical View* (London and New York: Macmillan, 1974); and Robert R. Alford and Roger Friedland, *Powers of Theory: Capitalism, the State, and Democracy* (Cambridge: Cambridge University Press, 1985).

22. A theory of power in this sense was initiated by the work of the late French sociologist Michel Foucault. For a useful introduction to Foucault's theory of power, see Hubert L. Dreyfus and Paul Rabinow, *Michel Foucault: Beyond Structuralism and Hermeneutics* (Chicago: University of Chicago Press, 1982).

23. This idea of a political "zone" was developed in Howard Lamar and Leonard Thompson, eds., *The Frontier in History: North America and Southern Africa Compared* (New Haven and London: Yale University Press, 1981): 3-13.

24. ROBERT H. JACKSON, "The Supreme Court as a Political Institution," in *The Supreme Court: Views from Inside*, ed. Alan F. Westin (New York: W.W. Norton, 1961): 163.

25. See James A. Aho, *Religious Mythology and the Art of War: Comparative Religious Symbolisms of Military Violence* (Westport, Connecticut: Greenwood Press, 1981); and Edward Tabor Linenthal, *Changing Images of the Warrior Hero in America: A History of Popular Symbolism* (New York: Edwin Mellen Press, 1982).

26. DONALD EUGENE SMITH, *Religion and Political Development* (Boston: Little, Brown, and Co., 1970): 6.

27. *Ibid.*: 57.

28. See Carlton Hayes, *Nationalism: A Religion* (New York: Macmillan, 1960); David E. Apter, "Political Religion in the New Nations," in *Old Societies and New States*, ed. Clifford Geertz (New York: Free Press, 1963); Christel Lane, *The Rites of Rulers: Ritual in Industrial Society—The Soviet Case* (Cambridge: Cambridge University Press, 1981); and Ninian Smart and Peter Merkl, eds., *Religion and Politics in the Contemporary World* (New York: New York University Press, 1983).

29. SIDNEY VERBA, "Comparative Political Culture," in *Political Culture and Political Development*, eds. Lucian Pye and Sidney Verba (Princeton: Princeton University Press, 1965): 513.

30. These three examples were suggested by George Armstrong Kelly, "Politics and the American Religious Consciousness," in *Religion in America*, eds. Douglas and Tipton: 210-11; see Kelly, *Politics and Religious Consciousness in America* (New Brunswick: Transaction Books, 1984).

31. MAURICE CRANSTON, ed., *John Locke on Politics, Religion, and Education* (New York: Collier Books, 1965): 134-5.
32. CHARLES LOUIS DE SECONDAT MONTESQUIEU, *The Spirit of the Laws*, ed. David Wallace Carrithers, trans. Thomas Nugent (Berkeley: University of California Press, 1977): 328; see Melvin Richter, *The Political Theory of Montesquieu* (Cambridge: Cambridge University Press, 1977): 297.
33. KARL BARTH, *Community, State, and Church* (Garden City, New York: Doubleday, 1962): 31, 33, 80.

CHAPTER ONE
THEOCRACY

The earliest English settlers ventured into the New World wilderness convinced that they carried a direct mandate from God to carve out a new religious and political order. These colonists in a strange and foreign land saw themselves as a divinely chosen people responding to the call and commandments of their God on a sacred mission into a new world. The entrepreneurial ambitions of the Virginia planters, the separatism of the Pilgrim community, and the utopian idealism of the Massachusetts Bay Puritans were all infused with a sense of religious power. They felt that their enterprises were directed by the hand of God, and the new political orders they established were consciously designed to conform to the demands of their religious commitments. These new religious and political establishments were experiments in theocracy.

The settlement in Virginia began in 1607 as a joint-stock corporation to acquire real estate, cultivate tobacco, and extend the influence of the British empire. But, at the same time, religious motives pulsed through this economic enterprise. John Rolfe, a leader among these Virginia colonists, described the settlers as "a peculiar people, marked and chosen by the finger of God."[1] Reporting back to England the *Good Newes from Virginia*, Alexander Whitaker confirmed this interpretation of the expedition by declaring: "We must confess that God has opened this passage unto us, and led us by the hand unto this work."[2] They saw themselves as a chosen people on a special mission to possess the wealth of this new land. They were confident that God was present in their work. This confidence produced a sense of harmony, therefore, between the ambition for profit and the advancement of religion. The Virginia Company declared that seeking profit was subservient to spreading religion, and their charter specified that "our primary end is to plant religion, our secondary and subalternate ends are for the honor and profit of our nation."[3]

By 1611 Governor Thomas Dale had supervised the establishment of religion in the colony. Strict laws punished heresy, impiety, and neglect of religious duties. These laws enforced the hierarchy of interests in the Virginia settlement. And Alexander Whitaker reminded the colonists of their priorities when he exhorted them to "remember that the Plantation is God's, and the reward your country's."[4] The Virginia Company was an economic extension of the British empire, but it was also an extension of the Church of England as a religious establishment in the New World.

The settlements in Massachusetts, however, resulted from separations from the Church of England. They were founded by Puritan separatists fleeing various forms of religious and political discrimination in the Old World to establish an independent religiopolitical order in America. Those religious separatists known as Pilgrims were English Puritans who objected to the political authority the Church of England exercised over their independent congregations. After a brief sojourn in the Netherlands, they set out for America. While still on board the *Mayflower* in November of 1620 they entered into an agreement, signed by thirty-one men, which described the purpose of their expedition. It was undertaken "for the glory of God, and advancement of the Christian faith, and honor of our king and country." This Mayflower Compact seemed to echo the religious and political sentiments of the Virginia planters. But this new agreement indicated that the Pilgrims intended to establish a separate and independent religiopolitical arrangement to fulfill their aims. The Mayflower Compact declared that the Pilgrims "in the presence of God, and of one another, covenant and combine ourselves together into a civil body politic."[5]

The Mayflower Compact was both a social contract and a divine covenant. As a contract it signified a social agreement to draft the necessary laws, ordinances, acts, constitutions, and offices to facilitate an organized political life. But this social contract was based on a prior covenant with God that unified the community. The idea of covenant was derived from the biblical precedent of the chosen people of Israel. The God of the Bible entered into a covenant, a unique relationship, with a particular people. The promise of this covenant was revealed to Abraham and his descendants; its conditions were established in the laws of Moses; and its power to unify the community of Israel was reinforced through the annual covenant renewal ceremonies in the promised land.

This image of a covenant between God and a community was central to the theocratic establishment in America. As the idea of covenant was transposed into a Christian context, a typological self-understanding emerged: Conversion became a sign of election; the church became the covenant community; and America became the new Israel. For the Pilgrim separatists, the existence of their church, knit together by a covenant of grace, was the prior condition that justified their efforts to form a "body politic."

The most effective theocratic experiment in America was the Puritan theocracy of the Massachusetts Bay Colony. The Puritans also felt they had embarked upon a divine errand into the wilderness. As preparations were being made for the great migration of Puritans from England in 1630, John Winthrop observed that their undertaking "appears to be a work of God . . . He has some great work in hand which he has revealed to his prophets among us."[6] And while still at sea aboard the *Arabella,* John Winthrop delivered a sermon that dedicated the Puritan community to a unique covenant relationship with God. "Thus stands the cause between God and us," Winthrop declared, "we are entered into Covenant with him for this work."[7] Winthrop was elected the first governor of the Massachusetts Bay settlement, and he supervised the implementation of religious and political policies that would establish the colony as a theocracy. It was a new order for a new world.

The sense of expectation that animated the Puritan community was captured by the historian of the first migration, Edward Johnson, when he declared that here is "the place where the Lord will create a new Heaven, and a new Earth, new churches, and a new commonwealth together."[8] The new churches and new commonwealth, in cooperation with each other, would shape the Puritan theocratic order; but the new heaven and earth signified something more. The Puritans saw themselves at the center of a fundamental reordering of the cosmos. Their errand into the wilderness signalled the coming of the millennium; it was the cosmic act that would usher in the kingdom of Christ on earth.

The Puritans self-consciously placed themselves at the very center of this sacred drama of human history. They looked to the Bible to understand their unique role in that drama. First, they referred back to the example of ancient Israel: the captivity in Egypt, the wandering in the wilderness, and the triumphant entry into the promised land to eventually establish the sacred city of Jerusalem. Second, they looked forward to the promise of the apocalyptic kingdom of Christ contained in the Book of Revelation. In that apocalypse, the old order was expected to be destroyed, a new heaven and earth to be established, and the New Jerusalem to descend from the skies. The ancient Jerusalem and the new Jerusalem were conflated in the self-understanding of the Massachusetts Bay community. The Puritan migration to America was a reenactment of the biblical typology of the history of ancient Israel; it was a fulfillment of the biblical prophecy of a New Jerusalem. The migration was conceived as a collective rite of passage from the old world to the new. This transition was symbolized in three stages: (1) captivity in the Old World; (2) separation, trials, and ordeals in the wilderness; and (3) a theocratic covenant in the New World. As one Puritan divine, Samuel Wakeman, summarized this self-understanding of the new theocratic community: "*Jerusalem* was, *New England* is, they were, you are God's own, God's covenant people."[9]

The Puritan theocratic system had clearly defined and tightly drawn boundaries. Power was centralized in the covenant, but it radiated from that single sacred center through the institutions of both church and government. Individuals who could demonstrate the acknowledged evidence of conversion, the workings of God's grace in their lives, were clearly included in the covenant community. And those individuals embodied the religiopolitical authority to define, maintain, and defend the theocratic order of the settlement. The centripetal force of the sacred covenant that bound this community together, however, had a complementary centrifugal force that excluded all those who did not belong to the covenant. This force of exclusion pushed Native Americans, heretics, and dissenters beyond the periphery of the covenant community. The Native Americans experienced this centrifugal force; as the Puritan poet, Michael Wigglesworth, imagined God to declare: "My fury's flail them threshed, my fatal broom; Did sweep them hence, to make my people elbow-room."[10]

But a number of European immigrants to Massachusetts also were swept out of the community by the power of God's fatal broom. Any theocracy may employ the power of exclusion to maintain its internal purity, consistency, and uniformity. The Puritan theocracy sought to maintain its purity by clearly marking the legitimate boundaries of the covenant community. At each stage, those boundaries were reinforced by rituals of exclusion: (1) the boundaries were *defined* with the expulsion of religious dissenters, such as Anne Hutchinson and Roger Williams, in the 1630s; (2) the boundaries were *maintained* by a consistent policy of religious intolerance that led to the banishment and execution of Quakers in the 1650s; and (3) the boundaries were *disrupted* when the British government revoked the original charter in 1684. In the context of this disruption of political order, the Puritans made one last attempt to exercise the theocratic rituals of exclusion in the conviction and execution in 1692 of alleged witches.

The Puritan establishment of seventeenth-century America was a powerful theocratic experiment. It was animated by a unique sense of collective destiny that conformed to biblical models and biblical expectations; it produced an interrelated network of religious and political institutions in harmony with the sacred covenant; and it maintained the purity of that sacred center by forcing all *others* beyond the periphery of the covenant community. The Puritan imagination has had a deep and lasting impact on American religion and politics. And the particular sense of sacred destiny which that imagination has nurtured has had a profound influence on America's sense of collective identity.

THE PURITAN IMAGINATION

The Protestant Reformation of the sixteenth century disrupted the old religious and political order which had unified European Christendom. The Protestant movements of Luther, Zwingli, Calvin, and others did not simply question traditional religious beliefs and practices; they attacked the centralized religiopolitical authority which the Catholic Church had held over Europe. This reformation of religion coincided with the emergence of a new national self-consciousness among the European states—the conviction, in the words of the historian Carlton Hayes, that "each people, and each alone, possessed a pure faith and a divine mission."[11] Religious commitments and national aspirations conspired to create conflicts between rival political powers in Europe. By the Peace of Westphalia, which brought these religious wars to a close in 1648, a territorial compromise was sanctioned by an international agreement which divided Europe into religiopolitical regions. The nation states of Europe were divided along religious lines. The formula—*cuius regio, eius religio*—recognized the prevailing condition in Europe that whoever ruled a region determined the religion that was practiced therein.

Religious power was localized in the apparatus of the state, and the established state religion in each nation exercised the authority to persecute dissenters within its boundaries. This religiopolitical arrangement supported the development of national churches: Anglicanism was the established church in England; Lutheranism in Germany and the Scandinavian countries; Calvinism in Switzerland, Scotland, and the Low Countries; and Catholicism in Spain and France. The Puritan dissenters who settled in the Massachusetts Bay Colony in 1630 may have been fleeing the established Church of England, but they carried with them the religiopolitical ideal of an established "church estate."

In the Puritan imagination the condition of their independent congregational churches was equivalent to the bondage of Israel in Egypt. The centralized authority of the Church of England, which had been solidified in the Act of Supremacy in 1534 under King Henry VIII, placed the royal power at the head of the church. Uniformity in religious beliefs and practices was enforced by the power of the state church. Puritanism began as a religious reform movement within the Church of England. At the end of the sixteenth century Puritans were seeking to purify the Church of heretical clergy, unwarranted ceremony, and the ecclesiastical hierarchy of bishops and archbishops. The congregational model of church polity, whose membership was comprised of individuals who declared their experience of the inner workings of grace, and whose leadership was elected from among these members, was developed by English Puritans at the beginning of the seventeenth century. Under the Stuarts (1603-1649), a number of separatist congregational groups would not accept compromise with the Church of England, and they departed for Holland or the New World.

The Puritans of the Massachusetts Bay Colony adopted this congregational church polity; but in leaving England with a royal charter they went with the approval of the King, and without rejecting the churches of England. And yet they were convinced that those churches were destined for destruction. The Old World was coming under the judgment of God. "All other churches of Europe," Winthrop declared, "are brought to desolation, and it cannot be, but the like Judgment is coming upon us." The migration of these Puritans was the escape, the exodus, of Israel out of the spiritual bondage of Egypt. But it was also the rapture of the true church before the apocalyptic devastation of the last days. "And who knows," Winthrop continued, "but that God has provided this place, to be a refuge for many, whom he means to save out of the general destruction."[12] This church understood itself to be the saved remnant of the new Israel, rescued by the hand of God from the judgment and destruction that was waiting for the Old World.

Before entering the promised land, however, these Puritans were required to endure hardships, trials, and ordeals in the wilderness. The wanderings of Israel for forty years in the wilderness provided a biblical model through which the Puritans could interpret their own trials. The sea voyage was like an initiation by ordeals. During that crossing they were neither in the Old World or the New; but they testified to the miraculous power of God in this period of transition. Letters and journals written by these travellers revealed the extent to which biblical imagery of the exodus of Israel had permeated the Puritan imagination. The voyagers to the New World were passing "from *Egypt* land through seas with watery walls." And those ocean walls would soon form a barrier of separation from the Old World's spiritual bondage. In this rite of passage, the God of Israel "let us see all his power." With His "own immediate good hand [He] . . . assuaged the violence of the sea." They described this crossing as "an extraordinary and miraculous deliverance." They were like Noah surviving the flood; like the Israelites crossing the Red Sea to escape Pharoah's armies; like the fishers on the Sea of Galilee when Jesus said "peace ye waves, and . . . for all their height they fell down flat." In the words of one of these travellers, Roger Clap, the sea voyage showed the "absolute necessity of the *New-Birth* . . . that our Hearts were taken off *Old-England* and set upon Heaven."[13]

The Puritan imagination was set upon a heaven on earth in the New

World. But the New World appeared to them upon arrival as a frightening wilderness. The image of wilderness may have been a biblical prototype, but it took on new meaning for the Puritan colonists through their struggles to survive their hardships in America. Michael Wigglesworth, in his epic poem that detailed "God's Controversy with New England," described America as "a waste and howling wilderness." Not only was this land uncultivated, but it was perceived as uncivilized. It was a world inhabited by "hellish fiends" and "brutish men" who appeared to worship devils. All the frightening apparitions of Christian demonology seemed to contend with these first Puritan settlers. This wilderness was a vast expanse of "grim death" and "eternal night." America was a dark and deserted wasteland that had never beheld the "sun of righteousness." All this changed, however, when the Puritans arrived. Wigglesworth announced that all these shadows vanished in the radiant light of the Puritans' "glorious gospel-shine."[14]

This Christian community, however, was beset with numerous trials and tribulations in establishing what they assumed could only be a beacon of light for the New World. The Puritan historian Edward Johnson, in his narrative of the first migration, *Wonder-Working Providence* (1654), reviewed the hardships of the Puritans in Massachusetts. "As Israel met with many difficulties after their return from captivity, in building the Temple and the City," he observed, "so [did] these New England people." First, they confronted the terrible wilderness, "with many dreadful Engines set by Satan to intrap their poor souls." In carving out a settlement in the wilderness, therefore, the Puritans saw themselves in a cosmic battle against the forces of evil. Second, they were separated from the Old World by the "dangerous ocean." The ocean became a wall of water separating the New World from the Old. It prevented them from fleeing their present dangers and returning to the familiarity of civilized life in England. Third, as they looked back across that expanse of water, they imagined the "worldly prelates" of the Church of England, and they were convinced that they could not return to a church which they felt was corrupt. And even if they did return, they feared they would be oppressed, persecuted, and even imprisoned for their faith. All of these factors intensified the sense of spiritual danger in the Puritan errand into the wilderness.

The historian Johnson declared that Christ was resolved to fight with them against these dangers. "The Immovable Resolutions continued in these men," he declared, "to re-build the most glorious Edifice of Mount Sion in a Wilderness, knowing this is the place where the Lord will create a new Heaven and a new Earth in new Churches and a new Commonwealth." Like the Israelites returning from captivity in Babylon, the Puritans would rebuild the temple and the city of God. The wilderness would become the promised land. And this new creation was considered a miracle even more remarkable than the example of ancient Israel. Johnson put this assumption to verse:

The noble Act Jehova wrought, his Israel to redeem,
Surely this second work of his shall far more glorious seem.[15]

This second Israel, the new chosen people, saw themselves transforming the wilderness into the promised land. And, as Cotton Mather put it in his *Magnalia Christi Americana* (1702), "such was the way of this little Israel, now going into a wilderness."[16]

The new order that the Puritans imposed upon this wilderness was based on their sense of having a special covenant with God. Governor John Winthrop, in his sermon on board the *Arabella*, exhorted the community to dedicate itself to creating a new life. As a covenant community they would create new forms of government, "both civil and ecclesiastical." The purpose of such an order would be to create a safe harbor in an evil world in which these Puritans might work out their salvation. Winthrop announced his hope "that our selves and posterity may be better preserved from the Common corruptions of the evil world to serve the Lord and work out our Salvation under the power and purity of his holy Ordinances." The heart of their covenant was framed as a bargain with God. If they arrived safely at their destination in the New World, this was to be interpreted as a sign that God had ratified the covenant. From the very inception of the Puritan community, therefore, human events were interpreted as signs through which the will of God might be discerned.

In return for their safe passage to the New World, Winthrop asserted that God would expect that the Puritans would willingly dedicate their lives to the observance of divine laws. But if they should deviate from this obligation, Winthrop warned that special sanctions had been built into the covenant agreement. A curse attended the breaking of the covenant: "The Lord shall surely breake out in war against us and be revenged of such a perjured people and make us know the price of the breach of such a Covenant." If they ordered their lives, churches, and government, however, according to divine law, they would be rewarded with God's favor and blessings. "We shall find," Winthrop declared, "that the God of Israel is among us." With such help, ten Puritans would be able to resist a thousand enemies, and the Massachusetts community would become a model for all other plantations in the New World.

The Puritans were aware that this covenant was not simply made before God. They were self-conscious about their position in the eyes of the world. A Puritan leader such as John Winthrop was very concerned about the public status of their covenant community: "For we must Consider that we shall be as a City upon a Hill, the eyes of all people are upon us." This motif of the shining city on a hill has played a powerful and persistent role in forming America's self-image. Winthrop's vision of the city on a hill has often been invoked by those who would like to see America as a beacon of light for the rest of the world. But when John Winthrop introduced this image of the Puritan community, he was more concerned with the prospect that their theocratic experiment, exposed to the eyes of the world, would be vulnerable to public censure if it failed. The Puritans' failure to remain faithful to the covenant would bring discredit to the true religion. "If we deal falsely with God," Winthrop warned, "the curse of God's people shall be spread throughout the world."[17] The risks involved in such a public exposure of the covenant became standardized in the Puritan theology of the Massachusetts Bay Colony. Twenty years after the first migration, the theologian Peter Bulkeley echoed the concerns of John Winthrop in his summary of Puritan theology, *The General Covenant: Or the Covenant of Grace Opened:*

> We are as a city set upon a hill, in open view of all the earth, the eyes of the world are upon us, because we profess ourselves to be a people in covenant with God, and therefore not only the Lord our God, with whom we have made covenant, but heaven and earth, angels and men, that are witness to our profession, will cry shame upon us if we walk contrary to the covenant which we have professed and promised to walk in.[18]

The covenant community imagined itself at the center of the cosmic drama. The profession of a sacred covenant exposed the community before the eyes of the world. The Puritans saw grave risks in entering into this covenant before heaven and earth. But one of the ironies in the history of this Massachusetts covenant community was that the Puritans were able to flourish in the New World, and practice the demands of their covenant undisturbed, because they were largely ignored in the Old.

While the Old World remained relatively unconcerned with this covenant community, the Puritans in the Massachusetts Bay Colony were convinced that God was not. The difficulties that the Puritans experienced in establishing their settlements in the New World were interpreted as an expression of God's interest in the community. The various hardships of the settlement were understood as one of the conditions of the covenant. These were sacred afflictions reserved by God for his chosen people. The Puritan theologian Increase Mather wrote in his *Times of Men* (1675) that "God has covenanted with his people that sanctified afflictions shall be their portion . . . This is the usual method of divine Providence . . . by the greatest miseries to prepare for the greatest mercies."

The chosen people stood directly under the constant judgment of God. Other nations might be allowed to sin; they would eventually be destroyed for the accumulated evil of their ways. But this new Israel would be punished for each infraction of the divine law in order to be corrected and brought back into conformity with the covenant. The covenant community would thereby avoid the eventual general destruction promised for all other nations. Increase Mather captured both the Puritan confidence in the providence of God, as well as their anxiety before the judgment of God, when he declared that "Christ by a wonderful Providence has . . . caused as it were *New Jerusalem* to come down from

Heaven; He dwells in this place therefore we may conclude that he will scourge us."[19]

The Puritan imagination was nurtured by biblical symbols of ancient Israel and the coming kingdom. Their religious imagination occupied a sacred time that was contemporaneous with both. They were able to interpret the events of their recent history in terms of the biblical narrative of Israel's redemption. Samuel Fisher, in his *Testimony of Truth* (1679), declared: "Let *Israel* be . . . our glass to view our faces in."[20] But because their understanding of biblical typology collapsed any separations of ordinary, historical time in the workings of God's grace, a Puritan such as Benjamin Woodbridge was able to exclaim: "O happy Israel in America."[21] The covenant community was not ancient history; it was alive and well in the New World. It was taking shape in the New Jerusalem prefigured in the Book of Revelation, and now appearing in America, in the words of Cambridge minister Urian Oakes "as a little model of the glorious kingdom of Christ on earth."[22]

In the Puritan community religious imagination had definite political consequences. These religious images had to be sustained by specific institutional arrangements in both church and state. The philosophy of theocratic government was outlined in *The Laws and Liberties of New England* (1648). The theocratic model of ancient Israel was again invoked: "Our Churches, and Civil State have been planted . . . together like that of Israel in the wilderness." Both church and state must conform to a theocratic pattern. In the churches this meant an attempt to "set up the ordinances of Christ Jesus in them according to the Apostolic pattern." They felt they were recovering the original, pure pattern of church organization. And in government this meant an administration of society based on the demands of divine law. They sought "to frame our civil Polity and laws according to the rules of his most holy word." The result was a synchronized theocratic system of church and state. The Puritans of New England assumed that church and state should function in close cooperation; "each do help and strengthen the other (the Churches the Civil Authority, and the Civil Authority the Churches), and so both prosper."[23] The theocratic experiment of New England, therefore, required that both church and state conform to the pattern of the divine covenant that had captured the Puritan imagination.

THE THEOCRATIC EXPERIMENT

There were a number of important signs of the covenant that united this Puritan community. The first was *conversion*. The Puritan experience of inner conversion marked their entrance into the covenant; it was through the conversion experience that they became, in the words of Peter Bulkeley, "a people in covenant, i.e., Grace with God."[24] Their understanding of this divine grace was shaped by the Calvinist branch of the Protestant Reformation. They subscribed to the formulation of Calvinist doctrine worked out at the Synod of Dort in 1617. This Calvinist council responded to the position articulated by Jacob Arminius (1560-1609), a theological stance that came to be known as Arminianism, which placed confidence in the ability of human free will to choose salvation in cooperation with God's grace. The orthodox Calvinists rejected any reliance on human decisions, or personal merit, in the workings of grace. They reaffirmed the Calvinist doctrine of predestination. Due to original sin, they believed, all humanity deserved eternal damnation; but God would demonstrate his mercy by selecting a chosen few to receive the unmerited gift of grace. Salvation was predestined for those elect solely through the inexorable will of God.

Orthodox Calvinist doctrine produced certain inevitable tensions in practice. First, the doctrine of the *total depravity of humanity* convinced the Puritans that sin was a basic fact of life. Sinfulness pervaded the human condition. So regardless of how rigorously they obeyed divine laws, they were inevitably enmeshed in a world of corruption. Second, the doctrine of *unconditional election* insisted that salvation would not be based on good works. Personal merit would not be a condition of their election. This produced the dilemma in which Puritans valued a life of good works, but recognized that no amount of personal righteousness could merit salvation. Third, the doctrine of *limited atonement* suggested that only those who had been predestined for salvation would receive grace through Christ. The Puritans felt compelled to spread their Christian gospel, but were convinced that only the elect would have the ears to hear. Fourth, the doctrine of the *irresistibility of grace* indicated that humans have no power to achieve or interfere with God's gift of grace. They were exhorted to seek salvation, but could do nothing to achieve it. Finally, the doctrine of the *perseverence of the saints* promised the elect that they would not only be shown signs of God's grace, but that they would be given the power to continue in that grace and enter into the kingdom of heaven. This inspired the Puritans to search their hearts, minds, and actions for evidence of grace, but no evidence could be certain. And if a Puritan did find such proof of divine election, this could just as easily be interpreted as evidence of the sin of pride. The Puritan theologian Arthur Hildersam wrote in 1629 that uncertainty was even to be preferred over a false assurance of election. "A false peace and assurance," Hildersam suggested, is "one of the most grievous judgments that can befall a man . . . it were better for a man to be vexed with continuall doubts and feares, than to be lulled a-sleep with such an assurance."[25]

The Puritan community resolved some of this tension regarding salvation by making conversion the criterion for entrance into the church. To become a church member an individual would be required to stand before the church and give personal testimony of his or her experience of

God's grace. If the church members acknowledged this testimony as a legitimate witness to religious conversion, then the individual would be admitted into the body of Christ. This public authentication of personal conversion eased some of the tension surrounding the question of salvation. Personal uncertainty about election could be somewhat resolved through public consensus in the church. Yet for many Puritans the agonizing scrutiny of conscience for signs of grace persisted. In a revealing journal entry a mason from Quincy demonstrated the kind of soul searching that was involved: "I am now forty years old," he said, "and cannot but be ashamed to look back and consider how I have spent my lost time; being at a great loss whether any true grace be wrought in my soul or no."[26] And there were rare occasions when a Puritan would prefer the certainty of damnation to the uncertainty of election. John Winthrop wrote of a woman in the Boston congregation who was experiencing intense distress about her spiritual state. He recounted that "one day she took her little infant and threw it into a well, and then came into the house and said, now she was sure she would be damned."[27]

Second, a more tangible sign of the covenant was the Puritan commitment to a *calling*. This calling, or vocation, took the form of disciplined work in the world. It was a prevailing disposition, however, that invested any kind of undertaking with the ascetic discipline of hard work, self-denial, and conscientious service. The monastic communities of the Catholic Middle Ages had developed an ascetic discipline removed from the world in which "to work is to pray." Puritans transposed this monastic ideal into the day-to-day occupations, businesses, and enterprises of the community. They were called to an "inner-worldly asceticism." The Puritan ethic demanded that they not retreat from the world, as a monk or a hermit, but rather that they live a pure, disciplined, and productive life in the world. Work in the world became a test of faith. Rather than avoiding the worldly temptations of pride, greed, and lust, they were to confront and conquer them. As John Winthrop expressed it: "For such trials as fall within the compass of our callings, it is better to arm and withstand them than to avoid and shun them."[28]

The Puritan calling did not simply provide a form of personal spiritual discipline, it also encouraged Puritans to translate their self-denial into efforts that would benefit the community. John Cotton, who became the preeminent theologian of the Puritan establishment, referred to this as a "warrantable calling." A member of the covenant community was expected to labor in a vocation "not only . . . at our own, but at the public good." True faith would find its expression in a calling that would be of service to others. According to John Cotton, God approved of those who "live by faith in [their] vocations, in that faith, in serving God, serves men, and in serving men, serves God." But, "if thou hast no calling, tending to public good, thou art an unclean beast."[29] The Puritan calling placed great value upon disciplined, productive, and useful work; it was an ascetic spiritual discipline for the individual, and a source of support and service for the community. The social byproduct of all this disciplined, industrious, and ascetic labor was the accumulation of wealth and the increase in economic power.

The third sign of the covenant addressed directly this problem of the distribution of wealth. It was the religioeconomic ideal of *charity*. John Winthrop believed that the Puritan community was knit together by bonds of love; but it was also divided by the unequal distribution of wealth. In his sermon on board the *Arabella* Winthrop maintained that the unequal distribution of wealth was a condition of God's design for humanity. "God Almighty in his most holy and wise providence," Winthrop declared, "has so disposed the Condition of mankind, as in all times some must be rich some poor, some high and eminent in power and dignity, others mean and in subjection."[30] According to Winthrop, inequalities in the distribution of wealth and power were built into God's providential plan for human societies. Winthrop proceeded to give two basic reasons for this arrangement.

First, these inequalities were designed to demonstrate God's power to order the variety of creation so that all its parts served the good of the whole. The poor served the interests of the rich and powerful to whom they were subjected. But the wealthy served the poor through their exercise of charity. They had been selected as stewards of the earth's resources, and they were responsible for redistributing that wealth through gifts of charity to the poor. Winthrop claimed that in selecting many stewards for this purpose, God was more honored "in dispensing his gifts to man by man, then if he did it by his own immediate hand."[31] This economic theory of providence, stewardship, and charity was an important aspect of the covenant; these economic assumptions were important ingredients in the theocratic system of religiopolitical power. To understand the political implications of religious power it is important to be aware of the ways in which wealth is distributed, and the ways in which that distribution is legitimated by religion. For Winthrop, God's plan for creation called for two kinds of people: rich and poor. The rich were defined as "all such as are able to live comfortably by their owne means duely improved; and all others are poor according to the former distribution."[32] The rich were responsible for the good of the entire theocratic system through their stewardship of resources and acts of charity. Nevertheless, this system not only justified but even required inequalities in the distribution of wealth.

A second reason Winthrop gave for the unequal distribution of wealth suggested that these inequalities enabled God to administer his moral government over humanity. God's moral government, according to Winthrop, required the rich should not destroy the poor, nor should the poor rise up and shake off the yoke of the rich and powerful. To accomplish this political balance between the rich and the poor, God had prescribed the development of certain moral virtues. But different virtues were appropriate to different stations in life. The rich found themselves in a social status suited for the development of love, mercy, gentleness, and temperance. The poor, however, had the opportunity to cultivate a different set of virtues: faith, patience, and obedience. When all these virtues were activated, the unequal distribution of wealth created a synchronized mutual dependency, "so that every man may have need of each other."[33] This harmony of mutual need served to weave together a unified human community. In this harmonious vision Winthrop proposed a religious justification for the unequal distribution of wealth in human society. It was a design that encouraged charity and mutual dependence in the covenant community; but it is also clear that such a theocentric solution justified a hierarchy of needs and gave a religious aura to social inequalities.

By 1635 as many as twelve churches had been formed in the Massachusetts Bay Colony. In each the notion of covenant provided the basis for ecclesiastical organization. Legitimate authority in the church was derived from the gathering of individuals who had entered into the covenant through their conversions. It was believed to be a gathering of "visible saints." Thomas Hooker, who was instrumental in extending the Puritan experiment to Connecticut, described the basis of church organization as this "Visible Covenant agreement or consent whereby they give themselves unto the Lord, to the observing of the ordinances of Christ together in the same society, which is usually called the Church-Covenant." This church covenant, as a voluntary gathering of Puritan saints, determined the shape of organized religious power. "For we see not otherwise," Hooker continued, "how members can have church-power one over another mutually."[34] The members were admitted into the church after they had made a voluntary testimony of their faith. They could then participate in the election of ministers to preach the word of God and administer church affairs. But the church members who held this nascent democratic prerogative were distinguished from the congregation. Some in the community were not willing or able to provide a convincing testimony of the workings of grace in their lives. They were restricted from church membership, but they were nevertheless required by law to be members of the congregation. The Puritan theocracy required mandatory church attendance. So any given Sunday service could be divided into two parts: first, the entire community would be required to hear the sermon encouraging all people toward "more hearty and conscionable obedience"; and, second, the congregation would depart so that the church members could receive the holy communion.

This was the congregational model of church polity. Each church was separate; but they were all united with each other because, in the words of Urian Oakes, Christ served "not only as a mystical but a political head."[35] And even though each church independently selected its own ministers, and directed its own affairs, it could be subjected to the co-

ercive power of the state if it became schismatic and broke off communion with other churches. So although the congregational model of
church polity allowed for a considerable degree of independence for each
church, the various churches were unified in a larger pattern of cooperation between church and state.

In the Puritan theocratic system, church and state were seen as two
aspects of a single order. The eternal sacred order was preserved by the
church, while a temporal sacred order was maintained by the state. In the
churches the word of God was preached; in the courts it was enforced.
Religious persuasion and political coercion were synchronized in the theocratic system. As president of Harvard College, Urian Oakes insisted that
church and state were separate institutions in theory, but they were unified in actual practice. "The design of our founders and the frame of
things laid by them," he stated, made "the interest of righteousness in the
Commonwealth and holiness in the Church . . . inseparable."[36] And the
religious standards of holiness were translated into law. Magistrates were
charged to restrain and punish a wide range of religious offenses: "idolatry, blasphemy, heresy, venting corrupt and pernicious opinions that destroy the foundation, open contempt of the word preached, profanation
of the Lord's Day, disturbing the peaceable administration and exercise of
the worship and holy things of God and the like."[37] All manner of religious deviations appeared before the law as serious criminal offenses.

The Puritan theory of church and state was most clearly articulated
by the theologian John Cotton. In a letter to England in 1636, Cotton
outlined and explained their theocratic system of government. He began
by insisting that God had ordained church administration and civil government as separate spheres. They may be close, compact, and coordinated, but they should not be confused. Nevertheless, "both of them are
subordinate to spiritual ends." The ideal political blueprint for both
church and state was to be found in the Bible. The best political order,
according to Cotton's reading of scripture, was one that was devoted to
preserving the vitality of the church. The civil government must be
framed in such a way that it meets the needs of religion. The government
of the commonwealth must be suited to the church. "It is better," Cotton
insisted, "that the Commonwealth be fashioned to the setting forth of
God's house, which is His Church, than to accommodate the Church frame
to the civil state."[38]

The model of government which John Cotton proposed was one in
which the state revolved around the sacred nucleus of the church; it
would be designed to form a synchronized harmony of religious and political power around the fixed center of the covenant. Democracy, as a
more diffused, egalitarian distribution of political power, would be an unacceptable form of civil government in such a centralized system. Democracy was incompatible with the centralization of power at the heart of the
covenant community. Cotton observed: "Democracy, I do not conceive

that ever God did ordain as a fit government either for church or commonwealth. If the people be governors, who shall be governed?" Democracy was rejected as a legitimate form of government for two reasons: It was not considered scriptural, and it did not make the necessary distinction between the rulers and the ruled. But there was also a sense that a democratic arrangement would disperse power through the political system which John Cotton would prefer to reserve for the religious elite of the covenant. Cotton proceeded to observe that both monarchy and aristocracy seem to have been approved by scripture, but only to the extent that they ultimately referred all civil power back to the authority of God. This left the conclusion that the only acceptable system of power was one which "sets up Theocracy . . . as the best form of government in the commonwealth, as well as in the church."[39]

The role of the church in such a theocratic system was to prepare "fit instruments both to rule and to choose rulers."[40] Only godly men who were acknowledged members of the church covenant could perform these political functions. They would both rule and choose rulers to serve as magistrates of the General Court and as burgesses, who, with the magistrates, would make and enforce all laws. The political franchise in the Puritan theocracy was, therefore, reserved for the members of the church. And they would strive to administer the commonwealth according to divine law. The theocratic state would be ruled according to God's will as revealed in scripture. John Cotton, and other leaders of the Puritan community, saw this model of government as the promise of a Christian theocracy, fulfilled in New England.

John Winthrop the governor echoed the theocratic ideals of John Cotton the theologian. He imagined that the magistrates represented an aristocracy of "gifts and experience." This spiritual aristocracy would carry the power and authority over civil government. They would even hold a veto over decisions made by representatives of the people elected by church members. Democracy would be an unacceptable form of civil government. Winthrop repeated the two reasons for this which had been suggested by John Cotton. First, democracy did not appear to have any justification in the Bible. "Now if we should change from a mixed aristocracy to a mere democracy," Winthrop stated, "first, we should have no warrant in Scripture for it; there was no such government in Israel." The covenant demanded conformity to biblical precedents. This ruled out any democratic civil government as an unwarranted innovation.

Second, democracy did not make the proper delineation of civil authority between rulers and ruled. If the Puritans should adopt a democratic form of civil organization, Winthrop asserted, "we should hereby voluntarily abase ourselves, and deprive ourselves of the dignity which the providence of God has put upon us, which is a manifest breach of the Fifth Commandment." The fifth commandment mandated that "You shall honor your father and mother." Winthrop assumed that the magistrates, as a spiritual aristocracy, held a patriarchal authority over the community. This commandment to honor parental authority was invoked as a justification of theocratic power; it was interpreted as supporting the legal authority of the civil magistrates. The fifth commandment was periodically invoked in legal proceedings against dissenters such as Anne Hutchinson, and against heretics such as the Quakers, to reinforce the religious legitimation of magisterial authority.

Obedience to the theocratic authority of the magistrates was felt to be mandated by scripture. The Puritan authorities could point to the justification of obedience to civil authority in the New Testament letter of Paul to the Romans: "You must obey the governing authorities. Since all government comes from God, the civil authorities were appointed by God (Rom 13:1)." And the Puritan magistrates could claim this divine authority as their own. Such a theocracy, Winthrop felt, could not tolerate a democratic distribution of power. Governor Winthrop condemned this form of government: "A democracy is, among most civil nations, accounted the meanest and worst of all forms of government."[41] Although there were certain democratic impulses operating in the congregational church polity, in the election of ministers, as well as magistrates, by church members, that enfranchisement was held under the theocratic power of the covenant. And all people were bound to its obedience.

THEOCRATIC POWER

The Puritans in New England established institutions of both church and state in the service of theocratic power. These institutions required a high degree of uniformity in the community. Everyone had to attend church; everyone had to live in a family, rather than alone; and everyone had to learn to read in order to study the Bible. Behavior, habits, and even dress were carefully regulated. Church members were expected to monitor each other's moral behavior, so they could live together in a commonwealth "wherein the least known evils are not to be tolerated." The result of such a meticulously ordered network of social relations was the tendency to perceive any departure from the established order as a dangerous threat to the entire social fabric.

Theocratic power is particularly threatened by any uncontrolled exercise of power within its domain. The theocratic power of the New England Puritans was reinforced by means of punitive acts—humiliation, confinement, banishment, and execution—which served as rituals of exclusion that maintained the purity of the social body by expelling any uncontrollable influences perceived to be dangerous. Those threats to the social order were symbolized as demonic, satanic, or evil forces attacking the theocratic community. The demands of theocratic purity required the expulsion of such dangers. The anthropologist Mary Douglas has suggested one way of understanding this process:

> Religious beliefs express society's awareness of itself; the social structure is credited with punitive powers which maintain it in being. This is quite straightforward. But I would like to suggest that those holding office in the explicit part of the structure tend to be credited with consciously controlled powers, in contrast with those whose role is less explicit and who tend to be credited with unconscious, uncontrollable powers, menacing those in better defined positions.[42]

The theocratic leaders punished religious dissenters, Quakers, and witches during the seventeenth century as forces of evil credited with unconscious and uncontrollable powers which threatened those in explicit centers of power.

The theocratic order could not tolerate any diversity in matters of religion. It was committed to a political regime of religious intolerance. The Puritan Nathaniel Ward assumed the role of spokesman for the theocratic ideal of intolerance. "I dare to take upon me to be the herald of New England," he declared, "as far as to proclaim to the world in the name of our colony, that all Familists, Antinomians, Anabaptists, and other enthusiasts shall have the liberty to keep away from us; and such as will come, to be gone as fast as they can, the sooner the better."[43] Rituals of exclusion are essential for the maintenance of a theocratic system. By reinforcing the boundaries of the community, the power of the theocratic center is renewed. The political history of the New England community can be viewed as a dynamic process of boundary definition, maintenance, and eventually disruption.

Boundary Definition

The religious controversies with Roger Williams and Anne Hutchinson occurred during the first decade of the New England settlement. Magisterial authority over the theocracy was still being defined, and these conflicts helped to clarify the position of the magistrates in the community. Roger Williams was variously described in New England as charming, sweet-tempered, God-intoxicated, and stubborn. He was a committed Puritan. But he struggled to achieve an even greater degree of religious purity than the ruling Puritans in Massachusetts. His conflict with the Massachusetts theocracy revolved around the issue of the relationship between church and state. Williams contended that only through an extreme separation from the institutional power of the civil state could the Puritans achieve religious purity.

Roger Williams arrived in New England in the year following the first migration of 1630. As a Puritan separatist, he had no hesitation about leaving England; he saw the Church of England, in allowing unregenerate persons to communion, as a contaminated body. When he arrived in Massachusetts he found that the Boston church followed the congregational model, but it did not actually renounce the Church of England. Williams refused to serve in such a church. "I durst not officiate to an unseparated people," he declared, "as upon examination and conference I found them to be."[44] He was offered a position in the Salem church; but the offer was withdrawn when Governor John Winthrop objected to his appointment. Williams then moved to Plymouth, but he soon left when he discovered that members visiting England on business would take communion with the Church of England. Williams went back to Salem to serve as an unofficial assistant to its pastor. There he created controversy by attacking some of the foundational principles of the theocracy. He questioned the right of the colonists to the land that had been granted by the King in the New World, referring to the King of England as liar and antichrist. And he further questioned the theocratic coordination between church and state that was being established in New England. For Williams, America was not the New Israel. In his interpretation of the Bible, Israel was "an unparalleled figure of the Spiritual State." It represented a spiritual redemption that was not of this world. But America, as well as Europe and all nations, "lies dead with sin." To fashion America into a political theocracy was to confuse the spiritual and the temporal orders; it was "to pull *God* and *Christ* and *Spirit* out of Heaven, and subject them unto *natural*, sinful, inconstant men."[45]

Under the influence of Roger Williams, the ministers of Salem declared congregational independence in 1635 in order to separate their church from the other churches in New England. Those other churches organized to petition the civil government to take punitive action against Williams, and he was brought to trial in Boston during October of the same year. Williams was confronted with two basic criminal charges. First, he was accused of fomenting dangerous opinions denying the authority of the civil magistrates over religious matters. He was advocating the separation of church from state. Second, Williams was accused of writing traitorous letters urging the Salem church to declare its independence from the other churches in New England. He was advocating the separation of church from church. After considering the evidence against Williams, the Magistrate Court ordered banishment. He was condemned to leave the colony within six weeks.

In January, 1636, Roger Williams departed for Rhode Island. There he was able to put his extreme separatism into practice, and his congregation of the faithful there were all rebaptized as evidence of their religious purity. From Providence, Rhode Island, Williams wrote back to John Winthrop attacking the Massachusetts theocracy. "Abstract yourself," Williams exhorted, "with a holy violence from the Dung Heap of this Earth."[46] Gradually however, Williams began to have doubts about the purity of his own congregation in Providence; and he finally reached the point where he could not conscientiously take communion with anyone but his own wife. Here Williams seemed to reach the limit of separation. Reversing his practice of rigorous separatism, he began to embrace a policy of open toleration of religious diversity. As John Winthrop reported this change, "having, a little before, refused communion with all, save his own wife, now he would preach to and pray with all comers."[47] Rhode Island became a haven of religious toleration. But from the perspective of John Winthrop it was the "cess pool of the world."

Roger Williams expressed his theory of church and state in the metaphor of the ship of state. A commonwealth is like a ship setting out to sea with hundreds of passengers, who all may have different religious commitments. It may happen that the ship contains Catholics, Protestants, Jews, and Muslims, and all must coexist. Religious freedom under such conditions is guaranteed by two principles. First, "that none of the papists, protestants, Jews, or Turks, be forced to come to the ship's prayers or worship, nor compelled from their own particular prayers or worship, if they practice any." Liberty of religious belief, practice, and association would be assured. Second, "notwithstanding this liberty, the commander of this ship ought to command the ship's course, and also command that justice, peace and sobriety, be kept and practiced, both among the seamen and all the passengers."[48] The civil authorities of the ship of state, therefore, are charged to maintain the public peace and order. They may establish and enforce laws in order to preserve and protect the common good, and they may restrain and punish transgressors. But their authority does not extend over matters of religion that do not disturb the public peace. Roger Williams articulated the basic elements of the separation of church and state that would define the relation between religious and political power in subsequent American history.

The Puritan theocracy, however, could not tolerate such a division within its unified field of religiopolitical power. All forms of religious diversity had to be pushed beyond the boundaries of the commonwealth in order to maintain the unified power of the theocratic state. A second threat to that power and authority was posed by the antinomianism of Anne Hutchinson. Anne arrived in Massachusetts with her husband William in September of 1634. She was described by John Winthrop as "a woman of a ready wit and bold spirit"; her husband was described by Winthrop as "a man of a very mild temper and weak parts and wholly guided by his wife."[49] Anne Hutchinson was denied church membership for two years, because some of her fellow passengers on the crossing had been disturbed by her unorthodox religious opinions. But after serving two years as a midwife, and with the support of the Reverend John Cotton, she was admitted into membership of the Boston church.

Anne Hutchinson began to hold Sunday meetings in her home after church services in which she would explain the sermons of Reverend Cotton and expound upon points of religious doctrine. Her message was a radical spirituality. She adopted the characteristic Calvinist assumption that human beings were helpless before the irresistible workings of God's grace. But she held that a radical spiritual transformation occurred when God acted upon a person; the person was totally changed by the indwelling power of the Holy Spirit. The person was no longer under God's law, but was now free in the spirit of God's grace. For this reason her teachings were labeled *antinomian*, signifying that the Christian who had received grace was beyond the law (*nomos*). No external behavior could indicate whether or not this transformation had occurred. So there was an important distinction, according to Anne Hutchinson, between *sanctification*—manifested in a holy life within God's laws—and *justification*—which signified that a person had been chosen by God for salvation. The sanctity of a person's behavior gave no indication of his or her justification. Anne Hutchinson's position ran against the Puritan mainstream which, although it recognized that there could be no certainty of election, nevertheless looked to the good lives of the saints as an indication of their salvation.

Anne Hutchinson's weekly lectures on justification posed a threat to the Puritan establishment for a number of reasons. First, she claimed independent access to divine authority through the indwelling of the Holy Spirit. Hutchinson claimed that "the person of the Holy Ghost dwells in a justified person." This represented an alternative source of spiritual authority that was independent of the theocratic system represented by the magistrates. Second, she showed a disregard for the system of divine laws upon which the Puritan establishment was based. A justified person had no concern for the enforced sanctity of laws, duties, and obligations. "Tell me not of duties," Anne Hutchinson said, "but tell me of Christ."[50] The theocratic system could not allow anyone to claim a higher authority than the divine law. Third, Anne Hutchinson claimed that a justified person could discern through the spirit who was justified and who was not. She apparently divided all Puritans into two groups: those of the *covenant of grace* (who were genuinely among the elect) and those of the *covenant of works* (who were deluded and damned because they relied upon good works rather than grace). When it came to discerning who among the Puritan clergy were in the covenant of grace, she apparently could find only two: John Cotton and her minister from England John Wheelwright.

In October 1636, the contingent following Anne Hutchinson proposed that John Wheelwright be installed as preacher in the Boston church. His nomination was defeated by John Winthrop. By the beginning of 1637 Boston was divided into two hostile factions. Wheelwright preached against the covenant of works. He attacked the established clergy. "The more *holy* they are," Wheelwright declared, "the greater enemies they are to Christ . . . We must kill them with the word of the Lord."[51] John Winthrop and the magistrates had the last word, however, and

Wheelwright was banished in August, 1637. In November Anne Hutchinson was called before the Magistrate Court to be tried for heresy.

Anne Hutchinson was charged with three criminal offenses. First, she was accused of encouraging Wheelwright's faction against the government of Massachusetts. In participating in this opposition movement, the Court contended, she broke the fifth commandment; she was accused of dishonoring the governors who were the fathers of the commonwealth. At the trial, John Winthrop told her: "We do not mean to discourse with those of your sex but only this: you do adhere unto them and do endeavor to set forward this faction and so you do dishonor us."[52] But Anne Hutchinson had not signed a general petition that had been circulated by the Wheelwright supporters against the government, so the Court's case was weak on this particular point.

Second, she was accused of holding illicit weekly meetings at her home of both men and women. The Court claimed that such mixed meetings were not fitting in the sight of God and were not appropriate for someone of her sex. Anne Hutchinson responded to this charge by citing two biblical verses that seemed to provide a precedent for women giving religious instruction in the early Christian community. But the Court was not satisfied by these examples. The following exchange between Anne Hutchinson and John Winthrop was recorded:

AH: "I call them not, but if they come to me, I may instruct them."

JW: "Yet you show not a rule."

AH: I have given you two places of scripture.

JW: But neither of them will suit your practice.

AH: Must I show my name written therein?[53]

On this point too the Court's position was considered inconclusive.

Third, Anne Hutchinson was accused of slandering the ministers of Massachusetts by claiming that they were in the covenant of works. Numerous ministers gave testimony to this, but John Cotton came to her defense. He claimed that he had never heard her denounce these ministers. Although he was challenged by other ministers, Cotton stood firm. This point also might have remained inconclusive if Anne Hutchinson had not volunteered to speak of her personal revelations. She announced that since she arrived in New England she had been persecuted like Daniel in the lion's den, and she warned the magistrates to deal carefully with her, because "God will ruin you, and your posterity and this whole state." The Court asked how these things were revealed to her.

JW: How do you know that it was God that did reveal these things to you, and not Satan?

AH: How did Abraham know that it was God that bid him offer his son . . . ?

JW: By an immediate voice.

AH: So to me by an immediate revelation.

JW: How! an immediate revelation?

AH: By the voice of his own spirit to my soul.[54]

Anne Hutchinson's claim to direct revelation from God was too much for the Court to tolerate. Such independent divine authority challenged the centralized power structure of the theocratic system. She was excommunicated and banished with her followers to Rhode Island.

In the first decade of the Puritan establishment the boundaries of the theocratic system were defined by what it excluded. The trials of Roger Williams and Anne Hutchinson were test cases for theocratic power. In a sense, both were attempting to be more authentic Puritans than the Massachusetts Puritan establishment. But, because of the challenge they represented to the authority of that establishment, they were not permitted to remain within the same civil space that was marked out by the theocratic system.

Boundary Maintenance

As the Massachusetts theocracy entered its third decade it confronted the problem of maintaining its rigid boundaries against the incursion of outside influences. At this point the first generation of leaders was passing from the scene. John Winthrop died in 1649; John Cotton died in 1652. In addition to this transition in leadership, the colony felt increasingly isolated from England. England was enmeshed in its own religious controversies; and the ascendancy of Cromwell marked a new era of religious toleration. The New England community felt even more compelled to maintain the rigid intolerance of its theocratic boundaries and to reaffirm its theocratic power by exercising the rituals of exclusion. In this context, the first missionaries of the Society of Friends, known as Quakers, entered into the New England theocracy.

The founder of the Society of Friends was George Fox (1624-1691). He was born in Leicestershire, England, and apprenticed as a shoemaker. Although Fox was of a serious religious disposition, he despaired of finding God in any of the existing churches. Suddenly he began to have personal religious experiences which convinced him that each individual could have direct access to God through the Holy Spirit. In rejecting the churches, Fox felt that he had found Christ within. "When all my hopes in them and in all men were gone," Fox declared, "I heard a voice which said, 'There is one, even Christ Jesus, that can speak to thy condition.'"[55] Fox began to travel around England preaching a religious message based upon this direct inner experience of God, and he was ridiculed by mobs, beaten, and imprisoned.

In 1652 George Fox formed the Society of Friends. This was a religious association dedicated to a mysticism of the inner light. Fox promised that whoever discovered this inner light would find the indwelling power of Christ. "Now I was sent to turn people from darkness to the light," Fox stated, "that they might receive Christ Jesus, for to as many as should receive him in his light, I saw that he would give power to become the sons of God."[56] These early Quakers cultivated a religious *enthusiasm*—a sense that God's power lived within them. For the Puritan establishment this was a serious heresy similar to the claims of personal spiritual inspiration and power that had been made by Anne Hutchinson. But even religious leaders such as Roger Williams, dedicated to the principle of religious toleration, found the Quaker enthusiasm theologically unacceptable. "They perceived not Jesus Christ but themselves," Williams observed, "yea, they preached the Lord Jesus to be themselves."[57] And Quaker missionary activities in preaching the enthusiasm of the inner light brought them to the New World; first they went to Barbados, and then in 1656 the first missionaries arrived in Massachusetts.

The response of the Puritan establishment to the Quaker missionaries indicated the extent to which it was willing to employ punitive measures to maintain the theocratic boundaries. The first two Quaker missionaries, Mary Fisher and Ann Austin, were arrested in Boston; they were taken to jail, stripped and searched for marks of witchcraft, their books were burned, and they were deported back to Barbados. But soon others followed. The magistrates drafted a series of anti-Quaker laws. Three distinguishing features of Quakers were identified: Quakers employed the expressions "thee" and "thou" in their conversation; they gathered in small groups for private religious meetings; and they refused to take off their hats before magistrates. The first feature simply set them apart from the orthodox Puritans, but these other characteristics signified that the Quakers represented an alternative source of religious and political power which was perceived as a threat by the Puritan establishment. In order to maintain the legitimate boundaries of the theocratic system, the Puritan leaders were determined to eliminate this new danger.

The increased activity of Quaker missionaries showed a desire for confrontation and perhaps an appetite for persecution. Harsher punishments were introduced. For the first offense of entering Massachusetts, the Quaker was to have one ear cut off. A second offense would cost the other ear. Women could keep their ears, but would be severely whipped. A third offense was punished by boring a hole through the Quaker's tongue with a hot iron. All of these corporal punishments were finalized by banishment. These same laws applied to any Massachusetts resident who converted to the Society of Friends. As missionary activity continued, the General Court, in October of 1658, simplified the prescribed punishment: banishment or death. The Quakers tested this new law. One announced: "All these as one come together in the moving and power of the Lord to look your bloody laws in the face." Governor Endicott responded by selecting two for execution. Endicott was reluctant to resort to capital punishment, but was convinced that it was necessary to maintain the integrity of the theocratic system. Other Puritans were more enthusiastic; John Wilson was reported as exclaiming: "Burn all the Quakers in the world."[58]

Persecution seemed to inspire the Quakers to greater missionary activities. It was reported that some ran naked in the streets, disrupted church services, and challenged the authority of the anti-Quaker laws. Many made themselves available for execution. Mary Dyer was executed in 1660, and William Leddra in 1661. By one account the waiting list became so long that if all were executed it would have been one of the bloodiest massacres on record. But in 1661 the King intervened. Charles II prohibited any form of corporal punishment of Quakers in the colonies. The Massachusetts magistrates wrote letters of protest back to England, but they were forced to suspend their laws against Quakers. As the intensity of persecution was thereby diminished, however, the Quaker missionaries seemed to lose interest in Massachusetts. They found a more congenial home in Rhode Island, and by 1681 the Quaker, William Penn, had established the colony of Pennsylvania in which the Society of Friends could flourish.

Violence directed against alternative religious movements was one means by which the Puritan establishment reinforced its absolute power, revitalized the theocratic system, and maintained its strict boundaries. This centrifugal force of exclusion was combined with a centripetal force of discipline. Church members were bound within the power of a disciplinary regimen. In order to maintain the purity of the covenant community all impurities had to be excluded from its center, as well as its periphery. Thomas Shepard, the pastor of the Cambridge church, indicated this need for internal purity when he insisted that if hypocrites within the church could be identified, "we should exclude them now." Vigilance was required to maintain the purity of the sacred center of the covenant community, for, as Shepard continued, "one man or woman secretly vile, which the church has not used all means to discover, may defile a whole church."[59] The purity of the center was maintained through a church discipline of mutual surveillance; the purity of the periphery was maintained by the punitive power of the state. Church and state were thus synchronized to maintain the boundaries of the covenant community.

The original covenant of faith, however, was subjected to certain internal pressures by the 1650s, with a growing population of second-generation Puritans who had been baptized, but who remained without the necessary experience of faith to become church members. A compromise which came to be called the Half-Way Covenant was worked out in a general church council in 1662. The leadership of the churches agreed that the offspring of church members would be eligible for a partial membership, and that any subsequent children of these children could also be baptized and accepted into this halfway church membership. These descendants of the original Puritan saints, who were not willing or able to make the necessary testimony of faith, could nevertheless "own the covenant" and enter into the discipline of the church. Some historians have seen the Half-Way Covenant as a sign of a decline in the original covenant ideal of a church of visible saints. The church was becoming a mixed body in which it was harder to tell the elect from the unregenerate. It is more likely, however, that the Half-Way Covenant was an attempt to extend the power and the scope of the original covenant to accommodate the descendants of its founders. Voting in church and state elections was still reserved for full members; political power, therefore, remained largely concentrated in the faithful elite. But the Half-Way Covenant, supported by covenant renewal ceremonies in which the whole community was encouraged to participate, sought to broaden the base of those who were connected to the church covenant. In this way, the Puritan establishment tried to maintain the religiopolitical structure of the covenant.[60]

Boundary Disruption

The churches were actually rather slow to accept the innovation of the Half-Way Covenant. By 1675 only 40 percent of the churches in Massachusetts had adopted this new policy. The years between 1675 and 1690, however, were times of crisis for the Puritan experiment. King Phillip's War in 1675 involved all of New England in a devastating full-scale military conflict with the Native Americans. Almost every town experienced death and destruction. This was followed by disastrous fires, widespread epidemics, and political turmoil. To many Puritans it seemed as if the afflictions that attended the covenant of a chosen people were being visited upon the community. And to make matters worse, England was showing an increased interest in the colony. Under royal authority the Anglican Church was required to be tolerated in Boston in 1679, and the King intervened in 1684 to revoke the original charter of the Massachusetts Bay Colony. A provincial government was enforced under Governor George Andros, but it met with such opposition that it was overthrown in a bloodless coup in 1689. Massachusetts was in effect without a government until a new charter was issued in 1692. It was in the context of these disturbances to the established order of the community that accusations of witchcraft were raised during the year of 1692 in the village of Salem, Massachusetts.

The fascination that subsequent generations have had for the Salem witchcraft trials is perhaps out of proportion to the importance of these events for the history of New England. The historian Perry Miller observed that the witchcraft crisis "had no effect on the ecclesiastical or political situation, it does not figure in the institutional or ideological development."[61] The Salem witchcraft crisis of 1692, in which at least 150 people stood trial as witches, was simply one episode in the long-term battle against supernatural forces of evil. Puritans shared the medieval assumption that certain people were in fact agents of the devil, and between 1647 and 1692 periodic outbreaks of witchcraft accusations had resulted in the execution of as many as fifteen convicted witches. But the intensity and scope of the witchcraft trials in Salem provide an important indication of the religious response in one community to the disruption of the Puritan experiment at the end of the seventeenth century.

At the beginning of 1692 a small group of young girls, between the ages of eight and eleven, in the household of the Reverend Samuel Parris, were experimenting with magical fortune telling. They met in informal gatherings to discuss their futures, and even devised a primitive crystal ball in which they tried to see signs of the character and status of their future husbands. By February these curiosities had turned into panic. The girls experienced strange disturbances: "odd postures," "foolish ridiculous speeches," "distempers," and "fits." Reverend Parris consulted with doctors and ministers about this strange behavior, but it was only after a month that he became convinced that the girls were being tormented by witches. By this time seven or eight other girls, ranging in age between twelve and twenty, also began to experience such disturbances. Under intense questioning by adults they named their tormenters, and on February 29, 1692 warrants for the arrest of three village women were issued.

One of these women, Tituba, a West Indian slave, confessed to being a witch and described the devil as "a thing all over hairy, all the face hairy, and a long nose." Another died in jail of natural causes. And the third was soon accompanied in prison by three other women as the accusations by the girls began to expand in scope. Abigail Williams accused the former Salem minister, George Burroughs, of being the wizard behind the entire outbreak, and a warrant was issued for his arrest and extradition from Maine. No trials could be held, however, because the colony of Massachusetts without a charter lacked any legal authority. But a new charter was brought from England by the new governor, William Phips, on May 14, 1692; and the witchcraft trials began. On June 10 a Salem Village woman, Bridget Bishop, was hanged for witchcraft; five more were executed in July; and in August another five were put to death, including Reverend George Burroughs. By the end of September, nineteen had been executed, two died in prison, and one died under torture. In all there were twenty-seven convictions, but those who confessed were reprieved from execution. In October Governor Phips intervened to stop any further imprisonments or trials for witchcraft. Over the next few months more than one hundred accused witches were eventually released from jail. The entire episode lasted less than a year.

The witchcraft hysteria was symptomatic of three types of conflict within the Salem community; these were conflicts that were endemic to the Puritan establishment. First, there was a *generational conflict*. The accusers were usually young unmarried women; the accused were middle-aged married or widowed women.[62] Disturbed by their uncertainty about the future, which must have been intensified by the recent social, economic, and political disruptions of New England, these girls projected their fears upon vulnerable members of the older generation. Second, the strange behavior of the girls occurred in the context of an intense *political conflict* within Salem Village. The village had recently hired and fired a number of ministers in rapid succession, one of whom was the unfortunate George Burroughs, later executed as a wizard. Factional divisions within the church contended with each other for political control. It is significant that the original accusations emanated from the home of the current minister, Samuel Parris, and continued accusations of witchcraft were sustained by supporters of his political faction in the church. Records from Salem Village indicate that of the twenty-seven adults who supported the trials by providing testimony against the accused witches, twenty-one can be clearly linked to the pro-Parris faction. And of the twenty who opposed the trials, by defending an accused person or questioning the accusations of the girls, nineteen were in the opposition faction.[63] This indicates that the witchcraft hysteria fed into political conflicts within the church; but it also suggests that witchcraft accusations may have been a political strategy exploited by Parris and his supporters to solidify their religious power in the church.

Third, the witchcraft accusations of 1692 are evidence of a *conflict of interpretation*. The strange behavior of the girls was interpreted in the vocabulary of demonology, but it could just as easily have been interpreted in another set of terms. The initial unusual behavior of the girls was described, by Robert Calef in 1700, as "getting into holes, and creeping under chairs and stools . . . , [with] sundry odd postures and antic gestures, [and] uttering foolish, ridiculous speeches which neither they themselves nor any others could make sense of."[64] The girls were encouraged by adults in the community to interpret their experience in terms of witchcraft. "When these calamities first began," Reverend Samuel Parris reported, "the affliction was several weeks before such hellish operations as witchcraft was suspected."[65] Only under the intense questioning about witchcraft did the girls begin to accuse others of being witches.

Similar afflictions occurred in Northampton in 1734. As in Salem, a number of people, particularly young women, began to experience anxiety, distress, and even terror. Unusual behavior was reported. But these afflictions, under the direction of the young minister of Northampton, Jonathan Edwards, were interpreted not as signs of demonic possession, but as evidence of a dramatic revival of religion. Public enthusiasm for this dynamic experiential religion ushered in the Great Awakening.

Spiritual afflictions were interpreted as evidence of a great outpouring of the Holy Spirit upon New England. But in the 1690s such afflictions, in the context of the general disruption of Massachusetts society, were interpreted as the work of the devil. The Massachusetts church leader, Cotton Mather, saw the witchcraft controversy as evidence of the demonic disruptions that threatened the boundaries of the Puritan establishment. "The wilderness through which we are passing to the Promised Land," he wrote in 1693, "is all over filled with fiery flying serpents . . . All our way to Heaven, lies by the Dens of Lions and the Mounts of Leopards; there are incredible Droves of Devils in our way."[66] The boundaries of the Puritan establishment were threatened by supernatural forces of evil; and the Salem witchcraft trials represented one of the last attempts to reinforce those boundaries through the exercise of punitive measures against uncontrollable forces that seemed to threaten the community.

By the end of the seventeenth century the center of theocratic power in New England had been displaced. The colonies were under the direct political control of England; they were provinces of a larger empire. And the ideal of an independent theocratic covenant community was largely dissolved in the new political realities of the eighteenth century. But the legacy of the Puritan experiment has carried a strong residual influence throughout American history. Subsequent generations of Americans abandoned the aspirations of a theocratic religiopolitical system, but they tended to incorporate many elements of the Puritan imagination in the formation of a corporate self-image: new world, chosen people, unique destiny. And the idea of a special covenant relationship between God and America has been periodically revived to render American experience in religious terms. The resonance of these themes in American history suggests the depth of that substratum of America's collective memory which is occupied by the Puritan theocracy.

NOTES

1. JOHN ROLFE, *A Relation of the State of Virginia* (1616); cited in Perry Miller, *Errand into the Wilderness* (Cambridge: Harvard University Press, 1956): 119.
2. ALEXANDER WHITAKER, *Good Newes From Virginia* (1613); in *God's New Israel: Religious Interpretations of American Destiny*, ed. Conrad Cherry (Englewood Cliffs, New Jersey: Prentice-Hall, 1971): 36-7.
3. *A True Declaration of the Estate of the Colonie in Virginia* (1610); cited in Maureen Henry, *The Intoxication of Power: An Analysis of Civil Religion in Relation to Ideology* (Dodrecht, Holland: D. Reidel Publishing Co., 1979): 25.
4. WHITAKER, *Good Newes From Virginia*, in *God's New Israel*: 37.
5. BENJAMIN PERLEY MOORE, ed., *The Federal and State Constitutions, Colonial Charters, and other Organic Laws of the United States* (Washington, DC: U.S. Government Printing Office, 1877); see *American Political Theology: Historical Perspective and Theoretical Analysis*, ed. Charles W. Dunn (New York: Praeger, 1984): 20.
6. JOHN WINTHROP, *Conclusions For the Plantation in New England* (1629); cited in Sacvan Bercovitch, *The Puritan Origins of the American Self* (New Haven: Yale University Press, 1975): 61.

7. JOHN WINTHROP, "A Modell of Christian Charity (1630)," in *The Puritans: A Sourcebook of their Writings*, eds. Perry Miller and Thomas H. Johnson, 2 vols. (New York: Harper and Row, 1963): I:198.

8. EDWARD JOHNSON, *Wonder-Working Providence of Sions Saviour* (1654), in *The Puritans*, I:145.

9. SAMUEL WAKEMAN, *Sound Repentance* (Boston, 1685); 18; cited in Bercovitch, *The Puritan Origins of the American Self*: 61; see Peter Toon, ed., *Puritans, the Millennium, and the Future Israel: Puritan Eschatology, 1600-1660* (Cambridge: James Clarke, 1970).

10. MICHAEL WIGGLESWORTH, "God's Controversy with New-England (1662)," in *The Puritans*, II:611.

11. CARLTON HAYES, *Nationalism: A Religion* (New York: Macmillan, 1960): 36.

12. Cited in Edmund S. Morgan, *The Puritan Dilemma: The Story of John Winthrop* (Boston: Little, Brown, and Co., 1958): 40.

13. BERCOVITCH, *The Puritan Origins of the American Self*: 117-19.

14. WIGGLESWORTH, "God's Controversy with New-England," in *The Puritans*, II:611-616.

15. JOHNSON, *Wonder-Working Providence of Sions Saviour*, cited in Bercovitch, *The Puritan Origins of the American Self*: 103-4; see Cecilia Tichi, "The Puritan Historians and Their New Jerusalem," *Early American Literature* 6 (1971): 147.

16. COTTON MATHER, *Magnalia Christi Americana* (1702); (New York: Russell and Russell, 1967): 50; see Peter N. Carroll, *Puritanism and the Wilderness: The Intellectual Significance of the New England Frontier* (New York: Columbia University Press, 1969).

17. JOHN WINTHROP, "A Modell of Christian Charity," in *The Puritans*, I:198-9.

18. PETER BULKELEY, *The Gospel Covenant: Or the Covenant of Grace Opened* (1651); in *The annals of America* (Chicago: Encyclopedia Britannica, 1968): I:212.

19. INCREASE MATHER, *The Times of Men* (Boston, 1675): 7.

20. SAMUEL FISHER, *The Testimony of Truth* (1679); cited in Perry Miller, *The New England Mind: The Seventeenth Century* (Cambridge: Harvard University Press, 1954): 475.

21. BENJAMIN WOODBRIDGE, "Upon the Tomb of . . . Cotton," in *Colonial American Poetry*, ed. Kenneth Silverman (New York: Hafner Publishing Co., 1968): 133.

22. Cited in Thomas Jefferson Wertenbaker, *The Puritan Oligarchy* (New York: Charles Scribner's Sons, 1947): 70.

23. Cited in Henry, *The Intoxication of Power*: 34-5.

24. Cited in Bercovitch, *The Puritan Origins of the American Self*: 116.

25. ARTHUR HILDERSAM, *Lectures upon the Fourth of John* (1629); cited in David E. Stannard, *The Puritan Way of Death: A Study in Religion, Culture and Social Change* (Oxford: Oxford University Press, 1977): 74.

26. CHARLES FRANCIS ADAMS, *Three Episodes of Massachusetts History* (Boston: Houghton Mifflin, 1903): III:718; cited in Kai T. Erikson, *Wayward Puritans: A Study in the Sociology of Deviance* (New York: John Wiley and Sons, 1966): 51.

27. STANNARD, *The Puritan Way of Death*: 75.

28. MORGAN, *The Puritan Dilemma*: 11.

29. JOHN COTTON, *The Way of Life* (1641); in *The Puritans*, I:320.

30. WINTHROP, "A Modell of Christian Charity," in *The Puritans*, I:195.

31. *Ibid.*: I:195.

32. *Ibid.*: I:196.

33. *Ibid.*: I:195.

34. Cited in Herbert W. Schneider, *The Puritan Mind* (Ann Arbor: University of Michigan Press, 1958): 19.

35. Cited in Wertenbaker, *The Puritan Oligarchy*: 72.

36. *Ibid.*: 70.

37. *The Platform of Church Discipline*, cited in Henry, *The Intoxication of Power*: 33.

38. JOHN COTTON, "Copy of a Letter from Mr. Cotton to Lord Saye and Seal in the Year 1636," in *The Puritans*, I:209; see Paul E. Lauer, *Church and State in New England* (Baltimore: Johns Hopkins University Press, 1982).

39. *Ibid.*: 209-10.

40. *Ibid.*: 210; see T.H. Breen, *The Character of the Good Ruler: A Study of Puritan Political Ideas in New England, 1630-1730* (New Haven: Yale University Press, 1970).

41. JOHN WINTHROP, in *The Annals of America*, I:169.

42. MARY DOUGLAS, *Purity and Danger* (London: Routledge and Kegan Paul, 1966): 101.

43. NATHANIEL WARD, *The Simple Cobler of Aggwam* (1647); in *The Puritans*, I:222; For an analysis of Puritan religious conflicts, see Philip F. Gura, *A Glimpse of Sion's Glory: Puritan Radicalism in New England, 1620-1660* (Middletown, CT: Wesleyan University Press, 1984).

44. Cited in Morgan, *The Puritan Dilemma*: 117.

45. ROGER WILLIAMS, *Complete Writings* 7 vols. (New York: Russell and Russell, 1963): VII:37.

46. Cited in Morgan, *The Puritan Dilemma*, 130.

47. *Ibid.*: 131.

48. ROGER WILLIAMS, "Letter to the Town of Providence (1655)," in *The Puritans*, I:255; see Perry Miller, *Roger Williams: His Contribution to the American Tradition* (Indianapolis: Bobbs-Merrill, 1953).

49. MORGAN, *The Puritan Dilemma*: 134; see David Hall, ed., *The Antinomian Controversy, 1636-1638: A Documentary History* (Middletown, CT: Wesleyan University Press, 1968).

50. Cited in Perry Miller, *Nature's Nation* (Cambridge: Harvard University Press, 1967): 62.

51. MORGAN, *The Puritan Dilemma*: 143.

52. Cited in *Ibid.*: 149.

53. *Ibid.*: 149.

54. *Ibid.*: 152.

55. GEORGE FOX, *The Journals of George Fox*, ed. John L. Nickalls (Cambridge: Cambridge University Press, 1952): 11.

56. *Ibid.*: 34.

57. ROGER WILLIAMS, *Complete Writings*, V:72.

58. ERIKSON, *Wayward Puritans*: 120.

59. THOMAS SHEPARD, *The Parable of the Ten Virgins* (1659); in *The Works of Thomas Shepard*, 3 vols., ed. John A. Albro (Boston: Doctrinal Tract and Book Society, 1853; New York: AMS Press, 1967): II:628.

60. See Robert G. Pope, *The Half-Way Covenant* (Princeton: Princeton University Press, 1969).

61. PERRY MILLER, *The New England Mind: From Colony to Province* (Cambridge: Harvard University Press, 1953): 191.

62. See John Demos, "Underlying Themes in the Witchcraft of Seventeenth-Century New England," in *Colonial America*, ed. Stanley N. Katz (Boston: Little, Brown 1971): 113-33.

63. PAUL BOYER and STEPHEN NISSENBAUM, *Salem Possessed: The Social Origins of Witchcraft* (Cambridge: Harvard University Press, 1974): 185.

64. ROBERT CALEF, *More Wonders of the Invisible World* (1700); in *Narratives of the Witchcraft Cases, 1648-1706*, ed. George Lincoln Burr (New York: Charles Scribner's Sons, 1914); New York: Barnes and Noble, 1968): 342.

65. SAMUEL PARRIS, "Church Records, March 27, 1692;" cited in Boyer and Nissenbaum, *Salem Possessed:* 24.

66. COTTON MATHER, *The Wonders of the Invisible World* (1693); in *The Witchcraft Delusion in New England*, ed. Samuel G. Drake (Roxbury, Massachusetts: Elliot Woodward, 1866): 94-5.

CHAPTER TWO
DEMOCRACY

The democratic religiopolitical system that emerged in the revolutionary era resulted from a constellation of religious and political forces very different from the corporate ideals of the Puritan theocracy. Yet many Puritan ideals persisted in the formation of the revolutionary imagination and the democratic experiment in America. The powerful symbolic image of a covenant people, the millennial drama of God's work in history, the linkage between political order and a moral virtue sustained by religion— these were all residual elements of the Puritan imagination that influenced the religious and political self-consciousness of the United States at its inception. These themes were transposed, however, into a new religiopolitical key in the organization of democratic power. The Puritans had been adamant in their rejection of democracy as a legitimate form of government. They were convinced that democracy had no basis in their sacred scriptures, that it did not make the necessary distinction between the rulers and the ruled, and that it could not accommodate the strong centripetal power of a theocratic covenant community. There was a certain degree of democratic participation in the congregational polity of the Puritan churches, but this participation was reserved for those who had demonstrated signs of election by God. The extension of democratic organization to the state represented a radical individualization of political identity. As it came to be imagined in the eighteenth century, a democracy was a voluntary agreement among individuals in society—a social contract— designed to protect their individual lives, liberties, and properties. It was an arrangement of power based on the contractual agreement of individuals, rather than a covenant between God and a community. This individualization of power was supported by a remarkable coalition between two very different groups of Americans who have often been referred to as *pietists* and *rationalists*. These religious options in eighteenth-century America reshaped the distribution of religious and political power, and contributed to the American historical trajectory away from Puritanism and toward a revolution of the religious and political order.

Emerging out of the Great Awakening of the 1740s, the pietistic trend in American religion was influenced by John Wesley's rejection of all the religious controversies of his century in the interest of an inner emotional experience of religious power. Wesley's Methodist movement made religion a private matter of "the heart strangely warmed." Jonathan Edwards, George Whitefield, Gilbert Tennant, and other ministers of the Awakening, exhorted their congregations to experience this private, personal, and individual conversion of the heart. The revival swept across denominational lines. Religious doctrines, ritual practices, and forms of association were regarded as less immediately significant than the intense inner experience of conversion. John Wesley had insisted on this point when he observed:

> Methodists do not impose in order to their admission any opinions whatever. Let them hold particular or general redemption, absolute or conditional decrees; let them be churchmen or dissenters, Presbyterians or Independents [i.e. Congregationalists], it is no obstacle. Let them choose one mode of baptism or another, it is no bar to their admission. The Presbyterian may be Presbyterian still; the Independent and Anabaptist use his own worship still. So may the Quaker; and none will contend with him about it. They think and let think. One condition, and only one is required—a real desire to save the soul. Where this is, it is enough; they desire no more; they lay stress upon nothing else; they only ask, "Is thy heart herein as my heart? If it be, give me thy hand."[1]

This toleration of differences in doctrines, rituals, and organization stood in marked contrast to the centripetal force of uniformity in Puritan religion. It was considerably removed from Nathaniel Ward's praises of intolerance, George Wilson's zeal for persecution, and the general demands for total conformity in religious beliefs, practices, and association that sustained the Puritan covenant community. The more established denominations in America—Congregationalists and Presbyterians—were divided between supporters and opponents of the spirituality of the Awakening. But the Baptist pietists and the emerging Methodist movement were closely aligned with this individualized, personalized, and experiential Christianity. This style of highly personalized religious power dominated

American religious life to such an extent that one hundred years later the Methodists and Baptists would be the largest Protestant denominations in America. This personalized religious power was consistent with a more democratic distribution of political power. One of the major religious supports for the revolution and the new democratic order was drawn from the resources of Protestant pietism.

The moving forces behind independence, revolution, and a new constitutional order, however, were rationalists of a very different spirit. Benjamin Franklin, Thomas Jefferson, James Madison, John Adams, Thomas Paine, and others, were inheritors of the European Enlightenment.[2] They were influenced by the deistic approach to God of Samuel Clarke, the rational approach to man and society of John Locke, and the scientific approach to nature of Isaac Newton. Religion was conceived as a rational enterprise. The God of rational deism was regarded as ultimately unknowable, but the natural laws of the universe, society, and moral order were felt to be within the grasp of reason. Religion, in this sense, played an important role in the political arena if it provided practical support for the public moral order. Beyond this social function, religion was regarded as a matter of personal opinion, private conscience, and individual preference. The rationalists were in league with the pietists on this one issue: Religion was meant to be circumscribed within the private sphere. For the pietists this was the inner movements of the heart; for the rationalists it was the mind's awakening to the clear light of reason. Whether religion was conceived as private feeling or private opinion, this shifting pattern of religious commitment represented by pietists and rationalists signified an individualization of religious power that ultimately supported a new democratic order in the political arena.

The revolutionary era in American history was imagined by its participants to be the creation of a new world. The events of this period have subsequently assumed a mythic proportion in the American popular imagination analogous to the primordial sacred time of creation itself. The revolution was also a cultural rite of passage from an old world to a new world, from the bondage of captivity to liberation, and the biblical images of the exodus of the Israelites often provided a frame of reference for the meaning and significance of the revolution. Contemporary participants in the revolution showed some disagreement about the precise time frame of the revolutionary rite of passage. The revolutionary statesman and second president of the United States, John Adams, was convinced that the true revolution was a transformation in the hearts and minds of the American people. "The Revolution was in the Minds of the People," Adams suggested in 1783, "and this was effected, from 1760 to 1775, in the course of fifteen Years before a drop of blood was drawn at Lexington."[3] The revolution, in this sense, was essentially a reorganization of American consciousness which occurred before the actual conflict was entered on the battlefield. The American patriot and physician Benjamin

Rush, however, felt that the true revolution in America was only beginning when the revolutionary war came to a close. "The American war is over," Rush said in 1787, "but this is far from being the case with the American Revolution, on the contrary, nothing but the First Act of the great drama is closed."[4] Rush's observation suggested that the revolution was an ongoing reordering of the political arena in America which was only initiated with those revolutionary events which separated that arena from direct foreign control.

It will be important to consider this continuing revolutionary drama in the transformation of American religious and political power from the 1760s into the early nineteenth century. The revolution was the first act in that drama, but it was supported by a fundamental reorientation in religious and political thought which might be regarded as the revolutionary imagination. The democratic experiment which grew out of the revolutionary era represented a new distribution of religious and political power. But that democratic power remained subject to shifting social, economic, and political forces as it continued to be defined and redefined into the nineteenth century. Revolutionary concepts such as liberty, equality, and government by the people continued to assume new significance during the early national period in the formulation of democratic power. And these new configurations of political power corresponded to fundamental realignments of religious power in the democratic religiopolitical system.

THE REVOLUTIONARY IMAGINATION

The revolutionary era remains more vividly alive in the American collective imagination than any other period in American history. The American bicentennial celebrations in 1976 demonstrated the quasi-religious patriotic fervor evoked by the formative events of the revolution. The revolution is the primordium to which the collective mythic imagination of America constantly refers for its holy texts, revered ancestors, and paradigmatic sacred history which form the basis for a shared civil religiosity. This revolution is recollected in the ordinary, mundane, and nonrevolutionary situations and circumstances of American life as a unique, radical breakthrough of sacred power in human history. For the participants in that historical event, the revolution was also enveloped in various configurations of sacred meaning and power. The revolution can certainly be attributed to social, economic, and political factors. But these factors were simultaneously wrapped in religious motives, images, and justifications that gave the revolution a sacred aura—even for those who saw revolution as a dangerous work to be accomplished, rather than a meaningful ritual to be celebrated. Socioeconomic factors, ideological motives, and this aura of religious significance were interwoven during a period of historical crisis in the American revolutionary imagination.

The economic conflict between Great Britain and the colonies revolved around issues of taxation, custom duties, and regulations. The Sugar Tax of 1764, designed to raise revenues for Great Britain rather than simply to regulate trade, was the first of a series of economic actions imposed upon the colonies which were considered oppressive. The Stamp Act of 1765 was a direct tax that inspired civil disobedience (in the form of minor riots, intimidation of tax collectors, and economic boycotts) with such disturbing effects that the act was repealed the following year. But various taxes and custom duties continued to be imposed on the colonies and to be met with resistance by the colonists. It is significant that the so-called Boston Massacre of 1770, in which five colonists were killed when British troops opened fire on an angry mob of protesters, occurred in front of the customs house. The closing of Boston harbor in response to the Tea Party in 1774 was part of a series of tax measures, economic sanctions, and new laws that were experienced as coercive acts against economic interests in the colonies. The popular perception of those acts as oppressive, including the resentment at the officials, customs agents, and troops that enforced these acts, was reflected in the passage of the Declaration of Independence that listed one of the grievances of the revolutionaries as the "swarms of new officers" which "harass our people and eat out our substance."[5]

These economic grievances, however, were not sufficient to account for the widespread colonial perception that they were being subjected to an unjust, tyrannical rule by a foreign power. Taxation without representation, as the revolutionary patriot James Otis claimed, may well be tyranny. But British rule over the colonies, while it might have been intolerable to the revolutionaries, was probably not the evil empire that appeared in American revolutionary rhetoric. Many scholars in the twentieth century have tried to argue that the portrayal of Britain as an oppressive tyrant was largely overdrawn by the American rhetoric of the revolution.[6] The revolutionary imagination was not simply shaped by practical social and economic events; it took form out of certain basic ideological commitments which allowed Britain to register in the American consciousness as a tyranny.

First, the revolutionaries had been deeply informed by a reading of the political philosophy of John Locke. Locke's *Treatises on Government* (1690) were the basis of a school of political thought throughout the eighteenth century which developed specific notions of natural law, the consent of the governed, and the symptoms of political tyranny. From this perspective, a republic required a measure of consent on the part of the governed. A republic was regarded as a civil contract into which individuals, based on the free exercise of their understanding and will, entered for the mutual protection of their lives, liberties, and properties. The protection of these rights was regarded as the primary purpose of government. But a republic, unless its contractual agreement is constantly renewed, inevitably descends into corruption, despotism, and tyranny. The republican form of government must be wary of any symptoms of this trajectory toward tyranny. When such signs appear, the people under the rule of government were regarded as having the right to reform, alter, or abolish that political order.

John Locke outlined this trajectory toward tyranny, and the justification for revolt against tyranny, in his *Second Treatise*: "But if a long train of abuses, prevarications, and artifices, all tending the same way, make the design visible to the people, and they cannot but feel, what they lie under, and see, whither they are going; 'tis not to be wonder'd, that they should then rouse themselves, and endeavor to put the rule into such hands, which may secure to them the ends for which government was at first erected."[7] The economic, social, and political abuses perpetrated by the British government in the colonies entered the revolutionary imagination as early symptoms of an inevitable trend toward tyranny. The colonists felt the need to rouse themselves because they were convinced that they knew where events were leading.

This ideological definition of tyranny was appropriated by the American revolutionaries to interpret their political experience. The Virginia Bill of Rights, issued in June, 1776, anticipated the Declaration of Independence in declaring that the majority of a community, under certain extreme circumstances, has "an indubitable, inalienable, and indefeasible right to reform, alter, or abolish [the government] in such manner as shall be judged most conducive to the public weal."[8] The extreme circumstances were defined in the revolutionary imagination as that moment when a republican form of government moves toward tyranny. When political power becomes arbitrary, irrational, and therefore tyrannical, the revolutionary impulse was necessary to restore government to its original purpose in protecting the liberty of the governed. Such a revolution, based on principles of government appropriated from Locke and his interpreters, would not be seen as the creation of a new order. Rather, it would be a necessary intervention to restore the original order for which government was intended. The Declaration of Independence characterized British political power in these terms. Jefferson's rough draft of the document described Great Britain as an "arbitrary power," the final version replaced this phrase with "Absolute Despotism," but in either case it was regarded as a political force that exercised an "absolute tyranny over these states."[9] The immediate political implication of such a diagnosis was clear: Revolutionary acts were required to restore government to its original order, pattern, and design in the protection of the rights of individuals.

Second, the revolutionary imagination identified tyranny with moral corruption. Countless sermons before and during the Revolutionary War castigated the British for luxuriant vices, decadence, and corruption. Political tyranny was felt to have a moral content. Corruption in the political order could be diagnosed from the symptoms of corruption in the moral order. This moral concern was certainly reminiscent of the Puritan preoccupation with moral virtue in government. But the notion of republican civic virtue as a precondition for fulfilling the demands of the social contract was also an important ingredient in Lockean political philosophy of the eighteenth century.

On the level of imagination, however, these themes were woven together in a composite picture of Britain as an aging, decrepit, and corrupt power that was infecting the youthful purity of the American colonies. The American educator, Noah Webster, captured this theme of moral corruption and tyranny in the introduction to his *Spelling Book* in 1783; but this was an important connection in the American imagination throughout the revolutionary period. "Europe is grown old in folly, corruption and tyranny," Webster declared, "in that country laws are perverted, manners are licentious, literature is declining and human nature debased. For America in her infancy to adopt the present maxims of the old world, would be to stamp the wrinkles of decrepit age upon the bloom of youth and to plant the seeds of decay in a vigorous constitution."[10] These images of sickness and health, moral corruption and innocence, political tyranny and freedom, were all interwoven in the revolutionary imagination. They served as powerful symbolic images by which Americans organized their perceptions of Great Britain as an oppressive tyrant.

Finally, the revolutionary perception of tyranny was supported by a variety of religious motives. One of these was the tendency to transpose the mythological imagination of the Puritan covenant community onto the colonies. The Puritan ideal of a single covenant community was appropriated in the religious self-understanding of America as a whole. As the historian Perry Miller noted, the religious leaders of the colonies "virtually took over the New England thesis that these colonial peoples stood in a contractual relationship to the 'great Governor' over and above that enjoyed by other groups."[11] The exclusive covenant theology of the Puritans was thereby transformed into a broader interpretive framework in order to incorporate the historical experience of Americans during the colonial, revolutionary, and early national periods. The "elect" became the entire nation of the United States.[12]

This religious transposition of the covenant theology assumed a number of different forms in the revolutionary imagination. First, the religious imagination of the colonial period was infused with a kind of civil millennialism. The religious revivals of the 1740s and 1750s were interpreted by many as signs of an outpouring of the Holy Spirit in anticipation of the millennial reign of Christ on earth. The Book of Revelation provided a religious vocabulary for this expectation. It allowed Americans to interpret the New World as the place appointed by God for the end of the Old World, and the creation of a radically new heaven and earth. This apocalypse has traditionally been imagined as a sudden, cataclysmic event that will destroy the forces of evil that dominate the earth and institute a thousand-year reign of Christ and his saints. But in eighteenth-century America, a postmillennial imagination translated this into a gradual transformation by which Christ would work his will upon the world through conversions, outbreaks of religious enthusiasm, and the expansion of churches in America.

The revival leader Jonathan Edwards proposed this post millennial interpretation of American destiny in his *Thoughts Concerning the Present Revival of Religion in New England.* Edwards suggested that God's work in human history promised to renew the world, and that "there are many things that make it probable that this work will begin in America."[13] The indications that this millennial work was destined for America included the assumption that the millennium would begin in a remote part of the world, in a new continent that was not heavy with the corruptions of the old, and in that youngest, most vital part of the world where the Christian churches had most recently been planted. Edwards even supposed that because the sun sets in the west, the sun of righteousness in the millennial kingdom of God on earth would arise in the west. All of these indications suggested for Jonathan Edwards that the religious revivals provided "abundant reason to hope that what is now seen in America, and especially in New England, may prove the dawn of that glorious day, and the very uncommon and wonderful circumstances and events of this work, seem to me strongly to argue that God intends it as a beginning or forerunner of something vastly great."[14] These millennial expectations expressed by Edwards clearly remained grounded in the Puritan covenant theology of New England; but in the enthusiasm of the religious revivals, mass conversions, and the intensely personalized character of the pietistic spirituality that emerged, Edwards initiated an extension of that covenant theology to all of America. America as a whole began to be conceived as the cutting edge of Christ's millennial kingdom on earth.

This assumption became commonplace in sermons, religious pamphlets, and the mythic imagination of revolutionary religious leaders who saw the revolution against British tyranny as ushering in "the universal REIGN of the SON OF GOD in glories of the latter days."[15] An election day sermon by the Reverend Samuel West in Massachusetts, 1776, insisted that in these latter days, the apocalyptic symbol of the antichrist had "better be understood as political than ecclesiastical tyrants." The British were to be regarded as the antichrist, the "horrible wild beast" of the Book of Revelation. The conclusion Samuel West drew from this symbolic association was shared by many other religious leaders in the revolutionary era: "We must beat our plowshares into swords and our pruning

hooks into spears."[16] The revolutionary contest against Britain, therefore, was conceived as a holy war against cosmic forces of evil which de-
fied the divine work of establishing God's millennial kingdom in America.
This civil millennialism provided powerful symbolic resources for involving the revolutionary imagination in what was regarded as a sacred conflict between the forces of good and evil.

Second, and closely related to this civil millennialism, the religious
imagination of the revolutionary period was sustained by the religious
symbols of a civil election by God. The notion of America as God's new
Israel, a theme that had been such an important ingredient in the Puritan
self-understanding of their calling, mission, and destiny, was transposed
upon the entire American experience in the revolution. The powerful
biblical themes of captivity, exodus, and promised land were again invoked to interpret the historical experience of America. The revolution
was imagined as the liberation of "God's American Israel" from the bondage of Egypt. A sermon by the Reverend Nicholas Street preached in
Connecticut, April 1777, called upon Americans to recognize their special
role in the sacred drama of human history. "We in this land," Reverend
Street declared, "are led out of Egypt by the hand of Moses." The Americans were transformed in this mythic imagination into the children of
Israel, and the British became the oppressive tyrants of Egypt. As in the
biblical model, when the Israelites "endeavored to make their escape from
this cruel and oppressive tyrant, Pharaoh pursued after Israel with a great
army unto the Red Sea (Exod. 14:7-10). So that the British tyrant is only
acting over the same wicked and cruel part, that Pharaoh king of Egypt
acted towards the children of Israel above 3000 years ago."[17] In the imagery of civil millennialism the British king registered as the antichrist;
but in this symbolic context of civil election, the British king appeared in
the mythic guise of the tyrannous Pharaoh of ancient Egypt.

If King George III became Pharaoh in the mythic imagination of the
revolutionary era, George Washington became a complex mythological
figure who combined the sacred offices of prophet and holy warrior.
Washington was both the Moses and the Joshua of this new American
Israel. A sermon preached by the Reverend Ezra Stiles in Hartford, Connecticut, 1783, captured this tendency to mythologize the role of Washington in leading the American Israelites out of captivity and into the
promised land. Ezra Stiles declared that "Congress put at the head of this
spirited army the only man on whom the eyes of all Israel were
placed. . . . this American Joshua was raised up by God and divinely
formed by a peculiar influence of the Sovereign of the Universe for the
great work of leading the armies . . . and conducting this people through
the severe, the arduous conflict, to Liberty and Independence."[18]
Although many ministers warned against this tendency to deify the American general, George Washington was transformed into a powerful symbolic figure of divine election by God in the American mythic imagina-

tion. The apotheosis of Washington was part of a larger symbolic complex of religious imagery in which America claimed a special status among the nations of the world as God's new chosen people.

Third, this sense of chosenness was associated with the conviction of the corporate nature of sin in the covenant community. The Puritan covenant theology believed that God's chosen people would be tried, tested, and punished for their sins. Because the Puritans felt they were chosen by God, they were also convinced that they had a unique collective responsibility for remaining faithful to the covenant. Protestant ministers of the revolutionary period were also deeply influenced by the biblical linkage between divine election and divine punishment for sins. The Book of Amos informed them that "You only have I known of all the families of the earth; therefore I will punish you for your iniquities (Amos 3:2)." The extention of the covenant theology to the entire American experience encouraged a perception of the injustices perpetrated by Great Britain as a divine punishment for national sinfulness. This confidence in a divine covenant and a conviction of collective sinfulness were the two sides of the implicit doctrine of election in the revolutionary religious imagination. Because the new American Israel supposedly had special status before God, it could expect to be immediately punished for its national sins.

This conviction of sinfulness was demonstrated in the convocation by the Continental Congress in Philadelphia of a day of public humiliation, fasting, and prayer on July 20, 1775. The Continental Congress called for a public confession of sins before the "all-wise, omnipotent, and merciful Disposer of all events." The colonists were exhorted by Congress to ask for forgiveness before asking for divine deliverance from the trials of revolutionary war into which they were entering. Only after America had made a full confession of its collective sinfulness before God could it expect the divine Governor of the universe "to remove our present calamities, to avert those desolating judgments with which we are threatened." The persistence of the covenant theology in the American revolutionary imagination was evident in this assumption that a public confession of sin would clear a space of religious and moral purity in the colonies from which America might request "a gracious interposition of Heaven for the redress of her many grievances."[19]

It has been suggested that such confessions of sin and invocations of divine aid were nothing more than calculated attempts to cover political interests with a veneer of religious propaganda.[20] But it is likely that this public day of humiliation, fasting, and prayer was a significant continuation of the covenant theology in the revolutionary imagination. Even a rationalist like Thomas Jefferson was impressed by how the deep symbolic chords struck by this call for public repentance resonated within the American imagination. "The effect of the day through the whole colony," Jefferson reported, "was like a shock of electricity, arousing every man and placing him erect and solidly on his center."[21] It is important to remember that rationalist revolutionary leaders may have called the colonies to the cause, but the resources of religious piety, including the symbolic resources of the covenant theology, were instrumental in inspiring them to respond.

Fourth, the resources of religious pietism were mobilized to support civil disobedience against centralized authority in both religion and politics. Both political and religious tyranny were felt to be embodied in British rule. That the British monarch was the nominal head of the Church of England supported this perception. Independent Congregational and Presbyterian church leaders in the mainstream American denominations feared the imposition of an Anglican bishop in America. A sermon by the Reverend John Mayhew, on the centenary of the execution of Charles I in 1749, anticipated justifications of civil disobedience that would be evoked during the revolutionary era. Mayhew declared himself "on the side of liberty, the Bible, and common sense, in opposition to tyranny, priestcraft, and nonsense."[22] There was a close linkage in his perceptions between civil and religious tyranny. Both may seem small in their beginnings, but civil and ecclesiastical tyranny could be expected to inundate political and religious freedom in a torrent of intolerable oppressions. The victims of such oppression, Mayhew argued, were not bound to accept the rule of arbitrary, centralized power in either state or church. The people did not have to passively submit to tyranny, but could look to the deposing of Charles I as an example of "a most righteous and glorious stand, made in defense of the natural and legal rights of the people, against the unnatural and illegal rights of arbitrary power."[23] The fear of an imposition of centralized ecclesiastical authority (in the form of an Anglican bishop for America) awakened powerful religious motives for resisting both religious and civil tyranny as two sides of the same oppressive power.

The Stamp Act of 1765 and subsequent political grievances mobilized this religious justification for the resistance of tyranny in the service of active civil disobedience. The Reverend Stephen Johnson delivered a fast-day sermon in Connecticut, in 1765, which declared that passive obedience was a "doctrine of iniquity" when fundamental rights and liberties were at stake. Johnson insisted that the actions on the part of the British government, in abolishing customary legal charters, rights, and privileges, had effectively abolished any bond of allegiance the colonies had with Great Britain. He implied that a government that does not govern justly is no government. In these terms, the colonists were under no legitimate government. "And their government being thus dissolved, without any act of theirs," Stephen Johnson argued, "they are absolutely in a state of nature and independency."[24]

Therefore, more than a decade before the Declaration of Independence, religious leaders in the colonies were marshaling arguments to justify the independence of America from Great Britain. After the Boston

Massacre, John Lathrop, minister of Boston's Second Church, gave religious sanction to the rights of the subjects of an unjust political order to "reduce matters to their original *good order*, whatever be the fate of those *wicked men* who for ends of their own would subvert the RIGHTS of the people."[25] Where the civil millennialism of the revolutionary imagination looked *forward* to the creation of God's kingdom in America, such calls for civil disobedience, resistance, and rebellion looked *backwards* to the restoration of the good order for which government (in the Lockean terms that had become common in eighteenth-century republican thinking) had originally been intended. This image of original order was defined in terms of the mutual protection of life, liberty, and property which was threatened with destruction by the centralized, arbitrary, and despotic power of tyranny.

Congregationalist and Presbyterian supporters of the revolution agreed to reject the British monarchy as both a religious and political tyranny. This interpenetration of religion and politics was captured in the slogan that was frequently repeated by both ministers and politicians in the revolutionary era: "No King but King Jesus."[26] Anglican loyalists to British rule, however, also demonstrated this connection between religion and politics by opposing revivalism in religion and republicanism in the political arena. Samuel Johnson, an Episcopalian leader in Connecticut, condemned the "prevalency of rigid enthusiastical conceited notions and practices in religion and republican mobbish principles and practices in policy." From this perspective, personalized pietistic spirituality corresponded to the republican insistence on personal liberties and the rights of the people in politics. These were perceived as the religious and political dimensions of the revolution. But from the vantage point of the Anglican loyalist Samuel Johnson, they were a prescription for the destruction of a necessary hierarchical order in both church and state. Revival religion and republican politics both resulted in a situation, Samuel Johnson argued, in which each person regarded himself as "an able divine and a statesman: hence perpetual feuds and factions in both."[27] Therefore, religious motives in the revolutionary era infused loyalties to the church and crown of England, as well as justifications for civil disobedience, resistance, and ultimately revolution against that centralized authority. The Protestant pietism which emerged from the revivals of the Great Awakening provided a supportive environment in which the revolutionary impulse could grow.

Fifth, rationalists in religion also enveloped the revolutionary cause in a sacred aura. The radical deist and revolutionary, Thomas Paine, vehemently attacked what he regarded as the superstitions of organized religion and the oppressions of political tyranny in his revolutionary tract, *Common Sense* (1776). Paine rejected the very foundations of pietism in revelation, scriptures, and faith for a religion based on reason alone. But if his deism were not so apparent, there are passages in Paine's *Common*

Sense that would appear to invoke a pious civil millennialism. Paine demanded: "But where, say some, is the King of America? I'll tell you, friend, he reigns above, and doth not make havoc of mankind like the Royal Brute of Great Britain."[28] The deistic "great Governor" of the universe, as a universal, abstract, and unknowable divine sovereign, may not have been the personal "King Jesus" of the pietists. But the divine ruler was counterposed against the tyrant of Great Britain to provide a similar sacred aura for the revolutionary conflict. And when Thomas Paine reflected upon the historical significance of that conflict, he intoned a similar millennial vision of a new heaven and new earth in America. "We have it in our power to begin the world over again," Paine declared. "A situation similar to the present has not happened since the days of Noah until now."[29] These symbolic resources of civil millennialism ran so deeply through the revolutionary imagination that they even permeated the self-understanding of the revolution's most committed rationalists.

The Declaration of Independence against Great Britain embodied a constellation of sacred doctrines which formed the basis for the rationalist justification of revolution. These doctrines were described as self-evident truths; but in his original rough draft, Thomas Jefferson declared that they were "sacred and undeniable."[30] The document of the Declaration began with a kind of creedal statement of five sacred truths. First was the truth of *equality*. The Declaration asserted that all men are created equal; it would remain for subsequent constitutional clarification to place conditions upon that equality. Second was the truth that *natural rights are divine rights*. People are endowed by their Creator with certain inalienable rights. These individual rights or powers belonging to the people were regarded as integral to the original design for human societies. Third was the specification of some of these *inherent human rights*. These basic human powers included the rights to life, liberty, happiness, and the right to preserve those rights from any political encroachment. Fourth was the truth of the *social contract*. Following the Lockean political philosophy of the eighteenth century, the Declaration specified that governments were created as contractual arrangements with the consent of the governed and for the purpose of securing human rights. Fifth, and finally, was the sacred truth of *revolution*. The Declaration announced that "Whenever any form of government becomes destructive of these rights, there is the further right of the people to alter or abolish such government and institute a new government." If a government does not fulfill the conditions of the social contract, the Declaration implied, it has made itself null and void. The people can then reform that government or revolt against it to restore the original terms of the social contract for the mutual recognition, protection, and support of individual rights.

Thomas Jefferson placed upon his seal a motto which captured the sacred logic which he felt permeated the revolutionary struggle: "Rebellion to Tyrants is Obedience to God."[31] This was a perception that came to be shared, perhaps for different reasons, by a wide cross section of the American public during the revolutionary era. This was considered a sacred commitment to resist tyranny that could be supported by both religious pietists and religious rationalists. The Declaration of Independence described the political, social, and economic symptoms that were the beginnings of a trajectory toward British tyranny. And it posed the distinction between tyranny and liberty in terms of the sacred rights and responsibilities which required a radical restoration of the intended purposes of civil government. The consequences of such religious and political logic were felt to be inevitable. As Jefferson insisted, "The tree of liberty must be refreshed from time to time with the blood of patriots and tyrants."[32] In order for there to be patriots, there must also be tyrants. Religious motives, such as civil millennialism, civil election, and civil disobedience against centralized religious and political authority, supported the perception of Great Britain as a tyranny in the revolutionary imagination. This was the fertile religious imagination which prepared American soil to be watered by the blood of patriots and tyrants in the Revolutionary War. This revolutionary imagination elevated the conflict to a sacred drama in human history which cleared the stage for a new democratic experiment in America that would represent a reordering of religious and political power.

THE DEMOCRATIC EXPERIMENT

The democratic religiopolitical system that emerged out of the revolutionary era initiated a redistribution of power in American society. The centripetal force of the sacred covenant was largely displaced in political thought by the notion of the social contract. This line of political reflection, associated with Locke, Rousseau, Montesquieu, and their eighteenth-century interpreters such as John Jacques Burlamaqui and Francis Hutcheson, perceived contractual agreement as the basis of civil society. The terms in which John Locke formulated the social contract were probably the most influential political vocabulary for the American theorists of the democratic experiment. Locke provided the basic conceptual terminology for a political order based upon a social contract.

In his *Second Treatise*, John Locke proposed that political thought should begin by considering the original state of nature that existed before human society. That state of nature was a condition of natural equality of human beings. This was an equality defined by the sheer biological similarity of humans, but more importantly it was determined by their common mortality. An element of violence was regarded by Locke as inherent in humanity's natural state; each person was equal because each was capable of killing the other under the right circumstances. This basic equality was the first characteristic of the state of nature. A second characteristic was revealed by Locke in his assumption that property rights were inherent in the natural condition of human beings. Prior to the formation of civil society, human beings had the right to acquire, possess, and use property. Equality and property rights, therefore, were regarded by Locke as two basic features of the state of nature.

This natural situation, however, offered no protection for the basic human right to property. The purpose of entering into a political arrangement, according to Locke, was "the protection of our property." The social agreements represented by civil society, law, and order were designed to serve the mutual protection of property rights and economic interests. Civil laws were created to insure the protection of natural rights by establishing mutually accepted social forms, agreements, and procedures for organizing social life. The social contract of civil society, for the protection of "life, liberty, and estate," was regarded by John Locke as an arrangement where government existed by the consent of the governed. Recognizing that their natural rights, and property interests, could not be protected in the natural state, human beings entered into voluntary contractual agreements for the protection of their natural rights. These themes in the political philosophy of John Locke—equality, natural rights, voluntary consent of the governed, and social contract—became part of the common vocabulary of republican political theory in the eighteenth century.[33]

These notions were essential ingredients in the political philosophy which animated the formation of the democratic experiment in America. The revolutionary theorist and statesman, Samuel Adams, provided an outline of such a political philosophy in his tract on *The Rights of the Colonists and a List of Infringements and Violations of Rights* (1774). Samuel Adams repeated the Lockean trinity of natural rights by insisting that Americans had the natural rights to life, liberty, property, and the right to defend those rights. These rights were conceived as natural, God-given human powers—the power to live, to be free, and to own property. An important distinction, however, was made by Samuel Adams, and the Lockean theorists of democracy, between the state of nature and the state of society. Human beings were born into nature; but they entered into society by voluntary consent. Civil society was regarded, by definition, as a social contract into which human beings entered through mutual consent. "When men enter into society," Samuel Adams insisted, "it is by voluntary consent; and they have a right to demand and insist upon the performance of such conditions, and previous limitations as form an equitable original compact."[34] This commitment to a government based on the voluntary assent of the governed—a mutual social contract for the protection of natural rights by civil society—was the theoretical foundation for the democratic experiment. But it remained to be seen how such a commitment could possibly be put into practice.

The basis of democratic power was an assumption that political power ultimately resided in the equal enfranchisement of the people to express their will through voting. The agreement, or disagreement, of the people to the social contract was demonstrated through their vote. In democratic power, the majority had the right to govern, and the minority had the duty to obey; as John Adams observed, "There can be no other rule." But who were *the people* who were enfranchised with this democratic power? When John Locke, or Thomas Jefferson for that matter, suggested that all were created equal, they did not assume that all human beings were created with equal abilities, merits, or even political rights in civil society. All human beings may have been created equal by God in the state of nature, but not all have the necessary understanding and will to enter into civil society as equal partners in the social contract. The Constitution of the United States served to clarify the conditions which defined *the people* who were invested with political power by excluding women, children, blacks, and the poor from enfranchisement. Access to democratic power was qualified by establishing a property requirement for voting rights.

Certain classes of persons were disenfranchised because they were regarded as lacking the necessary understanding and will to participate in the political process. Women were excluded because, as John Adams insisted, "their delicacy renders them unfit for practice and experience in the great business of life, and the hardy enterprise of war, as well as the arduous cares of state. Besides, their attention is so much engaged with the necessary nurture of their children, that nature has made them fittest for domestic cares." Children also were excluded from democratic power because, as John Adams suggested, they "have no judgment or will of their own."[35] Black Americans were disenfranchised in the original constitutional arrangement because, in a sentiment echoed by Thomas Jefferson, they were regarded as lacking in the necessary rational powers that would give them equal status with whites.[36] The disenfranchisement of blacks was further supported by the Lockean interpretation of slavery. Slaves were not regarded as equal partners in the social contract designed for the protection of property because, on the assumption that slaves were legitimately captured in war, they had themselves become property to be protected.[37] In all these cases, women, children, and blacks were regarded as lacking independent understanding and will because of their dependent social and economic status. Therefore, they had no independent political rights to exercise a vote in the democratic system.

The arguments invoked for excluding women and children from enfranchisement were also applied in the case of men "wholly destitute of property." John Adams insisted that men without property were like women in the sense that they were unacquainted with public affairs and unable to form a proper understanding, and that they were like children by being too dependent on other men to have a will of their own. Again, a dependent social and economic status supported the conclusion that men without property lacked the independent understanding and will that were necessary to enter into the social contract. To give men without property the vote was, according to John Adams, a "provision for corruption."[38] The exclusion of the poor from the democratic franchise was supported by property requirements for voting rights. John Adams and other theorists of the democratic experiment were convinced that it was a natural political law that "power always follows property." The balance of power in society, Adams held, always corresponds to the distribution of property in land. Adams was convinced that democratic power could be expanded by making land acquisition easy for every member of society. By apportioning land in smaller quantities, and making it available to the multitude, democratic power could be extended over a larger base of the American public. "If the multitude is possessed of the balance of real estate," John Adams suggested, "the multitude will have the balance of power, and in that case the multitude will take care of the liberty, virtue, and interest of the multitude in all acts of government."[39] But without a basis in the ownership of land, democratic power could not be legitimately extended to the multitude without property. Power had to be reserved for those who had an equal interest in protecting property for which the social contract of government was originally instituted.

In this original constitutional arrangement, democratic political power was balanced between the extension of political power to the people and the reservation of political power for those with vested interests in ownership of property. Certain tensions in American political thought were generated by the notion that political power should be vested in the people. Thomas Jefferson insisted that the people were the ultimate guardians of their own liberty. In his *Notes on the State of Virginia* (1781-82), Jefferson suggested that "every government degenerates when trusted to the rulers of the people alone. The people themselves, therefore, are its only safe depositories." But Jefferson's political confidence in the people was qualified when he added that "to render even them safe, their minds must be improved to a certain degree."[40] Strong reservations were expressed during the constitutional convention of 1787 to this version of Jeffersonian populism. Representative Elbridge Gerry of Massachusetts felt that he had been "taught by experience the danger of the leveling spirit"; Edmund Randolph of Virginia insisted that the evils of the times had "originated in the turbulence and follies of democracy"; Timothy Dwight of Connecticut maintained that democracy would destroy civilization and force mankind back into a savage state; and Fisher Ames of Massachusetts declared that the United States was in danger of becoming "too democratic for liberty." Alexander Hamilton summed up the opposition to Jeffersonian populism when he exclaimed: "Your people, sir—your people is a great beast!"[41]

The apprehension that animated these political reservations to democracy was a fear that the political order of the United States might degenerate into a "tyranny of the majority." At least three constitutional structures were put in place to avoid such an eventuality. First, a limited franchise was implemented based on a property requirement for voting rights. Only tax-paying, property-owning citizens, which at the end of the eighteenth century amounted to about one-third of the adult male population, could participate directly in electoral government. Second, a Bill of Rights was amended to the Constitution to insure the protection of individual liberties from the infringement of any political majority that might be in power. And, third, the Constitution provided for three branches of government—executive, legislative, and judicial—with sufficient independence to provide the necessary checks and balances against centralized political power, and to diffuse power through a more complex network of decision-making bodies. These political structures for the distribution of power through American society were designed to prevent the degeneration of the democratic experiment into a tyranny of the majority. They were regarded as necessary limits on the principle of majority rule by the people. John Adams once remarked that "to expect self-denial from men, when they have a majority in their favor, and consequently power to gratify themselves, is to disbelieve all history and universal experience . . . My fundamental maxim of government is, never to trust the lamb to the custody of the wolf."[42] The modified democratic system that was instituted by the constitutional convention was an experiment broadening the base of political participation, while at the same time keeping John Adam's maxim of government in mind.

This new constitutional order was based on a commitment to broadly based political participation, but it was also felt to be sustained by religion. John Adams, who served as the first vice-president of the United States, declared, "We have no government armed with power capable of contending with human passions unbridled by morality and religion. Our constitution was made only for a moral and a religious people. It is wholly inadequate to the government of any other."[43] George Washington, in his Farewell Address after two terms as the first president, concurred with this assessment by maintaining that "of all the suppositions and habits which lead to political prosperity, Religion and morality are indispensable supports."[44] These sentiments were held by rationalists who were convinced that the democratic order required practical support from the moral resources of religion. While the new constitutional dispensation clearly sought to prevent religious controls over government in the provision of Article Six against religious tests for public office, and the First Amendment prohibition of the establishment of a state religion, the framers of the Constitution were nevertheless convinced that religion provided a necessary moral support for the democratic political system.

A rationalist such as Benjamin Franklin provided a good example of the kind of religion that was felt to contribute to the maintenance of the democratic order. Franklin's theology, when he reflected on it at all, was primarily a practical one. He insisted that any religious doctrine should be judged by its effectiveness in cultivating moral virtues. Franklin wrote to his parents: "I think Opinions should be judg'd of by their Influences and Effects; and if a Man holds none that tend to make him less Virtuous or more vicious, it may be concluded he holds none that are dangerous."[45] Religious opinions had to be more than unconventional to be regarded as dangerous; though this had been sufficient for the Puritan orthodoxy. But for Benjamin Franklin, the test of any doctrine was its effect in molding the character of the individual who holds it. Religious doctrines were evaluated by Franklin in terms of their effectiveness in making people better citizens within civil society.

This disregard for standards of orthodox belief, which would regulate the private domain of religious opinion, was expressed in Benjamin Franklin's conviction that "Religion has always suffer'd when Orthodoxy is more regarded than Virtue."[46] This latitude in religious belief extended to an acceptance of skepticism, agnosticism, and uncertainty about traditional religious doctrines. Issues of orthodoxy were regarded by Franklin as largely irrelevant, as he observed toward the end of his life, "especially as I do not perceive, that the Supreme takes it amiss, by distinguishing the Unbelievers in his Government of the World with any peculiar Marks of his Displeasure."[47] This was an evident departure from any traditional Puritan notion that the faithful believers who had entered into a covenant with God would be rewarded in this world with signs of divine pleasure. Franklin excluded religious beliefs as operative forces in the social, political, and economic spheres; they only had an impact on those areas if they supported the development of republican civic virtues which would contribute to the freedom and stability of the public order.

Similar rationalist positions on the relation between religion and politics were expressed by other leaders in revolutionary America. Their considerations of religion seemed to revolve around three basic assumptions about the nature of religious power. First, ultimate religious power was thought to be abstract and unknowable. The divine being was regarded less as a personal God who enters into human experience than as a transcendent, universal power beyond human comprehension. John Adams described God as "an Essence that we know nothing of, in which Originally and necessarily reside all energy, all Power, all Capacity, all Activity, all Wisdom, all Goodness."[48] This absolute power cannot be known, and John Adams insisted that "it is not only vain but wicked for insects to pretend to comprehend it."[49] The common vocabulary for God among the revolutionary rationalists, which owed much to the theology of deism, symbolized God as a creator, architect, or governor who created the world according to the rational pattern of natural laws. It was the responsibility of human beings to exercise their own natural reason to discern these laws and to regulate civil laws according to their pattern. But the divine legislator behind the pattern could never be known.

Second, there was a tendency among these religious rationalists to perceive any established, institutionalized religious power as potentially oppressive. Thomas Paine was the most forceful critic of the special interests of revealed religion. He felt that any organized religious tradition based on revelation had the potential for suppressing the free exercise of reason under the weight of orthodoxy, tradition, and superstition. But this was especially the case in any establishment of a national religion. In his *Age of Reason*, Thomas Paine insisted that "every national church or religion has established itself by pretending some special mission from God, communicated to certain individuals—as if the way to God were not open to every man alike."[50] These revealed religions were perceived as coercive, oppressive, and divisive power structures which, under the cover of religious authority, sought only to monopolize political and economic power. Paine continued: "All national institutions of churches—whether Jewish, Christian or Turkish—appear to me no other than human inventions, set up to terrify and enslave mankind and monopolize power and profit."[51] Paine was convinced that any revealed religion exercised a coercive force over the political arena; but that coercion became even more acute when such a revealed religion was established as a national institution.

Some religious rationalists suggested that the social value of organized religion was its instrumental use as a mechanism for the social control of the masses. Benjamin Franklin affirmed this social value of religion when he asked his colleagues "to think how great a portion of mankind consists of weak and ignorant men and women . . . who have need of the motives of religion to restrain them from vice."[52] And Thomas Jefferson once observed that there were religions "of various kinds, indeed, but all good enough; all sufficient to preserve peace and order."[53] These religiopolitical convictions of the social role of organized religion probably owed much to Montesquieu and the ideal of a cooperation between religion and politics in the social production of good citizens. But the more radical and populist position, voiced by revolutionaries like Thomas Paine and Ethan Allen, held that all revealed religions had the potential to become oppressive forces. All the rationalists basically agreed that religion should be a private concern, and individuals should be free to use their natural reason, freedom of opinion, and liberty of conscience.

Finally, the rationalists held that legitimate religious power could only be found in the form of moral reason. The sacred authority embodied in the doctrines of organized religion was to be analyzed through reason. Only doctrines that could pass the test of reason could be considered legitimate by the rationalists. Thomas Jefferson provided a remarkable example of this exercise of reason in relation to revelation. Jefferson carefully extracted from the Gospels the words of Jesus to which he could give rational assent, and then pasted them together in his own version of the

Bible. He explained that "by cutting verse by verse out of the printed book and arranging the matter which is evidently his and which is easily distinguished as diamonds in a dunghill," he was able to extract "The Philosophy of Jesus of Nazareth." Jefferson determined that this moral code could pass the test of rational assent and practical application. This philosophy, he declared, was "the most sublime and benevolent code of morals which has ever been offered to man."[54] The religious implication of Jefferson's Bible was that religious doctrines should be extracted from the "dunghill" of sacred authority and submitted to the demands of reason.

The political consequences of these assumptions about religious power were: (1) religion was treated as a matter of personal opinion; (2) opinions could be judged by their practical consequences in cultivating private and civic virtues; and (3) religious associations must be persuasive—but never coercive—in their appeals to religious reason. The public position of the new government that emerged from the revolutionary debates over the status of religion was embodied in Article Six of the Constitution and in the First Amendment. Article Six specified that "no religious test shall ever be required as a qualification to any office or public trust under the United States." The First Amendment asserted a basic civil right to the freedom of religion, and it specified that "Congress shall make no law respecting an establishment of religion, or prohibiting the free exercise thereof." The First Amendment proceeded to guarantee other basic rights to speech, free press, assembly, and petitioning against grievances. But the religion clauses of the First Amendment had a particularly decisive effect in theoretically separating the two major powers in the collective life of the new nation: religion and politics.

The establishment clause of the First Amendment suggested a constitutional separation of church and state. This was proposed when Christian churches were for the most part still enjoying tax subsidies for their ongoing financial support. Insight into the concerns behind the establishment clause can be gained by looking at the debate in the Virginia legislature which had been conducted three years earlier (in 1784) over the establishment of religion in that state. The Virginia legislators agreed that no one particular religious denomination should be supported, subsidized, or established by the state. But Patrick Henry presented a proposal that all recognized Christian denominations should benefit from government financial support. Patrick Henry proposed, in his "Bill Establishing the Christian Religion," that "The Christian Religion shall in all times coming be deemed and held to be the established Religion of this Commonwealth; and all Denominations of Christians demeaning themselves peaceably and faithfully, shall enjoy equal privileges, civil and religious."[55] Henry declared that Christianity was the true religion and that it should be encouraged and supported so that it might flourish in the Commonwealth of Virginia. To this end, he proposed that money be allocated yearly for the ongoing financial support of religious teachers and places of worship in the major Christian denominations.

James Madison argued strongly against this proposal. In his response, "A Memorial and Remonstrance on the Religious Rights of Men," Madison countered Henry by insisting that such an establishment of religion by the state would be "a dangerous abuse of power." Madison was convinced that democratic power required a different arrangement of authority, a different distribution of power, in the relation between government and religion. Religion should "be directed only by reasons and conviction, not by force or violence." As a rationalist, Madison assumed that religion was a persuasive appeal to moral reason. Any attempt at coercion in matters of religion led inevitably to the corruption of religion. And any establishment would make religion a coercive, oppressive, and tyrannous force in human society. James Madison made this point by observing that, "experience witnesses that ecclesiastical establishments, instead of maintaining the purity and efficacy of Religion, have had a contrary operation. During almost fifteen centuries the legal establishment of Christianity has been on trial. What have been its fruits? More or less in all places, pride and indolence in the Clergy; ignorance and servility in the laity; in both, superstition, bigotry and persecution."[56]

The resolution of this debate against the proposal for a financial establishment of the Christian denominations in Virginia suggested that the restriction against an establishment of religion was not simply a reluctance to select one Christian denomination over others for financial support or to establish Christianity as a nationally endowed religion; nor was it merely the reluctance to entangle religion in the affairs of government, or government in the affairs of religion. The First Amendment provision against an establishment of religion was animated by a deeper conviction that organized, institutionalized, and established religions tended to be counterproductive to the free exercise of religious and moral reason. If established religion had been prone to "superstition, bigotry and persecution," as James Madison insisted, then it was a form of religion contrary to the legitimate, free exercise of religious power through reason. In the religious thought of James Madison, therefore, there was a natural transition from the establishment clause to the free exercise clause of the First Amendment.

In specifying that Congress shall not pass laws to restrict the free exercise of religion, the Constitution embodied another rationalist assumption that religion was essentially a matter of opinion. This clause has been interpreted as guaranteeing unrestricted freedom of religious opinion, but not necessarily freedom of religious actions that might be perceived as posing a threat to public order, health, and morals. The United States Supreme Court cases which have tested the provisions for free exercise in matters of religion have all been concerned with matters of religious practice. Religiously sanctioned polygamy, refusal to salute the American flag, and the use of controlled substances in religious rituals are a few examples of religious practices which, at one time or another, the Supreme Court has ruled are not protected under the free exercise clause of the First Amendment. In these and other cases the Court weighed competing interests between religion and the state. When state interests in protecting society have been compelling, then the free exercise of certain religious practices could be prohibited. These issues in the First Amendment provisions for the relation between religion and the state, and the ongoing interpretation of that relation by the United States Supreme Court, will be developed in more detail in the third section of this book. But this interpretation of the free exercise clause of the First Amendment appears to be consistent with the rationalist religious conception of religion as essentially a matter of opinion. Religious opinion had to be free from political coercion in order to exercise its free exploration of religious truth.

It has often been conjectured that perhaps John Adams, James Madison, and Thomas Jefferson hoped to see their particular form of rationalism become an established American religion in this constitutional arrangement. Jefferson thought that some version of Unitarianism would become the dominant religious force animating the democratic distribution of political power.[57] But this arrangement was also attractive to Baptists, Methodists, and religious dissenters in general who had not benefited from the colonial establishments of the Anglican, Congregational, and Presbyterian churches. A Baptist church leader such as Isaac Backus was very supportive of the separation of church and state. He was convinced that faith also required a freedom of religious conscience from any form of political coercion in order for it to be authentic.[58] The coalition of pietists and rationalists instrumental in forming the revolutionary imagination, therefore, was also a decisive force in the formation of the distinctive distribution of religious and political power that characterized the beginnings of the democratic experiment in American society.

DEMOCRATIC POWER

The distribution of power within the democratic system was theoretically grounded in the self-government of the people. This democratization of political power was intended to broaden the base of participation in government by investing decision-making in the people and their elected representatives. Any democratic order involves the problem of scale in effectively implementing mass participation in government. The ancient democracy of Athens, for example, had a voting population of around 40,000 citizens; a quorum on any issue could be obtained at 6,000. At its inception, the democratic experiment in America was already operating at a vastly expanded scale. By the mid-twentieth century, American democratic participation would be operating at a scale 2,500 times that of ancient Athens. The largest representative democracy in human history, India in the twentieth century, would be operating at a scale of five to six thousand times the number of voters in ancient Athens' democracy.[59] The sheer size of these democratic experiments has raised important issues about mass participation in the political process. Some of these issues were already being raised in the formation and transformation of the democratic experiment in America in the early years of the nineteenth century.

First, there was the question of the relation between majorities and minorities within a political system based on democratic power. James Madison affirmed the political principle of majority rule when he observed that "no other rule exists, by which any question which may divide society can be ultimately determined, but the will of the majority." But Madison also expressed the growing concern that such majority power had the potential for violating the independent rights of minority groups in American society. "It is also true," he observed, "that the majority may trespass on the rights of the minority."[60] The Bill of Rights, the constitutional system of checks and balances, and the limitation of voting rights to landowners were all designed to protect minority interests. But the limitation on voting rights frustrated the democratic intention of widening political participation. A series of internal revolutions continued through the national period to transform the distribution of democratic power.

A "Jeffersonian revolution" beginning in 1800 pressed the case for self-government by the common man against the vestiges of power and prestige held by the wealthy and wellborn in the United States. Jefferson's first inaugural address expressed his enduring confidence in the majority will of common individuals to form the basis of self-government. "Sometimes it is said," Jefferson noted, "that man cannot be trusted with the government of himself. Can he, then, be trusted with the government of others? Or have we found angels in the forms of kings to govern him? Let history answer this question."[61] The result of this Jeffersonian populism was a marked shift in the base of political power in the United States from the Northeastern states, with their powerful commercial interests, financial elite, and aristocratic heritage, to the agrarian masses in the South. But these agricultural landowners were still largely under the control of a kind of Southern landed aristocracy. The real expansion of democratic political power was closely tied with the expansion of the United States toward the West.

The centrifugal force of democratic power realized its potential in the westward expansion into the territories of Kentucky, Tennessee, Ohio, and Illinois. George Flowers, an English immigrant who settled in the prairies of Illinois in 1817, paid tribute to this expansive force represented by the West. He declared that "A real liberty is found in this country, apart from all its political theories. The practical liberty of America is found in its great space and small population. Good land, dog-cheap everywhere, and for nothing, if you will go for it, gives as much elbow room to every man as he chooses to take . . . This is the real liberty of America."[62] In the wake of this centrifugal force of expansion into the open spaces of the West, where individual initiative seemed to be given free liberty to carve out a new world, voting rights were extended to all adult males. The American public exercised this new "manhood suffrage" in 1828 to elect a representative of the rugged, enterprising, and expansionist West in Andrew Jackson.[63]

The "Jacksonian Revolution" enshrined both an enterprising individualism and the collective will of the common people as the two corresponding forces of democratic power. Andrew Jackson's first inaugural address demonstrated the sacred energy that infused these two aspects of political power in American society. Jackson declared:

> I believe man can be elevated; man can become more and more endowed with divinity; and as he does he becomes more God-like in his character and capable of governing himself. Let us go on elevating our people, perfecting our institutions, until democracy shall reach such a point of perfection that we can acclaim with truth that the voice of the people is the voice of God.[64]

The religious fervor of the Jacksonians promised to transform the democratic order into a sacred celebration of the majority will in government. Democracy seemed to be divinized as the ultimate sacred self-realization of human potential. This is what the political economist C.B. Macpherson has called the "developmental power" of any democratic system.[65] Presumably, democratic power has released power in each individual to develop and exercise—unrestrained by any imposed limitations by government—all the talents, abilities, and initiatives necessary for self-realization. This was the promise of democratic power in the early republic.

This developmental power, however, was only one dimension of democratic power. The other dimension, what C.B. Macpherson has called "extractive power," was the relatively unlimited power of owners, employers, and entrepreneurs to extract the value of labor from workers, and to translate that value into commodities and capital investments.[66] Democratic power in the early republic was closely aligned with the expansion of an aggressive, entrepreneurial capitalism in America. Democratic capitalism placed few limits on the acquisition and exploitation of economic power. At the end of the 1820s, in the midst of the Jacksonian expansion of political power to the American masses, workers called for a revision of the Declaration of Independence to guarantee rights denied by their employers. As the historian Michael Kammen has recorded, trade unions in New York issued "The Working Men's Declaration of Independence" in 1829, newspaper editorials in 1830 suggested that working men were oppressed by a mercenary foe as the patriots had been in 1776, and some even suggested that another revolution would be necessary against economic exploitation and tyranny.[67] By the 1840s the Transcendentalists Orestes Brownson and Theodore Parker distinguished between these two forces in democratic power. What they called "the organized trading power" animated a quest for economic gain, without regard for social justice, "amenable only to the almighty dollar." This was contrasted with the second force of the democratic order, "the organized political power," which they were convinced was usually subservient to the extractive force of purely economic power. The historian Sidney Mead described Parker's hope that this political power might be used to gain control over organized trading power in America as "an act of faith."[68] All of this suggests that there was a basic tension in democratic power as it was implemented in the United States. A persistent tension existed between the *developmental* power vested in the political rights of the majority and the *extractive* power invested in the economic interests of powerful minorities in American society.

Second, there was the need for voluntary associations in American society that would support smaller scale participation in political power. Political parties were, of course, one form of voluntary association that allowed participation; and emerging trade unions formed another vehicle of small-scale political organization. But the early republic was a political arena where many voluntary organizations vied for public support, allegiance, and commitment in the interests of a number of different political causes. Voluntary associations dedicated to the temperance crusade, the public school movement, prison reform, the peace society, women's rights and suffrage, and the abolition of slavery provided dynamic and vital avenues for political expression and participation. Most of these voluntary associations were supported by, or closely aligned with, religious commitments emerging from the Second Great Awakening. This second major eruption of religious enthusiasm, mass conversions, and intensely personal Protestant piety infused these voluntary associations with a kind of evangelical and missionary zeal during the first half of the nineteenth century. Political participation in voluntary associations for moral reforms in American society was directly related to the renewal of religious enthusiasm in Protestant revivalism.[69]

The religious revivals of the early nineteenth century—with their enthusiastic tent revival preaching, impassioned convictions of sin and conversions to Christ, and often extravagant demonstrations of religious ecstasy—had very practical political consequences for the democratic order of the early republic. The expansion of the American frontier and the political base of the republic led to various regional, sectional, and geographic political divisions which threatened to divide American society. The political and economic interests of the North were in conflict with the South, and both conflicted with the expanding economic power and political interests of the Western frontier. The religious revivals cut across these sectional conflicts. As the historian Sidney Mead has observed, "If this configuration posed a threat of centrifugal force, then that had to be countered by the centripetal force of the Revival."[70] The centrifugal expansion of American society was to a certain degree unified by the centripetal cohesion provided by the national enthusiasm for religious revival.

The revivals may have generated a unifying force in an expanding American society, but they also engendered a host of new religious organizations, associations, and movements which served as voluntary associations with their inherent political dimension. Active participation in such religious organizations was already an involvement in a voluntary political movement. And, as the historian Cushing Strout has noted, "By encouraging popular participation in religious organizational life, the evangelical sects were training grounds for popular participation in the organization work of politics that Jacksonians invited."[71] Even before such religious organizations began to actively support various crusades for moral, social, and political reforms, they prepared individuals for a more direct involvement in the larger political process. Small-scale, voluntary associations mobilized the active involvement of individuals, families, and communities in democratic power. And the religious movements that emerged from the early nineteenth-century revivals were important components in the general distribution of democratic power in American society.

Third, there was the question of religion's role in supporting mass participation in democratic power. The importance of voluntary religious associations, and the political reform movements they engendered, already suggested how religion could enter the political life of the early republic. But religious sentiments, convictions, and commitments permeated the collective political life of American society in another way. The French sociologist, Alexis de Tocqueville, who toured the United States in 1831-32, was immediately impressed by the religious character of American society. "On my arrival in the United States," Tocqueville wrote, "the religious aspect of the country was the first thing that struck my attention; and the longer I stayed there, the more I perceived the great political consequences resulting from this new state of things."[72] On the one hand, Tocqueville recorded the separation between church and state in America which allowed for the division of religion and politics into two separate spheres. He noted that Americans had "divided the intellectual world into two parts: in the one they place the doctrines of revealed religion, which demand their assent; in the other they leave those truths, which they believe to have been freely left open to the researches of political inquiry."[73] This nominal separation of church and state divided American religious and political domains. It cleared an open space for independent political thought.

But on a deeper level, the political arrangements of democratic power had elevated this relatively independent exercise of political opinion to a sacred status in America. Public opinion had become, Tocqueville suggested, "a species of religion, and the majority its ministering prophet."[74] The Jacksonian claim that the voice of the people should be regarded as the voice of God gave shape to a type of democratic faith that assumed the sacred aura of religion. Even the organized religious denominations seemed to adapt to this godlike voice of public opinion. Tocqueville reported:

> All the American clergy know and respect the intellectual supremacy exercised by the majority; they never sustain any but necessary conflicts with it. They take no share in the altercations of parties, but they readily adopt the general opinions of their country and their age, and they allow themselves to be borne away without opposition in the current of feeling and opinion by which everything around them is carried along.[75]

This suggestion that American religion was essentially a culture religion adapting to the demands of public opinion implied that there was a deep connection between religion and the majoritarian political, social, and cultural sentiments in the early republic. If this amorphous public opinion of the majority assumed the shape of a religion, then the particular religious denominations in American society appeared to a large extent to be subspecies of this more general culture religion born out of democratic power.

Alexis de Tocqueville had some pointed comments to make about both the potential and the limitations of this religion of public opinion. The "equality of condition" within democratic power led in two directions. First, it supported a certain independence of mind which placed its trust in the authority of private judgments. Tocqueville noted that social equality led human beings to "seek for the sources of truth in themselves or in those who are like themselves."[76] But, second, it encouraged a sense of personal insignificance in contrast to the great faceless mass of humanity that theoretically held democratic power. The sheer weight of public opinion had the effect of inhibiting independent thought. "In the principle of equality," Tocqueville wrote, "I very clearly discern two tendencies, one leading the mind of every man to untried thoughts, the other prohibiting him from thinking at all."[77] In this quasi-religious force that seemed to permeate democratic power, the god of public opinion threatened to assume the shape of an oppressive tyranny of the majority. This tension within democratic power, as Tocqueville suggested, generated both the potential for the actualization of independent, personal power, and the danger that this individual power might be absorbed in the sea of mass public opinion. This was regarded as both the promise and the peril of democratic power in American society.

The new American Israel, sacred and undeniable rights, public opinion as a species of religion, the voice of the people as the voice of

God—all of these themes suggest religious sentiments that pervaded the formation of democratic power in American society. This was an American religiosity that drew from the resources of the Puritan heritage, the rational religion of the Enlightenment, and the popular enthusiasm of the revivals. But these religious motifs seemed to be independent of any of the organized religious denominations in America. They were elements in the complex American ethos which Sidney Mead has called the "Religion of the Republic."[78] There is an important sense in which democratic power was supported by a quasi-religious ideology. As a system of political power, democracy itself assumed an aura of the sacred.

A twentieth-century enthusiast for the democratic faith has argued for its religious status in American society: "Americans must come to look upon the democratic ideal (not necessarily the practice of it) as the Will of God, or, if they please, of Nature . . . Americans must be brought to the conviction that democracy is the very Law of Life . . . The state must be brought into the picture; governmental agencies must teach the democratic idea *as religion* . . . Primary responsibility for teaching democracy as religion must be given to the public schools."[79] This democratic faith has been closely aligned with public institutions, but it also has permeated American collective consciousness as a civil religiosity independent of both church and state. In the space opened up by the separation of church and state appeared what has been called a civil religion. The theoretical and institutional separation of religious and political spheres has been ambiguous in the actual functioning of American society. The various forms of civil religion in America have been expressions of the interpenetration of religion and politics in American life.

NOTES

1. Cited in W.W. Sweet, *The American Churches: An Interpretation* (New York: Abingdon-Cokesbury Press, 1945): 46-7; see Alan Heimert, *Religion and the American Mind: From the Great Awakening to the Revolution* (Cambridge: Harvard University Press, 1966); Edwin Gaustad, *The Great Awakening* (New York: Harper and Row, 1964); and Alan Heimert and Perry Miller,eds., *The Great Awakening: Documents Illustrating the Crisis and its Consequences* (New York and Indianapolis: Bobbs-Merrill, 1967).
2. See Henry E. May, *The Enlightenment in America* (Oxford: Oxford University Press, 1976); and Adriene Koch, ed. *The American Enlightenment* (New York: G. Braziller, 1965).
3. JOHN ADAMS, "To Jefferson, August 24, 1815," in *The Adams-Jefferson Letters*, ed. Lester J. Cappon (Chapel Hill: University of North Carolina Press, 1959): II:455.
4. BENJAMIN RUSH, *An Address to the People of the United States* (Philadelphia, 1787); in Hezekiah Niles, *Principles and Acts of the Revolution in America*, ed. Alden T. Vaughn (New York: B. Franklin, 1971): 334.
5. For a survey of the causes of the revolution, see Gordon S. Wood, *The Creation of the American Republic, 1776-1787* (Chapel Hill: University of North Carolina Press, 1969); On the economic factors in the revolution, see Arthur M. Schlesinger, *The Colonial Merchants and the American Revolution* (New York: Columbia University Press, 1918); Charles Beard, *An Economic Interpretation of the Constitution of the United States* (1913; New York: Macmillan, 1967); Beard, *The Economic Origins of Jeffersonian Democracy* (1915; New York:

Macmillan, 1949); Louis M. Hacker, "The First American Revolution," *Columbia University Quarterly* 27 (1935): 259-95; Hacker, *The Triumph of American Capitalism* (New York: Simon and Schuster, 1940); John C. Miller, *The Origins of the American Revolution* (1943; Stanford: Stanford University Press, 1959); and Evarts B. Greene, *The Revolutionary Generation, 1763-1790* (New York: Macmillan, 1943).

6. For British perspectives on the revolution, see Charles M. Andrews, "The American Revolution: An Interpretation," *The American Historical Review* 31 (1926): 219-32; Lawrence H. Gipson, *The Coming of the Revolution, 1763-1775* (New York: Harper and Row, 1954); and Gipson, *The British Empire Before the American Revolution* (New York: Knopf, 1949): XII:363-7.

7. JOHN LOCKE, *Two Treatises of Government*, ed. Peter Laslett, 2nd ed. (Cambridge: Cambridge University Press, 1970): II:225.

8. JULIAN BOYD, *The Declaration of Independence: The Evolution of the Text as Shown in Facsimiles of Various Drafts by Its Author, Thomas Jefferson* (Princeton: Princeton University Press, 1945): 12-14.

9. BOYD, *Declaration of Independence*: 19; Carl Becker, *The Declaration of Independence* (New York: Harcourt, Brace & Co., 1922): 186-7.

10. HARRY R. WARFEL, *Noah Webster, Schoolmaster to America* (New York: Macmillan, 1936): 59-60.

11. PERRY MILLER, "From the Covenant to the Revival," in *Religion in American History: Interpretive Essays*, eds. John M. Mulder and John F. Wilson (Englewood Cliffs, New Jersey: Prentice-Hall, 1978): 148.

12. See Ernest Lee Tuveson, *Redeemer Nation: The Idea of America's Millennial Role* (Chicago: Universtiy of Chicago Press, 1968); John F. Berens, *Providence and Patriotism in Early America, 1640-1815* (Charlottesville: University Press of Virginia, 1978); and Robert Middelkauff, "The Ritualization of the American Revolution," in *The Development of an American Culture*, eds. Stanley Coben and Lorman Ratner (Englewood Cliffs, New Jersey: Prentice-Hall, 1970): 31-43.

13. JONATHAN EDWARDS, "Some Thoughts Concerning the Present Revival of Religion in New England," *The Works of President Edwards* (New York: S. Converse, 1830): IV:128-33; *God's New Israel: Religious Interpretations of American Destiny*, ed. Conrad Cherry (Englewood Cliffs, New Jersey: Prentice-Hall, 1971): 55.

14. *Ibid.*: 59; see C.C. Goen, "Jonathan Edwards: A New Departure in Eschatology," *Church History* 28 (1959): 25-40.

15. JAMES F. MACLEAR, "The Republic and the Millennium," in *Religion in American History*: 182.

16. Cited in Nathan O. Hatch, *The Sacred Cause of Liberty* (New Haven: Yale University Press, 1977): 55.

17. NICHOLAS STREET, "The American States Acting Over the Part of the Children of Israel in the Wilderness and Thereby Impeding Their Entrance into Canaan's Rest (1777)," in *God's New Israel*: 69-70.

18. EZRA STILES, "The United States Elevated to Glory and Honour (1783)," in *God's New Israel*, 85; see Paul F. Boller, Jr., *George Washington and Religion* (Dallas: Southern Methodist University Press, 1963); and Catherine Albanese, *Sons of the Fathers* (Philadelphia: Temple, 1976).

19. Cited in Miller, "From the Covenant to the Revival," *Religion in American History*: 146.

20. See Philip Davidson, *Propaganda and the American Revolution* (Chapel Hill: University of North Carolina Press, 1941).

21. B. F. MORRIS, *Christian Life and Character of the Civil Institutions of the United States* (Philadelphia, 1864): 526-27; cited in Miller, "From the Covenant to the Revival," in *Religion in American History*: 146.

22. JONATHAN MAYHEW, "A Discourse Concerning Unlimited Submission and Non-Resistance to the Higher Powers (1750)," in *Religion and the Coming of the American Revolution*, ed. Peter N. Carroll (Waltham, Massachusetts: Ginn-Blaisdell, 1970): 30.

23. *Ibid.*: 45; On the colonial fear that England might appoint a Bishop for America, see Carl Bridenbaugh, *Mitre and Sceptre: Transatlantic Faiths, Ideals, Personalities, and Politics, 1689-1775* (New York: Oxford University Press, 1962): 171-340.

24. STEPHEN JOHNSON, *Some Important Observations, Occasioned by . . . the Publick Fast* (Newport, 1766): 18; cited in Cushing Strout, *The New Heavens and New Earth: Political Religion in America* (New York: Harper and Row, 1974): 58.
25. JOHN LATHROP, *Innocent Blood Crying to God* (Boston, 1771): 16; cited in Strout, *The New Heavens and New Earth*: 60.
26. EDMUND S. MORGAN and HELEN MORGAN, *The Stamp Act Crisis: Prologue to Revolution* (Chapel Hill: University of North Carolina Press, 1953): 254.
27. Cited in Richard L. Bushman, *From Puritan to Yankee: Churches and Social Order in Connecticut, 1690-1765* (New Haven: Yale University Press, 1967): 273.
28. THOMAS PAINE, *Common Sense* (1776), in Thomas Paine, *Complete Writings*, ed. Philip S. Foner, 2 vols. (New York: The Citadel Press, 1945): I: 29.
29. *Ibid.*, I: 3; see David Freeman Hawke, *Paine* (New York: Harper and Row, 1974).
30. BOYD, *The Declaration of Independence*: 19-21.
31. DANIEL BOORSTIN, *The Lost World of Thomas Jefferson* (New York: Henry Holt, 1948): 203.
32. Cited in Morton White, *The Philosophy of the American Revolution* (New York: Oxford University Press, 1978): 4.
33. See John Dunn, *The Political Thought of John Locke* (Cambridge: Cambridge University Press, 1969).
34. SAMUEL ADAMS, *The Rights of the Colonists and a List of Infringements and Violations of Rights* (1774); in *American Ideas*, eds. Gerald N. Grob and Robert N. Beck (New York: Free Press, 1963): I: 176-77.
35. JOHN ADAMS, *The Works of John Adams*, ed. C. F. Adams, 6 vols. (Boston, 1850-56): IV: 375-6.
36. See Jefferson's remarks on the rationality of blacks, in *The Life and Selected Writings of Thomas Jefferson*, ed. Adrienne Koch and William Peden (New York: The Modern Library, 1944): 261.
37. See David Brion Davis, *The Problem of Slavery in Western Culture* (Ithaca, New York: Cornell University Press, 1966): 119-20.
38. ADAMS, *Works*: IV: 376.
39. *Ibid.*: IV: 376-7.
40. THOMAS JEFFERSON, *Notes on the State of Virginia*, ed. William Peden (Chapel Hill: University of North Carolina Press, 1954): 148.
41. Cited in Alice Felt Tyler, *Freedom's Ferment* (New York: Harper and Row, 1944): 12.
42. ADAMS, *Works*: VI: 61.
43. Cited in John R. Howe, Jr., *The Changing Political Thought of John Adams* (Princeton: Princeton University Press, 1966): 185.
44. GEORGE WASHINGTON, *The Basic Writings of George Washington*, ed. Saxe Cummins (New York: Random House, 1948): 637.
45. BENJAMIN FRANKLIN, *Autobiography and Other Writings*, ed. L. Jesse Lemisch (New York: New American Library, 1961): 319.
46. *Ibid.*: 320.
47. *Ibid.*: 338; on Franklin's religion, see A. O. Aldridge, *Benjamin Franklin and Nature's God* (Durham: Duke University Press, 1967).
48. JOHN ADAMS, "To Jefferson, January 20, 1820," in *The Adams-Jefferson Letters*, ed. Lester J. Cappon 2 vols. (Chapel Hill: University of North Carolina Press, 1959): II: 560.
49. JOHN ADAMS, "To Jefferson, September 14, 1813," in *The Adams-Jefferson Letters*, II: 375; see H. O. Fielding, "John Adams: Puritan, Deist, Humanist," *Journal of Religion* 20 (1940): 33-46.
50. ARTHUR WALLACE PEACH, ed., *Selections from the Works of Thomas Paine* (New York: Harcourt, Brace, and Co., 1928): 232.
51. *Ibid.*: 232.
52. Cited in Thomas L. Hall, *The Religious Background of American Culture* (Boston: Little, Brown, and Co., 1930): 172.
53. SAUL K. PADOVER, ed. *The Complete Jefferson* (New York: Duell, Sloan, and Pearce, 1943): 676.
54. HENRY WILDER FOOTE, *Thomas Jefferson: Champion of Religious Freedom, Advocate of Chris-*

tian Morals (Boston: Beacon Press, 1947): 52; see *Jefferson's Extracts from the Gospels: 'The Philosophy of Jesus' and 'The Life and Morals of Jesus,'* ed. Dickinson W. Adams (Princeton: Princeton University Press, 1983).

55. H. J. ECKENRODE, *Separation of Church and State in Virginia* (1910; New York: Da Capo Press, 1971): 58-61.

56. SAUL K. PADOVER, ed., *The Complete Madison* (New York: Harper and Row, 1953): 299-306; on Madison's religion, see Ralph J. Ketcham, "James Madison on Religion—A New Hypothesis," *Journal of the Presbyterian Historical Society* 28 (1960): 65-70; and Ketcham, *James Madison* (New York: Macmillan, 1971).

57. BOORSTIN, *The Lost World of Thomas Jefferson*: 704.

58. See William G. McLaughlin, *Isaac Backus and the American Pietistic Tradition* (Boston: Little, Brown, 1967); and Stanley Grenz, *Isaac Backus—Puritan and Baptist* (Macon, GA: Mercer University Press, 1983).

59. DANIEL BELL, *The Winding Passage: Essays and Sociological Journeys, 1960-1980* (Cambridge, Massachusetts: ABT Books, 1980): 26.

60. JAMES MADISON, "A Memorial and Remonstrance on the Religious Rights of Man," in *Cornerstones of Religious Freedom in America*, ed. Joseph L. Blau (Boston: Beacon Press, 1949): 82.

61. THOMAS JEFFERSON, "First Inaugural Address, March 4, 1801," in *God's New Israel*, 107: See Richard Buel, Jr., *Securing the Revolution in American Politics, 1789-1815* (Ithaca, New York: Cornell University Press, 1972).

62. Cited in Tyler, *Freedom's Ferment*: 18; see T. Scott Miyakawa, *Protestants and Pioneers: Individualism and Conformity on the American Frontier* (Berkeley: University of California Press, 1964).

63. On the broadening of suffrage, see Chilton Williamson, *American Suffrage from Property to Democracy, 1760-1860* (Princeton: Princeton University Press, 1960).

64. Cited in Tyler, *Freedom's Ferment*, 77; see Marvin Meyers, *The Jacksonian Persuasin: Politics and Belief* (Stanford: Stanford University Press, 1957).

65. See C. B. MacPherson, *Democratic Theory: Essays in Retrieval* (Oxford: Clarendon Press, 1973): 3-76.

66. *Ibid.*; also, see MacPherson, *The Political Theory of Possessive Individualism: Hobbes to Locke* (Oxford: Oxford University Press, 1967): 226.

67. MICHAEL KAMMEN, *A Season of Youth: The American Revolution and the Historical Imagination* (New York: Oxford University Press, 1978): 45.

68. SIDNEY MEAD, *The Lively Experiment: The Shaping of Christianity in America* (New York: Harper and Row, 1963): 99-100.

69. See John R. Bodo, *The Protestant Clergy and Public Issues, 1812-1848* (Princeton: Princeton University Press, 1954).

70. MEAD, *The Lively Experiment*: 157.

71. STROUT, *The New Heavens and New Earth*: 111.

72. ALEXIS DE TOCQUEVILLE, *Democracy in America*, ed. Phillips Bradley (New York: Alfred A. Knopf, 1945): I: 319; see Joachim Wach, "The Role of Religion in the Social Philosophy of Alexis de Tocqueville," *Journal of the History of Ideas* 7 (1946): 74-90.

73. *Ibid.*: I:312.

74. *Ibid.*: II:12.

75. *Ibid.*: II:29.

76. *Ibid.*: II:10.

77. *Ibid.*: II:12.

78. SIDNEY E. MEAD, *The Nation with the Soul of a Church* (New York: Harper and Row, 1975): 64ff.

79. J. PAUL WILLIAMS, *What Americans Believe and How They Worship* (New York: Harper and Row, 1951): 71, 78, 368, 374; cited in Will Herberg, "America's Civil Religion: What it is and Whence it Comes," in *American Civil Religion*, eds. Russell E. Richey and Donald G. Jones (New York: Harper and Row, 1974): 84.

CHAPTER THREE
CIVIL RELIGION

The French philosopher Jean-Jacques Rousseau introduced the notion of a civil religion at the end of his meditations on the republican system of government in his *Social Contract* (1762). Rousseau's arguments for a political system based on the sovereignty of the general will of the people, the necessity for the voluntary agreement of individuals to the conditions of the social contract, and the significance of religion in such a social order had a tremendous, formative influence on the democratic experiment in the United States. Reflecting on the place of religion in the political arena, Rousseau was convinced that traditional religions represented potentially disruptive forces in the political order. A republic required committed citizens convinced of the ultimate validity of the social contract. But organized religions—with their alternative institutional structures, traditional sources of authority, and other-worldly interests—created divided loyalties in society. Religions exercised arbitrary power that could become tyrannical; they were divisive forces which undermined the unity of the social order; and they subjected human beings to exclusive, other-worldly aspirations which, Rousseau contended, "prevents them from being devoted at once to god and country."[1] Christianity in particular was regarded by Rousseau as a religion which created divided loyalties between a kingdom of God and the social contract.

The solution proposed by Rousseau for this tension created by traditional religions was a purely civic religious faith that would support the social order. This civil religion would be, in Rousseau's terms, "a purely civil profession of faith whose articles the sovereign is competent to determine, not precisely as religious dogmas, but as sentiments of sociability without which it is impossible to be a good citizen or a faithful subject."[2] In this sense, civil religion is a supportive system of religious sentiments, convictions, and commitments that emerges from the separation of church and state. The doctrines of such a civil faith, according to Rousseau, should be few, simple, and clearly stated.

First, a civil faith should affirm the existence of a powerful, intelligent, and good Divinity. That divine being should be regarded as exercising foresight and providence in the destiny of a community. Second, a civil faith should hold a belief in the survival of the soul after death. A belief in the ultimate happiness of the just, and punishment for the wicked, would provide supernatural sanctions for a just social order. Third, a civil faith should be committed to the sanctity of the social contract and the laws of the land. In this civil religion, the social contract becomes a sacred contract infused with religious power. Beyond these simple doctrines, the civil religion should be tolerant of the diversity of private religious opinions, as long as they do not disrupt the unifying sentiments generated by the civil religion.[3]

America has never had precisely this form of established civil religion prescribed by the state for the allegiance of all citizens, as it was proposed by Rousseau. And yet, sentiments have taken shape in American public life that might be characterized as a civil religiosity. Benjamin Franklin came close to Rousseau's definition of a civil religion when he noted in his *Autobiography*, "I never was without some religious principles. I never doubted, for instance, the existence of the Deity; that he made the world, and govern'd it by his Providence; that the most acceptable service of God was the doing of good to man; that our souls are immortal; and that all crime will be punished, and virtues rewarded, either here or hereafter. These I esteem'd the essentials of every religion." Franklin considered these elements of a general religiosity necessary in a unified social order. Religious doctrines supporting morality, virtues, and dedication to public service were necessary for the unity of a republic. However, like Rousseau, Franklin was convinced that traditional religions tended to disrupt that moral, spiritual, and essentially religious unity. In such traditional religions, Franklin observed, the simple doctrines of a civic faith were often found to be "more or less mix'd with other articles, which, without any tendency to inspire, promote, or confirm morality, serv'd principally to divide us, and make us unfriendly to one another."[4] Particularist religions could be tolerated in the democratic system, but the divisive religious commitments they represent should be ultimately resolved in a unifying civic faith.

Civil religion may be regarded as a third distribution of religious and political power in American historical experience. As a more or less organized system of religiopolitical power, civil religion has displayed persistent elements of the theocratic system, in such themes as divine providence, a unique American destiny, and a type of civil millennialism that has regarded America as the central arena of God's work in human history. Likewise, civil religion has represented the elevation of the democratic system to a sacred status. In treating democratic principles, institutions, and the voice of the people as sacred elements in an overarching religious faith, civil religion in America has infused the democratic system with a unique, sacred aura.

Civil religion, however, has provided a relatively independent religiopolitical system in American historical experience in three basic respects. First, it has signified the interdependence of religion and politics in that space opened up by the separation of church and state. Public symbols, beliefs, and values have emerged in that space; collective rituals, a sacred calendar of holy days, and a sacred history have taken shape; and social institutions, such as the public schools, have arisen to instill a general, shared religious commitment to a common national identity. Second, civil religion has signified the legitimation of American politics by religious convictions. Clearly, particular religious groups have provided resources to support national purposes throughout American history, but a relatively independent religious nationalism has emerged which legitimizes American institutions, authority, and actions. Vague references to God in presidential inaugural addresses, the inscription of "In God We Trust" on American money, the phrase "One nation under God" in the pledge of allegiance to the flag, all suggest an underlying conviction that the causes and conduct of the American nation are infused with an ultimate religious significance. Third, civil religion has signified the formulation of political principles of government as if they were transcendent religious doctrines. In this sense, the theocratic sacred covenant has become a civil religious covenant in which the nation stands under the judgment of God; and the democratic social contract has become a civil religious contract which embodies sacred principles to be enacted in the American political order. Civil religion in America, therefore, may be considered as a religiopolitical system, independent of both organized religions and the institutions of government, which represents a set of collective religious symbols, a sacralized national identity, and a system of transcendent, quasi-religious principles of political order.

These distinct yet often overlapping senses in which civil religious power appears to operate in American society can be identified as three types of civil religion. The first type might be characterized as *American culture religion*. This is the operative religion of American society, viewed from a perspective derived from Emile Durkheim's understanding of the necessary interdependence between religion and society, as a set of collective representations symbolizing a common American identity. American culture religion, folk religion, or what the sociologist Will Herberg referred to as the "American Way of Life," involves powerful symbols, values, and practices that to a certain extent unify American society.[5] The symbols of this culture religion are independent of church and state, but their symbolic resonance has permeated both religion and politics. This diffuse system of collective representations can be described, interpreted, and analyzed in the same way that a cultural anthropologist might try to reconstruct the religious worldview which gives a certain degree of coherence to a tribal society. American culture religion signifies the dimension of civil religion that has the potential for providing such a symbolic unity for American society.

Second, civil religion may assume the form of an *American religious nationalism*. This perspective draws on Max Weber's insights into the power of religion to legitimize the state. But in religious nationalism, the sacred power of transcendence is invested directly in the state itself. Many, if not all, of the elements of American culture religion may be present in religious nationalism, but these symbolic resources are used to legitimize the aims, goals, and purposes pursued by the nation. One of the consequences of modernization, as we noted in the introduction to this book, has been the transfer of religiopolitical power from religious institutions to the state. As the sociologist of religion Phillip Hammond has noted, "religion declines as power coalesces in the institutions of the state."[6] The political power consolidated in the state assumes a religious character.

In this sense, the United States adopted an aura of sacrality very early in its history, and has continued to represent itself in terms of a unique national destiny as the central locus of God's interaction with the world. This dramatic elevation of the nation to the sacred status of a mediating power between God and the world is the essence of religious nationalism; but it is also a reason why this form of civil religion has been regarded by adherents of traditional religions as a form of idolatry. Religious nationalism appears to be the idolatrous worship of national identity, purposes, and destiny as the primary frame of reference for the experience of sacred transcendence. Nevertheless, the impulse of religious nationalism has been a powerful force in shaping American history. To some extent, the religiopolitical belief in a sacred, manifest destiny has been a kind of self-fulfilling prophecy. The motivations of religious nationalism have helped mobilize and direct generations of Americans to expand the power, territory, and influence of the United States in the world.

A third version of American civil religion might be regarded as the *transcendent religion of America*. The sociologist Robert Bellah revived the term civil religion in 1967 to describe this type of transcendent religion in American history. In this sense, civil religion involves "a genuine apprehension of universal and transcendent religious reality as seen in or, one could almost say, as revealed through the experience of the American people."[7] As in religious nationalism, the historical experience of American society provides the context for the relationship between God and the world. But in the transcendent religion of America, that national experience is judged by powerful religious values and sacred ideals. The American nation, in this form of civil religion, "stands under transcendent judgment and has value only insofar as it realizes, partially and fragmentarily at best, a 'higher law.' "[8] This sense that American historical experience must be measured against a higher law is derived from the biblical notion of a divine covenant and the Enlightenment principle of natural law embodied in a sacred social contract. These become transcendent reference points for evaluating the American nation.

Robert Bellah's concept of civil religion owes something to Durkheim, for example, when he describes civil religion as "a collection of beliefs, symbols, and rituals with respect to sacred things and institutionalized in a collectivity."[9] In this sense, religious and political spheres interpenetrate in the formation of collective symbols of American civil religion. But Bellah also owes a debt to Weber in describing how civil religion generates motivational symbols which serve "to mobilize deep levels of personal motivation for the attainment of national goals."[10] These symbols mobilize religious sentiments in the service of political action. They have surfaced and crystallized during particularly intense national crises. The most powerful collective symbols of American civil religion have arisen out of episodes of national trial: the Revolutionary War, the Civil War, and the Vietnam War. In those periods, a transcendent civil religion mobilized Americans to action in the interest of national goals, but it also reinforced a conviction that during such times of crisis America stands most directly under the shadow of religious judgment. Bellah has insisted that this transcendent religion of America is to be distinguished from religious nationalism. It is "not a form of national self worship but . . . the subordination of the nation to ethical principles that transcend it and in terms of which it should be judged."[11] It will be useful to examine how these civil religious dimensions of American society—culture religion, religious nationalism, and a transcendent religion of America—have functioned as more or less organized systems of religiopolitical power in the historical experience of the United States. Although America has not had an established civil religion in Rousseau's sense, civil religious power has permeated American beliefs, practices, and experience as a relatively unifying religious dimension of American political order.

AMERICAN CULTURE RELIGION

The notion of a culture religion is a synthetic concept which tries to draw together the most basic religious sentiments, motivations, and ideals which actually operate in a given cultural context. Culture religion demonstrates the Durkheimian thesis that a society is held together by collective religious symbols, practices, and forms of interaction. The sociologist Robin Williams maintained that "every functioning society has to an important degree a *common* religion. The possession of a common set of ideas, rituals, and symbols can supply an overarching sense of unity even in a society riddled with conflicts."[12] Religions in a plural society may be sources of division, opposition, and conflict as competing sources of religious authority. But the common culture religion of a community can provide a more or less systematic vocabulary of sacred symbols which allows for a certain degree of cooperation, integration, and solidarity in an otherwise divided society. From this perspective, the collective symbols that serve this unifying function may be regarded as the culture religion of the community.

To regard such shared symbolic representations as a culture religion is also to acknowledge a necessary relationship between religion and culture. It is to regard religion as the meaningful inner core of culture, and culture as the outer manifestation of religion. The theologian Paul Tillich suggested this relation between religion and culture when he noted that "Religion as ultimate concern is the meaning-giving substance of culture, and culture is the totality of forms in which the basic concern of religion expresses itself. In abbreviation: religion is the substance of culture, culture is the form of religion."[13] Religion, in this sense, is the ultimate internal power which drives the shared, common, cultural life of a community. That power is not identified exclusively with organized religious institutions, but it is an inherent force which finds expression in the basic patterns of a culture. In this respect, culture religion is the "invisible religion" of a community which is manifested in its shared symbols, values, and ideals that represent a relatively coherent and unified worldview.[14] As a culture religion, folk religion, or common religion, civil religion may function as precisely such a religious dimension inherent in American culture.

Like any religion, American culture religion can be analyzed in terms of its interrelated aspects of belief, practice, and experience. The collective representations of American cultural religion take on all the aspects of traditional religion. First is the aspect of *myth*. The powerful symbolic narratives of Pilgrims and Puritans, founding fathers, and heroic battles and adventures all have assumed the proportion of religious myth in American culture. The mythic transformation of history into sacred history began even while the revolution was still in progress. But the transformation of America into the New Israel, George Washington into Moses, and the Declaration of Independence into a sacred text only signified the beginning of a continuous process of mythic interpretation. When the founding fathers searched for symbols that would be appropriate for the seal of the new nation, they rejected the image of Moses parting the Red Sea (suggested by Benjamin Franklin) and the image of the children of Israel wandering in the wilderness (suggested by Thomas Jefferson) to formulate a new set of sacred symbols that would signify national identity. The eagle with olive branch and thirteen arrows and the unfinished pyramid topped by the all-seeing eye of God were visual symbols of the new nation. They were supplemented by two mottos: *Annuit Coeptis*, "God has smiled on our beginnings"; and *Novus Ordo Seclorum*, "A New Order of the Ages." These symbols captured the mythic perception of America as a nation formed under divine providence with a sacred cosmic destiny in human history.

The mythic transformation of the founding fathers accelerated in the early national period as they were regarded as sacred figures, revered ancestors, or cultural heroes who exemplified the primordial sacred time of American origins.[15] John Adams and Thomas Jefferson further insured their places in this mythic pantheon by both dying on the same day: July 4, 1826. And President James Monroe added to the sacred correspondence of coincidence in American sacred history by dying on the Fourth of July five years later. Newspaper accounts of all three deaths gave evidence to the symbolic reverberations such sacred coincidences held in the public imagination. These events seemed to testify to an underlying sacred pattern in American history.[16] Martyrdom has traditionally been regarded as the road to sanctification in the western religious imagination; the assassinations of Abraham Lincoln and John F. Kennedy elevated both presidents to a special sacred status in American culture religion. The obelisk of Washington, the imposing statue of Lincoln, and the eternal flame of Kennedy memorialize in the nation's capital this trinity of American saints. The living presence of sacred narratives, sacred persons, and sacred events in American history signify a mythic dimension in American culture religion.

The second aspect of American civil culture religion is *doctrine*. The author G.K. Chesterton is often recalled in discussions of American civil religion for his remark that "America is the only nation in the world that is founded on a creed."[17] America may not be unique in this regard, but its political identity is clearly grounded on what may be regarded as basic religious premises. This American creed has been shaped by two major sources of religious belief: the Enlightenment ideals embodied in the Declaration of Independence; and the persisting, residual traces of a Puritan covenant theology. Chesterton maintained that the first source of the American creed was clearly articulated in the Declaration of Independence. He noted:

> That creed is set forth with dogmatic and even theological lucidity in The Declaration of Independence . . . It enunciates that all men are equal in their claim to justice, and that governments exist to give them that justice, and that their authority is for that reason just. It certainly does condemn

anarchism, and it does also by inference condemn atheism, since it clearly names the Creator as the ultimate authority from whom these equal rights are derived.[18]

These theological doctrines of equality, liberty, and justice—all derived from the sacred power and authority of the divine Creator—were, however, integrated into a civil theology with deep biblical roots. Doctrines of divine election, special providence, and manifest destiny reflected the persistent influence of the Puritan doctrine of a sacred covenant between God and community which represented a second source for the American creed. This civil theology of American culture religion is not a systematic, prescribed formula of religious belief, but a rather loosely organized set of ideals and assumptions that have provided important religious resources in shaping American self-understanding as a nation. These elements create a theological vocabulary for achieving ideological consensus and for conducting ideological conflicts in American culture religion.

A third aspect in this culture religion is *ritual*. Every religion is sustained by ritual practices that activate sacred power, carve out regions of sacred space, and observe the sacred times of a religious calendar. American culture religion has its significant ritual practices. The American sacred calendar of holidays represents a cycle of holy days with their traditional ritual practices. These are sacred times marked out, and set apart, from the ordinary, mundane, or profane flow of time. Some of these holy days have a sacred significance directly related to American history and political life. The Fourth of July, Memorial Day, Veterans Day, Presidents Day, Martin Luther King Day, and Thanksgiving all carry some degree of sacred relevance for the common religious and political life of American society. Other holy days, such as New Year's, Christmas, Halloween, Valentine's Day, Father's Day, Mother's Day, and Labor Day reflect certain shared quasi-religious values of celebration and renewal in their commemoration of familial, public, and even primordial dimensions of American culture religion.

The central holy day in this American sacred calendar is certainly the Fourth of July. Traditionally celebrated by patriotic prayers, sermons, and speeches, this holy day is honored by ritual practices which evoke the primordial powers of American origins. By the 1830s the ceremonial reading of the Declaration of Independence on this day had become an important element in its ritual celebration, and a visitor to the United States in 1837 recorded his observation that "it is with the solemnities of religion that the Declaration of Independence is yet annually read to the people from the pulpit, or that Americans celebrate the anniversaries of the most important events in their history."[19]

Memorial Day, which had been celebrated in a number of different regions of the United States throughout the nineteenth century, was institutionalized after two world wars into a ritual cult of the dead who had been sacrificed in American wars. This collective ritual commemoration of the dead has demonstrated the potential in American culture religion for producing unifying religious symbols and practices which may, to a certain extent, operate to sanctify and revitalize American society. The anthropologist Lloyd Warner certainly regarded Memorial Day ceremonies in this light when he observed that they "are rituals which are a sacred symbol system, which functions periodically to integrate the whole community, with its conflicting symbols and its opposing autonomous churches and associations . . . Memorial Day is a cult of the dead which organizes and integrates the various faiths, ethnic and class groups into a sacred unity."[20] Warner's idealized description of the unifying effect of these sacred ceremonies raises the question of how effective civic rituals actually are in achieving cultural unity. Religious rituals, even of this civic variety, can easily become arenas of competition between different religious communities, ethnic groups, and class interests to claim a privileged possession of the sacred symbols evoked by these rituals.[21]

But even when such rituals involve competing social claims, the ritual order embodied in the sacred calendar, ceremonial practices, and sanctified places sets the terms within which any conflicts are conducted. The sacred status of the American flag, for example, as a ritual object which focuses powerful religious sentiments in American culture, has often been claimed by special social, political, or religious interest groups. During the political protests of the 1960s, it was the sacred status of the flag that made any public, ceremonial burning of this ritual object a potent symbolic statement against political interests in America that claimed sole access to its sacred power. Ritual practices associated with the sacred calendar, presidential inaugurations, state funerals, and even the electoral rituals of voting reveal a dynamic ritual dimension in the American civil culture religion.

A fourth aspect of American culture religion is *ethics*. Ritual refers to religious practices in extraordinary, set apart, or sacred times and places; ethics represents a more or less systematic set of standards for ordinary action. In terms of ethical standards, American culture religion has been deeply informed by the personal and social commitments embodied in its creed. These ethical commitments, born out of the coalescence between Enlightenment rationalism and Puritan piety, have been summarized by the sociologist Will Herberg as the American dedication to "individual freedom, personal independence, human dignity, community responsibility, social and political democracy, sincerity, restraint in outward conduct, and thrift."[22] Like Warner's description of American ritual, Herberg's list of American ethical standards represents a highly idealized description of the "American Way of Life." Nevertheless, it suggests that American culture religion embodies a loosely integrated set of ethical values for personal conduct and social relations.

The ethical character of American culture religion has been captured by Robert Bellah in the phrase "utilitarian individualism."[23] This orientation to personal and social ethics in American society reflects a generally practical set of standards suggesting that things are to be used and people are to be useful. Utilitarian individualism measures the usefulness of people and resources. This practical orientation toward utility has been an important ethical dimension in American collective life. The organized conception of how things ought to be, or how people ought to act and interact, may be defined as the *ethos* of a culture.[24] The distinctive ethos of American culture religion has been shaped by the cultural forces of pragmatism, materialism, and an abiding faith in human progress through technological development.

The pragmatic orientation toward ethics, what the historian Richard Hofstadter has called the "cult of religious practicality," measures any religious value in terms of its practical consequences.[25] Religion's role in society can be justified by its capacity for cultivating individual self-improvement and public civic virtues. Materialism pervades the American ethos in the aspirations for material wealth, abundance, and prosperity. The Gospel of Wealth that emerged at the end of the nineteenth century represented the extent to which the American religious imagination could invest material prosperity with a sense of ethical righteousness. Reverend William Lawrence of Massachusetts, declaring in 1901 that "godliness is in league with riches," saw this gospel of material wealth as a "rekindling of the spirit, that, clothed with her material forces, the great personality of this nation may fulfill her divine destiny."[26]

Finally, what might be called the "myth of progress" through technological advancement has pervaded the American ethos. Mechanization, industrialization, and technological innovations have promised a new technical millennium in the American religious imagination—a new heaven and new earth through technological advancement. But a perennial dilemma in technology remains: In harnessing the power of machines, human beings have not discovered how to avoid being controlled by those very machines. The demands of mechanical efficiency, regularity, and uniformity have tended to be transposed upon the realm of human actions and interactions. The ethos of American culture religion has become increasingly conditioned by precisely these practical, material, and mechanical values. There may be a certain degree of tension in that ethos between those mechanical values and the ethical aspirations toward individual freedom, personal independence, and human dignity in American culture religion.

A fifth aspect of culture religion is the domain of *personal experience*. Love of country, devotion to national ideals, and fervent patriotism are not necessarily religious experiences. But in American culture religion they become infused with a sense of the sacred. Patriotism becomes a sacred emotion. The ultimate power of such a religious commitment may be reflected in a person's willingness to make the supreme sacrifice for his or her country. This willingness to die for God and country—perceiving them as a single, unified object of devotion—may be one indication of a depth of personal commitment to American culture religion. It is difficult, however, to measure degrees of personal involvement in this religious dimension of American culture. There also seems to be an almost endless variety of ways to express that involvement. The poet Walt Whitman, in his *Leaves of Grass* (1855), described his experience as "an American, one of the roughs, a kosmos, disorderly, fleshy and sensual."[27] The Congregational minister and theologian, Horace Bushnell, speaking at a graduation ceremony at Yale University in 1865, spoke of a new American culture that was infused with "great sentiments, and mighty impulsions, and souls alive all through in fires of high devotion."[28] In one respect, therefore, this cultural religious experience has been imagined as a dynamic power, energy, and enthusiasm awakened through personal involvement with America.

American presidents have functioned as the exemplary prophets and ceremonial priests of an American cultural faith. The religious experience of faith, devotion, and surrender to a higher divine power is exemplified in presidential invocations of divine aid and guidance. The American faith of Abraham Lincoln, for example, weaving together the sacred texts of the Bible and the Declaration of Independence, set a type of exemplary model for religious experience in American culture religion. Speaking of his faith in a God that directs American destiny, Lincoln once remarked: "I have had so many evidences of His direction, so many instances when I have been controlled by some other power than my own will, that I cannot doubt that this power came from above."[29] This faith in a divine agency directing American destiny became institutionalized in American culture religion. It has been a religious faith not specifically tied to any church, sect, or religious tradition in America. President Dwight Eisenhower exemplified this rather diffuse, general faithfulness in American culture religion during a period of revival in the American faith after the second world war. "I am the most intensely religious man I know," Eisenhower declared. "Nobody goes through six years of war without a faith. That does not mean that I adhere to any sect."[30] One critic of this faith represented by American culture religion insisted that "the faith is not in God but in faith; we worship our own worshipping."[31] But that ultimate value placed on faithfulness has represented an important element in the dimension of religious experience within American culture religion. This is a faith that is general, vague, and amorphous enough to embrace the wide variety of divergent faith communities in American society.

In American culture religion, that personal experience of faith is ultimately focused into patriotism. This patriotic faith is the point at which American culture religion tends to intersect with religious nationalism. The nation itself tends to become a sacralized object of religious devotion. The Catholic Church leader, Monsignor C.F. Thomas, sought to mobilize this patriotic devotion in the interest of national purposes in World War I. Thomas declared: "No nation, no people, have endured who were not endowed with the deepest instincts of patriotism and the most unselfish spirit of devotion and sacrifice . . . our trust cannot be fulfilled without the loyalty, love, personal and patriotic efforts of each and every individual."[32] Monsignor Thomas was certainly not alone in evoking from the pulpit a spirit of devotion, commitment, and sacrifice to the sacred trust of patriotism during times of war. But the fact that he was a spokesman for the Catholic Church suggests, again, that the cultural religious faith was a general, diffuse religious sentiment that had the potential for bridging sectarian differences among religious groups in America. Nevertheless, the mantle of patriotism in American history has periodically been claimed as the exclusive privilege of particular social, political, and religious interest groups. The author and journalist Susan Sontag, during the political unrest of the sixties, observed that "Ever since World War II, the rhetoric of patriotism in the United States has been in the hands of reactionaries and yahoos; by monopolizing it, they have succeeded in rendering the idea of loving America synonymous with bigotry, provincialism, and selfishness."[33]

Patriotism, like any religious experience, can mobilize sectarian interests; it can reinforce a narrow, exclusive definition of American nationalism. Religious experience, even in American culture religion, creates a certain tension between ideal expectations which are embodied in its religious creed, and the actual experience of those involved in that religion. Personal experience in American culture religion has not simply taken the form of fervent devotion to America—it has also taken shape in feelings of resentment, frustration, and discontent among those who have been systematically excluded from full participation in American society. These *others*, as the historian of religion Charles Long noted, have largely been "invisible" in American culture religion.[34] One of the most powerful representatives of this *other* side of American civil religion, Martin Luther King, Jr., wrote in 1963 from the Birmingham jail about the personal experience of black Americans in American culture.

> The Negro has many pent-up resentments and latent frustrations, and he must release them. So let him march; let him make prayer pilgrimages to the city hall; let him go on freedom rides—and try to understand why he must do so. If his repressed emotions are not released in nonviolent ways, they will seek expression through violence; this is not a threat but a fact of history. So I have not said to my people: "Get rid of your discontent." Rather, I have tried to say that this normal and healthy discontent can be channeled into the creative outlet of nonviolent direct action.[35]

King's eloquent statement regarding the personal experience of black Americans suggests that tensions in American culture are also tensions in

American culture religion. The personal experiences of Native Americans, blacks, immigrants, and women have revealed basic tensions in the American culture religion. First, the overarching symbols of a civil faith provide the potential for a unifying, all-inclusive religious devotion to America, but many have felt excluded from this cultural faith. Second, the sacred contract of American culture religion has held that all persons are created equal, but not all Americans have had equal opportunity in American society, or equal access to the political process. And third, the sacred covenant of American culture religion has often served not as a religious image of divine judgment, but a warrant for the self-righteous vindication of national purposes and policies. The accommodation of *otherness* within a unified culture religion is perhaps the greatest challenge in American collective religious experience. The personal experience of all *others* reveals basic, inherent conflicts in the overarching American culture religion.

The sixth aspect of American culture religion is the role of *social institutions*. Civil faith is, in a sense, marginal to American society because it is not formally institutionalized in either church or state. There is no church of American culture religion, and its beliefs and practices are not officially mandated by the institutions of government. And yet certain social institutions in American society have served as social carriers of American culture religion. The most important of these institutions has been the public school system. The public school has periodically been an arena of religious conflicts as sectarian religious interests have been frustrated by strict definitions of the separation of church and state in American public institutions. But it is also clear that the shared, common mythic narratives of American sacred history, the doctrinal propositions of the American creed, the ritual observances of flag and sacred calendar, the ethical values of utilitarian individualism, and the patriotic sentiments of a common, cultural religious experience have all been sustained and supported by public schools. As the historian of American religion, Robert Michaelsen noted, "the common school has been the primary center in and around which this common religionizing has gone on."[36] As a social institution for the transmission of a sacred cultural tradition, the American public school system has provided a social basis for American culture religion. While it may not quite be the "established church" of an American civil religion, the public school has been an important social carrier of a general religious dimension in American culture.

As a culture religion, common religion, or folk religion, American civil religion has represented an underlying religious structure (or an overarching sacred canopy, to use a phrase of the sociologist Peter Berger) which has registered American historical experience in essentially religious terms. The pattern of American culture religion has provided a powerful symbolic context, as the sociologist John Coleman has observed, for linking America's distinctive "place in space, time, and history to the conditions of ultimate existence and meaning."[37] Human beings do not simply live in a world; they live in a meaningful world. And this culture religion has provided a symbolic vocabulary for articulating a general, shared sense of meaning in the social world of American society. The power invested in American culture religion has manifested in at least three important ways: (1) a cohesive, centripetal force which has the potential for binding Americans into a common community; (2) an adaptive force which has tended to temper, modify, and Americanize the various particular religious groups in American society; and (3) an exclusive force which tends to reject certain forms of *otherness* that cannot be, or are not allowed to be, assimilated into a relatively homogeneous Americanism. This exclusive force, what the sociologist Robert Bellah has referred to as "a pull toward archaic regression in the American civil religion," has tended to identify a particular constellation of Americans (traditionally white, Protestant, and of Anglo-Saxon origin) as the exclusive representatives of a uniquely American community of righteousness.[38] This exclusive claim to religiopolitical power, both within American society and in relation to other societies, is the central element in religious nationalism as a form of civil religion in America.

AMERICAN RELIGIOUS NATIONALISM

Religious nationalism takes the form of devotion to the nation as an ultimate locus of sacred meaning and power. This devotion may be supported and sustained by all the elements of a culture religion; but it specifically signifies the legitimation of national identity, purposes, and political policies in terms of specifically religious beliefs. Nationalism itself, as the historian Carlton Hayes observed, becomes a species of religion in which the state strives to mold each citizen by "tutoring him in a national catechism, teaching him by pious schooling and precept the beauties of national holiness, fitting him for a life of service . . . to the state."[39] In religious nationalism, the state—and not simply a general, collective, shared culture—becomes the ultimate sacred reference point for religious devotion, commitment, and ultimately self-sacrifice on behalf of the sacralized nation-state. Nationalism and nationalistic ideologies have mobilized the most powerful religious energies in the modern world. American religious nationalism has provided a powerful source of legitimation for political order in American society and the sense of a sacred national mission in the world.

Varieties of religious nationalism formed early in the national period in American history. Elements of a religious nationalism were already present in the themes of chosen people and millennial destiny that infused the religious rhetoric surrounding the Revolutionary War. These themes persisted because, as the historian Elwyn Smith has noted, "the

Republic—both its morals and its unity, and therefore its power to survive—rested on a pervasive religious and moral consensus."[40] The first decades of the nineteenth century witnessed different attempts to articulate this religious unity upon which the nation was based. A public merger between Protestant religion and American politics revealed two different, yet complimentary ways of defining American religious nationalism: a revival democracy or a republican theocracy.

The Protestant revivals of the early nineteenth century unleashed a religious enthusiasm for personal salvation, the spiritual value of the individual, and active participation in voluntary religious and social organizations that contributed an evangelical dimension to American religious nationalism. Revival preachers, camp meeting evangelists, and itinerant frontier ministers on horseback preached personal salvation and moral perfectionism, combined with a nascent American nationalism. The revivals not only supported the emergence of Jacksonian democracy and public participation in movements for social reform, but they also infused national life with a revival spirituality that persisted throughout the nineteenth century and into the twentieth. The historian William McLoughlin has suggested how deeply revival religion permeated American nationalism. "The story of American Evangelicalism," McLoughlin noted, "is the story of America itself in the years 1800 to 1900, for it was Evangelical religion which made Americans the most religious people in the world, molded them into a unified, pietistic-perfectionist nation, and spurred them on to those heights of social reform, missionary endeavor, and imperialistic expansion which constitute the moving forces of our history in that century."[41] American religious nationalism, as a revival democracy, was infused with a particular style of Protestant spirituality in its ardent individualism and sense of crusading religiopolitical mission to the world. Even when divorced from its expressly religious context, the style, tone, and rhythm of revival spirituality has remained an important ingredient in American political life and nationalism.

A second Protestant definition of religious nationalism was worked out in the early nineteenth century by a group of Calvinist theologians who have been referred to as "republican theocrats."[42] These theologians, such as Timothy Dwight, Nathaniel W. Taylor, and Lyman Beecher, all from Connecticut, sought to integrate the new constitutional arrangement of the United States into a more traditional Puritan understanding of the relation between God and the world. Rousseau, it might be recalled in this context, was convinced that a Christian republic was a contradiction in terms. He argued that Christianity introduced divided loyalties into the republic, and could not accept the separation of church and state, the ultimate sanctity of the social contract, and the individual freedom of conscience necessary for each citizen to agree to that contract. While at first resisting the disestablishment of Christian churches required by a separation of church and state, the republican theocrats came to embrace these republican political ideals. They retained the theocratic notion, however, that God exercises moral government over the state. But they adapted this theocratic concept of religiopolitical power by maintaining that the divine moral government of America was carried out, in the words of Lyman Beecher, by awakening "the voluntary energies of the nation itself."[43] In this sense, the democratic order was interpreted as God's theocratic order. Beecher even asserted that "the civil constitution of the Old Testament was a federal republic."[44] God's divine laws for human government were felt to be embodied in the Constitution of the United States. Lyman Beecher declared that "Our own republic, in its constitutions and laws, is of heavenly origin. Our constitution borrows from the Bible its elements, proportions, and power. It was God that gave these elementary principles to our forefathers."[45] This theocratic interpretation of the democratic order constructed a sacred bridge between the Puritan conviction of divine election and the new constitutional arrangements of religion and politics in the early republic. With a sophisticated theological precision, Lyman Beecher, and the other republican theocrats, affirmed a residual Puritan heritage in the notion of America as a chosen people with a unique destiny under the moral government of God, which formed a major current in American religious nationalism.

The Civil War provided the supreme test of American religious nationalism. A deeply divided society, with economic differences between the agrarian-plantation economy of the South and the urban-commercial economy of the North, and with social differences over the status of slavery, invested the political dissolution of the nation with conflicting religious significance. Not only were major Protestant denominations broken into Northern and Southern branches, but competing religious nationalisms emerged to interpret the religious significance of the conflict between North and South. As expected, both sides evoked the sacred symbols of religious nationalism in the interest of their cause. The theologian Horace Bushnell recorded in 1864 the devotion with which the North was convinced that God was on its side. "Our cause, we love to think," Bushnell noted, "is especially God's and so we are connecting all most sacred impressions with our government itself, weaving in a woof of holy feeling among all the fibres of our constitutional polity and government."[46] From this perspective, the secession of eleven Confederate states was a cosmic disruption of the sacred order represented by national union. As the divine governor of that union, God could only be expected to restore order.

Theologians of religious nationalism in the Confederacy, however, were often equally convinced that God was on their side. The Presbyterian minister, Benjamin Palmer, delivered a fast-day sermon in New Orleans in 1861 which summarized the powerful symbols of a sacred national mission which were integral elements in an emerging Southern religious nationalism. Palmer evoked the civil religious themes of both the sacred covenant and the social contract in American history. Appropriating the perennial imagery of the exodus of Israel, Palmer assumed the mantle of divine election for the Confederate States who were, like Israel in the wilderness, fleeing the political bondage of the Northern pharaoh. These Southern states were the new chosen people. The United States, Palmer insisted, had betrayed its divine mission by neglecting to mention God in its Constitution. He announced with a certain pride that the new Confederate Constitution "is indeed no ordinary State Paper. . . . But a religious unction pervades every clause and line; and the child of God can recognize the dialect which his ear loves to hear. It summons us to 'recognize our dependence upon God,' to 'humble ourselves under the dispensations of divine providence,' to 'acknowledge his goodness' and 'supplicate his merciful protection.' "[47] This invocation of divine power and authority in the Confederate Constitution was interpreted by Benjamin Palmer as a sure sign that the South had renewed the covenant relationship with God that was essential for a vital religious nationalism.

Reverend Benjamin Palmer also called upon the sacred principles of the social contract embodied in America's national heritage. The Declaration of Independence provided the textual precedent in American religious nationalism for the divine right of a people, when they are convinced that they suffer under political tyranny, to alter or abolish that government and to institute a new political order. This was precisely what Palmer understood as the basic justification for the South's secession from the Union and its institution of a new order of government. The Southern states were simply consistent with the sacred political principles embodied in the Declaration of Independence. "The last hope of self-government upon this Continent," Benjamin Palmer declared, "lies in these eleven Confederate States. We have retained the one, primary truth upon which the whole fabric of public liberty was reared by our fathers, and from which the North has openly apostasized."[48] Palmer imagined the South to be the true inheritor of the divine covenant and the sacred principles of self-government which had been basic elements in American religious nationalism. The possibility that slavery might be inconsistent with the proposition that all men are created equal was not regarded as a serious problem by Benjamin Palmer and other defenders of the righteousness of the Southern cause. Slavery was regarded as a beneficent social institution which extended protection, civilization, and the Christian religion to a people who were not believed to have been created equal. Slavery was an institution, Palmer argued, which had "the support of God's immovable Providence."[49]

North and South, therefore, both claimed special access to and guidance from God's providence. Both were convinced that God was on their side, and that they were the legitimate heirs to the social covenant and the sacred contract which defined American religious nationalism. President Abraham Lincoln, who is often described as the preeminent theologian of American political religion, wrestled with the religious significance of this contest between North and South. Convinced that a divine providence guided American destiny, Lincoln nevertheless suggested that the divine will might in fact not be aligned with the political interests of either side. In the midst of that conflict, reflecting on the inscrutable will of God in American national experience, Lincoln meditated on a sacred power that transcended the political interests of all factions. Lincoln wrote:

> The will of God prevails. In great contests each party claims to act in accordance with the will of God. Both *may* be and one *must* be wrong. God cannot be *for* and *against* the same thing at the same time. In the present civil war it is quite possible that God's purpose is something different from the purpose of either party—and yet the human instrumentalities, working just as they do, are of the best adaptation to effect His purpose. I am almost ready to say this is probably true—that God wills this contest, and wills that it shall not end yet. By his mere quiet power, on the minds of the now contestants, He could have *saved* or *destroyed* the Union without a human contest. Yet the contest began. And, having begun, He could give the final victory to either side any day. Yet the contest proceeds.[50]

Lincoln's agonizing struggles to discern a divine will operating in human history seemed to move beyond the parameters of religious nationalism (with its invocation of sacred power to legitimate a particular social, political, or military program) into what has been called a transcendent religion of America. American destiny was imagined to be under the direction of a divine will, but that will of God was an instrument of judgment, rather than vindication. Lincoln regarded sacred power as an impenetrable mystery, despite how close he might have felt at times to sensing the contours of its design. Yet that power was felt to infuse American destiny by adapting human beings to its purposes and placing them under its transcendent judgments. In many respects, Lincoln was an exceptional representative of American civil religion. He evoked the biblical imagery of a sacred covenant and the egalitarian principles of a social contract in his religiopolitical meditations on American destiny. But Lincoln employed these resources of American culture religion and religious nationalism in a difficult and often agonizing scrutiny of American collective conscience. Lincoln's suggestion that both sides may be wrong mitigated against American religious nationalism's tendency to manipulate sacred symbols in order to legitimate national purposes and policies. The tensions in American civil religion, revealed by the Civil War, were intensified after the War with the failure of Reconstruction, the emplacement of legalized segregation, and the entrenchment of white supremacy. As the historian Cushing Strout observed, "The civic religion, most memorably expressed in the judgment on American Negro slavery, threatened to become only a white tribal cult."[51] That white, predominately Anglo-Saxon, and Protestant religious nationalism became increasingly dedicated to a sacred destiny felt to be revealed through the expansion of American national power.

The term *manifest destiny* was introduced by a journalist for the *New York Morning News*, John L. O'Sullivan, in 1845 to capture a prevalent national conviction that the United States was entitled to possess territory from coast to coast in North America. This notion of a sacred destiny, revealed in the expansion of American territorial control, was, as the historian Albert Weinberg has noted, a quasi-religious faith in "geographical predestination." Manifest destiny was "a dogma of supreme self-assurance and ambition—that America's incorporation of all adjacent lands was the virtually inevitable fulfillment of a moral mission delegated to the nation by Providence itself."[52] In American historical experience, land has served as both a political and religious symbol. The doctrine of manifest destiny held that the expansion of American territory signified a sacred entitlement to a promised land that was increasingly expanding in scope and dimension as divine providence unfolded. Initially, manifest destiny provided a quasi-religious justification for the extension of American political power over the continent. By the end of the nineteenth century, American religious nationalism displayed an ardent enthusiasm for extending the centrifugal force of that political control over the rest of the world.

As the frame of reference for this national manifest destiny expanded, religious nationalists regarded the United States not only as God's chosen nation occupying a promised land, but as a willing instrument in God's millennial design for the transformation of the world. One of the most enthusiastic exponents of the national-millennial vision, Josiah Strong, wrote a tract for the American Home Missionary Society, entitled *Our Country* (1885), which combined the civil religious symbols of sacred covenant and social contract into a manifesto of American expansionism. Strong contended that the world would be brought to millennial perfection through the expansion of American revival Christianity and American democratic principles and institutions. America was imagined to be God's agent in the regeneration of the world. "For if this generation is faithful to its trust," Josiah Strong declared, "America is to become God's right arm in his battle with the world's ignorance and oppression and sin."[53] The thrust of Strong's version of manifest destiny exhorted Americans to maintain religious and political purity at home, and to extend American cultural, religious, and political influence abroad. This conception of American destiny was deeply imbued with notions of historical progress, the evolutionary survival of the fittest, and racial theories of white supremacy. But it was also consistent with the undercurrent of millennial thinking which has animated American religious nationalism throughout its history.

The sacred destiny of expansion was apparently confirmed by the annexation of the Philippines in 1900. Albert J. Beveridge, a United

States senator from Indiana, celebrated this event with a speech that represented a sermonic rededication to America's sacred destiny. God was preparing, Beveridge announced, the "English speaking and Teutonic peoples" to be "the master organizers of the world to establish system where chaos reigns." This enterprise of political expansion was justified, in Beveridge's terms, because "God marked the American people as His chosen nation to finally lead in the regeneration of the world." God's hand was felt to be guiding this expansion; His plan was being unfolded in America's sacred destiny; His guidance was directing "the eternal movement of the American people toward the mastery of the world." This divine mission, as Senator Beveridge declared, "is a destiny neither vague nor undesirable. It is definite, splendid and holy."[54] This persistent millennial vision of America's central role in the regeneration of the world remained an important element in American religious nationalism. As America entered the twentieth century that vision was tested, and for most religious nationalists resoundingly confirmed, through America's victorious intervention in two international wars. By the middle of the twentieth century, religious nationalism experienced a powerful revival as American political power seemed to encircle the globe.

The ceremonial high priest of a revived American religious nationalism during the fifties was President Dwight Eisenhower. Eisenhower has often been cited in discussions of American civil religion for his conviction that "our government makes no sense unless it is founded in a deeply felt religious faith—and I don't care what it is."[55] That national religious faith promoted by Eisenhower had all the cherished attributes of American culture religion. It was a faith in the power of faithfulness itself, emphasizing a deep emotional commitment and concern for the practical, utilitarian consequences of such a faith in embracing American religious communities and mobilizing a general devotion for national purposes. The historian of American religion and politics, William Lee Miller, summarized the characteristics of this national faith proclaimed by Eisenhower during the fifties.

> Mr. Eisenhower voiced exactly the standard themes of the popular 'revival' that took place during his period in office: the belief in 'believing' or in 'faith,' independent of its object ('These devoted people here,' he said to the World Council of Churches at Evanston, 'believe, first of all, always in faith . . . '); the emphasis on feeling rather than content or meaning ('a *deeply felt* religion'); the recommendation of religion for its usefulness ('faith is the mightiest force that man has at his command'); the connection of this generalized religion with America's 'foundation,' as he said over and over again; and finally, the differentiation of America from the Communist world chiefly on the basis of this 'religious' view.[56]

This American faith was particularly mobilized in the cold war/holy war against the political and military forces of communism. Religious faith and free enterprise were perceived as poised against the evil, threatening forces of communism in the world. This was conceived as essentially a religious contest. Communism was defined by Eisenhower as a negation of the spiritual premises upon which the American nation was founded. "According to that doctrine," Eisenhower said in a commencement address at Baylor University in 1956, "there is no God; there is no soul in man; there is no reward beyond the satisfaction of daily needs. Consequently, toward the human being, Communism is cruel, intolerant, materialistic."[57] As embodied in the political power of the Soviet Union, communism was regarded as a denial of the fundamental religious faith which sustained America, and therefore was seen as the focus of evil in the world. In the cold war mythology of American religious nationalism, which has remained an integral part of that national faith, the conflict between these two religiopolitical systems assumed cosmic proportions and the zone of conflict opened up by their encounter encompassed both the heavens and the earth. "We sense with all our faculties," Eisenhower announced in his first inaugural address, January 20, 1953, "that forces of good and evil are massed and armed and opposed as rarely before in history."[58] It would require a revival of American religious nationalism, Eisenhower and other cold war warriors were convinced, to effectively counter the spiritual dangers posed by the evil forces of communism.

The perennial themes of American religious nationalism—America as the locus of God's agency in the world, as the primary context for defining personal religious experience, and as the collective representation of a community of righteousness—were defined in opposition to the uncontrollable religiopolitical forces represented by communism. In the popular mythology of religious nationalism since the fifties, America's millennial role has not simply been the regeneration of the world, but the salvation of humanity from the demonic domination of an absolute evil. American nuclear capabilities, military power, and self-appointed role as the moral policeman of the world intensified the practical consequences of American religious nationalism in the international arena. The mantle of the high priesthood of this religious nationalism fell upon Richard Nixon from 1968 until he was, in effect, deposed from that office in 1974. It has often been noted that Nixon invested his personal vision of the American nation with all the religious attributes of sacred transcendence. One critic of the "Nixon theology" complained that "Nixon systematically appropriates the vocabulary of the church—faith, trust, hope, belief, spirit—and applies these words not to a transcendent God but to his own nation, and worse, to his personal vision of what that nation should be . . . Lacking a transcendent God, he seems to make patriotism his religion, the American dream his deity."[59]

From the perspective of the historic faith communities in American society, this transference of sacred power from a transcendent God to the state has often been regarded as a form of idolatry. Such religious nationalism certainly allows for worshipping the idol of the tribe as if it were an ultimate sacred object. But this proclivity for self-referential national worship has been a major ingredient in American religious nationalism throughout its history. This was not a new doctrine introduced by Richard Nixon, but a residual impulse in a historical American religious nationalism which has periodically engaged religious symbols, beliefs, and emotions in the interests of national objectives.

Civil religion, in the form of religious nationalism, has always had the religious potential to legitimate political power. This religious nationalism may be regarded as parochial, exclusive, and self-righteous in its prevalent imagery of American chosenness and sacred destiny. Critics have argued that it has exacerbated conflicts, divisions, and resentments in the larger world. America's sacred mission to regenerate the world, it has been suggested, has been counterproductive as it creates deeply entrenched enemies by violating the principles of equality, liberty, and freedom in its international relations. Religious nationalism has supported the sacrifice of such principles in the interest of doing battle against international communism, the "Great Satan."[60]

The justification of American economic interests in the international arena in terms of the special mission of American religious nationalism has been inevitably linked with American military power. Military force has reinforced economic, political, and ultimately religious interests in relation to the rest of the world. The exercise of military power has continued to be legitimated within American religious nationalism by commitments to a special mission and destiny regarded as uniquely American. The sociologist Robert Bellah has suggested that "any archaic claims to our own special righteousness or messianic mission, however, can only further the process of global disintegration."[61] American religious nationalism, particularly as it has become armed with the almost limitless destructive capabilities of a nuclear arsenal, appears from Bellah's and other critics' remarks to have become increasingly problematic in the modern world.

THE TRANSCENDENT RELIGION OF AMERICA

American religious nationalism has drawn forceful criticisms from theologians, sociologists, and historians on a number of counts. First is the argument proposed by theologians that religious nationalism is a species of idolatry. Will Herberg criticized American culture religion in this regard when he argued that its national religious symbols were not an adequate substitute for the transcendent God of Protestantism, Catholicism, and Judaism. Herberg suggested that even though civil religion may be regarded as an operative religion in America, it remains somehow less authentic than the historical and traditional faiths of America's major religious communities. "Because they serve a jealous God," Herberg insisted, "these biblical faiths cannot allow any claim to ultimacy and absoluteness on the part of any thing or any idea or any system short of God . . . To see America's civil religion as somehow standing above or beyond the biblical religions of Judaism and Christianity, and Islam too, as somehow including them and finding a place for them in its overarching unity, is idolatry, however innocently held and whatever may be the subjective intentions of the believers."[62]

The theologian Herbert Richardson has also argued that American civil religion, particularly when taking the form of religious nationalism, has been a misdirection of religion. Civil religion is problematic not only when its symbols are mobilized for what might be regarded as the wrong ends, but also when a religious identification with the state displaces people from the traditional faith communities that alone have the spiritual resources to limit abuses of political power by the state. "We, as citizens," Richardson announced, "affirm that civil religion is idolatry and limit the power of the state only when we affirm and act on the basis of alternative allegiances that restrict our participation in its cult and values."[63] These theological critiques reveal a tension between worship of God and worship of country from the perspective of traditional religions in America. Although American religious groups have certainly accommodated themselves to civil religion, these accusations of idolatry suggest that this accommodation has not always been comfortable.

A second criticism raised regarding religious nationalism has been directed against the tendency of civil religious symbols to be mobilized for national vindication, rather than self-analysis and a sense of divine judgment of American political actions. The exploitation of civil religious symbols to produce a sense of American self-righteousness, infinite innocence, and unquestioned divine support has placed the nation beyond moral or religious criticism. Again, religious nationalism may involve a certain flattening of transcendence as the nation becomes invested with attributes of divinity. A nation *of* God, in this sense, is not necessarily a nation *under* God. Robert Bellah, in particular, has fashioned his definition of civil religion to avoid the closed, self-justifying religious vindication of America. Bellah has argued for the vitality of a transcendent civil religion of America which insists that the nation must be measured against the sacred principles embodied in its founding documents and must be judged by a transcendent divine authority. "At its best," Bellah has observed, "civil religion would be realized in a situation where politics operates within a set of moral norms and both politics and morality are open to transcendent judgment."[64] In the sense of a transcendent religion of America, civil religion represents a set of religious ideals distilled from American foundational principles, but perhaps never fully achieved in American historical experience. These ideals, imbued with a sacred transcendent power, are the ultimate standards against which that actual experience can be evaluated.

A third criticism directed toward civil religion, particularly in the form of religious nationalism, is that it has been too exclusive in practice to be true to its first principles of equality, liberty, and justice for all Americans. Civil religious symbols have been exercised in the interests of a relatively exclusive political power base. The experience of those who have been systematically excluded from full political participation in that system of power has testified to serious tensions in American civil religion. Martin Luther King, Jr. spoke from the perspective of a transcendent civil religion of America, deeply informed by the sacred principles of its founding documents, when he sought to identify a certain cultural schizophrenia between putative beliefs and historical practices in American society. In a speech entitled "The American Dream," in 1961, King said:

> Ever since the founding fathers of our nation dreamed this noble dream, America has been something of a schizophrenic personality, tragically divided against herself. On the one hand we have proudly professed the principles of democracy, and on the other hand we have sadly practiced the antithesis of those principles. Indeed slavery and segregation have been strange paradoxes in a nation founded on the principle that all men are created equal.[65]

The "American Dream," in King's terms, may be the unfulfilled promise contained in the principles of equality, liberty, and justice upon which the nation was expressly founded. Although those principles have not been realized, the sacred precepts of a transcendent civil religion in America are not thereby invalidated. Civil religion may be regarded as a transcendent condemnation of the past, a judgment of the present, and an exhortation for the future which requires American society to align with its most fundamental ideals.

Many theoretical formulations of a transcendent, American civil religion have been proposed. Robert Bellah's definition of civil religion as, "an understanding of the American experience in the light of ultimate and universal reality," has perhaps been the most prominent in recent discussions of civil religion in America.[66] The historian Sidney Mead's formulation of the "Religion of the Republic" is closely aligned with this definition in its concentration on the ultimate and universal principles of a republican reality which are embodied in the Enlightenment religio-political ideals of the founding fathers, and imbued with a prophetic character in the biblical mold.[67] And the sociologist of religion Phillip Hammond, in characterizing civil religion as the "moral architecture" of America, has suggested that the legal separation of church and state, combined with a vital, dynamic pluralism in American society, has supported a civil religion devoted to putting basic moral principles of republican government into practice in the United States.[68] All three of these definitions of civil religion present this religiopolitical system as a transcendent cultural ideal against which actual political practices may be evaluated.

But proponents of this transcendent civil religion intend more by this concept than simply a set of ideals for measuring the performance of American society. Robert Bellah has suggested the political implications of such a transcendent civil religion; it is America's attempt to make "any form of political absolutism illegitimate."[69] A transcendent civil religion of America, in this sense, would operate within the religiopolitical system of American society to limit arbitrary employments of political power. Political power would be constrained and conditioned by the religious precepts embodied in the founding principles of government. This claim for civil religion has not been born out in the habitual patterns of American culture religion, nor in the often arbitrary excesses of political power in religious nationalism. These dimensions of civil religious power have taken on a life of their own, unrestrained and unrestricted by any necessary fulfillment of the sacred limits on political power prescribed by the liberal, democratic principles of the founding documents of the United States. A transcendent civil religion, in the sense of a sacred limit on American political power, has not necessarily provided a consensus on the role of power in the religiopolitical system of the United States. And transcendent symbols of American civil religion have increasingly become objects for competition among mutually exclusive definitions of that American system.

Perhaps this competition over American sacred symbols does, in fact, reveal a transcendent dimension in American politics. For political interests to establish themselves in or near the center of the American political arena, they are obligated to make some claim to these transcendent symbols. Recent political experience in America has demonstrated this competition over sacred symbols. In the 1984 election, religiopolitical figures such as Jerry Falwell and Jesse Jackson, although they definitely played different roles in the political campaigns, were Baptist ministers who quoted in prophetic tones from the Bible, and claimed special access to the inner significance of transcendent civil religious principles of American government. Such competition over sacred symbols obviously reveals that one person's transcendence can be regarded by another as oppression, illusion, or heresy. To occupy a space in the American political arena, however, is to evoke the reverberating resonance of those sacred symbols. And those transcendental symbols have proven to be a vocabulary for both consensus and conflict in American politics.

The critical dimension of a transcendent civil religion has been activated in recent political experience, particularly during the period from 1965 to 1985, by special interest groups seeking to carve out a space in the territory of American politics. The invocation of these transcendent symbols has not simply been the province of fundamentalist Protestants redefining America as a Christian nation, nor of their liberal opponents who insist that such a religious nationalism would violate the sacred principles of democratic government which Christian nationalists have attempted exclusively to co-opt. Many religious and political movements during this period have struggled to appropriate civil religious symbols in the interests of a particular cause. The opposition to the Vietnam War, which took shape in an activist antiwar movement, has been interpreted as an attempt to revitalize American commitment to transcendent civil religious principles. "The conflict over Vietnam," argued the theologian Richard Neuhaus, "is between the government (under both Johnson and Nixon) and the American civil religion, a conflict within the American political enterprise, broadly understood."[70] Antiwar activists, from this perspective, struggled to remind the American government of transcendent moral commitments violated by America's involvement in Vietnam. Likewise, the civil rights movement, particularly under the leadership of Martin Luther King, Jr., attempted to recall America to its transcendent civil religious precepts of equality, liberty, and justice for all persons regardless of race, religion, situation, or circumstance in American society. The feminist movement in America, perhaps most politically visible in the campaign for an Equal Rights Amendment which would insure the civil rights of women against arbitrary discrimination, has also involved an implicit (and often explicit) invocation of civil religious principles and a critique of civil religious practices in the interest of a transcendent ideal of equality.[71] Environmentalist groups, farm workers unions, and even new religious movements, such as the Unification Church of Sun Myung Moon, have all had recourse at one time or another to transcendent symbols of American civil religion.

At this point, it may be more realistic to speak of civil religion*s* in America. This is not only because culture religion, religious nationalism, and a transcendent civil religion are three different ways in which a religious dimension has appeared in American history and society. There are multiple civil religions in America because different groups have inevitably located the signals of transcendence in American politics differently. These differences seem to have intensified during the twenty years from 1965 to 1985. At the midpoint of that period, Robert Bellah lamented that civil religion in America had become "a broken and empty shell."[72] Perhaps the demise of civil religion as a coherent, unifying set of collective representations could be regarded as a symptom of the social disruptions in the late sixties and early seventies. Perhaps a note of betrayal was evident in the widespread notion during this period that the American ship of state had lost its moorings in the sacred principles and ideals that had defined its origins. But the transcendent symbols of American civil religion seemed to remain a vital vocabulary for social conflict in American political life. They remained powerful symbols to be appropriated, owned, and operated by contending groups in American society. The symbols may retain their transcendence because anyone can claim them—but no one can own them. The ideals of a transcendent civil religion are the common property of American historical experience. One thing revealed by recent conflicts over American sacred symbols is the malleability of religious symbols in general. Although they may provide a basic symbolic pattern, the elements of that configuration can be appropriated and adapted to almost any political purpose. Perhaps the symbols of American civil religion have always been empty signifiers which can only be filled by Americans struggling to define themselves and work out their destinies through hints contained in those sacred symbols.

As a religiopolitical system, civil religion in America has revealed a variety of different ways to negotiate the relations between religion and politics. Civil religion can be analyzed in at least three basic dimensions: It has been the folk religion of a people; the religious legitimation of a nation; and a set of transcendent ideals against which the American people and nation have been assessed. These are three different ways in which the term civil religion has been used to explore the distributions of religiopolitical power in American historical experience. The plurality of civil religions should not disguise the fact that these systems of religious and political power in America have often achieved a relatively unified consensus by excluding *others* from full participation. Religiopolitical systems in American society, whether theocratic, democratic, or civil religious, have inevitably been implicated in zones of conflict which have arisen from the encounter with otherness. The promise of a vital, dynamic pluralism in American religion and politics has been presented by these encounters, but the result in American historical experience has more often been the emergence of sustained zones of conflict between alternative religiopolitical systems.

NOTES

1. JEAN-JACQUES ROUSSEAU, "The Social Contract," in *Rousseau: Political Writings* trans. and ed. Frederick Watkins (New York: Nelson and Sons, 1953): 148.
2. *Ibid.*: 153.
3. *Ibid.*: 153; see Louis J. Voskuil, "Jean-Jacques Rousseau: Secular Salvation and Civil Religion," *Fides et Historia* 6 (1975): 11–26; Fred H. Willhoite, Jr., "Rousseau's Political Religion," *The Review of Politics* 27 (1965): 501–515; Ronald Grimsley, *Rousseau and the Religious Quest* (Oxford: Clarendon Press, 1968); Roger D. Masters, *The Political Philosophy of Rousseau* (Princeton: Princeton University Press, 1968); and Hilail Gildin, *Rousseau's Social Contract: The Design of the Argument* (Chicago: University of Chicago Press, 1983).
4. FRANK LUTHER MOTT and CHESTER E. JORGENSON, eds., *Benjamin Franklin: Representative Selections* (New York: American Book Co., 1936): 69–70.
5. WILL HERBERG, "Religion and Culture in Present-Day America," in *Roman Catholicism and the American Way of Life*, ed. Thomas T. McAvoy (Notre Dame: University of Notre Dame Press, 1960): 11–12; see Herberg, *Protestant, Catholic, Jew* (Garden City, New York: Doubleday, 1955).
6. ROBERT N. BELLAH and PHILLIP E. HAMMOND, *Varieties of Civil Religion* (Berkeley: University of California Press, 1980): 77.
7. ROBERT N. BELLAH, *Beyond Belief: Essays on Religion in a Post-Traditional World* (New York: Harper and Row, 1970): 179.

8. ROBERT N. BELLAH, "American Civil Religion in the 1970s," in *American Civil Religion*, eds. Russell E. Richey and Donald G. Jones (New York: Harper and Row, 1974): 255.
9. ROBERT N. BELLAH, *The Broken Covenant: American Civil Religion in Time of Trial* (New York: Seabury Press, 1975): 175.
10. BELLAH, *Beyond Belief*, 181.
11. *Ibid.*: 168.
12. ROBIN M. WILLIAMS, *American Society: A Sociological Interpretation* (New York: Alfred A. Knopf, 1951): 312.
13. PAUL TILLICH, *The Theology of Culture* (New York: Oxford University Press, 1959): 42.
14. On the concept of "invisible religion," see Thomas Luckman, *The Invisible Religion: The Problem of Religion in Modern Society* (New York: Macmillan, 1967).
15. See Catherine L. Albanese, *Sons of the Fathers: The Civil Religion of the American Revolution* (Philadelphia: Temple University Press, 1976).
16. MICHAEL KAMMEN, *A Season of Youth: The American Revolution and the Historical Imagination* (New York: Oxford University Press, 1978): 44.
17. RAYMOND T. BOND, ed., *The Man who was Chesterton* (Garden City, New York: Doubleday, 1960): 125.
18. *Ibid.*: 125−6; see Sidney E. Mead, *The Nation with the Soul of a Church* (New York: Harper and Row, 1975): 20.
19. FRANCIS J. GRUND, *The Americans in Their Moral, Social and Political Relations* (1837); cited in Mead, *The Nation with the Soul of a Church*: 134, n. 37.
20. W. LLOYD WARNER, *The Living and the Dead: A Study of the Symbolic Life of Americans* (New Haven: Yale University Press, 1959): 249.
21. See Michael W. Hughey, *Civil Religion and Moral Order: Theoretical and Historical Dimensions* (Westport, Connecticut: Greenwood Press, 1983): 109−123.
22. HERBERG, *Protestant, Catholic, Jew: An Essay in American Religious Sociology*, new rev. ed. (Garden City, New York: Doubleday, 1960): 80.
23. BELLAH and HAMMOND, *Varieties of Civil Religion*: 169−171.
24. On this definition of ethos, see Robert Redfield, *The Primitive World and Its Transformations* (Ithaca, New York: Cornell University Press, 1953): 85.
25. RICHARD HOFSTADTER, *Anti-Intellectualism in American Life* (New York: Knopf, 1963): 264.
26. GAIL KENNEDY (ed.) "Democracy and the Gospel of Wealth," *Problems in American Civilization* (Boston: D.C. Heath, 1949): VI: 76.
27. WALT WHITMAN, *Leaves of Grass, The First (1855) Edition* (ed.) Malcolm Cowley (New York: Penguin, 1976): 48.
28. HORACE BUSHNELL, "Our Obligations to the Dead (1865)," in *God's New Israel: Religious Interpretations of American Destiny*, ed. Conrad Cherry (Englewood Cliffs, New Jersey: Prentice-Hall, 1971): 204.
29. WILLIAM J. WOLF, *Lincoln's Religion* (Philadelphia: Pilgrim Press, 1970): 156; see Glen E. Thurow, *Abraham Lincoln and American Political Religion* (New York: State University of New York Press, 1976).
30. Cited in Mead, *The Nation with the Soul of a Church*, 25.
31. WILLIAM LEE MILLER, *Piety along the Potomac: Notes on Politics and Morals in the Fifties* (Boston: Houghton Mifflin, 1964): 43.
32. MONSIGNOR C.F. THOMAS, "Patriotism," in *God's New Israel*, 281.
33. SUSAN SONTAG, *Trip to Hanoi* (New York: Farrar, Strauss and Giroux, 1968): 81−2.
34. CHARLES H. LONG, "Civil Rights—Civil Religion: Visible People and Invisible Religion," in *American Civil Religion*: 211−221.
35. MARTIN LUTHER KING, JR., *Why We Can't Wait* (New York: Harper and Row, 1963): 91−2.
36. ROBERT MICHAELSEN, "Is the Public School Religious or Secular?," in *The Religion of the Republic*, ed. Elwyn A. Smith (Philadelphia: Fortress Press, 1971): 43.
37. JOHN COLEMAN, "Civil Religion," *Sociological Analysis* 31 (1970): 70.
38. BELLAH and HAMMOND, *Varieties of Civil Religion*: xiii.
39. CARLTON HAYES, *Nationalism: A Religion* (New York: Macmillan, 1960): 164ff.
40. ELWYN A. SMITH, "The Voluntary Establishment of Religion," in *The Religion of the Republic*: 155; see Paul C. Nagel, *The Sacred Trust: American Nationality, 1798−1898* (New York: Oxford University Press, 1971).

41. WILLIAM G. MCLOUGHLIN, ed., *The American Evangelicals, 1800–1900: An Anthology* (New York: Harper and Row, 1968): 1.
42. SMITH, "The Voluntary Establishment of Religion," in *The Religion of the Republic*: 168.
43. LYMAN BEECHER, *The Memory of Our Fathers* (Boston: Marvin, 1828): 28.
44. LYMAN BEECHER, *Republican Elements in the Old Testament: Lectures on Political Atheism and Kindred Subjects* (Boston: Jewett, 1852): 177–8.
45. *Ibid.*: 189.
46. HORACE BUSHNELL, *Popular Government by Divine Right* (Hartford: L.E. Hunt, 1864): 12.
47. BENJAMIN M. PALMER, "Natural Responsibility Before God (1861)," in *God's New Israel*, 183.
48. *Ibid.*: 192–3.
49. *Ibid.*: 193.
50. WOLF, *Lincoln's Religion*: 147–8.
51. CUSHING STROUT, *The New Heavens and New Earth: Political Religion in America* (New York: Harper and Row, 1974): 204.
52. ALBERT K. WEINBERG, *Manifest Destiny* (Gloucester, Massachusetts: Peter Smith, 1958): 1–2; see Frederick Merk, *Manifest Destiny and Mission in American History* (New York: Alfred A. Knopf, 1963).
53. JOSIAH STRONG, *Our Country* (New York, 1885) 253–4; see J.F. Maclear, "The Republic and the Millennium," in *The Religion of the Republic*: 209–212; and Ernest Lee Tuveson, *Redeemer Nation: The Idea of America's Millennial Role* (Chicago: University of Chicago Press, 1968): 165–8.
54. Cited in *God's New Israel*: 116, 153.
55. PATRICK HENRY, " 'And I Don't Care What It Is': The Tradition History of a Civil Religion Proof-Text," *Journal of the American Academy of Religion* 49 (1981): 35–50.
56. MILLER, *Piety along the Potomac*: 19–20.
57. DWIGHT EISENHOWER, "Freedom in the Destiny of Man," in *Peace with Justice* (New York: Columbia University Press, 1961): 159.
58. *Ibid.*: 25. Even an anti-McCarthy senator in 1953 such as Ralph Flanders could render the cold war in cosmic religious imagery: "In very truth, the world seems to be mobilizing for the great battle of Armageddon. Now is a crisis in the agelong warfare between God and the Devil for the souls of men." Ralph E. Flanders, *Senator from Vermont* (Boston: Little, Brown, 1961): 255.
59. CHARLES B. HENDERSON, *The Nixon Theology* (New York: Harper and Row, 1972): 193.
60. See Jonathan Kwitny, *Endless Enemies: The Making of an Unfriendly World* (New York: Congden and Weed, 1984).
61. BELLAH and HAMMOND, *Varieties of Civil Religion*: xiv.
62. WILL HERBERG, "America's Civil Religion: What It Is and Whence It Comes," in *American Civil Religion*: 87.
63. HERBERT RICHARDSON, "Civil Religion in Theological Perspective," in *American Civil Religion*: 182.
64. ROBERT BELLAH, "American Civil Religion in the 1970s," in *American Civil Religion*: 271.
65. MARTIN LUTHER KING, JR., "The American Dream (June 6, 1961)," in *The Voice of Black America: Major Speeches by Negroes in the United States, 1797–1971*, ed. Philip S. Foner (New York: Simon and Schuster, 1972): 934.
66. BELLAH, *Beyond Belief*: 186; see John F. Wilson, *Public Religion in American Culture* (Philadelphia: Temple University Press, 1979).
67. MEAD, *The Nation with the Soul of a Church*: 65–9; 115–121.
68. BELLAH and HAMMOND, *Varieties of Civil Religion*: 142–6.
69. BELLAH, *Beyond Belief*: 172.
70. RICHARD JOHN NEUHAUS, "The War, the Churches, and Civil Religion," *The Annals of the American Academy of Political and Social Sciences* 387 (1970): 138.
71. See, for example, Rosemary Radford Reuther, *Liberation Theology: Human Hope Confronts Christian History and American Power* (New York: Paulist Press, 1972).
72. BELLAH, *The Broken Covenant*: 142.

CHAPTER FOUR
NATIVE AMERICANS

The peoples who inhabited the North American continent when European colonists arrived were forcibly excluded from participating in the dominant religiopolitical systems that emerged. This was primarily because the Europeans perceived them to be lacking in two things: Christianity and civilization. These two concerns formed the basis for excluding the Native Americans from the new social forms that were being produced, and they set the rigid terms under which Native Americans might be considered for inclusion. Christian missionaries, whether Catholic or Protestant, assumed that native customs, practices, and traditions were tremendous stumbling blocks to their conversion to Christianity. So the missionary was more than the social agent of a new religion. He also promoted the specific life styles of western Europe under the banner of civilization. As one missionary observed, it was necessary to "civilize Savages before they can be converted to Christianity, & that in order to make them Christians, they must first be made Men."[1] This, of course, represented an extremely ethnocentric view of what it is to be human. We will need to look more closely at the European assumptions that influenced perceptions of Native Americans, and the systems of classification the Europeans brought to the New World for dealing with *otherness*.

The entry of Europeans into North America opened up a frontier zone between intruder groups and indigenous groups. Each side in this zone of conflict had very different religious worldviews, as well as different technologies, economic practices, and forms of social organization. The diversity of cultures is suggested by the five basic language groups in which Native North Americans can be divided: (1) the Algonkian speakers, who lived in the Northeast woodlands in small groups supported by hunting, fishing, and small scale agriculture; (2) the Hokan-Sioux speakers who comprised the Six Nations of the Iroquois, living in the Northeast on wild rice, hunting, and fishing; the groups of the central prairies, where buffalo hunting and farming were practiced; and even extending into the hunting and gathering societies of California; (3) the Uto-Aztecan speakers of the Southwest and West who developed efficient forms of agriculture with the use of irrigation in a desert environment; (4) the Athabascan speakers who formed hunter and warrior societies in the Southwest; and (5) the Penutian speakers, who developed a rich woodland existence in the Pacific Northwest based on fishing, hunting, and food gathering.[2] These different cultures confronted a similar set of crises with the advent of Europeans, which led to the destruction of lives and life styles.

The invasion and colonization of America was supported by religion. Spanish Catholic conquistadors and missionaries invaded the Pueblo communities of the Southwest; French Jesuit missionaries followed the new trade routes among the Iroquois and the Huron of the Canadian North; and Puritan Protestants missionized and fought the Massachusetts and Wampanoags of the Northeast.[3] In addition to the military, political, and religious disruption that ensued, imported diseases for which the Native Americans had no immunity rapidly reduced native populations. Disease was the most important factor in reducing the populations to between 60 and 98 percent of their precontact size by the end of the nineteenth century.[4] Those who survived were displaced in a new network of power relations. The history of Native Americans after the arrival of the whites is a narrative of displacement.

Native American religions were characterized by diversity, but they all seemed to have an inclusive spirit open to the introduction of new beliefs and practices, and a tolerant disposition toward divergent religious beliefs, which came up against the intolerant and exclusive spirit of a missionizing Christianity. Native American religions had a highly developed sensitivity to the dynamics of religious power.[5] Sacred power was assumed to be diffused throughout the world, intimately infused in human life, and manifested in specific people, places, and objects. Among the Algonkian this power was called *manitou*; the Iroquois called it *orenda*; the Sioux, *wakantanka*. In the case of the Sioux, for example, one who showed evidence of sacred power was *wakan*. Although Native American religions often included beliefs in a creator god, high god, or supreme being, their primary concern was with those persons, places, and practices that were focal points for sacred power. Religious leaders who displayed sacred power—such as the shaman, the priest, or the healer—simply demonstrated a highly developed ability to focus spiritual power that was felt to be available to everyone. Religion was not institutionalized in a professional priesthood, but in the shared ritual and ethical life that sustained Native American communities.

The community of the living was in close contact with the community of the dead. Native American communities were acutely aware of continuing bonds of love, obligation, and commitment that connected the living and the dead. Departed ancestors remained in contact with the living, and they represented sources of spiritual guidance, support, and communion. Contact was established with ancestors in specific places: burial grounds, valleys, hillsides, mountains, and rivers. These were often sanctified as sacred space. One of the central features of Native American religion was the sanctification of place. The land itself was regarded as a natural religious symbol invested in very specific ways with sacred power. The earth, as the maternal womb of both the living and the dead, provided a common image in Native American religions of the land as an inherently sacred symbol.

The Europeans, of course, were largely unconcerned with all this. When it did come to their attention, any commitment to the sacred character of the land registered as demonology, idolatry, and superstition in their Christian worldview. For the Puritans who settled in the Massachusetts Bay Colony, sacred space was not environmental. It was architectural. The model Puritan town placed the religious meeting house at the center, so that the place of worship could stand "at the center of the whole circumference."[6] This architectural order was imposed on the chaos of the wilderness; it was simultaneously a Christian order and a civilized (from the Latin, *civitas*, or city) order. The civil space itself was sanctified by revolving around a constructed, central, sacred axis. And, even when it was not convenient to place the house of worship at the actual center of the settlement, as in Boston, the architects of Puritan sacred space placed the meeting house next door to John Winthrop's house, which represented the virtual center of political, social, and even religious authority in the community.

For the Europeans, the land was not sacred because it expressed a living, sacred power. It could only be sanctified by imposing a strict human design upon its inherent disorder. Land was made sacred only when it was converted to human patterns, intentions, and uses. This revealed something important about European Christian attitudes toward land as a religious and political symbol in the New World. Its religious and political value resided solely in human efforts to mold, shape, and conform it to European ideals. In this sense, the Native Americans were perceived as not using the land properly, and, therefore, as ultimately having forfeited their right to occupy it. These two themes—that Native Americans were not fully human, and that they had no rights to the land—formed the basis for the strange, and ultimately tragic, historical possibility that Europeans with highly developed weapons, technologies, and economies could come to a place already occupied for centuries by a rich variety of cultures, and perceive it as uninhabited.

IMAGES OF OTHERNESS

The European explorers, colonists, and administrators in the New World brought with them specific assumptions about otherness, which had a long history in the Old World. The dominant European system for classifying others informed the encounter with foreign, strange, and different people in the Americas. There were basically three categories by which the *other* might be classified: (1) savage, (2) slave, or (3) subhuman. All three of these categories were illustrated in the dealings of Christopher Columbus with the native population of Hispaniola (present day Haiti and the Dominican Republic), which came under his jurisdiction. His first impressions of the Arawaks were governed by the image, often invoked in critiques of European society, of the noble savage. This romantic notion of the savage, living in primitive, childlike simplicity, echoed in his earliest reports of the Arawaks who "showed as much lovingness as though they would give their hearts . . . they remained so much our friends that it was a marvel." But, Columbus quickly shifted to the next category in perceiving these people as natural slaves. He reported back to Spain, that "from here, in the name of the blessed Trinity, we can send all the slaves that can be sold." And in 1495 he sent 500 Arawaks to Spain, of which 300 arrived and soon died from European diseases. Seeing that the Arawaks were unsuitable as slaves in Europe, Columbus saw them as a potential source of gold. He required each Arawak over the age of thirteen to provide a certain quota of gold dust every three months. Those who supplied the quota would receive a stamped token to be hung around their necks. Whoever was found without the necessary token would be killed by having his hands cut off. The Arawaks worked all day in the streams, but there was no gold supply on the island. Those who fled were hunted and killed like animals, and there were reports of mass suicides. Within two years the population, which has been estimated as high as 500,000, was cut in half; by 1515 there were 6,000 left; and by 1540 the Arawaks had ceased to exist.[7] This illustrated a policy of dehumanization of native peoples, which was reinforced by the third classification of otherness: the tendency to treat the *other* as subhuman.

The notion of the noble savage was attractive to social critics like Montaigne, who saw it as an image against which to compare the sophisticated failings of European societies. It was also useful to Christian communities that wanted to actively expand their base of power in the new worlds; the conquistadors might claim the natives' bodies, but the church would claim their souls. Of course, this latter claim must have been based on the assumption that these people did in fact have souls. In 1537, Pope Paul III issued a declaration (*Sublimus Dei*) that the native inhabitants of the Americas were not "dumb brutes created for our service," but "truly men . . . capable of understanding the Catholic faith."[8]

But, if these were humans, what kind of humans were they? The religious imagination may at times have speculated about whether or not these people were the lost tribes of Israel; but the classifications in the *Systema Naturae* of Linnaeus gives us some idea of the kinds of stereotypes that were built into the European perception of otherness. Humans were divided by Linnaeus into four classes: (1) *Europaeus*, who were "white, sanguine, muscular"; (2) *Asiaticus*, "sallow, melancholy, stiff"; (3) *Afer*, "black, phlegmatic, relaxed;" and (4) *Americanus*, who were characterized as "reddish, choleric, erect."[9] The species of human being was first divided by color. It is some indication of how strange the Europeans found color differences among humans, when we notice how often they saw them as something temporary, caused by weather conditions, greasing the body, diet, and so on.[10] The implication was that human beings should be white, and differences in color were local aberrations.

The second division was based on emotional disposition. The medieval theory of the humors was employed to characterize the different kinds of humans; and it is interesting that the Native Americans were stereotyped by choleric, wild, and unpredictable emotions. Much of the European effort spent trying to change the natives went into strategies for making them more docile, tame, and predictable in their behavior.[11]

Finally, humans were characterized by body posture. Again, it is interesting to speculate that the image of the erect—and we might infer stiff, stubborn, resistant—Americanus posture was depicted in contrast to the muscular, dynamic, and strong self-image of the European. These stereotypes in the taxonomy of Linnaeus embodied important elements in the European imagination of otherness.

But where the category of savage implied that the other was human (however different), the Europeans had a second category at hand in which to place the Native Americans. They could invoke Aristotle's doctrine of natural slavery. As Lewis Hanke has observed, this doctrine assumed that slavery was the natural condition for "persons of both inborn rudeness and of inhuman and barbarous customs."[12] Civilized men were regarded as the natural masters of such barbarians. If the barbarians would not recognize their natural condition of slavery, then they could be compelled to come under the rule of civilization. This was at the heart of the Valladolid debate (1550-51) in Spain between the jurist Juan Gines de

Sepulveda and the Dominican monk Bartolemé de las Casas. And where the ideal of kindness and conversion, represented by las Casas, remained the official position of the Church, in practice Sepulveda's position that Europeans had a right according to natural law to subdue and dominate the native peoples was more often the rule. Where such practice needed religious legitimation, it was possible to turn to a biblical interpretation, such as that proposed by Johann Boemus, which understood all barbarous people to be the cursed descendents of Noah's son Ham, while all civilized people descended from his sons, Shem and Japheth.[13]

The final classification in which the *other* might appear in the European imagination was the category of subhuman. Ever since Pliny, the European popular imagination was intrigued by those "marvels of the east" that existed beyond the boundaries of civilized society: those strange, almost human, inhabitants of India who had dogs' heads, or two heads, or no heads (but who did have eyes, nose, and mouth conveniently located in the area of the chest), or those remarkable one-legged, semihuman beings who ran like the wind and, when the weather was hot, used their one huge foot for an umbrella.[14] These strange creatures were located somewhere between animals and humans in the chain of being. The images of these subhumans conditioned the European expectations of what they would discover in their explorations. Sir Walter Raleigh, for example, actually believed that the natives of Guyana "have their eyes in their shoulders, and their mouths in the middle of their breasts."[15] The subhuman Plinian people that occupied a purely imaginary realm in medieval encyclopedias now seemed to occupy the New World. And, although on closer inspection the inhabitants of these lands did not precisely fit the descriptions in the encyclopedias, it was difficult to escape the prejudice that they were still somehow less than human.

Each of the three images of otherness, in fact, dehumanized the Native Americans in the eyes of the Europeans. In the first case, as savages, the Native Americans were perceived as not fully human to the extent that they had not cultivated the humane virtues of civilized society. Next, as natural slaves, the Native Americans were not fully human because they did not have the individual human right to own property—they *were* property. And, finally, in many cases the Native Americans appeared to be subhuman, part of the natural environment of the wilderness, to be rooted out like wild brush, trees, and animals to make way for the progress of European civilization. The inherent element of dehumanization in these images of otherness had important religious and political implications. The Native Americans were perceived as having neither religion nor politics. The solution for both problems was a uniform imposition of Christian civilization.

This sense of religiopolitical mission was expressed in the royal charter which established the Virginia companies of London and Plymouth in 1606. It set out the basic religious and political intentions behind the efforts in colonization,

> which may, by the Providence of Almighty God, hereafter tend to the Glory of His divine Majesty, in propagating of Christian Religion to such people, as yet live in darkness and miserable ignorance of the true knowledge and worship of God, and may in time bring the Infidels and Savages living in these parts, to human civility and to a settled and quiet Government.[16]

The "yoke of Christ" introduced by these colonists was a disciplinary regimen intended to reduce the savages from what was perceived as their wild state to Christian civility. This meant introducing the Native Americans to three dimensions of civilized life that the Europeans assumed were lacking in their lives: order, labor, and manners.

There was an assumption in western thought dating back to Aristotle that barbarians had no politics. Aristotle was convinced that the barbarian peoples, because they could not speak Greek, were unable to organize themselves in order to act politically; they could not achieve a political life.[17] The European colonists made the same assumption about the Native Americans. They could not imagine a form of social order based on kinship, tradition, and mutual cooperation, but only a political order that extended over a territory and was anchored in the settled life of the town. They assumed that the Native Americans needed the Europeans to "bring them to Political Life, both in Ecclesiastical society and in Civil."[18] In this regard, it is significant that the Puritan missionary, John Eliot, constructed "praying towns" to accomplish both these tasks: to bring religious and political order into the lives of the Indians.

Although Native Americans may not have had organized systems of social authority that resembled the western European model of the state—as an organized exercise of violence over a territory—they did develop distinctive systems of power relations that could be regarded as political. The Northeastern Americans encountered by the French and English colonizers, for example, based their power relations on kinship. Among the Iroquois and Huron, each clan selected two leaders: a civil leader responsible for maintaining ordered relations among clans and a military leader responsible for the conduct of warfare. These clan headmen were not invested with coercive power, but had to rely on powers of persuasion, diplomatic negotiations, and administrative skill to fulfill their leadership roles. Village councils were presided over by these civil and military leaders, but everyone was allowed to participate in the decision-making process. Rulings that emerged from these councils, therefore, represented a certain degree of consensus within the community, although decisions were not legally binding upon every member.[19]

A similar political arrangement was found among the Massachusetts, Wampanoags, and other groups encountered by the Puritans. These mobile, seminomadic groups were supported by small scale agriculture (planting in the spring and harvesting in the fall), but they spent most of the year fishing, hunting, and gathering nuts and berries in different locations. Social authority was also based on clan arrangements. Several clans might be unified under the leadership of a *sachem*. Civil and military leadership provided by the sachem was the result of the personal power, diplomatic abilities, and military skills of the leader. This office was not a hereditary kingship, but a position of respect and authority often filled by a distinguished individual over a lifetime. The sachem ruled by persuasion rather than coercion. Even when several clans were mobilized for a military expedition, participation was purely voluntary and no sanctions would be taken against a person who refused to participate.[20] While these political arrangements may not have matched the western European definition of politics, they provided social systems which allowed for a high degree of personal freedom and initiative within cohesive patterns of mutual cooperation and support. As in the case of Native American religion, however, the European colonizers failed to recognize the legitimacy of these systems and insisted that the Indians lacked any form of political order.

A second assumption was that legitimate labor took the form of agriculture. The economic base of a settled civil society was the cultivation of the land. The colonists were disturbed to encounter native societies where small scale agriculture was an occupation for women, while the men were engaged primarily in hunting and fishing. In England, hunting was the leisure time pursuit of a gentleman. The forests were the private preserves of the aristocracy, and poachers who entered these reserves were punished. The Indians were perceived as violating the class privileges of the aristocracy in spending their time in these kinds of leisure activity. William Penn could observe that "we sweat and toil to live; their pleasure feeds them, I mean, their hunting, fishing and fowling."[21] Their pleasure, however, not only violated assumptions about class privilege; it ignored the biblical injunction that man is to labor by the sweat of his brow in tilling the earth. So the natives had to be directed into legitimate forms of labor. John Eliot claimed that "we labour and work in building, planting, clothing our selves, etc. and they doe not."[22] In order for this situation to be corrected, the Indians had to be disciplined in the civilized practice of settled agricultural labor.

Finally, the Native Americans were lacking in civilized manners, and it was felt that an essential part of the conversion process was a dramatic change in Indian modes of clothing, hair styles, and appearance. The wild and colorful attire of the Indians, the animal skins, bird feathers, and bright paint had to be replaced by the civilized clothing of English society. Likewise, the long hair of the males, which stood as a symbol of the sin of pride in Puritan eyes, had to be shorn in order for these "proud savages" to enter into the regimen of Christian humility. These meticulous details of civilized discipline were important elements in the conversion process.

The disciplinary technology of Christian conversion carefully regulated all aspects of daily life. European dress became an important symbol of conversion. As James Axtell has observed, "the infallible mark of a Protestant 'praying Indian' was his English appearance: short hair, cobbled shoes, and working-class suit."[23] An Indian's progress toward Christian civilization could be read in his appearance.

The notion of a European adopting Indian customs, however, was abhorrent to the Puritans; it represented a descent into the horrors of paganism, barbarism, and chaos. One Puritan settler who horrified the leadership of the community by fraternizing with Indians was Thomas Morton. He arrived in New England in 1625 and began trading extensively with the Indians. Two years later he raised a Maypole on Merry Mount to celebrate the rites of spring with them. King James had issued a decree in 1618 to encourage Maypole dancing, and Morton invited the Native Americans to join in the celebration by erecting an 80-foot pole and introducing dances to Pan, the spirit of Nature. In 1628 Miles Standish from Plymouth captured Morton, shipped him back to England, and accused him of selling guns and alcohol to the Indians. The case was dismissed for lack of evidence, and the following year Morton returned to Plymouth and reestablished Merry Mount. Then, in 1630, Morton was arrested again for not submitting to "good order and government." John Winthrop and John Endicott had him tried and put in stocks. His goods were sold to pay for his deportation, and his house was burned down "in the sight of the Indians." Merry Mount was also burned to the ground, "because the habitation of the wicked could no more appear in Israel."

During his stay in England, Morton wrote a book about his experiences in the New World, *New England Canaan*. He described an "enchanting green land with friendly red men." He praised the intelligence of the Native Americans: "These people," he remarked, "are not, as some have thought, a dull, or slender-witted people, but very ingenious, and very subtile." Morton demonstrated a sensitivity to their religious practices that was uncommon among the Puritans. The Native Americans showed a reverence for their ancestors through sacred sites, burial grounds, and grave ornaments that the New England Puritans failed to appreciate. The grave of the mother of one chief, for example, was decorated with two bearskins sewed together and placed over it "which the Plymouth planters defaced because they accounted it an act of superstition." Morton described how the Puritans had come to rid the land of all pollution, and that this ultimately included its inhabitants. The Puritan consensus may have been that the Indians were subhuman; but, Morton concluded, "I have found the Massachusetts Indians more full of humanity than the Christians."[24] Where Morton experienced a green world peopled with friendly human beings, a Puritan such as William Bradford, the Governor of Plymouth, perceived a "hideous and desolate wilderness, full of wild beasts and wild men." [25] Thomas Morton was a rare example of the celebration of otherness in the New World.

The Puritan efforts to conform the natives to the disciplinary regimen of Christian civilization were largely unsuccessful. There were converts; but the vast majority of the Indians resisted the missionary advances. It was not long before the Europeans turned to harsher measures of control in order to impose their will upon the wilderness. In 1636 John Winthrop sent out an expedition to take revenge upon the Indians who were living on Block Island for the death of an Englishman. He instructed John Endicott, with eighty men in armor, "to put to death the men of Block Island, but to spare the women and children and to bring them away, and to take possession of the island."[26] This began the Pequot War in which between 800-900 Indians were killed, homes and fields of corn were destroyed, and the land was taken into the possession of the European settlers. As one of the Puritan leaders, John Mason, observed, "thus was God pleased to smite our enemies and to give us their land as an inheritance."[27] This set the pattern of religious legitimation for the dispossession and displacement of the Native Americans from the land.

DISPLACEMENT

In 1675 the leadership of Plymouth executed three Indians accused of murdering another Indian and sparked off what came to be known as King Phillip's War. Four tribes joined battle against the Europeans, not only in response to this event, but also because the Puritans were trying to enforce laws that required the observance of the Sabbath and required capital punishment for blasphemy. The war resulted in the destruction of twelve New England towns and the death of over 1,000 whites. But the whites emerged victorious, and with the deaths of approximately 5,000 Native Americans, King Phillip's War marked the effective displacement of Indians from the areas of Massachusetts, Connecticut, and Rhode Island.[28] It also signaled the dismantling of most of the fourteen praying towns that had been established for Indian converts. Missionary optimism regarding the prospect of molding the natives into the image of Christian civilization dimmed considerably.

The eighteenth century continued the pattern of displacement as the cutting edge of the frontier zone pushed west. And the displacement of the Indians from their lands was accompanied by increasingly sophisticated legal justifications. The eighteenth-century Swiss jurist, Emmerich de Vattel, specified that possession of land implied an obligation to cultivate it. When he applied this principle to the land use of native populations, he observed that "natives cannot exclusively appropriate to themselves more land than they have occasion for, and which they are unable to settle and cultivate."[29] The Native Americans of the Northeast tended to base their political arrangements, as we have noted, on cooperation through kinship, custom, and tradition, but not on territory. Many groups maintained a relatively nomadic, wandering, or migratory life-style, rather than a settled existence. In these cases, land was a shared, supportive environment for all life, rather than something to be exclusively owned, exploited, and cultivated for agriculture. All of these characteristics of Native American life indicated to the Europeans that the Indians were not using the land, and therefore had no right to possess it.

These asumptions were applied directly to the American case by H.H. Brackenridge in 1782. Brackenridge revealed how persistent European prejudices continued to dehumanize the Native Americans, and suggested the religious and political logic under which they might be deprived of land. Brackenridge asked, "What do these ringed, streaked, spotted, and speckled cattle make of the soil? Do they till it? Revelation said to man, 'Thou shalt till the ground.' This alone is human life."[30] From this perspective, the Native Americans stood convicted by the Word of God of misusing the land by not utilizing it for settled agriculture. The Europeans were able to marshal this set of legal, religious, and political arguments to justify taking Indian lands. Brackenridge concluded: "I am so far from thinking the Indians have a right to the soil, that not having made a better use of it for many hundred years, I conceive they have forfeited all pretense to claim, and ought to be driven from it."[31]

Europeans, therefore, not only perceived that the Indians had no rights to the land, but that they had an ethical and religious obligation to take control of it and use it according to the demands of scripture. This linkage of the Bible and agriculture was institutionalized in the "Civilization Fund" established by Congress in 1819. Funds in the amount of $10,000.00 per year were allocated for the purpose of instructing the Indians in the techniques of agriculture and in literacy so they could read the Bible. Congress declared: "The Bible will be their book, and they will grow up in the habits of morality and industry, leave the chase to those of minds less cultured, and become useful members of society."[32] Unless the Native Americans were themselves useful in using the land for biblically mandated settled agriculture, the land could be legitimately appropriated by those determined to put it to such a use.

This notion of legitimate legal rights to the land was coupled with another powerful ideal in the eighteenth century: the individual ownership of private property. During the French Revolution the immense property holdings of the Church had been confiscated and parceled out by sale to the highest bidder. This represented a tremendous shift in the distribution of wealth; but it also created a great number of property owners, with unlimited rights to the use and disposal of their property, who were protected by law. This same ideal—the value of private property— was enshrined in the American Revolution, and the new government was dedicated to the protection of life, liberty, and private property. This ethical ideal, which has been called utilitarian individualism, implied that personal identity plus the ownership, use, and disposal of private property went hand-in-hand. In the light of this ideal, the presence of Indian communities, which held land in common, or, as was often the case, had no notion of the private ownership of land, was a disturbing anomaly. T.H. Crawford, in 1838, spoke on behalf of the United States government in observing that "at the foundation of the whole social system lies the individuality of property."[33] And toward the end of the nineteenth century, Carl Schurz, Secretary of the Interior, was able to say that "the enjoyment and pride of the individual ownership of property is one of the most effective civilizing agencies."[34]

These two assumptions about land—settled cultivation and individual ownership—were embodied in treaty agreements fashioned by the United States in an attempt to relocate the Native American populations, and, at the same time, to conform them to the persistent ideals of western civilization. For example, in all treaties since 1854 a special provision was written in the allotment of Indian lands which would cancel the assignment to "any such person or family [who] shall at any time neglect or refuse to occupy and till a portion of the land assigned, and on which they have located, or shall rove from place to place."[35] The assumption again was that the right to ownership of land implied the use, cultivation, and exploitation of its resources, preferably in settled agricultural life. An example of the emphasis on individual ownership is found in those treaties that insisted on allocating land to individuals or families, and not to tribal groups. The General Allotment Act of 1887 was the most comprehensive attempt to break up tribal allegiances, communal ownership, and traditional associations by parceling out reserve land to Indians as individuals. Parcels of 160 acres were given to heads of households; 80 acres to each unmarried male over eighteen. Any "surplus" was sold to white settlers. By the time the allotment was ended in 1934, almost 90 million acres of Indian lands, amounting to over 60 percent of land held before 1887, had been transferred to the ownership of non-natives.[36]

These policies reflected the central role that land played in the ongoing efforts of the United States government to adapt the Indians to the demands of Christian civilization. Thomas McKenney, who was the architect of America's Indian policy between 1816 and 1830, offered the Native Americans two choices: civilize or relocate. They stood as a resistant force to the manifest destiny of civilization, an obstacle that must be removed. The Indians, according to McKenney, persisted in their traditional ways, "in this state of helpless ignorance and imbecility."[37] They howled, greased their bodies, and adorned their hair as they had done for centuries, and they "have never been taught the lessons of morality, and cleanliness, and industry."[38] The European prejudices of his Puritan predecessors, echoed by McKenney, had also remained unchanged during the 200 years of contact. But, the power of the legal apparatus and military force that could be marshaled by the European descendants had changed. And the United States was able to pursue a policy of forced removals, containment, and war that would reshape the political geography of America. McKenney maintained that "we believe if the Indians do not emigrate, and fly the causes, which are fixed in themselves, and which have proved so destructive in the past, they must perish."[39]

The continuing tragic irony of Indian displacement was that they could in fact relocate and continue to perish in the process. For example, after gold was discovered on Indian lands in 1830 in Georgia, the state put into action a policy of forced removal enacted on all native Cherokee within its borders. Christian missionaries were ordered to leave Indian lands to prevent them from interfering with the removals. Eleven clergy and several assistants were subsequently arrested and sentenced to four years in prison for being on Indian land and obstructing the removal of the Indians. Their case was appealed to the United States Supreme Court in 1832, but the Court's ruling in favor of the clergy was ignored by the state of Georgia and not enforced by President Andrew Jackson. The last of the Cherokee in Georgia were forced out along the "trail of tears" in 1838–39. Many died from the hardships of the journey, while many others died in Indian wars caused by forcing the Cherokee into territory occupied by other tribes in the West.[40] This was an era of negotiations, treaties, and wars with Indian nations in the West. But as the territorial expanse of the United States continued to increase, Native American political and military power was shattered.

After 1871, the United States Congress no longer regarded Native American groups as sovereign, independent nations, but as collections of individuals to be contained on remote reservations, or, in some cases, to be assimilated into American society. The United States' "manifest destiny" would allow no other sovereign national unit to obstruct it from achieving political and military domination from coast to coast. The Board of Indian Commissioners made this explicit in 1871:

> The Anglo-Saxon Race will not allow the car of civilization to stop long at any line of latitude or longitude on our broad domain. If the Indian in his wildness plants himself on the track, he must inevitably be crushed by it.[41]

By the end of the nineteenth century, the United States had not only extended its territorial domination over the length of the North American continent, but had begun its "Open Door Policy" of extending its reach westward to the Pacific Islands. Secretary of State John Hay was able to see U.S. expansion as "a cosmic tendency."[42] International expansion appeared as an American tendency because it had already been demonstrated in the defeat and displacement of the Native Americans.

The religious and political aspirations that motivated the conquest of a continent began to extend to other lands.[43]

NATIVE AMERICAN RESPONSES

A limited number of responses were open to the Native Americans in the face of such overwhelming displacement, disruption, and destruction of their traditional worlds. Armed resistance resulted in few victories and many defeats. The victory over General George Armstrong Custer at the Battle of Little Big Horn in 1876 was followed by the unconditional surrender of Chief Joseph's Nez Percé the following year. Even in defeat, however, Native Americans found ways to draw upon traditional religious resources, and also fashioned a number of creative religious innovations to respond to their new political situations. Native American responses to displacement took three major forms. First, *introversionist responses* sought to turn within and turn back to reaffirm traditional Native American religious values in the face of the overwhelming encroachment of white domination. Second, *revolutionist responses* mobilized traditional and Christian religious symbols in anticipation of the overthrow of white power, the destruction of the whites, and the restoration of traditional patterns of life. And, third, modern *Pan-Indian movements* emerged in the twentieth century to fashion new, cohesive forms of Native American identity. All of these responses generated alternative sources of power for Native Americans disempowered by the white military and political domination of America.

Introversionist Responses

One option open to Native Americans was withdrawal from the religiopolitical system that dominated white American society. Retreat was of course forced upon Native American tribes by the overwhelming military, political, and economic power of the whites, but traditional religious resources could be reaffirmed in order to retain a sense of integrity while accommodating to the new political situation of subjection and oppression. The sociologist Bryan Wilson analyzed introversionist responses to the larger social environment as attempts to "retain a social system and a form of religious practice different from those of the dominant culture, and representing the continuance of the native past."[44]As Native American tribal groups were violently disrupted by wars, removals, and containment on reservations, accompanied by desperate social problems of disease, poverty, alcoholism, and despair, some religious and political leaders found ways to restate traditional Native American values in a new world.

In response to the new situation of the Iroquois at the end of the eighteenth century, as a dominated minority in a white, Christian world, a new religion, *Gai'wiio'*, or the Good Word, was formed to reaffirm traditional Iroquois values.[45] The prophet of this new faith was an Iroquois known as Handsome Lake. Born in 1735, Handsome Lake had fought in the American Revolutionary War on the side of the British. His half-brother, Cornplanter, was a military leader among the Seneca who had gone to Washington on behalf of his tribe to negotiate a postwar settlement with the United States. After the war, however, Handsome Lake had succumbed, like many other Iroquois, to alcoholism and despair. In June 1799 Handsome Lake "died" and experienced the first of a series of visions of the world of the dead from which he returned with new ethical and ritual instructions that formed the central message of the religion of the Good Word. This message was introduced in Cornplanter's village in February of 1800, and soon spread among the various Iroquois tribes of the Northeast. The visions and teachings of Handsome Lake were told and retold to call Native Americans to a new life of ethical discipline, repentance, and mutual cooperation that would allow traditional religious values to survive in a new political environment.

The teachings of Handsome Lake gave new power to traditional beliefs and practices by adapting them to the religiopolitical situation of white, Christian domination in America. Since the values of military glory, honor, and prestige could no longer be realized, the religion of the Good Word emphasized personal salvation through following an ethical code of moral purity. In Handsome Lake's vision of the world of the dead, the prophet saw the punishments that awaited the wicked and the rewards promised for those who repented of their sins. This new ethical orientation emphasized personal discipline, renouncing alcohol, dishonesty, laziness, adultery, and other personal sins, and advocated strong family ties and intertribal cooperation. Personal salvation was possible through moral discipline and the confession of sins. Although preservation of traditional beliefs and practices was central to the teachings of Handsome Lake, there was nevertheless some ambivalence about the ancestors. In his visions of the other world, Handsome Lake did not find the ancestors in either heaven or hell:

> [They] have never reached the true lands of our Creator, nor did they enter the house of the tormenter, Ganos'ge. It is said that in some matters they did the will of the Creator, and in others they did not. They did both good and bad, and none was either good or bad. They are therefore in a place separate and unknown to us, we think, enjoying themselves.[46]

Perhaps this uncertainty regarding the ancestors reflected a sense of being cut off from traditional religious beliefs and practices, which were now "separate and unknown," even while struggling to preserve the values that the ancestors represented.

This new religion, however, did not simply preserve tradition. Elements of the new religiopolitical environment were also appropriated in the religion of the Good Word: The very name of the religion was reminiscent of the Christian gospel, or "good news." In Handsome Lake's vision of the other world, symbols of the white religiopolitical system appeared. The prophet saw the prison and the church, new symbols of American political and religious power, and he saw the house of George Washington, who had treated the Iroquois fairly in the postrevolutionary settlement, as well as a savior whom the whites had killed. To some extent, these visions of new religious and political symbols absorbed the power represented by white domination. The vision of the savior killed by the whites, for example, suggested that the Indians were more deserving of such a savior. By absorbing the power of these new symbols, the Iroquois who adopted the religion of the Good Word could preserve the basic, traditional patterns of a separate way of life, while accommodating to the dominant religiopolitical system in America.

Above all, the religion of Handsome Lake embodied a message of peace. If the Native Americans lived in peace and cooperation, they could be assured of rewards in the next life. Although the teachings of Handsome Lake were spread among one of America's most martial tribes, they advocated a spirit of peace devoted to fulfilling traditional ethical obligations in separation from and accommodation with the white world. Obviously, this spirit of peace corresponded to white political and military interests. When the teachings of Handsome Lake came to the attention of President Thomas Jefferson, the President commended the prophet and recommended his message to all Native Americans. "If all the red people follow the advice of your friend and teacher, Handsome Lake, and in the future will be sober, honest, industrious, and good," President Jefferson wrote to the Six Nations of the Iroquois, "there can be no doubt but the Great Spirit will take care of you and make you happy."[47] The teachings of Handsome Lake did spread among the Iroquois providing one viable response to the religiopolitical situation of white domination in America. By the 1950s, the religion of the Good Word was still practiced by 7,000 of the 15,000 Iroquois in New York State and Ontario.[48] The introversionist response advocated by Handsome Lake represented a religious vehicle for reaffirming a separate, continuous Iroquois identity in a hostile world.

Another eloquent illustration of traditional Native American religious resources surviving in a hostile environment is found in the speech of Chief Seattle, recorded January 9, 1855, in response to a treaty proposal that would relocate his tribe in the Washington territory.[49] Seattle's speech gave poignant and poetic testimony to the enduring power of Native American religion in relation to the realities of an impossible political situation. Seattle responded to the overtures of friendship and goodwill offered by the governor of the Washington territory on behalf of the United States government by saying, "this is kind of him since we know

he has little need of our friendship in return. His people are many, like
the grass that covers the plains. My people are few, like the trees scattered
by the storms on the grasslands." The great white chief had sent word that
he wanted to buy the Indian lands. The state, in return, made two promises. The first was that the Indians would be given enough land to live
comfortably. Seattle noted that "this seems generous, since the red man
no longer has rights he needs respect." The people, "who once covered
this land like a flood-tide moving with the wind," were gone and almost
forgotten. The second promise was that the United States would provide
military protection for Seattle's people from their traditional enemies, and
would create a protective wall around his people who would be like children in its care.

But Seattle questioned this protection. In calling this protective care
into question, Seattle offered a critique of the imagery of divine father-
hood that had run throughout the European notion of Christian civilization. He asked: "But how can this be? Your God loves your people and
hates mine." This God had guided, protected, and provided for the white
man; but he had abandoned his red children. Seattle observed, "He
makes your people stronger every day. Soon they will flood all the land.
But my people are an ebb-tide, we will never return." It seemed impossible that the God of the whites could also love the red man, and, Seattle
lamented, "Now we are orphans. There is no one to help us." He maintained that the white and red were separate races, with no common father, no common heritage, no common future. And, Seattle continued,
"How can we be brothers? How can your father be our father, and make
us prosper and send us dreams of future greatness? Your God is prejudiced. He came to the white man. We never saw him, never even heard
his voice."

This God gave the white man laws, written on tablets of stone by the
iron finger of an angry God; but the red man's religion was written on the
hearts of the people. In response to white religion, Seattle invoked the
spiritual resources of the ancestors. He observed, "To us the ashes of our
fathers are sacred. Their graves are holy ground. But you are wanderers,
you leave your fathers' graves behind you, and you do not care." This
indictment of the whites was an ironic reversal of the symbolism of place
in the relations between these two peoples. The Indians, who appeared to
the Europeans as nomadic wanderers, pursuing unsettled roving exis-
tences in the wilderness, perceived the whites themselves, in a profound
sense, as wanderers. They had forsaken the graves of their ancestors, leaving land that should have been holy to them, to wander in the world cut
off from the ongoing connection with sacred space. Seattle accused the
whites of betraying their ancestors, and so, he told them, "Your dead forget you." But the Indian ancestors never forget: "Our dead never forget
this beautiful earth. It is their mother. They always love and remember
her rivers, her great mountains, her valleys. They long for the living, who

are lonely too and who long for the dead. And their spirits often return to visit and console us." Seattle did not mourn the dead; death was the common destiny of all humanity. In that common end, he suggested, the whites may be brothers after all.

Seattle concluded his response to the governor of the Washington territory with a powerful affirmation of the sacred character of the earth in Native American religion. His words gave resounding testimony to the sacred presence of the ancestors that continued to infuse the world. Chief Seattle declared:

> Every part of this earth is sacred to my people. Every hillside, every valley, every clearing and wood, is holy in the memory and experience of my people. . . . The ground beneath your feet responds more lovingly to our steps than yours, because it is the ashes of our grandfathers. Our bare feet know the kindred touch. The earth is alive with the lives of our kin.

The sacred earth was experienced as alive with the living presence of the dead ancestors, and their contact with the earth was sustained through specific sites, burial grounds, and sacred places. The dead were present in the ground itself. Therefore, Seattle warned the whites that even when the last red man had disappeared from the earth, the land would still be alive with the invisible dead of the Indian people. And even when whites should think they were alone, this presence would continue to surround them. Keeping this in mind, Seattle concluded, the whites should deal justly with the Native Americans, because "the dead have power too."

Revolutionist Responses

Evidence of the power of the dead in Native American religious responses to displacement was also found in the emergence of revolutionary revitalization movements in the eighteenth and nineteenth centuries. Many of these movements adapted what might appear to be a Christian theme in the millenarian expectation of a second coming. But they did not await the return of Christ. Their inspired prophets had visions of the imminent return of the ancestors. And, with the power of the ancestors, the world of the whites would be destroyed in order that the Native Americans might return to their former glory. These were apocalyptic religious movements that promised spiritual power to destroy the prevailing social and political order in which Native Americans were subjected. In many cases, sacred power and military action were combined in a struggle to invert the social world. Introversion, withdrawal, or personal salvation were not considered adequate means of addressing the condition of displacement in which Native Americans found themselves. The situation called for a mobilization of religious power that would overthrow the whites and reestablish the Native Americans' place in America.

An early revolutionist response was initiated in 1762 by the prophet

Neolin, known as the Delaware Prophet.[50] The Delaware, and other tribes, had been forcibly expelled from Pennsylvania into the Great Lakes and Ohio regions in 1759. In this context of displacement, the Delaware Prophet appeared with a promise of victory over the whites. The Prophet recounted a visionary journey, led by a woman clothed in white, in which he had learned the will of the Master of Life. The Delaware Prophet returned from this journey with a sacred prayer stick, a prayer to be recited every morning and evening, and a skin map called "The Great Book of Writing." This map illustrated how the ways of the ancestors had been obstructed by the whites. The prophet made copies of this map to remind his followers that if they returned to the ways of their ancestors, and purified themselves of all the sins they had absorbed from the whites, the Master of Life would give them the power to drive their oppressors from the land. The Delaware Prophet predicted a great war that would mobilize the spiritual power of the ancestors to bring victory over the whites. Many tribes came to hear these teachings of the Delaware Prophet, and his message was disseminated widely in the Great Lakes region.

One military leader in this area who adopted these teachings was the Ottawa Chief Pontiac. The British victory over the French in Canada in 1760 had left Pontiac and other leaders discontented with British rule. In 1762, Pontiac heard the prophet's message, perhaps from the Delaware Prophet himself, and perceived it as a unifying, mobilizing religious vision that could bring together different tribes in concerted military action against the British. At a meeting of various tribes on April 27, 1763, Pontiac delivered his version of the Delaware Prophet's teachings. The result was a confederacy of Ottawas, Potawatomies, Hurons, Algonkians, Wyandots, Senecas, and Winnebagos united by the religious vision of victory in warfare against the whites. Pontiac directed their attack on twelve frontier posts; nine were taken. Detroit was besieged for fifty days until the siege was broken by British reinforcements. Finally, the tribal confederacy was forced to disband with the start of the hunting season, as warriors had to break up into smaller groups in search of game. Although the military victories were short-lived, the confederacy drawn together by the religious inspiration of the Delaware Prophet and the military organization of Chief Pontiac demonstrated the power of religious vision animating revolutionary responses to Native American displacement.

A second revolutionist response was inspired by the militant Seneca prophet Tenskwatawa of the Northern Lakes, a contemporary of the pacifist prophet Handsome Lake. Tenskwatawa assumed his name, which meant "the Open Door," and announced himself as a prophet in 1805. Half-brother of the miltary leader Tecumseh, the prophet Tenskwatawa preached a return to traditional customs, traditional dress, respect for elders, and the communal holding of property. Whites had power, the prophet argued, because the Native Americans had abandoned the ways of their ancestors. Three years later, in 1808, Tecumseh and Tenskwatawa had assembled a confederacy of 400 warriors committed to stopping white encroachment into Indian territory and to recovering land that had been unjustly taken. Prophet Tenskwatawa predicted the imminent return of the ancestors and a cataclysm that would destroy the whites. This religious vision of redemption through the destruction of the whites was a message that unified the tribes on the United States frontier. In 1808, Tenskwatawa declared: "The religion I have established in the last three years, has been attended to by the different tribes of Indians in this part of the world. Those Indians were once different peoples; they are now one."[51] The movement continued to grow over the next three years, extending from north to south along the United States border, as these tribes worked to form a "union" like the "seventeen fires" of the United States. This Indian union was imagined as a dam that would stop the expansion of that white union and turn back the tide of white power.

This confederacy dissolved, however, in the wake of a military expedition of October and November 1811, led by the prophet in the absence of Tecumseh, against a United States army regiment under the command of William Henry Harrison. Before the battle at Tippecanoe, the prophet Tenskwatawa assured the warriors that they could not be harmed by the bullets of the whites. In spite of promises of invulnerability and victory by their religious leader, the warriors suffered heavy losses against the United States troops. The unity forged by prophetic religious and military alliance was broken. Warfare continued, but the cohesive power provided by religious vision was lacking. When the war of 1812 broke out, Tecumseh led a contingent of 2,000 warriors on the side of the British against the United States. The prophet Tenskwatawa, however, retreated west of the Mississippi where he lived on a British pension until his death in 1834. The millenarian teachings of Tenskwatawa, based on a religious vision of the imminent destruction of the whites through the supernatural, spiritual powers of the ancestors, had served as a catalyst for tribal unity. Combined with the leadership of Tecumseh, this religious vision almost became the basis of a viable military and political policy of resistance to white power.

Throughout the nineteenth century various nativist religious revivals spread through the Creek, Cherokee, Sioux, and other Plains tribes, bringing spiritual power, renewal, and hope for the overthrow of white political domination. The most powerful of these revitalization movements was the Ghost Dance Religion that was widespread among the Indians of the Plains in the last decades of the nineteenth century.[52] Since the arrival of horses, brought by the Spanish, the plains tribes had flourished as buffalo hunters and warriors. As a warrior culture, the Plains Indians valued skill, courage, and success in battle. But, with the destruction of their way of life, with the elimination of the buffalo by white hunters, the encroachment of white farmers, and the containment of the tribes by the United

States military, these values had no opportunity for expression. Traditional ways of demonstrating power, prestige, and integrity were destroyed, and the prospect of a settled life of farming, wage labor, or subservience to white missionary and military powers offered no acceptable substitute. It was in this context that a Pan-Indian revitalization movement was able to activate resources in traditional American Indian religion to offer hope of spiritual renewal.

This movement drew on traditional resources that had been present in the Sun Dance: the ceremonial religious and political gathering of the tribes in the Plains for ritual dancing, competitive games, and exercises in self-torture and endurance.[53] The Sun Dance had provided an opportunity for the tribes to renew their allegiances and settle disputes. It was a religious celebration of a common political identity. The Ghost Dance shared many of these characteristics. The practices included singing, chanting, falling into trance, stripping naked, and wearing special clothing that would make the wearer invincible. But the purpose of the Ghost Dance was not simply to unify the various tribal groups; it was designed to achieve union with the ancestors, to realize the presence of the power of the dead, and, by recovering the lost power of the ancestors, to effectively overthrow the pattern of white domination over the living.

One version of the Ghost Dance religion prophesied an imminent catastrophe that would bring in the new age. There would be earthquakes, storms, and floods that would destroy the present world order, and out of that destruction all distinctions between the races would be obliterated. The prophet Wovoka brought this message to the Plains Indians. In the late 1880s this prophet appeared among the Paiute in Nevada. Wovoka was out chopping wood when he heard a great noise which seemed to come from the direction of the mountains. He started in the direction of the noise, but he fell down "dead" and "God took him to heaven." Wovoka described his experience: "I went up to heaven and saw God and all the people who had died a long time ago. God told me to come back and tell my people they must be good and love one another and not fight or steal or lie. He gave me this dance to give to my people."[54] The prophet entered into death to renew contact with the ancestors, and the ecstatic dance he returned with was a means by which all the living might restore this connection. This dance did in fact spread throughout the Plains Indian tribes; it was adapted to the various mythic frameworks of each tribe, yet served a similar function in revitalizing tribal identities, hopes, and expectations.

The Ghost Dance religion also had specific military consequences. In many variants it was aggressively antiwhite, and its expectation was that the whites would be totally destroyed with the return of the ancestors, buffalo, and power. Chief Short Bull, inspired by the millenarian visions of the Ghost Dance religion, led the Sioux into the battle of Wounded Knee in 1890. Before entering into battle, he told his people that God had shown him what was to happen. He had been shown that a tree would sprout where they gathered, and that there they would see their dead ancestors; and they would be rewarded for their sacred way of life. Chief Short Bull continued:

> My father has shown me these things, therefore we must continue this dance [the Ghost Dance]. If the soldiers surround you four deep, three of you, on whom I have put holy shirts [supposedly bullet proof], will sing a song, which I have taught you, around them, when some of them will drop dead. Then the rest will start to run, but their horses will sink into the earth. The riders will jump from their horses, but they will sink into the earth also. Then you will do as you desire with them. Now, you must know this, that all the soldiers and that race [the whites] will be dead.[55]

The actual battle was a massacre of the Sioux. Although there is some dispute as to how the engagement started, the result was the slaughter of over 300 Indians, most of them women and children, by the United States troops. Again, military defeat seemed to disperse the spiritual energy generated by the revolutionist religious movement. Wovoka himself apparently disavowed the military purposes for which his message had been used. Nevertheless, the Ghost Dance religion represented a final attempt to recover a traditional form of religious power and redemption. The Ghost Dance was simultaneously a religious and political response to white domination, and its symbolic power resided in its ability to invert the order of domination and to recover the spirit of independence, integrity, and glory represented by the ancestors. By the beginning of the twentieth century, this traditional spirit had become almost impossible to sustain.

Modern Pan-Indian Movements

Survival of traditional Native American social, religious, and even political identity depended to a large extent on the emergence of Pan-Indian religious movements in the twentieth century. Like the revolutionist responses, these movements unified Native Americans across tribal lines; but, like the introversionist movements, they tended toward pacifism, separatism, and withdrawal from the dominant religiopolitical system of white American society. Religious movements such as the Sun Dance, and the peyotism of the Native American Church, refocused traditional religious resources to address the lack of self-esteem endemic to the poverty, slum conditions, and white domination of reservation life.

The Sun Dance was a ritual cycle of celebration, healing, visions, and heroic endurance, often involving ordeals of self-torture, which had its origin among the Algonkian tribes of the Plains prior to contact with whites.[56] By the early nineteenth century, the Sun Dance had become the most widespread ritual in the plains region. The elaborate, beautiful ceremony lasted three days and two nights. Participants, supervised by the warrior and hunting societies of the community, danced around a central, sacred pole, and went without food and water. At the culmination of the ceremony, dancers collapsed in a trancelike state to commune with the spirits. Austerities, ordeals, and visions were felt to provide access to power and instill the strength to achieve personal distinction in hunting and warfare. Christian missionaries and government agents tried to suppress the Sun Dance on the reservations, and had almost succeeded in eliminating it by the end of the nineteenth century. Repression of the Sun Dance was simply part of a government policy that prohibited all traditional Native American religious practices in the interests of Christianizing and civilizing the Indians. Clearly, the First Amendment protection of the freedom of religion was not interpreted as extending to Native American religions.

The revival of the Sun Dance was undertaken by the Wind River Shoshone between 1890 and 1915.[57] Through active propagation of the dance, its practice was adopted by a number of different tribes in Idaho, Utah, and Nevada. Personal power could still be gained through dancing and visions, but greater emphasis was placed on the mutual solidarity of Indian communities in the face of white domination. Certain Christian elements were adapted to the dance: The central pole was identified with Christ, the number of surrounding poles was increased to correspond to the number of the twelve apostles, and physical ordeals in the dance came to be identified with the sufferings of Christ. But these changes were incidental to the practice of the Sun Dance as a collective reaffirmation of traditional spirituality, ethical values, and life styles which were at the heart of the dance. The Bureau of Indian Affairs remained hostile to the Sun Dance, but its persistence among the Shoshone, Utes, and other tribes revealed a commitment to maintaining a sense of traditional Native American power despite overwhelming political opposition.

The use of peyote in religious ritual has been at the center of a second Pan-Indian movement which reaffirmed traditional Native American identity.[58] By eating the dried top of this small desert cactus, participants in peyote rituals experienced a sense of euphoria, vivid perceptions, heightened sensations of sound and color, and perhaps hallucinations. Ritual use of peyote was found among the Pueblo Indians by the Spanish in the sixteenth century. Peyotism was adopted by the Mescalero Apaches, Kiowas, and Commanches, however, as a central feature in their ceremonial dances between 1870 and 1890. In the wake of the Ghost Dance, peyote use spread rapidly throughout the Plains tribes. By 1910, Oklahoma had become the center of the peyote ritual, but its practice was common throughout the Midwest and the Southwest. Traditional peyote religion, which used peyote to communicate with the Great Spirit, with guardian spirits, and with the thunderbird, absorbed many Christian elements into its beliefs and practices. God, Christ, and the Holy Spirit were identified with the traditional supernatural powers, and peyote became the true sacrament of a distinctively Native American Christian church. The first legally recognized peyote church was the First Born Church of Christ founded in Redrock, Oklahoma in 1914. Under the pressure of state laws prohibiting peyote, and a proposed congressional bill that would outlaw peyote religion, a larger, intertribal organization was formed in 1918 representing 12,000 adherents of peyotism, and the Native American Church was founded. This national federation of peyote churches represented twelve states in 1934 and eighteen states by 1945. By 1980 the Native American Church of North America numbered as many as 250,000 members in its congregations.

Native American Christian peyotism encountered serious legal difficulties. At one time, thirty-four different states had passed laws prohibiting the use of peyote. But landmark court cases in the Arizona Supreme Court in 1961, and the California Supreme Court in 1964, determined that peyote use within the context of religious ritual was not addictive, harmful, or destructive, and that its use for religious purposes should not be restricted. In fact, adherents of peyotism had maintained that its use was beneficial for spirituality and a moral life. The founders of the Native American Church had declared in 1918 that the church used the peyote sacrament "to teach the Christian religion with morality, sobriety, industry, kindly charity and right living, and [to] cultivate the spirit of self-respect, [and] brotherly union among the members of the native race of Indians." [59]

Clearly, this was a unique form of Native American Christianity. In this respect, peyotism had much in common with the Sun Dance as a Pan-Indian, Native American movement. First, both provided access to personal power through dreams, trances, and visions for people who had been disempowered in the prevailing network of white domination in America. The deprivations, hardships, and poverty of reservation life could be counteracted by these alternative sources of spiritual power. Second, both movements emerged out of a new, unified definition of Indian identity. Tribal identities were increasingly subsumed within this shared identification. Of course, that identity had been forged out of a long conflict and struggle with white oppression in America. In this regard, both the Sun Dance and peyotism served to refocus that identity into common religious and political concerns shared by all Native Americans by virtue of their situation in America. [60]

The United States had been committed to a course of action designed to eliminate tribal groups. Government policies attacked their political autonomy by refusing to acknowledge them as separate nations; they attacked their religious cohesion by prohibiting tribal ceremonials; and they attacked the social and economic order of tribal groups by reallocating land to individuals rather than to communities. Even when all Indians were enfranchised in 1924, this policy was an attempt to assimilate Native Americans into the political system as individuals. Beginning with the Indian Reorganization Act (IRA) of 1934, however, Native American groups were allowed more autonomy in the areas of political organization, religious practices, and ownership of land.[61] Although tensions persisted, a growing recognition that Native American religious practices might be protected under the free exercise clause resulted in a number of important court decisions: The ceremonial use of peyote, as we noted, was upheld by the Supreme Court of California; the Supreme Court of Alaska exonerated an Athabascan Indian who had violated game laws by killing a moose for a religious ritual; and a Congressional Act returned Blue Lake to the Taos Pueblo Indians because it was perceived to be central and necessary for ongoing traditional religious practices.[62] This trend toward a growing climate of support for Native American religions culminated in the American Indian Religious Freedom Act of 1978. This act stipulated that traditional religious practices of Native Americans are integral to their cultural identity; and that it shall be the policy of the United States to protect and preserve the inherent right of freedom of Native Americans to believe, express, and exercise their traditional religions.[63]

Nevertheless, the centrality of land to Native American religions has led to a number of recent court cases in which Indian groups have tried to recover sacred sites. Most of these land claims have been denied.[64] Recovery of sacred land is an important issue in the protection of traditional Native American religions. As Robert Michaelsen has noted, "Land is central in most Native American religions. All land traditionally experienced, not just specific sites, has a sacred quality. Land forms as such may be highly significant. And the opportunity to carry on sacred—essentially secret—ceremonies in specific areas is crucial."[65] Land cases coming before United States courts put the protection of Native American religions in the balance against the competing interests of the government. The result in most of these cases has been that if the Native American group cannot prove that a particular sacred site is central and indispensible to its religious practice, then government interests (and the interests of private enterprise or recreation) are deemed more compelling.

These court cases test a set of interests on both sides that go back to the first encounters between European intruders and the indigenous populations of America. Deeply ingrained cultural values on both sides continue to be in conflict, and the religious and political forces that constellate around these values continue to create tensions in American society. Native Americans, who have been forcibly excluded from the dominant religiopolitical system of the United States, are seeking to restore meaningful enclaves of religious and political power. The source of this power is deeply tied to land and specific sacred sites. The government has put forth a greater effort to accommodate Native American power interests within the protection of the First Amendment. But the very existence of these alernative forms of power call into question the values of Christianity and civilization that have been powerful forces in shaping the American religiopolitical culture by excluding all *others*.

NOTES

1. JAMES SULLIVAN, et al.,eds., *The Papers of Sir William Johnson*, 14 volumes (Albany, 1921–65): VII:506; cited in James Axtell, "The Invasion Within: The Contest of Cultures in Colonial North America," in *The Frontier in History: North America and Southern Africa Compared*, eds., Howard Lamar and Leonard Thompson (New Haven and London: Yale University Press, 1981): 240.
2. For a brief overview of Native American cultures, see Peter Farb, *Man's Rise to Civilization as Shown by the Indians of North America from Primeval Times to the Coming of the Industrial State* (New York: Dutton, 1968.)
3. See Henry Warner Bowden, *American Indians and Christian Missions: Studies in Cultural Conflict* (Chicago: University of Chicago Press, 1981): 25–133. For bibliography on relations between Native Americans and Euro-Americans, see Francis Paul Prucha, *A Bibliographic Guide to the History of Indian–White Relations in the United States* (Chicago: University of Chicago Press, 1977); *Indian–White Relations in the United States: A Bibliography of Works Published 1975–1980* (Lincoln: University of Nebraska Press, 1982).
4. ROBERT F. BERKHOFER JR., "The North American Frontier as Process and Context," in *The Frontier in History*: 48; Some estimate that the Indian population of North America declined to one twenty-fifth of its precontact size. See Wilbur R. Jacobs, "The Tip of the Iceberg: Pre-Columbian Indian Demography and Some Implications for Revisionism," *William and Mary Quarterly* 31 (1974): 125; and Francis Jennings, *The Invasion of America: Indians, Colonialism, and the Cant of Conquest* (Chapel Hill: University of North Carolina Press, 1975): 16–31.
5. On Native American religions, see Walter Holden Capps, ed., *Seeing with the Native Eye: Essays on Native American Religion* (New York: Harper and Row, 1976); Vine Deloria, Jr., *God is Red* (New York: Grosset and Dunlap, 1973); Sam Gill, *Native American Religions* (Belmont, California: Wadsworth Publishing Company, 1982); Åke Hultkrantz, *The Religions of the American Indians* (Berkeley: University of California Press, 1979); and Ruth M. Underhill, *Red Man's Religion* (Chicago: University of Chicago Press, 1965).
6. JAMES P. WALSH, "Puritans and Sacred Places," in *Christianity in America*, eds., Mark A. Noll, et al. (Grand Rapids, Michigan: Eerdmans, 1983): 39–41.
7. H. KONIG, *Columbus: His Enterprise* (New York: Monthly Review Press, 1976): 53; see Alfred W. Crosby, Jr., *The Columbian Exchange: Biological and Cultural Consequences of 1492* (Westport, Connecticut: Greenwood Press, 1972).
8. Cited in Lewis Hanke, *Aristotle and the American Indians: A Study of Race Prejudice in the Modern World* (Bloomington: Indiana University Press, 1959): 19.
9. Cited in J. S. Slotkin, ed., *Readings in Early Anthropology* (Chicago: Aldine Publishing, 1965): 177–78.
10. MARGARET T. HODGEN, *Early Anthropology in the Sixteenth and Seventeenth Centuries* (Philadelphia: University of Pennsylvania Press, 1964): 213–14; Wesley Frank Craven has observed that "the view best suited to the European's preconceptions was one holding that the native American was born white and that the distinctive complexion of his skin was artificially achieved." *White, Red, and Black: The Seventeenth-Century Virginian* (Charlottesville, Virginia: University of Virginia Press, 1970): 40.
11. AXTELL, "The Invasion Within": 250.
12. HANKE, *Aristotle and the American Indians*: 44–5.
13. WILCOMB E. WASHBURN, *Red Man's Land/White Man's Law: A Study of the Past and Present Status of the American Indian* (New York: Charles Scribner's Sons, 1971); Hodgen, *Early Anthropology*: 234–5.
14. RUDOLF WITTKOWER, "Marvels of the East: A Study of the History of Monsters," in *Allegory and the Migration of Symbols* (London: Thames and Hudson, 1977). John Block Friedman has noted that "the sense of the alien or 'other' in the marvelous races of the East was so

great as to disqualify them, in the Greco-Roman view, from the epithet 'men.'" And through-out the Middle Ages it was generally agreed that these races "could perform many human actions without at the same time being men." *The Monstrous Races in Medieval Art and Thought* (Cambridge: Harvard University Press, 1981): 34, 179.

15. RICHARD HAKLUYT, *Voyages and Discoveries*, ed., Jack Beeching (Harmondsworth, England: Penguin Books, 1972): 402.

16. Cited in Roy Harvey Pearce, *Savagism and Civilization: A Study of the Indian and the American Mind* (Baltimore: Johns Hopkins Press, 1965): 6.

17. See Hayden White, "The Forms of Wildness: Archaeology of an Idea," in *The Wild Man Within: An Image in Western Thought from the Renaissance to Romanticism*, eds. Edward Dudley and Maxmillan E. Novak (Pittsburgh: University of Pittsburgh Press, 1972): 19.

18. *New England Historical and Genealogical Register*, 36 (1882): 296; cited in Axtell, "The Invasion Within": 241.

19. BOWDIN, *American Indians and Christian Missions*: 63.

20. *Ibid.*:101–2; See Robert H. Lowie, "Some Aspects of Political Organization among the American Aborigines," in *Comparative Political Systems: Studies in the Politics of Pre-Industrial Societies* (Garden City, New York: Doubleday, 1967): 63–88; and Neil Salisbury, *Manitou and Providence: Indians, Puritans, and the Making of New England, 1500–1643* (New York: Oxford University Press, 1982).

21. ALBERT C. MYERS, ed., *Narratives of Early Pennsylvania, West New Jersey, and Delaware, 1630–1707* (New York, 1912): 233; cited in Axtell, "The Invasion Within": 244.

22. *Collections of the Massachusetts Historical Society*, 3rd series, 4 (1834): 50; cited in Axtell, "The Invasion Within": 242.

23. AXTELL, "The Invasion Within": 248.

24. RICHARD DRINNON, *Facing West: The Metaphysics of Indian-Hating and Empire-Building* (Minneapolis: University of Minnesota Press, 1980): 19; For analysis of Puritan misunder-standing of Native American religion, see William S. Simmons, "Cultural Bias in the New England Puritans' Perception of Indians," *William and Mary Quarterly* 3rd series, 38 (1981): 56–72.

25. DRINNON, *Facing West*: 14.

26. *Ibid.*: 34.

27. *Ibid.*: 46.

28. WILCOMB E. WASHBURN, *The Indian in America* (New York: Harper, 1975): 131–2.

29. EMMERICH de VATTEL, *The Law of Nations; or Principles of the Law of Nature, Applied to the Conduct and Affairs of Nations and Sovereigns* (1760); see Wilcomb E. Washburn, "The Moral and Legal Justification for Dispossessing the Indians," in *Seventeenth-Century America: Essays in Colonial History*, ed. J. M. Smith (Chapel Hill: University of North Carolina Press, 1959): 15–32; and Albert K. Weinberg, *Manifest Destiny: A Study of Nationalist Expansion in American History* (Baltimore: Johns Hopkins Press, 1935): 77–99.

30. WAYNE MOQUIN and CHARLES VAN DOREN, eds., *Great Documents in American Indian History* (New York: Praeger, 1973): 109.

31. VIRGIL J. VOGEL, ed., *This Country Was Ours: A Documentary History of the American Indian* (New York: Harper and Row, 1972): 105.

32. Cited in R. Pierce Beaver, *Church, State, and the American Indian* (St. Louis: Concordia, 1966): 68.

33. WILCOMB E. WASHBURN, *The American Indian and the United States: A Documentary History*, I (New York: Random House, 1973): 37.

34. Cited in D.S. Otis, "History of the Allotment Policy," *Hearings Before the House Committee on Indian Affairs in the Indian Reorganization Act of 1934*, 73rd Congress, 2nd session; cited in J. E. Chamberlin, *The Harrowing of Eden: White Attitudes Toward Native Americans* (New York: Seabury, 1975): 39.

35. CHAMBERLIN, *The Harrowing of Eden*: 39.

36. See Wilcomb E. Washburn, *The Assualt on Indian Tribalism: The General Allotment Law (Dawes Act) of 1887* (Philadelphia: Lippincott, 1975); and Kirke Kickingbird and Karen Ducheneaux, *One Hundred Million Acres* (New York: Macmillan, 1973).

37. THOMAS L. MCKENNEY, *Memoirs, Official and Personal*, 2nd ed. (New York: Paine and Burgess, 1846): II:39–40.

38. THOMAS L. MCKENNEY, *Sketches of a Tour to the Lakes, of the Character and Customs of the Chippeway Indians, and of Incidents Connected with the Treaty of Fond du Lac* (Baltimore: Fielding Lucas, Jr., 1827): 379.

39. McKenney, *Memoirs*, I:241; see Robert W. Mardock, *The Reformers and the American Indian* (Columbia: University of Missouri Press, 1971).

40. Grant Foreman, *Indian Removal: The Emigration of the Five Civilized Tribes of Indians* (Norman: University of Oklahoma Press, 1932): 267ff.; see Ronald N. Satz, *American Indian Policy in the Jacksonian Era* (Lincoln: University of Nebraska Press, 1975); and William G. McLoughlin, *Cherokees and Missionaries, 1789–1939* (New Haven: Yale University Press, 1984).

41. Loring B. Priest, *Uncle Sam's Stepchildren: The Reformation of Indian Policy, 1865–1887* (New Brunswick: Rutgers University Press, 1942): 219–20.

42. John Hay, *Addresses of John Hay* (New York: Century, 1907): 250.

43. An illustration of United States expansion to the Pacific islands, continuing the preoccupation with Christian civilization, is found in President McKinley's descripton of how he spent a sleepless night worrying about the Philippines, but then suddenly realized, "that there was nothing left for us to do but to take them all, and to educate the Filipinos, and uplift and civilize and Christianize them, and by God's grace do the very best we could by them as our fellowmen for whom Christ died. And then I went to bed and went to sleep, and slept soundly, and next morning I sent for the chief engineer of the War Department (our map-maker), and I told him to put the Philippines on the map of the United States." Cited in Charles S. Olcott, *The Life of William McKinley*: (New York: Houghton, Mifflin, 1916): II:111.

44. Bryan R. Wilson, *Magic and the Millennium: A Sociological Study of Religious Movements of Protest Among Tribal and Third-World Peoples* (London: Heinemann, 1973): 385.

45. See Merle H. Deardorff, "The Religion of Handsome Lake: Its Origin and Development," in *Symposium on Local Diversity in Indian Culture*, ed., William N. Fenton (Washington, D.C.: Smithsonian Institution, Bureau of American Ethnology, 1951): 77–107.

46. A.C. Parker, *The Code of Handsome Lake* (Albany: State University of New York, 1912): 56.

47. *Ibid.*: 10.

48. A.F.C. Wallace, "Handsome Lake and the Great Revival in the West," *American Quarterly* 4 (1952): 149.

49. Speech of Chief Seattle, January 9, 1855, as published in the *Seattle Star* (October 29, 1877); See Seattle, *The Great Chief Sends Word: Chief Seathl's Testament* (Leicester: Saint Bernard Press, 1977); and *Your Dead Cease to Love You: A Speech* (Sacramento: Press of Arden Park, 1976).

50. See A.F.C. Wallace, *The Death and Rebirth of the Seneca* (New York: Knopf, 1969): 115–21; and Howard H. Peckham, *Pontiac and the Indian Uprising* (Princeton: Princeton University Press, 1947).

51. Benjamin Drake, *Life of Tecumseh and of his Brother the Prophet* (Philadelphia: Quaker City Publishing House, 1856): 108.

52. James Mooney, *Ghost Dance Religion and the Sioux Outbreak of 1890* (Chicago: University of Chicago Press, 1965); and David Humphreys Miller, *Ghost Dance* (New York: Duell, Sloan and Pearce, 1959).

53. E.A. Hoebel, "The Commanche and the Messianic Outbreak of 1873," *American Anthropologist* 43 (1941): 301–3; Hoebel, *The Cheyennes* (New York: Holt, Rinehart and Winston, 1960): 11–16; John C. Ewers, *The Blackfeet* (Norman: University of Oklahoma Press, 1961): 174–84; 298ff.

54. Mooney, *Ghost Dance Religion*: 26–7; see Paul Bailey, *Wovoka: The Indian Messiah* (Los Angeles: Westernlore Press, 1957).

55. Mooney, *Ghost Dance Religion*: 31.

56. Joseph G. Jorgensen, *The Sun Dance Religion: Power for the Powerless* (Chicago: University of Chicago Press, 1972); Leslie Spier, *The Sun Dance of the Plains Indians: Its Development and Diffusion* (New York: Anthropological Papers of the American Museum of Natural History, No. 16, 1921).

57. Demitri B. Shimkin, "The Wind River Shoshone Sun Dance," *Bureau of American Ethnology Bulletin*, No. 151 (Washington, D.C.: U.S. Government Printing Office, 1953): 397–484.

58. James S. Slotkin, *The Peyote Religion: A Study in Indian–White Relations* (Glencoe, Illinois: Free Press, 1956); David F. Aberle, *The Peyote Religion among the Navaho* (Chicago: Aldine, 1966).

59. Cited in Omer C. Stewart, "The Native American Church and the Law," in *The Emergent Native Americans*, ed. Deward E. Walker, Jr. (Boston: Little, Brown, 1972): 385.
60. HAZEL W. HERTZBERG, *The Search for an American Indian Identity: Modern Pan-Indian Movements* (Syracuse: Syracuse University Press, 1971); Stan Steiner, *The New Indians* (New York: Harper and Row, 1968); Helen L. Peterson, "American Indian Political Participation," in *Annals of the American Academy of Political and Social Science*, eds. George E. Simpson and Milton Yinger, 311 (1957): 116–26.
61. See Kenneth R. Philp, *John Collier's Crusade for Indian Reform, 1920–1954* (Tucson: University of Arizona Press, 1977).
62. *People v. Woody*, 394 P. 2d 813 (Sup. Ct. Calif., 1964); *Frank v. Alaska*, 604 P. 2d 1068 (Alaska Sup. Ct., 1979); and Public Law 91–550, December 15, 1970); on this last issue, see John T. Whatley, "The Saga of Taos Pueblo: The Blue Lake Controversy," *The Indian Historian* 2 (Fall, 1969): 22–28; and John J. Bodine, "Blue Lake: A Struggle for Indian Rights," *American Indian Law Review* 1 (1973): 23–32.
63. ROBERT MICHAELSEN, "Red Man's Religion/White Man's Religious History," *Journal of the American Academy of Religion* 51 (1983): 677.
64. ROBERT MICHAELSEN, "The Significance of the American Indian Religious Freedom Act of 1978," *Journal of the American Academy of Religion* 52 (1984): 99.
65. *Ibid.*:105.

CHAPTER FIVE
BLACK AMERICANS

The Declaration of Independence stands as a sacred text in the canon of American civil religion. It enshrines a religiopolitical ideal of sacred human rights which must be protected by civil government. This document sets forth three kinds of basic rights. The first is *individual human rights*. These rights are inherent in the natural condition of being human and are held by all human beings equally. If everything is either to be used or to be enjoyed, then these rights are not instrumental values to be used toward some desired end, but rather they are natural human capacities to be enjoyed as ends in themselves. The Declaration makes a basic faith statement when it maintains that, "We hold these truths to be self-evident, that all men are created equal, that they are endowed by their Creator with certain unalienable Rights, that among these are Life, Liberty and the pursuit of Happiness." This list of human rights could probably be expanded; but it is a basic declaration of faith in the equal rights of individuals to the enjoyment of their inherent human powers.

A second kind of power, however, appears in the notion of *individual civil rights*. The form of government imagined in the Declaration of Independence is a voluntary social contract entered into by individuals for the protection of their human rights. Civil rights, in this sense, guarantee full participation in the political process; they are the powers reserved to individuals to consent to the forms of government designed to protect their human rights. As the Declaration continues, "to secure these rights, Governments are instituted among Men, deriving their just powers from the consent of the governed." If civil rights protect human rights, a denial of civil rights denies the full humanity of those excluded from the civil ceremonies of power.

Finally, a third kind of power is suggested in the notion of *collective civil rights*. The distribution of political power in government is intended to insure the individual freedom to enjoy human rights and the individual freedom from unnecessary limitations on that enjoyment. But, the Declaration asserts, "whenever any Form of Government becomes destructive of these ends, it is the Right of the People to alter or to abolish it, and to institute new Government, laying its foundation on such principles and organizing its powers in such form, as to them shall seem most likely to effect their Safety and Happiness." The "Right of the People" implies that those who are under the jurisdiction of any form of government have the collective authority to question, change, and even eliminate that government. This suggests that people have the collective right to alter the power arrangements of government when these interfere with the full enjoyment of basic human rights. The distribution of power suggested in the Declaration of Independence is based on a fundamentally religious commitment to human rights, and the individual and collective civil rights form the basis of political power to insure that these sacred human rights may be freely enjoyed.

Two hundred years of United States political history appears as a chronicle of the struggles to extend this ideal of human rights and powers to an ever increasing spectrum of American society. It has been a struggle to expand the circle of humanity in which these powers may be exercised. Though Jefferson may have been making an unconditional declaration of equal human rights, it was clear from the beginning that there was no intention of extending equal civil rights for all people to participate fully in the political process. Civil rights were the exclusive privilege of property-owning citizens, and those who fell outside this definition were excluded from full participation. Slaves, in particular, were thought to have forfeited any claims to civil rights. John Locke, in his *Two Treatises of Government*, maintained that slavery was "nothing else, but the state of War continued, between a lawful Conquerour, and a Captive."[1] As a captive subject of a conquering power, the slave lost any individual claims to the rights of life, liberty, and property, and was property in the eyes of the law, rather than a person with any social or political status. Slaves were, therefore, factored out of the social contract. They were denied any civil rights to participate in the political process that might recognize and protect their human rights.

The political dehumanization of black Africans in the institution of slavery was legitimized by a number of religious and political arguments; but those arguments could not be sustained in the face of the unconditional declaration of human rights embodied in the phrase "all men are created equal." The dilemma of equality struck at the root of the American religiopolitical system, called into question its most central commitments, and resulted in deep divisions in American society that still continue. The American dilemma, as Gunnar Myrdal called it, was the internal conflict between the "high-sounding Christian concepts embodied in the American creed as compared to the way Americans really behaved."[2] Slavery, segregation, and racial discrimination presented an ongoing critique of the religiopolitical ideal of equality. The struggle to extend the scope of civil rights can be seen as an effort to bring America into greater harmony with its own ideals.

But what is the political formula for equality? There have been three basic responses to the dilemma of equality in race relations in the United States. Each of these responses draws upon both religious and political resources to work out a formula for equal civil rights; but they are directed toward very different political goals. One formula is *separation*. A powerful image for both whites and blacks in American history, it assumes that equal civil rights can only be realized with a separation of the races. A second formula is *integration*. This ideal holds that civil rights can only be exercised in the shared community of American society when all people have equal opportunity to participate in the same political processes. The third formula is *liberation*. It is a concern with the present struggle of an oppressed people. While freedom from oppression may result in either a separation or integration of the races, this third response is more immediately concerned with the conditions of the struggle itself. All three of these responses to the American dilemma have been deeply identified with sources of religious power. They represent three definitions of black identity, consciousness, and power within the religiopolitical pattern of American society.

SLAVERY

The enslavement of black Africans was surrounded by both political and religious justifications. The political basis for enslaving Africans was grounded in the assumption that they had been legitimately conquered in war; or that they were criminals who had been sentenced to death within their own African societies. In either case, enslavement was seen as the alternative to execution. If these people had been properly condemned to slavery by the legitimate authorities of their African societies, then the Europeans argued that they were justified in obtaining them for enslavement in the New World. This was not, of course, an accurate representation of the situation in which Europeans forcibly captured their own cargoes of slaves, or where they encouraged, supported, and armed wars between African groups for the purpose of obtaining slaves. But it did serve to define in the European imagination the legal propriety of acquiring people as a form of property.

The religious arguments for slavery were of two kinds. The first was the missionary ambition for converting the Africans to Christianity. By bringing these people to the European colonies, it was assumed that they would be exposed to the benefits of Christian civilization. The most recent analogy for the enslavement of a population in European history was the capture of Muslim prisoners during the Crusades. These people were vulnerable for slavery, not only because they were taken in war, but also because they were considered barbarous heathens. It was a comforting justification for the practice of slavery to imagine that through enslavement in a Christian society, the Africans might lose their freedom but gain their salvation. The Africans were certainly not lacking in religious beliefs and practices: Traditional African religions held beliefs in creator gods, reverence for ancestors, and dynamic ritual practices that unified each community; many African groups, particularly on the west coast of Africa, had come under the influence of Islam; and there may even have been some Christians, as a result of the efforts of Portuguese and French missionaries, among those who were enslaved.[3] But from the exclusive vantage point of Christian civilization, Africans were all barbarous heathens or infidels who lacked religion. Presumably, they could only benefit from their contact with Christianity.

The other set of religious arguments was based on the mythic dehumanization of black Africans in the Christian world view. The story of Noah's curse of his son, Ham, in the Book of Genesis (9:18–27) was used to provide a mythological justification for the enslavement of blacks. According to the story, the descendants of Ham were condemned to be "servants of servants." His lineage was to be subservient to the descendants of his brothers, Shem and Japheth. In the popular interpretation of this narrative, Ham was distinguished by blackness and the black skin color of his descendants was seen as a punishment.[4] This mythic history of race relations had considerable popularity, particularly in the southern part of the United States before the Civil War, but it was part of a larger trend in American society which gradually justified slavery on purely racial grounds. Racial arguments emerged as the most prominent source of justification for continuing the practice of slavery. The clergyman Morgan Godwyn maintained in 1680 that the terms *Negro* and *Slave* were equivalent, and, as Winthrop Jordan has pointed out, the equation of whiteness with freedom and blackness with slavery came to dominate the imagination of Americans of European descent.[5]

The original religious justification for slavery was seriously undermined by a series of legal restrictions on black religious practices. One set of laws banned public funerals. A slave revolt in Virginia broke out in 1687, and it apparently developed out of a mass funeral. Such funerals were religious events, usually held at night, in which the emotional intensity of the mourners could be focused and directed against their masters. This particular funeral resulted in a riot; its leaders were executed and such events were legally banned.[6] A similar ban on public funerals for black slaves was passed in New York in 1712.[7] Other laws were issued to restrict any religious gatherings of slaves. It was feared that under the cover of religion blacks might plan revolution. A North Carolina law in 1715 stipulated that any master or slaveholder who allowed "Negroes to build . . . any house under the pretense of a meeting-house upon the account of worship, shall be liable to a fine of fifty pounds." A 1723 statute in Maryland restricted any independent religious meetings among blacks, and a Georgia law required punishment by whipping for slaves who gathered together in any form of assembly.[8] Other laws were passed against blacks preaching.

These restrictive laws were clearly designed to maintain control over slaves by diffusing any possibility that religious gatherings might result in revolt against the slave masters. But they were also part of a larger pattern of religiopolitical power which used Christian religion to protect the property interests of slaveholders. Religious leaders in the established Christian churches presented a form of Christianity designed to make slaves more docile in their station in life. As Winthrop Jordan has pointed out, "These clergymen had been forced by the circumstances of racial slavery in America into propagating the Gospel by presenting it as an attractive device for slave control."[9] Charles Colcock Jones, who was the leading figure in the interdenominational missions to the plantation slaves in the South and was himself a slaveholder, represented the culmination of these efforts to use Christianity in the control of slaves in the 1830s. His *Catechism for Colored Persons* (1834) was a widely used text in religious instruction for slaves. He exhorted slaves "to count their Masters 'worthy of all honour,' as those whom God has placed over them in this world . . . and let Servants serve their masters as faithfully behind their backs as before their faces. God is present to see, if their masters are not."[10] The Christian religion, in this sense, served as a useful system of invisible behavioral controls, and blacks might thereby be more tightly bound into the conditions of slavery.

There were, nevertheless, important independent developments in black Christianity in America that provided a range of vital religious resources. It was not until the Great Awakening of the 1740s that blacks turned to Christianity in large numbers. The enthusiastic preaching, outdoor revivals and meetings, and emotional appeals attracted considerable interest. This was the first stirring of a style of Christian worship that was to become characteristic of black spirituality in America; and it was a style that may have had important reverberations with traditional forms of African religious ritual.[11] The dramatic exhortations of the preachers, the vivid imagery of heaven and hell, and the emotional appeals for sinners to change their hearts, contrasted against the authoritative legalism in doctrine and practice that had dominated the Anglican, Congregational, and Presbyterian churches in America until then. But it wasn't simply the emotionalism of the Awakening that drew in black converts; as C. Eric Lincoln has observed, "what the Africans found in the camp meetings of the Great Awakening was *acceptance and involvement as human beings.*"[12] The more traditional religious leaders were shocked by these developments. As one New England minister complained, "So great has been the enthusiasm created by Wesley and Whitefield and Tennant . . . the very Servants and Slaves pretend to extraordinary inspiration, and under veil thereof cherish their idle dispositions, and in lieu of minding their respective businesses run rambling about to utter enthusiastic nonsense."[13] But blacks could participate in a new arena where their social status could be temporarily transcended through a direct experience of the spirit.

The egalitarian impulses generated by the religious awakening of the mid-seventeenth century were kept in motion by Methodists, Baptists, and New Light Presbyterians. These movements attracted a large black membership in both the North and South. By the time the Declaration of Independence was drafted, blacks formed a large segment of these Christian churches. In November 1787 a group of black Methodists were forced from St. George's Methodist Church in Philadelphia for violating its rule of segregation. In response to this event, two of the offenders, Richard Allen and Absalom Jones, founded the Free African Society, as a "self-improvement association which was designed to provide mutual aid in times of misfortune, and to exercise a kind of moral oversight over its membership by visitation and prayer."[14] Although it does not seem to have been their intention to start an independent black church, it was out of this initial organization that Jones formed the African Protestant Episcopal Church and Richard Allen founded the African Methodist Episcopal Church. It was out of Allen's independent church, and the expansion of African Methodist churches throughout the northern states, that the first independent national black denomination was formed in 1816.[15]

The Anglican Church had been established in the five southern colonies, and because of its close identification with the power interests of the plantation owners, it was unlikely that it would attract much black support. So the Methodist and Baptist revivals drew large numbers of blacks into those churches. By the turn of the nineteenth century, black membership accounted for about one-fourth of the total membership in both denominations. Church services were often mixed meetings, although whites and blacks would sit in separate areas of the building. Gradually, separate meeting places were formed. And blacks in towns and cities were permitted a greater "access to religious privileges."[16] The slaveholders were concerned that the egalitarian spirit of the revival religions would rise up in opposition to the institution of slavery, and, in fact, the leadership of the Methodist denomination took a public position against slavery. This may account for the greater scope given to Baptist missions in the South and the tremendous expansion of black membership in that denomination.

Fears of slave revolt were realized in the nineteenth century, and these uprisings were inspired by religious visions that translated into political action. The first important revolt was led by Gabriel, the twenty-five-year-old slave of Thomas Prosser, who planned an attack upon the city of Richmond, Virginia. He had been inspired by the recent revolutionary actions of Toussaint L'Ouverture against the British in Haiti; but, more significantly, he was motivated by a deep conviction drawn from his reading of the Bible that he was to be a black Samson, chosen by God to deliver his people. He wore his hair long like Samson, told people of his divine election, and planned to establish a black kingdom in Virginia under his rule. His plan was to lead a black army against Richmond, seize arms and ammunition, capture the state treasury, and reach an agreement with the slaveholders for the release of their slaves. A contingent of around 1,000 slaves gathered for the attack on Richmond on August 30, 1800. There may have been more involved. Gabriel claimed to have 10,000 soldiers, organized in cavalry and infantry, under his leadership. Witnesses gave figures that ranged between 2,000 and 6,000. But a storm intervened in this military operation and the attack had to be postponed. Many disbanded in confusion, and Gabriel was betrayed, arrested, and later executed. All together, 35 were hanged for their participation in the revolt. Gabriel's army was the first instance of an organized military operation against the institution of slavery in the United States; but it was also an important illustration of the power of religious visions of redemption in the formation of revolutionary movements.

A second major uprising occurred in 1822 under the leadership of Denmark Vesey. He had purchased his freedom in 1800 and became involved with the black Methodists in Charleston. The church was an organizational base for revolutionary activity, and its scriptures provided mythic resources for inspiration. Like Gabriel Prosser, Vesey was drawn to the military imagery of holy war in the Old Testament. He was particularly drawn to the story of Joshua and the battle of Jericho, and he understood his own military preparations to be guided by the Lord in the form of an angel with a sword in his hand. Like Joshua's conquest of Jericho, this would be a total war which would obliterate the enemy. These biblical images merged with traditional African magical practices. One of Vesey's associates, a slave from Angola called Gullah Jack, provided the conspirators with pieces of crab claw to keep in their mouths to protect them from harm during the attack. The actual attack, scheduled for June 16, 1822, was revealed to the white authorities by traitors, and out of 131 arrested, 37 were executed, including Denmark Vesey, Gullah Jack, and the leadership of the insurrection. The Methodist church which had served in the organization of the movement was closed down, and more severe restrictions were placed on black religious gatherings.[18]

A third revolt was led by the Baptist preacher Nat Turner in Southampton, Virginia, in 1831. Turner, born in 1800, was described as a precocious child who was considered by his parents to have certain birthmarks that indicated the special abilities of an African conjurer. He was introduced into the Christian religion in the Methodist meeting house sponsored by the master of his plantation, and it was in the context of Methodist evangelical piety that he was marked out to be a preacher. At one point he escaped, but returned to his master after thirty days in the woods. He recounted that "the reason of my return was the Spirit appeared to me and said I had my wishes directed to things of this world and not the Kingdom of Heaven." Turner's attention was directed to a messianic kingdom of heaven on earth. Shortly after returning to his plantation, he had another vision of white and black spirits in a great battle with streams of blood flowing. It was an apocalyptic vision of a battle between the forces of good and evil. Gradually, these visions increased, and soon Turner had embarked on a ministry that attracted large followings at a number of different churches. Additional signs, such as a solar eclipse in February and unusual atmospheric conditions in August, were interpreted to signal the beginning of the battle. Completing his preparations, Turner delivered a sermon on the night of August 21, 1831 declaring that God had chosen that night to deliver the black race from slavery. He insisted that the war was to be conducted on a Christian basis. By midnight Turner and his followers had set off the bloodiest slave revolt in American history. By Tuesday morning, August 23, at least 75 slaves had killed 57 whites within a 20-mile area around Southampton County. The Virginia militia was able to subdue the revolt; more than 100 slaves were killed; and 20, including Nat Turner, were hanged. As Turner was led to his execution he was asked if he thought he had been mistaken in his religious convictions; and he responded: "Was not Christ crucified?"[19]

These three revolts show how religious resources could be translated into political action. Each of the leaders cultivated a particular religious vision of his role in the struggle against the institution of slavery: Black Samson, Black Joshua, and Black Messiah. In each case the fluid character of religious myth was molded into an image of political action, and served as a powerful motive and inspiration for revolution. The response of white authorities was to tighten the restrictions on black religious freedom. As W. E. B. Du Bois noted, "A wave of legislation passed over the South prohibiting the slaves from learning to read and write, forbidding Negroes to preach, and interfering with Negro religious meetings."[20] From the perspective of the dominant white system of political authority in America there was an inherent ambivalence in the propagation of Christian religion among slaves. On the one hand, it was hoped that the influence of Christianity would have the positive effect of making the slaves better, and, therefore, making them better slaves. Christian preachers emphasized Christian virtues of obedience: Servants, obey your masters. Charles Colcock Jones reported the effect that this style of preaching had on one congregation:

> I was preaching to a large congregation on the Epistle of Philemon; and when I insisted on fidelity and obedience as Christian virtues in servants, and upon the authority of Paul, condemned the practice of running away one-half of my audience deliberately rose up and walked off with themselves; and those who remained looked anything but satisfied with the preacher or his doctrine. After dismission, there was no small stir among them; some solemnly declared that there was no such Epistle in the Bible; others, that I preached to please the masters; others, that they did not care if they never heard me preach again.[21]

Of course there was such a letter in the Bible, and of course Jones was preaching to protect the interests of the slave masters, and of course many slaves did refuse to listen to such a version of the gospel. And so, in contrast to those who would use religion to support slavery, there was a range of creative responses to Christianity on the part of slaves themselves. Some responses were directly political in nature, such as the appropriations of biblical imagery and inspiration in the revolts of Prosser, Vesey, and Turner. Other responses involved a more subtle inversion of the very mythic framework which was being exploited to justify the condition of enslavement for blacks in America. At the beginning of the Civil War, in 1862, Edward W. Blyden wrote in New York about the descendants of Ham. The lineage of Ham, which included Egypt and Ethiopia (Genesis 10:6 - 14), was being freed from the curse which had held it in bondage. Japheth (representing Europeans) and Shem (representing Jews) have had their glory; the descendants of Ham were ascending to theirs.

> The all-conquering descendants of Japheth have gone to every clime, and have planted themselves on almost every shore. By means fair and unfair, they have spread themselves . . . The Messiah-God manifest in the flesh was of the tribe of Judah. He was born and dwelt in the tents of Shem. The promise to Ethiopia, or Ham, is like that to Shem, of a spiritual kind. It refers not to physical strength, not to large and extensive domains, not to foreign conquests, not to wide-spread dominions, but to the possession of spiritual qualities, to the elevation of the soul heavenward, to spiritual inspirations and divine communications. 'Ethiopia shall stretch forth her hands unto God. Blessed, glorious promise![22]

With this promise the order of spiritual domination over the descendants of Ham was broken. This creative inversion of mythological elements in the biblical narrative revealed the capacity of myth to express new forms of identity in the religious lives of individuals and groups.

It was undeniable that religion provided an important source of power for black slaves in America. As the historian Albert Raboteau has observed, "that some slaves maintained their identity as persons, despite a system bent on reducing them to a subhuman level, was certainly due in part to their religious life."[23] But these vital resources of religious power did not necessarily translate into civil, social, or political rights, and certain white power interests were clearly very much concerned to prevent the inclusion of blacks in the civil ceremonies of power.

CIVIL RIGHTS

The earliest conversions of black African slaves to Christianity raised questions about their civil status. Would a person who converted to Christianity, received Christian baptism, and entered into a Christian church be freed from slavery? The orthodox Calvinist position was clearly stated by the Dutch Reformed Church at the Synod of Dort in the seventeenth century: Slaves who converted to Christianity "ought to enjoy equal right of liberty with other Christians."[24] And, for a time, it appeared that colonists in the Massachusetts Bay Colony would follow this guideline. Until 1664 in Massachusetts slaves who were baptized and became church members were in theory eligible for the full status of freemen in the community. But soon a distinction between the human right to participate in the Christian religion and the civil right to participate in the political processes of the community began to be enforced. Cotton Mather, for example, could affirm that black slaves had the "equal Right with other Men to the Exercises and Privileges of Religion."[25] But the insistence that this religious privilege did not extend to civil rights was captured in Thomas Secker's statement in 1740, that "the Scripture, far from making any Alteration in Civil Rights, expressly directs, that every Man abide in the condition wherein he is called, with great Indifference of mind concerning outward circumstances."[26] This distinction between religious and civil rights became embodied in a series of laws which specified clearly that baptism would not change the social status of a slave. The Virginia Assembly passed into law the proclamation "that the conferring of baptism doth not alter the condition of a person as to his bondage or freedom."[27] The conflict between the economic interests in maintaining the institution of slavery and the religious interests in winning souls for Christianity was resolved to protect the property rights of slaveholders. And those slaves who did convert to Christianity were assured that it would not affect their social status as slaves.

The Declaration of Independence, with its ideal of equality, did nothing to change this situation. Thomas Jefferson himself was a slaveholder, and in his *Notes on the State of Virginia* (1781–82) reflected the racial prejudices of his era by insisting that "the blacks, whether originally a distinct race, or made distinct by time and circumstances, are inferior to the whites in the endowments of body and mind."[28] How did the ideal of unalienable equal rights apply to black Americans? One strategy was to give priority to property rights, so that the rights of slave owners to their property took precedence over any rights those slaves might have had to equal liberties in American society. Another strategy was to refer back to John Locke's notion that slaves had no part in civil rights that were derived from the social contract which had been formed by equal individuals.

But whatever strategy was used to adapt the ideal of equality to the institution of slavery, clearly the new nation saw itself as a homogeneous republic of white Americans. This image of America was reinforced by the naturalization law passed by Congress in 1790 which limited the acquisition of American citizenship only to white immigrants. Jefferson's ambivalent opposition to the institution of slavery can be understood in these terms: He opposed the enslavement of blacks as human beings, but did not wish to see the inclusion of blacks as citizens. In his *Autobiography* (1821) he observed that, "nothing is more certainly written in the book of fate, than that these people are to be free; nor is it less certain that the two races, equally free, cannot live in the same government."[29]

The solution proposed by many white abolitionists in the North was the deportation of blacks to Africa. It is ironic that the first organized "Back to Africa" movements were led by whites who were convinced, like Jefferson, that blacks and whites could never live together within the same civil government. The American Society for Colonizing the Free People of Color in the United States was founded in 1816 by Reverend Robert Finley of New Jersey. By 1850 this organization relocated almost 8,000 freed blacks in settlements in Liberia on the west coast of Africa. So, while emancipation of blacks from slavery was its program, this did not include efforts to incorporate black Americans into an equal enfranchisement in American society. Even Abraham Lincoln, the "Great Emancipator," was caught up in this dilemma. In an 1854 election speech in Peoria, Illinois, he maintained that slavery was a gross outrage against the laws of nature; but, he continued, "my first impulse would be to free all the slaves, and send them to Liberia—their own native land."[30] Lincoln was concerned with avoiding what he called "racial amalgamation.'" As he insisted in a speech in 1857, the only way to prevent this was through "the separation of the races."[31] To a delegation of free blacks visiting the White House in 1862 he said, "It is better for us both, therefore, to be separated."[32] And shortly before his death Lincoln expressed his continuing ambivalence about the status of blacks after the emancipation. In a letter to General Benjamin F. Butler, April, 1865, he asked, "But what shall we do with the Negroes after they are free? I can hardly believe that the South and North can live in peace unless we get rid of the Negroes."[33]

There were also black leaders in America during this period who supported a policy of emigration as the only way for blacks to achieve equal political rights. The emergence of black nationalism during the nineteenth century was closely aligned with attempts to locate black political identity outside of the territorial limits of the United States. The most eloquent spokesman for this position during the mid-nineteenth century was the medical doctor and journalist, Martin R. Delany. He published a book in 1852, *The Condition, Elevation, Emigration and Destiny of the Colored People of the United States*. He referred to blacks in America as a nation within a nation. He saw their collective experience, however, as a people who had been denied their natural rights in American society. "We are Americans," Delany said, "having a birthright citizenship—natural claims upon the country—claims common to all others of our fellow citizens— natural rights, which may, by virtue of unjust laws, be obstructed, but never can be annulled." And yet, because these rights had been obstructed, blacks were "aliens to the laws and political privileges of the country."[34] The only solution was emigration. Delany considered the possibility of colonies in South America, Mexico, and the West Indies, but settled on a proposed new nation in East Africa.

Throughout the nineteenth century, the image of Africa was closely tied to the religious hopes of black clergy of returning there with the Christian gospel. Ministers such as Daniel Coker were convinced that the independent black churches had a mission to colonize and Christianize the African continent. He declared that "anyone who loves souls would weep over them, and be willing to suffer and die with them. I can say that my soul cleaves to Africa."[35] Reverend Lott Carey, a slave minister from Virginia, organized the African Missionary Society in 1815 and based his missionary efforts in Liberia. The Episcopal clergyman, Alexander Crummell, spent from 1853 to 1873 involved in missionizing in Liberia and Sierra Leone. He called for black Christians to colonize and missionize Africa out of a deep connection with the land of their fathers. He proclaimed that "We should live for the good of our kind, and strive for the salvation of the world."[36] And perhaps the most prominent spokesman for emigration at the end of the nineteenth century was the bishop of the African Methodist Episcopal Church, Henry M. Turner. In 1900 he declared that "Africa is our home, and is the one place that offers us manhood and freedom"; and he imagined "a highway made across the Atlantic: upon which regular and social intercourse between Black America and Africa could be carried on and self-reliant, energetic Black people could be permanently settled if they chose to do so."[37]

There were many black leaders, however, who were committed to realizing both their religious privileges and civil rights within American society. The first Negro convention, held in Philadelphia in 1831, condemned emigration to Liberia. The policy of emigration was viewed as divisive of the black community in the United States and damaging to the struggle for civil rights in America.[38] Even terminology was an important issue in the controversy between those who supported emigration from America and those who desired an equal integration in the American political system. Prior to the nineteenth century, American blacks referred to themselves as "Africans" or "free Africans." But, many were concerned that they might be forced to go back to Africa if they used these terms. So, the term "Negro" grew in usage, and Booker T. Washington even led a successful campaign to have it capitalized, as an important symbolic statement that blacks had a permanent place in American society.[39] The issue, of course, was what kind of a place that was. And after the Civil War even a committed emigrationist, such as Martin Delany, recognized that American blacks required equal access to political power through the guarantee of civil rights. In a letter addressed to President Andrew Johnson, Delany said that "what becomes necessary, then, to secure and perpetuate the union is simply the enfranchisement and recognition of the political equality of the blacks with the whites in all their relations as American citizens."[40]

Such guarantees of equal civil rights took the form of an amendment to the United States Constitution, and a series of civil rights acts culminating in the Act of 1875 which protected equality of rights in the United States, even including equal access to transportation, accommodation, and entertainment. But subsequent civil rights cases produced Supreme Court rulings that seriously undermined any effects this legislation might have had. The Court made the distinction between the rights of blacks as United States citizens and their rights as citizens of particular states, and decided that the federal government had no jurisdiction over discriminatory laws that might be passed within any given state. This curious interpretation of the Fourteenth Amendment effectively nullified its protection of political rights; and, as J.R. Pole has observed, "although conditions differed from state to state, there was a remarkable consistency in the manner in which Negroes were eventually driven out of political life."[41] The disenfranchisement of black Americans was particularly prevalent in the southern states. The short-lived confederacy of southern states had entered the Civil War immersed in a racial mythology directly opposed to the ideal that all men are created equal. The first vice-president of the Confederate States of America, Alexander H. Stephens, made this clear when he declared that, "Our new Government is founded upon exactly the opposite idea; its foundations are laid, its corner stone rests upon the great truth that the negro is not equal to the white man; that slavery, subordination to the superior race, is his natural and normal condition."[42] What Stephens called "this great physical, philosophical and moral truth," continued to undergird the commitment of southern states to the divided system of racial segregation.

The forces that held this divided system in place were both religious and political. The myth of the Hamitic curse may have been gradually replaced by the scientist mythology of Social Darwinism; but the result was to reinforce the exclusion of blacks in the dominant religious worldview of American society. And the political pressures that eliminated blacks from the political life of America forced them to turn to the black churches as the major arena for political activities. Throughout their history, black churches were an important source of support and a central locus of social identity. They were centers of power in black social life. In the twentieth century they became more effective in directing that power into political action. New theological orientations needed to be developed in order to redefine black power in American society. At the turn of the century, Bishop Henry M. Turner suggested one direction these theological developments might take in declaring that "God is a Negro." He observed that "We have as much right biblically and otherwise to believe that God is a Negro, as you buckra or white people have to believe God is a fine looking, symmetrical and ornamented white man." Every race has tended to imagine its god in its own image; and Turner remarked that he did not believe "that there is any hope for a race of people who do not believe they look like God." He made the subtler theological point that God is beyond color, and might better be symbolized by the blue sky. But he would accept any symbolic representation of God rather than believe that God was white, because of the unacceptable social consequences. As long as blacks imagine God to be white, "the Negro will believe that the devil is black and that he (the Negro) bears no resemblance to Him, and the effects of such a sentiment is contemptuous and degrading, and one-half of the Negro race will be trying to get white and the other half will spend their days in trying to be the white men's scullions in order to please the whites."[43] For Bishop Turner, and many other black religious leaders, it did not make either theological or political sense for blacks to imagine God as white. Many of the issues that emerged in nineteenth-century struggles for religious and political power continued into the twentieth century, and a series of important movements were initiated to reconceptualize the sacred in such a way that its social consequences might result in greater power for black Americans.

BLACK POWER

The term *black power* focused a wide range of concerns for self-determination in the cultural, economic, and political spheres. It symbolized the new militancy of black leaders taking direct control over the social institutions that affect the lives of blacks in America. It was a symbolic catalyst for a new sense of pride, as well as a sense of fear and apprehension in many blacks and whites. The term was apparently first used by the Reverend Adam Clayton Powell in an address at Howard University in 1966. He declared: "Human rights are God-given. Civil rights are manmade . . . our life must be purposed to implement human rights . . . To demand these God-given rights is to seek black power—the power to build black institutions of splendid achievement."[44] Here again we find the assertion that human rights are sacred resources of God-given power, and civil rights are institutional arrangements of political power. The challenge of black power was to change manmade civil institutions of political life to give greater scope to the expression of human rights. The fact that this was fundamentally a religious challenge is reflected in the role that religious leaders, organizations, and movements played in the struggle for black power. Three major religiopolitical strategies were pursued—separation, integration, and liberation—and each served to redefine the religious and political role of blacks in American society.

Separation

The most important religious movements that encouraged the separation between whites and blacks as the only realistic means of achieving black political identity were based not in the Christian tradition, but in varieties of the religion of Islam. The attraction of Islam was its potential for providing a source and center for religious identity that was clearly outside the territorial boundaries of the United States. To turn to Mecca was to look beyond American political society for a tradition that transcended the immediate situation of racial discrimination in the U.S. Since many of the Africans taken into slavery had in fact been Muslims there was a historical precedent; but in the present context Islam promised a powerful sacred center "out there" with which American blacks could identify.

The earliest Islamic movement was started by a black from North Carolina, Timothy Drew. In 1913 he founded the first Moorish Science Temple of America in Newark, New Jersey; and soon other temples appeared in major urban areas. The founder changed his name to Noble Drew Ali, beginning a custom of relinquishing slave names for new Islamic names, and presented himself as a prophet similar not only to Muhammad, but also to Confucius, Buddha, and Jesus. His sixty-four page Holy Koran, which was identical to the Muslim sacred text in name only, was the basis for religious belief and practice in the Moorish Science movement. Although it was relatively short-lived, the Moorish Science Temple revealed something of the attraction of Islam for American blacks.

The most successful of the Islamic groups was the Nation of Islam, more commonly known as the Black Muslims. The Nation of Islam traced its origin to the appearance of a mysterious silk merchant from the Orient, W. D. Fard, who appeared in Detroit in the 1930s preaching an unusual form of Islamic doctrine. His teachings revolved around a mythic revelation of the pattern of history. It began with the creation of the original black human race 66 trillion years ago. Blacks lived in an earthly paradise until about 6,000 years ago when an evil black scientist, by the name of Yakub, began to perform genetic experiments by interbreeding lighter skinned blacks until he began producing lighter and lighter skin colors—

first brown, then red, then yellow. Finally he created a race of bleached out white devils, who were physically and mentally inferior. But these whites succeeded in conquering the other races. Their dominion over the earth continued until around 1914. That time marked the beginning of the end for white power, and soon there would be an apocalyptic battle between the forces of good (represented by all blacks) and evil (represented by all whites). It was revealed that the blacks would emerge victorious from this battle; but in the interim it was important for blacks to separate themselves from whites as much as possible in order not to get caught up in the destruction that was awaiting the white race.

One of Fard's earliest converts, Elijah Poole, soon took over the movement as Elijah Muhammad and the group expanded into centers in Detroit, Chicago, and Washington, D.C. Under Elijah Muhammad's leadership the doctrines of the Nation of Islam were developed. He emphasized that blacks were not Americans; nor were they Christians; rather, they were identified with the world-wide Muslim community, the nation of Islam. Christianity was perceived to be a white doctrine, designed to keep blacks inferior. It was the religion of the slave masters. Elijah Muhammad said, "You have made yourselves the most foolish people on earth by loving and following after the ways of the slave masters, whom Allah has revealed to me to be none other than real devils, and that their so-called Christianity is not His religion of Jesus or any other prophet of Allah."[45] Islam provided a source of religious identity that was outside of the religiopolitical system of white domination in America. And ultimately, all blacks must separate themselves from that system: "We believe this is the time in history for the separation of so-called Negroes and so-called white Americans."[46]

The Nation of Islam remained a fairly small movement until the mid-1950s when the former street hustler, con man, and convict, Malcolm X, became Elijah's chief minister and established mosques in every major city on the east coast. Malcolm was born Malcolm Little and grew up in the ghetto of Lansing, Michigan. His father was a Baptist minister, influenced by the Back to Africa movement of Marcus Garvey, and was killed by a white mob when Malcolm was six years of age. In prison, Malcolm converted to Islam, and began a program of self-education. By the time he was released in 1952 he could assume an active role in the leadership of the Black Muslim movement. Throughout the mid-fifties and into the early sixties Malcolm preached a message of black integrity, nationalism, and power through Islam. He linked Christianity with the powers of racial slavery in America. In one sermon he said:

> My brothers and sisters, our white slavemasters' Christian religion has taught us black people here in the wilderness of North America that we will sprout wings when we die and fly up into the sky where God will have for us a special place called heaven. This is the white man's Christian religion used

to *brainwash* us black people! We have *accepted* it! We have *believed* it! We have *practiced* it! And while we were doing all of that, for himself, this blue-eyed devil has *twisted* his Christianity, to keep his *foot* on our backs . . . to keep our eyes fixed on the pie in the sky and heaven in the hereafter . . . while *he* enjoys *his* heaven right here . . . on *this earth* . . . in *this* life.[47]

Christianity was seen to be deeply embedded in the white power structure that kept blacks in an inferior position. There was no hope of trying to integrate blacks into that structure. Not only was American Christianity designed to keep blacks in a passive and subservient condition, but American democracy had betrayed its own central political ideals in the vision of all men created equal. Malcolm declared: "Not only do I refuse to integrate with you, white man, but I demand that I be completely separated from you in some states of our own or back home in Africa; not only is your Christianity a fraud, but your 'democracy' a brittle lie."[48] From Malcolm's perspective this call for separation was not racism; it was a positive reaction against white racism. It was designed to intensify the awareness among blacks of their situation in America in the hope that this would produce a new power to be channeled constructively.

In 1964 Malcolm broke with Elijah Muhammad and began to form his own organizations. The first was an orthodox Islamic religious movement, Muslim Mosque, Inc.; and the second was a secular movement designed to achieve a greater unity between the 100 million blacks in the western hemisphere and the 300 million Africans by taking black control over educational, economic, political, and cultural institutions in the black community. Although these were intended to be two separate organizations, Malcolm perceived a spiritual connection between them. There was a necessary connection between religion and politics; as Malcolm observed, "The only true world solution today is governments guided by true religion—of the spirit. Here in race-torn America, I am convinced that the Islam religion is desperately needed, particularly by the American black man."[49] In 1964 Malcolm went on pilgrimage to Mecca and was deeply affected by what he saw as a spirit of brotherhood displayed by people of all colors within the religious community of Islam. A new spirit of universal human rights began to emerge in his sermons, and he as convinced that it was a mistake to give blanket indictments of all whites. But this was not to absolve what Malcolm saw as a political system that nurtured white racism. He began to suggest that "the white man is *not* inherently evil, but America's racist society influences him to act evilly. The society has produced and nourishes a psychology which brings out the lowest, most base part of human beings."[50] This was a departure from the basic Black Muslim mythological vision of the essential evilness of whites, and it represented a movement toward humanizing all people who were caught up in dehumanizing social systems. It is hard to say how Malcolm would have developed these new insights. In February, 1965, he was assassinated at a rally in a Harlem ballroom, by unknown assailants.

The Black Muslim movement continued as an important group in American society; but with the death of Elijah Muhammad in 1975, the organization became divided. One group, under the leadership of Louis Farrakhan, retained the name of Nation of Islam, and continued to give expression to the separatist message of Elijah Muhammad. But the main body of the movement followed his son, Wallace Deen Muhammad, into the American Muslim Mission. The new Imam, who changed his name to Warith Deen Muhammad, set the group on a course of identifying more closely with orthodox Islamic beliefs and practices, thereby abandoning much of the unique mythology of the Black Muslims, and, at the same time, identifying more closely with American society. The American flag was flown over Muslim schools, the pledge of allegiance was made before morning prayers, and the Imam hoped that those students would become integrated into the American civil process. "My greatest desire," he said, "is to one day hear that a Muslim, a real Muslim, a genuine Muslim from our community has become a governor, or senator, or head of some big corporation."[51] Warith Deen Muhammad anticipated that Islam would soon become the second largest faith in America, next to Christianity, and thereby alter the distribution of religiopolitical power from within American society.

Integration

This momentum for greater inclusion within the power structures of American society was also found in the campaigns for civil rights associated with Martin Luther King, Jr. King did not seek black separation from white society, but an equality of education, opportunity, and access to political power that would integrate blacks on an equal basis in American society. King came from a long line of Baptist preachers, and, after completing an education which included a doctoral degree from Boston University, he began his ministry in the Dexter Avenue Baptist Church in Montgomery, Alabama. Within a year of assuming that position he was involved in social actions that would have widespread political consequences. On December 1, 1955, the refusal of black seamstress Rosa M. Parks to give up her seat on a bus to a white male passenger set off the Montgomery bus boycott. King was elected president of the movement. The boycott exerted economic pressure on the municipality of Montgomery to desegregate public transportation. Similar efforts spread into sixty communities throughout the South. The attention directed to the issue resulted in a Supreme Court decision against racial segregation in public transport.

In 1957 the Southern Christian Leadership Conference was formed with King as its first president. It was formed to carry on the kind of nonviolent activism started in Montgomery against the divided system in the South. Some religious leaders were critical of the political programs under King's leadership, and felt that such social activism was in conflict with the other-worldly emphasis of Christianity. But King insisted that there was a necessary relationship between his Christian commitment and social action. "I see a necessary relationship," he said, "between the experience of Jesus and our present action. If one is devoted to Jesus they will seek to rid the world of social evils." For inspiration, King drew upon the Christian identification with the poor, meek, and oppressed in the Sermon on the Mount; and on the example of *satyagraha*, the "soul force" of nonviolent resistance to injustice in order to bring about social change practiced by Mahatma Gandhi. As King observed,

> When I went to Montgomery as a pastor, I had not the slightest idea that I would later become involved in a crisis in which nonviolent resistance would be applicable. I neither started the protest nor suggested it. I simply responded to the call of the people for a spokesman. When the protest began, my mind, consciously or unconsciously, was driven back to the Sermon on the Mount, with its sublime teaching on love, and to the Gandhian method of nonviolent resistance.[52]

The techniques he adapted from these two examples employed nonviolence as a tactical weapon as well as a deep moral commitment. Nonviolent civil disobedience was a strategy of creative tension, in which public opinion could be mobilized to change unjust laws. King would march thousands of unarmed men, women, and children into a hostile community, defy the local law, and create a dramatic tension between the marchers and the local authorities. When the authorities responded with violence, dogs, firehoses, arrests, or beatings, the marchers would refuse to retaliate or defend themselves. Perhaps the central ingredient in the tactical effectiveness of this strategy was the media. Through the involvement of mass media enraged public opinion would take form and demand basic social changes.

Between 1960 and 1965 King's influence was at its peak. He led sit-ins, protest marches, and demonstrations throughout the South; he was imprisoned in Atlanta and Birmingham, led an interracial assembly of more than 200,000 people in a march on Washington, and conducted a series of demonstrations that led to the passing of the Voting Rights Act in 1965. Through all this social activism King maintained a focus upon the ideals of love and nonviolence. The ideal of love was expressed in his refusal to dehumanize the enemy and the suggestion that whoever dehumanizes someone else has failed in a fundamental way to be human. He saw his political strategy flowing directly from a Christian commitment to love:

> Love your enemies .... Let no man pull you so low as to make you hate him .... If you will protest courageously, and yet with dignity and Christian

love, when the history books are written in future generations, the historians will have to pause to say "There lived a great people—a black people—who injected new meaning and dignity into the veins of civilization." That is our challenge and our overwhelming responsibility.[53]

The ideal of nonviolence was expressed in the appeal to human moral conscience to effect social changes. For King, this was the source of spiritual strength. "Nonviolence is not a symbol of weakness or cowardice," he insisted, "but as Jesus demonstrated, nonviolent resistance transforms weakness into strength and breeds courage in the face of danger."[54]

King's strategy was a program for political action that drew upon deep religious resources in the black community and sought to awaken the sleeping conscience of the American public. As Lerone Bennett observed, "the peculiar genius of Martin Luther King is that he was able to translate religious fervor into social action, thereby creating political leadership under the rubric of his religious ministry."[55] This marriage of religion and politics was directed into social activism to achieve an equal access to power for blacks in American society. In this respect, Martin Luther King appeared as a prophet of American civil religion; or, as Gayraud Wilmore has put it, "the high priest of the religion of civil rights."[56] King's vision of equal civil rights was a dream of an America true to its own highest aspirations, an America that was able to solve its most disturbing internal dilemma by conforming its behavior to its own ideals. In his speech on the steps of the Lincoln Memorial, at the march on Washington in 1963, he called for continuing efforts to realize this American dream.

> There will be neither rest nor tranquility in America until the Negro is granted his citizenship rights. The whirlwinds of revolt will continue to shake the foundations of our nation until the bright day of justice emerges . . . I have a dream that one day this nation will rise up and live out the true meaning of its creed: "We hold these truths to be self-evident, that all men are created equal."[57]

By the mid-sixties, King's leadership began to be questioned by a younger, more militant generation of black leaders. The Student Nonviolent Coordinating Committee (SNCC), originally loyal to King, came under the direction of Stokely Carmichael and H. Rap Brown. Under the slogan, "Black Power," they supported a more aggressive campaign for political power. King encouraged them to give up this slogan. "It is absolutely necessary," he argued, "for the Negro to gain power, but the term Black Power is unfortunate because it tends to give the impression of black nationalism."[58] But this was exactly the course that more militant leaders wanted to pursue, and, as Stokely Carmichael responded, "the question of violence versus nonviolence was irrelevant. The real question was the need for black people to consolidate their political and economic resources to achieve power."[59] While King's authority was waning with the younger leadership, he experienced frustration after 1965 in trying to take his campaign to the industrial centers of the North. In 1968 he was planning a poor peoples' march on Washington, but interrupted his plans to go to Memphis to support a garbage workers' strike. There on April 4, 1968 he was killed by a sniper's bullet. In his last speech, King expressed the religious vision that had motivated his political action. He said: "It really doesn't matter with me now, because I've been to the mountaintop . . . I may not get to the promised land with you, but I want you to know tonight that we as a people will."[60]

King's efforts did result in important political changes in American society. They contributed to the breakdown of the divided system in the South and led to a greater involvement of blacks in the political process. In the state of Mississippi, for example, black voter registration went up from 8 percent in 1965 to 59 percent in 1968; and black elected officials in the country increased from 72 in 1965 to 461 in 1968.[61] And yet it would be hard to say that King's dream of equality has been realized. In 1983, only 1 percent of all elected officials in the United States were black; average black income was 56 percent of white income, which was down from a peak of 61 percent in 1970; and whereas 74 percent of black men over age 16 were employed in 1960, the figure in 1983 was around 55 percent.[62] This suggests that the American dilemma remains a persistent fact of life in American society, and that Martin Luther King's dream of an integrated promised land, where blacks have equal access to power, is yet to be achieved.

Liberation

A third religious response to this situation took the form of Christian theologies of liberation that identified Christianity with the black struggle for freedom from oppression. Blacks in America were perceived to be in a state of bondage, and God was present in their struggle for liberation. The National Committee of Negro Churchmen published a statement, entitled "Black Power," in the *New York Times* in 1966. They described the imbalance between conscience and power in American society: Whites got what they wanted through power; but blacks, following the kind of example set by Martin Luther King, could make their appeals only through conscience. As the situation existed, blacks could achieve their goals only if they awakened white conscience to make changes in an oppressive system. And, as the article suggested, "we are faced now with a situation where conscienceless power meets powerless conscience, threatening the very foundations of our nation."[63] Blacks had to consolidate their power, to coordinate their efforts in assuming control over their social, economic and political lives. Behind this new power was a sense of religious vocation. As the National Committee put it in 1969, "We believe it is God . . . who has chosen black humanity as a vanguard to resist the demonic powers of racism, capitalism and imperialism, and to so reform the structures of this world that they will more perfectly minister to the peace and power of all people as children of God and brothers of one another."[64] This vocation was the center of a redemptive process in which God had chosen black people to play a special role in human history. God had entered into a special covenant with blacks, analogous to the covenant relationship between God and the nation of Israel in the Hebrew Bible, to work toward their release from the bondage of captivity. The liberation of black people would play a central role in the liberation of all people from oppressive social structures.

The most articulate spokesman for a black theology of liberation has been James H. Cone, professor of theology at Union Theological Seminary in New York. Beginning in 1969, he produced a series of books of black theology which maintained that since Christianity was a religion of liberation, it must become a black theology identified with the lives, conditions, and conflicts of the oppressed. Any theology, according to Cone, which was not oriented toward the liberation of the oppressed was not a legitimate Christian theology. The goal of such a Christian theology was "to analyze the nature of the gospel of Jesus Christ in the light of the oppressed black people so they will see the gospel as inseparable from their humiliated condition, bestowing on them the necessary power to break the chains of oppression."[65] The God of a black theology of liberation must be black, as Cone insisted, for "either God is identified with the oppressed to the point that their experience becomes His or He is a God of racism."[66] God was identified with the struggles of oppressed people, present with them in their bondage, and working for their liberation. This suggested a source of spiritual power available to blacks in their struggle for political power. It was a religious dimension grounded in the immediate experience of the black community. "This means," according to Cone, "that it is a theology of and for the black community, seeking to interpret the religious dimensions of the forces of liberation in that community."[67] It also held, however, the potential for whites to liberate themselves from their own oppressive social structures. Whites could become involved in the religious work of liberation. For whites to receive this revelation of God's identification with blacks, Cone suggested, "is to become black with him by joining him in his work of liberation."[68]

A black theology that awakens the power necessary to break the chains of oppression almost advocates using any power to achieve this goal. Cone, and other liberation theologians, did not necessarily reject the use of violence in the pursuit of black power. They perceived their situation to be already violent: a condition of institutional, structural, or systemic violence where an entire class of people was forced into an inferior social position. The violence inherent in the subclassification of a race may be even more pervasive and dehumanizing than overt acts of violence against individuals. Where nonviolent appeals to conscience had been exhausted, many black liberation theologians advocated whatever means may be necessary "to remove the structures of white power which hover over their being."[69] A spirit of revolutionary black nationalism pervaded much of this literature. A theologian such as Albert Cleage saw the sources for a revolutionary black liberation movement in the example of Christ. He argued on historical grounds that Jesus was a black nationalist messiah, a "nonwhite leader of a nonwhite people struggling for national liberation against the rule of a white nation, Rome."[70] The spirit of this Black Messiah was present in the struggles of blacks for their liberation in the contemporary era. And, Cleage maintained, revolutionary black nationalism was inspired by the presence of Christ in their conflicts. "I believe," he declared, "that the revolutionary spirit of God, embodied in the Black Messiah, is born anew in each generation and that Black Christian Nationalists constitute the living remnant of God's Chosen People in this day, and are charged with responsibility for the Liberation of Black People."[71] These theologies of liberation left open the possibilites for the future distribution of power in American society; they tended not to specify separation or integration as the ultimate outcome of the struggle. Rather, they were concerned with the more immediate conditions of oppression in American society, and the religious power derived from a God that identified with their condition and worked to break the political bonds that held them in captivity.

These three black responses to the dominant religiopolitical system of American society—separation, integration, and liberation—have had a long history in black and white relations in America. They continue to provide three basic types of religious resources for meaning, identity, and power in black experience. Throughout American history they have represented powerful critiques of dominant white power structures; but, more fundamentally, they have indicted America for its failures to live up to its highest ideals. The dilemma of equality, embodied in the Declaration of Independence, has challenged white Americans to respond to *difference* in a common human community. The dominant political strategy has been one of exclusion. Religion has served as a powerful institutional legitimation for the exclusion of otherness from American society. Black religious movements have refused to accept the legitimacy of this exclusion, and they have sought to work out a variety of self-definitions of black identity that would affirm its basic integrity. The presence of these alternative identities in American society has also provided a valuable opportunity for whites to enter into an experience of otherness that could broaden and enhance their experience of what it means to be human. As Charles Long has noted, "We are not Western in the same way as our compatriots, and thus we afford within America an entree to the *otherness* of America and the otherness of mankind."[72] Black religious movements have helped clarify what it means to be *other* in American society, and thereby provide an important foundation upon which a more inclusive structure of American identity might be built.

NOTES

1. JOHN LOCKE, *Two Treatises of Government*; cited in David Brion Davis, *The Problem of Slavery in Western Culture* (Ithaca, New York: Cornell University Press, 1966):119–20.
2. C. ERIC LINCOLN, *Race, Religion, and the Continuing American Dilemma* (New York: Hill and Wang, 1984): xiv; see Gunnar Myrdal, *The American Dilemma* (New York: Harper, 1944).
3. On African religion, see Benjamin C. Ray, *African Religions: Symbol, Ritual, and Community* (Englewood Cliffs, New Jersey: Prentice-Hall, 1976); Geoffrey Parrinder, *West African Religions*, 2nd rev. ed. (London: Epworth Press, 1961); John S. Mbiti, *Concepts of God in Africa* (New York: Praeger, 1970); M. Fortes and G. Dieterlen, eds., *African Systems of Thought* (London: Oxford University Press, 1965).
4. THOMAS VIRGIL PETERSON, *Ham and Japheth: The Mythic World of Whites in the Antebellum South* (Metuchen, New Jersey: Scarecrow Press, 1978); Donald G. Mathews, *Religion in the Old South* (Chicago: University of Chicago Press, 1977); H. Shelton Smith, *In His Image, But . . . ; Racism in Southern Religion, 1780–1910* (Durham, North Carolina: Duke University Press, 1972): 130–2, 152–3; George M. Frederickson has suggested that the Hamitic hypothesis was used less frequently than other arguments for slavery and racial inferiority. See his *The Black Image in the White Mind: The Debate on Afro-American Character and Destiny, 1817–1914* (New York: Harper and Row, 1971).
5. WINTHROP D. JORDAN, *White Over Black: American Attitudes Toward the Negro* (Chapel Hill: University of North Carolina Press, 1968): 96–7).
6. JOSEPH C. CARROLL, *Slave Insurrections in the United States, 1800–1865* (Boston: Chapman and Grimes, 1938): 14; Herbert Aptheker, *American Negro Slave Revolts* (New York: International Publishers, 1965): 166.
7. BENJAMIN BRAWLEY, *A Social History of the American Negro* (New York: Macmillan, 1921): 36–40.
8. GAYRAUD S. WILMORE, *Black Religion and Black Radicalism*, 2nd ed. (Maryknoll: Orbis Books, 1983): 25.
9. JORDAN, *White Over Black*, 191; see Lester B. Scherer, *Slavery and the Churches in Early America, 1619–1819* (Grand Rapids, MI: Eerdmans, 1975).
10. Cited in Albert J. Raboteau, *Slave Religion: The 'Invisible Institution' in the Antebellum South* (New York: Oxford University Press, 1978): 162–3.
11. The argument for continuity between African traditions and the religiocultural life of Black Americans was made by Melville J. Herskovits, *The Myth of the Negro Past* (Boston: Beacon Press, 1958); The contrary argument, that there was a major disruption of the African way of life in America, was pursued by E. Franklin Frazier, *The Negro Church in America* (New York: Schocken Books, 1964); Raboteau recognizes the weight of Frazier's objections to Herskovitz, but observes that "nevertheless, even as the gods of Africa gave way to the God of Christianity, the African heritage of singing, dancing, spirit possession, and magic continued to influence Afro-American spirituals, ring shouts, and folk beliefs." *Slave Religion*, 92.
12. C. ERIC LINCOLN, *Race, Religion, and the Continuing American Dilemma*: 48.
13. LORENZO J. GREENE, *The Negro in Colonial New England* (New York: Atheneum, 1968): 276.
14. CHARLES H. WESLEY, *Richard Allen, Apostle of Freedom* (Washington, D.C.: Associated Publishers, 1969): 52–3.
15. On the formation of independent black denominations, see Harry V. Richardson, *Dark Salvation* (New York: Anchor/Doubleday, 1976).
16. CHARLES COLCOCK JONES, *Religious Instruction of the Negroes in the United States* (Savannah, GA: T. Purse Co., 1842); cited in Raboteau, *Slave Religion*: 137.
17. See Carrol, *Slave Insurrections in the United States*, 49–74; Aptheker, *American Negro Slave Revolts*, 226–61; Gerald W. Mullin, *Flight and Rebellion in Eighteenth-Century Virginia* (New York: Oxford University Press, 1972); 150–160.

18. JOHN LOFTEN, *Insurrection in South Carolina*)Yellow Springs, Ohio: Antioch Press, 1964); John O. Killens, ed., *The Trial Record of Denmark Vesey* (Boston: Beacon Press, 1970); Robert Starobin, "Denmark Vesey's Slave Conspiracy of 1822: A Study in Rebellion and Repression," in *American Slavery: The Question of Resistance*, eds., John Bracey, et al. (Belmont, California: Wadsworth Publishing Company, 1970): 142−57.

19. HENRY IRVING TRAGLE, *The Southampton Slave Revolt of 1831: A Compilation of Source Material* (Amherst: University of Massachusetts Press, 1971); Herbert Aptheker, *Nat Turner's Slave Rebellion* (New York: Humanities Press, 1966); F. Roy Johnson, *The Nat Turner Insurrection* (Murfreesboro, North Carolina: Johnson Publishing Col., 1966); Stepahn B. Oates, The Fires of Jubilee: Nat Turner's Fierce Rebellion (New York: Harper and Row, 1975).

20. W.E.B. DU BOIS, *The Negro Church* (Atlanta: Atlanta University Press, 1903): 25−6.

21. CHARLES COLCOCK JONES, *The Religious Instruction of Negroes in the United States:* 126.

22. HOWARD BROTZ, ed., *Negro Social and Political Thought, 1850−1900: Representative Texts* (New York: Basic Books, 1966): 121−2.

23. RABOTEAU, *Slave Religion:* 318.

24. Cited in George M. Frederickson, *White Supremacy. A Comparative Study in American and South African History* (New York and Oxford: Oxford University Press, 1981): 73.

25. COTTON MATHER, *The Negro Christianized? An Essay to Excite and Assist that Good Work, the Instruction of Negro Servants in Christianity* (Boston, 1706): 4−6.

26. THOMAS SECKER, *Sermon before the S.P.G.*, 1740; cited in Frank J. Klinberg, *Anglican Humanitarianism in Colonial New York* (Philadelphia: The Church Historical Society, 1940): 223.

27. JOHN CODMAN HURD, *The Law of Freedom and Bondage in the United States* (1858; New York: Negro Universities Press, 1968): I:232.

28. ADRIENE KOCH and WILLIAM PEDEN, eds., *The Life and Selected Writings of Thomas Jefferson* (New York: The Modern Library, 1944): 261; See John Chester Miller, *The Wolf by the Ears: Thomas Jefferson and Slavery* (New York: Free Press, 1977); and David Brion Davis, *The Problem of Slavery in the Age of Revolution, 1770−1823* (Ithaca, New York: Cornell University Press, 1975).

29. See Jordan, *White Over Black;* 542−82.

30. ROY P. BASLER, ed., *The Collected Works of Abraham Lincoln* (New Brunswick, New Jersey: Rutgers University Press, 1953): II:245.

31. *Ibid.*, II:255−6.

32. *Ibid.*, II: 409; see Benjamin Quarles, *Lincoln and the Negro* (new York: Oxford University Press, 1962): 115−17.

33. BASLER, ed., *The Collected Works of Abraham Lincoln*, V:370−75.

34. MARTIN R. DELANY, *The Condition, Elevation, Emigration and Destiny of the Colored People of the United States* (Philadelphia, 1852); cited in Theodore Draper, *The Rediscovery of Black Nationalism* (London: Secker and Warburg, 1969): 23−4; See Victor Ullman, *Martin R. Delany: The Beginnings of Black Nationalism* (Boston: Beacon Press, 1971).

35. DANIEL COKER, *Journal of Daniel Coker* (Baltimore: Press of Edward J. Coate, 1820); cited in John H. Bracey, Jr., August Meier, and Elliott Rudwick, *Black Nationalism in America* (Indianapolis: Bobbs-Merrill, 1970): 47.

36. BROTZ, ed., *Negro Social and Political Thought:* 176.

37. BRACEY et al., *Black Nationalism in America:* 172−3; Henry M. Turner, "The Races Must Separate," in: *The Possibilities of the Negro: In Symposium*, ed. Willis B. Parks (Atlanta: Franklin Co., 1904): 91−2; see Edwin S. Redkey, *Black Exodus: Black Nationalist and Back to Africa Movements, 1890−1910* (New Haven: Yale University Press, 1969); and Walter L. Williams, *Black Americans and the Evangelization of Africa, 1877−1900* (Madison: University of Wisconsin Press, 1982).

38. WILMORE, *Black Religion and Black Radicalism:* 102−3.

39. DRAPER, *The Rediscovery of Black Nationalism:* 19−20.

40. FRANK A. ROLLIN, *Life and Public Services of Martin R. Delany* (Boston: Lee and Shepherd, 1868): 279.

41. J.R. POLE, *The Pursuit of Equality in American History* (Berkeley: University of California Press, 1978): 182; See E. Morgan Kousser, *The Shaping of Southern Politics* (New Haven: Yale University Press, 1975).

42. Cited in James M. McPherson, *Struggle for Equality: Abolitionists and the Negro in the Civil War and Reconstruction* (Princeton: Princeton University Press, 1964): 61.
43. *The Voice of Missions*, February 1, 1898; cited in Bracey, et al., *Black Nationalism in America*: 154.
44. CHUCK STONE, "The National Conference on Black Power," in *The Black Power Revolt*, ed. Floyd B. Barbour (Boston: Porter Sargent, 1968): 189.
45. MR. MUHAMMED SPEAKS, May 2, 1959; cited in Wilmore, *Black Religion and Black Nationalism*: 173; see C. Eric Lincoln, *The Black Muslims in America*, rev. ed. (Westport, Conn.: Greenwood Press, 1982).
46. Cited in Alphonso Pinkney, *Red, Black, and Green: Black Nationalism in the United States* (Cambridge: Cambridge University Press, 1976): 157.
47. MALCOLM X, *The Autobiography of Malcolm X* (New York: Grove Press, 1964): 200–201; see John Henrik Clarke, ed., *Malcolm X: The Man and His Times* (New York: Macmillan, 1969).
48. Cited in PINKNEY, *Red, Black, and Green*: 67.
49. MALCOLM X, *Autobiography*: 369.
50. *Ibid.*: 377; see George Breitman, *The Last Year of Malcolm X* (New York: Schocken Books, 1967).
51. Cited in Lincoln, *Race, Religion, and the Continuing American Dilemma*: 167.
52. MARTIN LUTHER KING, JR., *Stride Toward Freedom* (New York: Harper, 1958): 101.
53. LERONE BENNETT, JR., *What Manner of Man?* (Chicago: Johnson Publishing Col., 1962): 66.
54. *Ibid.*: 82.
55. Cited in Wilmore, *Black Religion and Black Radicalism*: 174; see C. Eric Lincoln, ed., *Martin Luther King, Jr., A Profile* (New York: Hill and Wang, 1970); David L. Lewis, *King: A Critical Biography* (Baltimore: Penguin, 1970); Stephan Oates, *Let the Trumpet Sound: The Life of Martin Luther King* (New York: Harper, 1982); and Kenneth L. Smith and Ira G. Zepp, Jr., *Search for the Beloved Community: The Thinking of Martin Luther King., Jr.* (Valley Forge, Pennsylvania: Judson Press, 1974).
56. WILMORE, *Black Religion and Black Radicalism*, 182.
57. Cited in Robert A. Spivey, EDWIN S. GAUSTAD, and RODNEY F. ALLEN, eds., *Religious Issues in American Culture* (Menlo Park, California: Addison-Wesley Publishing Co., 1972): 78.
58. Cited in C. Nathan Wright, Jr., *Black Power and Urban Unrest* (New York: Hawthorne, 1967): coverflap.
59. MARTIN LUTHER KING, JR., *Where Do We Go From Here: Chaos or Community?* (New York: Harper and Row, 1967): 30; see Stokely Carmichael and Charles V. Hamilton, *Black Power: The Politics of Liberation in America* (New York: Random House, 1967).
60. Cited in Lerone Bennett, Jr., *What Manner of Man?* (Chicago: Johnson Publishing Co., 1968): 240.
61. DRAPER, *The Rediscovery of Black Nationalism*: 141.
62. LINCOLN, *Race, Religion, and the Continuing American Dilemma*: 10.
63. Cited in Pinkney, *Red, Black, and Green*: 165.
64. *Ibid.*: 167.
65. JAMES H. CONE, *A Black Theology of Liberation* (Philadelphia: Lippincott, 1970): 23.
66. *Ibid.*: 120–1.
67. *Ibid.*: 23.
68. *Ibid.*: 125.
69. JAMES H. CONE, *Black Therology and Black Power* (New York: Seabury, 1969): 118.
70. ALBERT CLEAGE, JR., *The Black Messiah* (New York: Sheed and Ward, 1968): 3.
71. ALBERT CLEAGE, JR., *Black Christian Nationalism* (New York: Morrow, 1972): xiii.
72. CHARLES H. LONG, "The Black Reality: Toward a Theology of Freedom," *Criterion* (September, 1969); cited in Wilmore *Black Religion and Black Radicalism*: 239.

CHAPTER SIX
IMMIGRANT AMERICANS

In its provisions for the separation between church and state, the First Amendment to the United States Constitution opened a space in American society for the proliferation of many different religious groups. Since the government was pledged to refrain from establishing one religious group, it allowed for the flourishing of many. The disestablishment of religion in American society was accompanied by two basic patterns of social organization in American religious groups. First was the *denominational pattern of organization*. Whereas a state church (which was the dominant organizational pattern in Europe during the colonial period) claimed an absolute monopoly on religious truth, maintained a broad, all-inclusive definition of membership, and was closely aligned with the political interests of the state, the denomination was more tolerant of other religious groups, placed more open requirements on membership, and was by definition separate from the state.[1] The American churches followed this denominational pattern. Not one of the major Protestant denominations—Congregational, Presbyterian, Anglican, Methodist, or Baptist—was strong enough to achieve a position of dominance in the early republic; so, in order to insure its own survival, each agreed to tolerate and guarantee the protection of the others.

The second major characteristic of the social organization of American religious groups was the *voluntary pattern of association*. Americans were free to affiliate with the religious groups of their choice. Association with a religious body was not imposed by the state. Americans could choose to join a religious group, leave it, or affiliate with no religious organization. This voluntary principle replaced the coercion of an established state church with the individual right of voluntary assent, and that assent was sought by the persuasive appeals of the various religious groups. After the last establishment was dropped from state constitutions, religious groups that made persuasive appeals for voluntary conversion—Baptists and Methodists—rapidly became the largest Protestant denominations in the United States.

These characteristics of denominational organization and voluntary association, supported by the separation of church and state in the United States Constitution, liberated religious groups from the coercive power of the state. But this wall that prevented the state from exerting coercive power over religion also isolated religion as a separate institution which would have no direct impact on the political affairs of the state. This differentiation of religion as a separate institution, alongside political, legal, economic, educational, medical, and other social institutions, was part of a larger process that we may refer to as secularization. To isolate religion was to open a large sphere of human activities that could be conducted independently without any direct reference to the sacred power invested in religion. This modern, secular arrangement contrasted dramatically with traditional distributions of religiopolitical power. We have seen how this separation of church and state, and the insistence on the independent status of the secular sphere in political life, was a central concern of the political theorists who shaped the United States Constitution. As enlightened rationalists, they feared the tyranny of established religious authority over the political lives of individuals. This was a development, however, that was also consistent with the fundamental Protestant rejection of the political authority of Pope, Church, and hierarchy in the Reformation. Separation of church and state could be easily reconciled with Protestant theology; but it was a strange, foreign, and incongruous arrangement for the Roman Catholic and Jewish traditions that continued to maintain a closer interrelation between religious and political authority in every aspect of the social life of their communities.

When the First Amendment was drafted, the religious character of American society was predominantly Protestant. Religious liberty could be guaranteed with the comfortable assumption that it would only allow for the freedom of individual choice among Protestant denominations; and the same assumption could also stand behind the prohibition of religious tests that might exclude members of some denominations from holding public office. But this Protestant, and largely Anglo-Saxon, dominance was dramatically altered by waves of immigrants coming to North America and bringing with them foreign languages, ethnic identities, cultural heritages, and religious traditions that appeared as fundamentally *other* in

American society. In a profound sense, America is a nation of immigrants. The Statue of Liberty, dedicated in 1886, bears on its base the words of the Jewish poet, Emma Lazarus, opening the golden door of America to the world:

> Give me your tired, your poor,
> Your huddled masses yearning to breathe free,
> The wretched refuse of your teeming shore,
> Send these, the homeless, tempest-tost to me . . .

Here is a powerful image of an open, inclusive, and free America welcoming the cultural diversity of immigrants with open arms. But there were Americans who rejected this image. Nineteenth-century immigration to America generated a Protestant backlash that took the form of a new nativism in American society. Nativist movements, advocating a closed, exclusive, and essentially Protestant vision of America, arose in the 1840s, 1880s and 1930s in response to the perceived religiopolitical dangers of immigrant Americans. The nineteenth-century nativist movements were ardently anti-Catholic; but the movements of the twentieth century began to focus their attacks on Jews.

The essential vision of American identity was at stake in these conflicts. Was the distribution of religiopolitical power in America to be open or closed? Inclusive or exclusive? An exclusive distribution of power would draw the boundaries very tightly around white, Anglo-Saxon, Protestant identity. As this American looked within these boundaries its vision would be conditioned by *ethnocentricism*; as it looked without, it would be motivated by *xenophobia*. Ethnocentricism rejoices in the preservation of particular cultural traits, while xenophobia is the fear of foreign elements. They are the centripetal and centrifugal forces of an exclusive distribution of power. But an inclusive distribution of power would open those boundaries to the world. It would encourage difference, diversity, and variety, affirming the irreducible integrity of otherness. The term for this is *pluralism*. Wilbur Katz has described the significance of pluralism for religion in an open society. "A religiously pluralistic society," he observed, "is one in which principal religious groups not only claim freedom for themselves, but affirm equal freedom for others, whatever their beliefs may be. Individuals are free to doubt or to believe. The model pluralism is also one in which there is a sensitizing to the differing needs of various groups and a disposition to accommodate these needs."[2]

The accommodation of different religious *groups* in America was the central religious problem posed by immigration. It was one thing to accommodate individuals, another to embrace a pluralism of groups with competing interests. The predominantly Protestant Americans of English origin could dream of an American melting pot that would reshape individuals from different cultural backgrounds into a common, shared

American identity. Immigrants could also nurture this American dream. Crèvecoeur could speak in 1782 of the process by which immigrants were able to *melt* into new men in America; and over a century later Israel Zangwill could declare that "all the races of Europe are melting and re-forming . . . God is making the American."[3]

But some did not want to be so reshaped; while others were not allowed this opportunity. The central challenge of pluralism for American Protestants was the need to accommodate in a plural society the irre-ducible interests of different ethnic and religious groups. The dominant strategy of accommodation has been the absorption of divergent religious groups into the denominational pattern of American religion. In this sense, Catholics and Jews in particular have registered in the American public arena as denominations alongside Protestants, and as voluntary associations with which Americans may freely affiliate. But this process of accommodation has worked both ways, and in order to appear as denomi-nations in American society both Catholics and Jews have been under pressures to conform their patterns of religious belief, practice, and asso-ciation to the dominant Protestant model. This has required each particu-lar tradition to adapt to a distinctive American style, to conform their particular interests to the democratic religiopolitical system of American society. But it also has involved a sacrifice of their most particular, exclu-sive, and even tribal claims to absolute truth.

J. Milton Yinger noted the social pressures on the three major American religious communities. "It is dysfunctional," he pointed out, "in a mobile and diverse society to have a group of religions, each of which claims some kind of ultimate superiority; the elements of Protestantism, Catholicism, and Judaism which sponsor such claims are disruptive. Claims by Protestants that the Bible is the final and literal truth, by Catho-lics that theirs is the only true church, by Jews that they are the chosen people, can only exacerbate the divisions of a society."[4] In order to achieve a greater functional harmony in American society, the price of accommodation for each of these groups has been a certain modification of their most central truth claims. They may continue to hold them in pri-vate; but the necessary political consequences of these claims must be kept out of the public sphere. An absolute claim to truth in theory must give way to a spirit of mutual acceptance in practice. "The constant interaction of people with different national and religious backgrounds," Yinger con-cluded, "makes tolerance as the minimum degree of accommodation a vital necessity."[5]

The result of this religiopolitical compromise in the plural society of America was the emergence of what Will Herberg called, in 1955, the "triple melting pot" of American religion. Americans identified them-selves as Protestants, Catholics, or Jews; but each of these affiliations had been tempered in the American context by a uniquely American way of life, which served as "the characteristic American religion, undergirding life and overarching American society despite indubitable differences of religion, section, culture and class."[6] The three faith communities were American Protestants, American Catholics, and American Jews, and the adjective before each indicated that while there may have been private religious differences among them, these differences were dissolved through the religious and political values of a common civil religion. It will be important to examine the religious and political conflicts that divided American society before this compromise was achieved. Various nativist movements indicate the extent to which Protestant Americans could perceive different religious traditions as direct political threats to American society. Following this, we will need to look more closely at what religious traditions in America have sacrificed in order to enter into the spirit of toleration demanded in a plural society.

CATHOLICS AND JEWS

History is not simply a catalogue of events. The telling of a historical narrative invests the recounting of events with a particular meaning, by selecting certain events as important, emphasizing some events over others, and organizing them in a particular pattern. American religious history has traditionally been informed by the interests of a Protestant majority; it begins with the Pilgrims and Puritans of Massachusetts and then moves west with the progress of the nation. But what if we retold the story of American religious history beginning in California? We would certainly begin with the religions of the Native Americans, but the first actors in the European drama would be the Russian Orthodox settlers in the Fort Ross area, and the Spanish Franciscans who eventually built the missions along the California coast. By the time we got to the east coast Protestants they might appear very foreign, strange, and different in the context of such a history. And yet the way the story is usually told, the Protestant hegemony over American religion and politics sets the norm for the historical record.

From the very earliest settlements on the east coast there was a Catholic and Jewish presence in America. Catholics found a haven from Protestant persecution in Maryland from 1632, and there were communities in Pennsylvania and New York. They presented a minority religious presence in early America, and, as Sidney Ahlstrom has observed, "outside of these three areas the colonial history of the Roman Catholic Church is almost nonexistent."[7] The earliest Jewish settlers had escaped from a Dutch colony in eastern Brazil when it was recaptured by the Portuguese in 1654. Jews had been driven from Spain in 1492, and from Portugal in 1496, and were subject to persecution in the imperial domains of both countries. Some came to New Amsterdam, the Dutch settlement that was later to become New York, and by the end of the seventeenth century this

Portuguese-speaking group had formed the first congregation, *Shearith Israel* (Remnant of Israel). Both the Catholic and Jewish communities have flourished in America. But from the perspective of the dominant Protestant majority in American history, they have been characterized by their separateness, their apartness, their otherness. As William Clebsch observed, "In a certain sense the history of Catholics and the history of Jews in America arise precisely as these people are viewed apart from their involvement in American society."[8] They have been dynamic elements in American society (particularly after the nineteenth-century immigrations changed the demographic distribution of religious affiliation in America) and important ingredients in shaping the plural society that emerged.

The Maryland settlement in 1632 was a royal bequest to Lord Baltimore, who as a Catholic allowed for the creation of a colony that would become a refuge for Catholics from the restrictive laws in England. The Catholics were, nevertheless, conscious of being a religious minority in the English Protestant colonies, and were careful not to give political offense to the dominant Protestant public through their religious practices. The instructions to governors of Maryland exhorted them to see that Catholics "suffer no scandal nor offense to be given to any of the Protestants, whereby any just complaint may hereafter be made."[9] Although Maryland governors allowed for religious liberty in the colony, they encouraged Roman Catholics to worship "as privately as may be," and not discuss religious matters in public. This division between private and public spheres was a compromise that all minority religious groups have been pressured to make in Protestant America. Rather than being a natural, internal development of Catholic religious thought (which has tended to see both the private and public lives of Catholics under the authority of the Church), this privatization of religious practice adapted to the dominant Protestant presence in the colonies.

This privatization of religion had political consequences in one of the first legal enactments of religious liberty in the colonies. The Maryland Act Concerning Religion (1649) specified the death penalty for anyone who would deny the Trinity, and punishments for blasphemy or violating the Sabbath; but it also legislated that no one (who believed in Jesus Christ) would be persecuted for the free exercise of religion and that no one would be compelled to practice a certain religion against his or her consent.[10] This situation changed in Maryland when it was absorbed into the system of Crown colonies in 1691, and the Church of England was established in 1692. The Catholic community continued to grow, however, and eventually Baltimore became the center of the Catholic Church in America. New York maintained a policy of religious liberty for Catholics, and there was a series of Catholic governors until, again in 1691, New York became a Crown colony. This led to a set of restrictions on Roman Catholic liberties: Catholics were denied the right to vote or to hold office, and Jesuit missionaries and Roman Catholic priests were excluded from the colony. Pennsylvania remained an exception to this legal persecution of Catholics in the colonies, but in 1705 it was forced to uphold laws against Catholics voting or holding office.

Catholics remained a very small proportion of the American population. Even in Maryland they accounted for only about 10 percent. By 1790 there were approximately 30,000 Catholics in the new nation out of a population of about three million. The United States Constitution had eliminated religious tests for holding public office on the national level; but states were still free to enforce restrictions on the political participation of Catholics in state politics. There were no restrictions placed on immigration, however, and by 1850 the number of Catholics had increased to approximately one million, and made up the largest single religious body in the United States.

This first wave of Catholic immigrants was primarily from Ireland, but also from Germany. This was a church of immigrants. The American Catholic Church hierarchy in 1852 had six foreign-born archbishops and seventeen foreign-born bishops; there were no American-born archbishops and only nine American-born bishops in positions of authority within the American Church. The second wave of immigration between 1880 and 1900 saw an increase in the Roman Catholic population from around 6 million to over 10 million. Protestants, as a whole, still held a majority with nearly 18 million; but the Protestant denominational system divided that number into smaller religious bodies. The largest Protestant denomination at the turn of the century, the Methodists, accounted for about 6 million. Some sense of the divisions in the Protestant community is given by the fact that the major denominations—Methodist, Baptist, Presbyterian, Lutheran, and Congregationalist—accounted for a little over half of the total number of Protestants in America. The Protestant tendency to decentralize religious authority through the proliferation of different denominations contrasted with the centralized authority of the Roman Catholic community within the structure of a single church hierarchy. By the turn of the century the Church had increased its status in America with the founding of a pontifical university in Washington, D.C., the appointment of an American Cardinal, and the sending of a papal delegation to the United States.

Catholics in America enjoyed considerable religious freedom. John Carroll, the first American bishop in the United States, wrote in praise of the tolerant conditions in American society. "The fullest and largest system of toleration," he said, "is adopted in almost all of the American states; public protection and encouragement are extended alike to all denominations; and Roman Catholics are members of Congress, assemblies, and hold civil and military posts as well as others."[11] The Pastoral Letter of the Roman Catholic Bishops in the American hierarchy in 1833 encouraged Catholics to embrace the American political system and to "discharge the duties of the government under which you live."[12] At the same time, the bishops perceived that American Catholics lived in a predominantly Protestant culture that was not entirely in harmony with Catholic interests. So the American hierarchy warned against the use of any "corrupt" translation of the Bible, specifically the Protestant King James version; planned the construction of Catholic parochial schools that would protect children from the Protestant influences that ran through public education; and actively encouraged conversions to Catholicism.[13]

The American hierarchy was supported in these goals by the authority of the Pope in Rome. But as the Catholic Church grew in the nineteenth century, some liberal American Catholic bishops wanted to embrace the principle of separation of church and state as the foundation of religious liberty in American society. One Catholic leader in America, John Ireland, saw the American experiment as an opportunity for Roman Catholicism to adapt to the religiopolitical conditions of the modern world. At a Church council in 1894, Archbishop Ireland declared that "there is no conflict between the Catholic Church and America . . . the principles of the Church are in thorough harmony with the interests of the Republic." The interests of the republic, in the separation of church and state, had been to remove religion from a direct exercise of power in the political sphere. Ireland declared this to be a development that was also in the best interests of the Catholic Church. In a tribute of praise to the United States, Archbishop Ireland said that its "mission from God is to show to nations that men are capable of the highest civil and political liberty."[14]

Rome reacted to these sentiments in a papal encyclical addressed to the American Church in 1895. This letter was part of a larger papal campaign against modernism, a resistance to any trend in the Church that adapted to modern theories (such as Darwinian evolution or critical biblical interpretation), or to changing political circumstances in the western democracies. Pope Leo XIII recognized in American society the "latent forces for the advancement alike of civilization and Christianity." But he rejected the principle of separation between church and state as the best religiopolitical model. "It would be very erroneous to draw the conclusion," he asserted, "that in America is to be sought the type of the most desirable status of the Church, or that it would be universally lawful or expedient for State and Church to be, as in America, dissevered and divorced."[15] Pope Leo XIII reasserted traditional Roman Catholic emphasis on the subservience of the secular state to the sacred authority of the Church. And he encouraged American Catholics to maintain the traditional bonds of allegiance to this sacred authority in their social and religious lives. Even in their daily lives, the Pope insisted, that, "unless forced by necessity to do otherwise, Catholics ought to prefer to associate with Catholics, a course which will be very conducive to the safeguarding of their faith."[16] This course would isolate American Catholics from the effects of modernism in American society and preserve the traditional identity of the faith.

The condemnation of the modernizing erosion of traditional beliefs and practices was sealed in another letter, four years later in 1899, in which the Pope maintained that "we cannot approve the opinions which some comprise under the head of Americanism."[17] The American question continued to be the central religiopolitical issue in the Roman Catholic Church throughout the twentieth century. And while the Church remained the largest single religious body in America, its relation to the larger society in which it lived remained ambiguous.

The year 1492 is significant in Spanish history, not only for the voyage of Columbus to the New World, but also for the expulsion of the Jews from Spain and the beginning of persecutions that led many to flee to Amsterdam, and some, by that route, to come to America. These Jews from the Iberian peninsula were called Sephardim (from the Hebrew word for Spain) and formed small communities in the British colonies during the colonial period. They were granted naturalization rights by the British parliament in 1740, and small communities formed in New York, Philadelphia, and other cities. They remained relatively small communities throughout the colonial period: the largest was composed of 500 in Charleston. They were free to build synagogues, maintain the traditional practices of Jewish orthodoxy, and develop a way of life in America based on an adherence to the Torah. Although there were no rabbis in these communities, the emphasis on literacy, education, and study of sacred texts allowed for a preservation of orthodox tradition in America.

At the beginning of the nineteenth century, Jewish immigrants began to come to America from northern Europe. The Ashkenazim (from the Hebrew word for Germany) that arrived in the United States had been under the influence of the culture and customs of western Europe, and the rapid increase in Jewish population in America was largely drawn from this background. By 1840 the American Jewish population had risen to 15,000; by 1850—50,000; by 1860—160,000; and by 1880 there were approximately 250,000 Jews in the United States. The western Ashkenazim spoke Yiddish, studied the Torah and Talmud, and sought to preserve traditional Jewish religious practice; but they had also been influenced by certain currents in western religious thought. The eighteenth century, with a relaxation of legal restrictions, brought new opportunities for Jewish assimilation into the nation-states of western Europe. This "emancipation" of European Jews, so that they might be fully participating citizens in European states, was accompanied by a religious and philosophical movement known as the "Enlightenment."

The new political and social conditions of assimilation seemed to require, for a number of influential Jewish thinkers, a corresponding reform of traditional religious beliefs and practices. An enlightened Jewish philosopher, such as Moses Mendelssohn, was able to embrace modern philosophical approaches to religion, techniques of critical biblical scholarship, and German culture, while at the same time maintaining the ortho-dox Jewish traditions of prayer, dietary laws, Sabbath observance, and holy days. Others saw these as incompatible with a modern Judaism. David Einhorn, for example, a German immigrant who assumed leadership of the Jewish community in Baltimore in 1855 declared that "Judaism has reached a turning point when all customs and usages as are lifeless must be abolished."[18] This meant discarding ceremonial rituals, traditional prayers, and forms of worship that did not conform to the modern, en-lightened spirit. It also meant adapting Jewish religious practice to the surrounding society.

The Reform movement in American Judaism was such an experi-ment in adaptation. Its leading organizer, Isaac Mayer Wise, came to Amer-ica in 1846 to serve an Orthodox congregation in Albany, New York. Soon he began to introduce principles of reform in Jewish thought and prac-tice, and moved to create a Reformed congregation in Cincinnati in 1853. In his *Reminiscences*, written in 1874, Wise insisted that "The Jew must be Americanized . . . The Jew must become an American, in order to gain the proud self-consciousness of the free-born man."[19] This was a free-dom from the status of second-class citizenship under which Jews had suffered in Europe; but it was a freedom based on an identification with American individualism, rather than the unique identity of Jewish tradi-tion. The Reform movement sought to abandon any traditional practices that were "not adapted to the views and habits of modern civilization."[20] This led to innovations in synagogue life: the use of organs and mixed choirs, seating of men and women together in worship services, and the translation of many prayers from Hebrew into English. Many aspects of Torah observance, including dietary laws and rituals in the home, became optional. The goal was to adapt tradition to the conditions of modern life; and by 1880 most of the 270 Jewish congregations in the United States had come under the influence of the Reform movement.

Many felt that the Reform had gone too far in trying to assimilate Judaism to the religiopolitical situation of American life. Often these reli-gious innovations appeared as strategies for giving Jews a greater mobility in American society. The Conservative movement emerged as a reaction against these rapid social changes. From its center in the Jewish Theologi-cal Seminary in New York, founded in 1885, it tried to produce an au-thentic American Judaism that would assist the new wave of immigrants, primarily drawn from the Ashkenazim of eastern Europe, to adapt to American society while still preserving the observances of the tradition. One of its most important leaders, Solomon Schechter, insisted that there was nothing in American citizenship that was incompatible with maintain-ing traditional Jewish practices. These rituals were an essential part of the religion, and, according to the Conservatives, the Reform movement failed to recognize their importance. In Europe, social and political emancipation required certain sacrifices of the Jewish heritage; but not in America. "In this great, glorious and free country," Schechter declared in 1904, "we Jews need not sacrifice a single iota of our Torah; and, in the enjoyment of absolute equality with our fellow citizens, we can live to carry out those ideals for which our ancestors so often had to die."[21]

The tremendous influx of immigrants to the United States around the turn of the century brought Jews from eastern Europe and increased the Jewish population from 250,000 in 1880 to 1 million in 1900; 3.5 million by 1917; and 4.2 million in 1927. The majority of eastern European Jewish immigrants had been raised in the traditional orthodox practices that had been maintained in the agricultural villages of Poland, Russia, and Lithuania. Many sought to maintain the orthodox life styles of these small-scale Jewish communities; but this was a difficult challenge in the urban centers of American society, where many immigrants lived in relatively isolated ghettos. This last wave of immigrants, however, changed the shape of Jewish affiliation in the United States so that American Judaism was divided into three groups—Orthodox, Conservative, and Reform—with roughly a third of the Jewish population affiliated with each group.

The immigrant traditions that entered the United States encountered certain social pressures: (1) the pressure of the denominational system put them in competition with other religious groups in the open market place of American religion; (2) the pressure of voluntarism encouraged them to fashion persuasive appeals to reason that would be recognized by generally shared intellectual criteria in American society; (3) the pressure of Protestant hegemony in American life forced many to sacrifice distinctive ethnic customs in the interest of social mobility; (4) the pressure of American political life forced them to relinquish allegiance to symbolic religious centers of authority—Rome and Jerusalem—outside of the territorial boundaries of the United States; and (5) the pressure of a common civil religion modified the unique particularity of each tradition, so that it was not identified by what set it apart from the mainstream of American society, but by those characteristics through which it was able to identify with America. For the immigrant religious communities that could adapt to these pressures, "being a Protestant, a Catholic, or a Jew," as Will Herberg observed, "is understood as the specific way, and increasingly perhaps the only way of being an American and locating oneself in American society."[22]

But at the same time there were forces resisting the assimilation of this "triple melting pot." One resistant force was exerted by the traditional (or orthodox) movements in Catholicism and Judaism that saw this assimilation as a sacrifice of the unique, distinctive, and vital characteristics essential to the life of the religious community. For many, this was a price too high to pay. The other force, however, was exercised by a largely Protestant, Anglo-Saxon resistance to the assimilation of immigrants into

American society. This resistance has emerged periodically in American history in the form of nativist movements.

NATIVISM

When the Declaration of Independence was signed, 80 percent of those Americans with religious affiliations could be found in one of the three major Protestant denominations: Congregational, Presbyterian and Anglican. Catholics and Jews together accounted for 0.1 percent of the religious population of America. By 1850 the Roman Catholic Church was the largest single religious body. It had benefited from the rapid influx of Irish Catholic immigrants, who had left famine, poverty, and starvation in Ireland to find a living in American cities. These poor, unskilled, and illiterate immigrants flooded the labor markets in urban centers, and they were perceived as a threat by two segments of the American population.

One source of conflict was with those urban industrial workers who felt threatened by the influx of cheap labor, and saw themselves in competition with Irish Catholic workers. The other segment of American society that felt threatened was the old agrarian establishment in America, as well as the still vast American farming communities, who saw the immigrants contributing to the rise of power in the cities. They saw their settled agrarian lifestyles threatened by the rise of the cities because, as Ralph Gabriel has observed, "the mores of a simpler agricultural and commercial era did not fit the conditions of an age characterized by the swift accumulation of industrial power."[23] They imagined the Irish Catholic immigrants to be at the center of this conflict between life styles in American society.

Both of these groups began to focus their fears upon Irish Catholics in the 1840s, and to attack Roman Catholicism as a religious symbol of all the dangers to the American way of life. The immigration occurred during the period of Jacksonian democracy, with its ideals of individualism in opposition to any forms of centralized authority. Roman Catholic presence in the United States involved a political contradiction; they were citizens of the republic, and yet seemed connected to the authoritative power of the Pope in Rome. Many questioned the loyalty of Roman Catholics to the democratic ideals of America. As James Olson observed, they "questioned Irish allegiance, doubting that they could become 'true Americans' because dual loyalty to a religious monarchy and a liberal democracy seemed impossible."[24]

Fear of political subversion took shape in the imaginations of many Protestants as, in the words of Ray Billington, "many Americans, particularly in the Middle West, viewed with mounting alarm the rapid accretion of Catholic power."[25] This power was thought to be dangerous to American society because it was concentrated in foreign hands. Romanism, or Popism, had always been a symbol of evil in Protestant religion; now it took on specific political content in the fear of foreign domination by the religiopolitical power of the Pope. If the Catholics were successful in establishing themselves in America, one writer of the period declared, "all knees would bend, or be broken before 'His Holiness' of Rome."[26]

Nativist attacks on Roman Catholics were orchestrated by specifically anti-Catholic groups, such as the American Protestant Association, the Protestant Reformation Society, and the American Protestant Union. They generated propaganda against the Church, including lurid exposés of convent life such as Rebecca Reed's *Six Months in a Convent*, and Maria Monk's *Awful Disclosures of the Hotel Dieu Nunnery*, which were sponsored, forged, and disseminated by nativist groups to paint a picture of scandalous sex, accumulation of wealth, and political subversion in the Catholic convents. And these attacks sometimes took the form of overt acts of violence against Catholics. In 1834 the Ursuline convent in Charleston, Massachusetts, was burned by a mob. There were rumors that a girl was being held inside against her will; but the mob was composed of local workers who were angered by Irish competition for jobs. The Kensington suburb of Philadelphia was the scene of the worst outbreak of mob violence. Thirteen people were killed and fifty wounded, two Catholic churches were burned, and the state militia had to be called in to restore order.

The political parties that were formed out of these sentiments originally appeared in cities where foreign-born populations made up large voting blocs. Native American parties (an ironic turn of phrase) sprang up in 1837 in Washington, D.C., and New York. They called for naturalization laws that would require an immigrant to be twenty-one years in residence in the United States before acquiring the right to vote. They were pledged to vote for no foreign-born candidates, to keep the Bible (in its Protestant translation) in the public schools, and to combat the influence of foreign powers in American society.

Throughout the 1840s nativist parties, in cities like New York and Philadelphia, carried local elections and began to have ambitions on the level of national politics. They were aided by the formation of two propaganda organizations: The American Protestant Union was led by Samuel F. B. Morse, known more for his invention of the telegraph than for his virulent anti-Catholic diatribes; and the American Protestant Association was organized in 1842 to coordinate the efforts of all anti-Catholic groups in promoting "vigorous opposition to the aggressive movements of the Papal Hierarchy against the civil and religious liberties of the United States."[27] The proliferation of secret nativist societies, such as the American Brotherhood, the Order of the Star-Spangled Banner, and the Order of the Sons of the Sires of '76, intensified anti-Catholic sentiment.

The most successful of the native American political parties started by nominating candidates in secret meetings and then writing in their names on election days. The strength of the party was such that this produced some electoral surprises. When members were asked how the party worked they were instructed to say that they knew nothing about it. So, the name "Know-Nothing" was given to the party. The "Know-Nothing" American party candidates ran on a loosely knit platform of antiforeign proposals, and their candidates achieved a considerable degree of success in a number of states. This nativist party was a force in Congress between 1854-56, and provided a temporary vehicle for the political expression of Protestant ethnocentricism and xenophobia. But, the slavery issue soon dominated public attention, and the Know-Nothing party was swept out of power before the Civil War.

A similar eruption of nativist fears emerged after the increase of immigration in the 1880s. One of the most influential spokesmen for Protestant nativism was Josiah Strong, general secretary of the Evangelical Alliance. He revived the nativist fears of Catholicism in America. In his book, *Our Country* (1885), he insisted that "there is an irreconcilable difference between papal principles and the fundamental principles of our free institutions."[28] Catholics were again perceived as a political threat. Although they may have appeared as patriotic Americans, Strong was convinced that their first loyalty was to the political power of Rome.

Josiah Strong combined this anti-Catholic sentiment, however, with a new concern with the classification of race. Various theories of racial classification were being proposed in the nineteenth century, the most popular tending to use Darwinian notions of evolution to rank racial groups in terms of their fitness to survive. Strong's second book, *The New Era* (1893), combined the xenophobia of his earlier work with an ethnocentricism based on the presumed superiority of an Anglo-Saxon race. The Anglo-Saxon race, he asserted, must emerge victorious from the competition of the races. He confidently predicted that, "this race is destined to dispossess many weaker ones, assimilate others, and mold the remainder, until in a very true and important sense, it has Anglo-Saxonized mankind."[29] Strong's books were widely read, and they focused a wide range of American Protestant sentiments against all forms of otherness.

The most prominent anti-Catholic organization during this period was the American Protective Association. It was founded in 1887 by H. F. Bowers, a sixty-year-old lawyer in Clinton, Ohio. Bowers formed the APA as a secret society. The movement combined American nativism, a rural antagonism to the power of the industrial urban centers in America, and fear of Catholic ecclesiastical power in the interest of defending an exclusively Protestant vision of America. He felt that freedom of religious conscience should be protected, but that foreign religious influences should be excluded from the political realm. In describing the aims of his organization, Bowers said that, "every man in this country has a right to worship God according to the dictates of his conscience, but we did not believe that the Constitution intended to convey the right to any set of men to

control and manipulate the political affairs of this country to the aggran-
dizement of any ecclesiastical power."[30] The group devised a set of rituals, drew up a creed, and maintained secrecy in their meetings, because,
"going to war, one does not divulge one's plans to the enemy."[31] Songs
were sung at the meetings as anthems of the holy war against Catholic
influence in American society, politics, and public schools. One song had
the following lyrics:

> Come ye sons of Uncle Sam,
> Come join the gallant band,
> Come unite with us to fight our country's foe.
> For our God is with the right,
> We will conquer by His might,
> And the slick and wily Jesuit must go.
> Noble men are in our ranks—
> We are not a band of cranks—
> We are not a lot of bigots or of fools.
> But, ye Roman Catholic hordes,
> We will buckle on our swords,
> If you dare to meddle with our public schools.[32]

The movement had about 70,000 members by 1893, and at its peak in
1896 the American Protective Association numbered around one million
members. Its primary efforts were in the area of propaganda: The APA
accused Catholics of attacking public schools and stockpiling weapons in
Catholic churches, and it suggested that priests under the direction of the
Pope controlled politics in large cities. The APA proposed that Catholics
should not be allowed to hold public office in municipal, state, or national
government; that they should not be allowed to teach in public schools;
and that restrictions should be placed on Catholic immigration to America.

The movement was divided as a political force in the 1896 election
when it was realized that both candidates, Bryan and McKinley, had considerable support among Catholics. It became harder to sustain the argument that there was a monolithic Catholic vote, or that Catholic money
and power were exercised to control American politics. Cardinal Gibbons,
Archbishop of Baltimore, made a public statement which acknowledged
that Catholics were to be found in both parties, and he hoped that there
would never be the "entire identification of any religious body with any
political party."[33] Gibbons encouraged both political parties to dedicate
themselves to the principles of religious freedom that underlie the Constitution. As an eloquent spokesman for the Church in the face of anti-
Catholic fervor, he maintained that, "Sixteen millions of Catholics live their
lives on our land with undisturbed belief in the perfect harmony existing
between their religion and their duties as American citizens." Through
the Church, he asserted, Catholics were brought into closer communion
with God, and nurtured the hope of eternal life, but, at the same time,

"they accept the Constitution without reserve, with no desire, as Catholics, to see it changed in any feature."[34] Cardinal Gibbons provided another example of a Catholic leader accepting the denominational role of the Roman Catholic Church in American society in the division between private religious commitments and public political participation. After the 1896 election the American Protective Association dissolved. But, the American question in Catholic church-state theory continued to linger throughout the twentieth century.

Opposition to otherness in American society began to focus more directly on Jews at the turn of the century. This shift in focus was initially part of the larger Protestant Anglo-American response to the large numbers of immigrants from southern and eastern Europe, which brought 2 million European Jews to America and resulted in the restrictive immigration laws of 1921 and 1924. By this time Jews had become a large enough population in the United States to attract the attention of nativist movements. In the 1920s, propaganda against Jews began to be circulated in America. The fraudulent *Protocols of the Elders of Zion*, a classic text in anti-Semitic propaganda, depicted an international conspiracy of Jews to take over the world. The fear that a Jewish conspiracy controlled international banking was juxtaposed with anti-Semitic literature that connected Jews with the recent Bolshevik revolution in Russia. This resulted in the strange and contradictory obsession of anti-Semitism which perceived Jews as alternatively a capitalist and a communist threat. The industrialist Henry Ford conducted an anti-Semitic campaign along these lines in the pages of the *Dearborn Independent* between 1920 and 1924.

The Ku Klux Klan was active throughout the twenties, with a membership reaching 3 million and considerable political power in several states. The KKK was a nativist movement which, in the words of John Higham, provided "a single outlet for every racial and religious hatred and every defensive anxiety that festered among the nation's white Protestant majority."[35] The Klan originally directed its hatred toward blacks; but during the twenties it expanded its efforts against Catholics and Jews. At the height of the Klan's power in 1923, its Imperial Wizard Evans addressed a crowd of 75,000 in Dallas, Texas: "Negroes, Catholics, and Jews are the undesirable elements in America, defying every fundamental requirement of assimilation. They are incapable of attaining the Anglo-Saxon level."[36]

Where the Ku Klux Klan included anti-Semitism on a larger agenda of racial prejudice, many groups sprang up in the 1930s that were specifically anti-Semitic in their focus. The House Un-American Activities Committee in 1935 listed 135 anti-Jewish organizations. Most of these groups had been inspired by the racism of Hitler's Germany. The German-American Bund had as many as 25,000 members who were able to declare that "I am of Aryan descent, free of Jewish or colored racial traces."[37] At a rally in Madison Square Garden attended by 19,000 people, they displayed banners that read: "Stop Jewish Domination of Christian America." The Bund saw itself as the American representative of the Nazi dictatorship. One of its publications declared, "We stand here as the heralds of the Third Reich, as preachers of the German world viewpoint, of National Socialism, which has displayed before the eyes of the world the incomparable German miracle . . . ."[38]

The Silver Shirts of William Dudley Pelley reached a peak membership of 15,000 in 1935. Pelley combined an interest in spiritualism with the desire to create a "Christian political machine." He even ran for president on a Christian Party ticket in 1936. He dreamed of driving Jews and revolutionaries from America under his leadership. In the official Silver Shirt newspaper, *Liberation*, Pelley encouraged his followers with the example of Hitler. "The Hitler Movement in Germany started from a sign painter making a speech from the top of a barrel," he recalled. "It is not too early to begin casting up our slates."[39] The Silver Shirts distributed pamphlets and books, including Hitler's *Mein Kampf* and the *Protocols of the Elders of Zion*. Other anti-Semitic groups, such as the Defenders of the Christian Faith, the American Vigilant Intelligence Association, and the Paul Reveres were also involved in similar propaganda campaigns. Perhaps the most influential source of anti-Semitic propaganda was Father Charles E. Coughlin. His radio ministry reached an audience of around 3.5 million listeners every Sunday, and his weekly newspaper, *Social Justice*, which began printing the *Protocols of the Elders of Zion* in 1938, was probably the most widely read anti-Semitic periodical in America.

While these groups may have gained considerable popular attention, and served as vehicles for anti-Semitic sentiments, they never rose to positions of political power in America. The horror of the holocaust in Nazi Germany, in which European Jewry was almost completely destroyed by a political power dedicated to genocidal racial hatred, demonstrated the terrible potential that such nativist movements hold in a plural society. Although such organizations did not achieve their political goals in America, there were nevertheless continuing undercurrents of anti-Semitic sentiment that sought to exclude Jews from American society. Any self-definition of America as a Christian nation comes up against the otherness of Judaism. Throughout Christian history Jews have been perceived as *other*: They have been accused of misunderstanding their own sacred texts, condemned with the responsibility for the death of Jesus, and persecuted for refusing to convert to Christianity. Jews were systematically excluded from Catholic societies during the Middle Ages, and when Martin Luther was disappointed that they did not convert to Protestantism he advocated burning their sacred texts, destroying their homes and synagogues, and driving them from Protestant countries. This religious tension has also been an undercurrent in Jewish-Christian relations in the United States.

Anti-Semitism has appeared as one feature of the recurring nativist desire to exclude all minorities from occupying legitimate places in American society.[40]

Ultimately, however, both religious and political nativism were contrary to a greater acceptance of pluralism in the twentieth century. As John Higham described it, "the pluralist outlook has comprised a generous and humane faith." Pluralism represented a new distribution of religiopolitical power in American society. Higham continued:

> Drawing upon our best traditions, it has helped in no small measure to make the United States a better homeland for many of its people, and few men of good will would want to impugn its basic values. Some affirmation of diversity, some pleasure in the sheer variety of the American people, would seem to be an essential element in the receptiveness and fluidity of our open society.[41]

In this vision of America as an open, receptive, and plural society, nativism itself became a minority position. The forces of ethnocentricism and xenophobia dissipated in the celebration of variety in American society. Rather than trying to establish one religiopolitical identity through the exclusion of the many, the many were allowed to participate on a more equal basis within the one common and shared community. But each was required to pay a price in order to enter into this public arena. We will need to look more closely at the consequences of pluralism in American religion and politics.

PLURALISM

Pluralism is the central fact of life in American religion. Dreams of Protestant hegemony, nurtured by American nativist movements, have dissolved in the irreducible diversity of American religious groups. And this diversity extends beyond the dominant coalition of Protestant, Catholic, and Jewish interests to include the proliferation of alternative religious movements. Buddhists in Hawaii and San Francisco, Hindu Swamis in Los Angeles and Oregon, Muslims in the Nation of Islam and the American Muslim Mission, and a vast array of new religious movements bring the traditional diversity of the religions of the world within the shared civil space of American society. Each tends to make absolute claims to truth; but in their civil relations they must subscribe to the principle of toleration. In the civil contract of American society the uniqueness of each group is maintained by a principle that protects the uniqueness of all. In the political terms of the social contract, tolerance is the minimum price of admission into American civil society. This principle of toleration was embodied in Rousseau's theory of the social contract. With the abolition of any exclusive, established national religion, Rousseau asserted, "we should tolerate all creeds which show tolerance to others."[42] If these groups do not interfere with individuals performing their duties as good citizens, they should have the right to exist, as long as they recognize that same right for others. This is the first condition of an open religiopolitical system.

But each particular religious group is empowered with strong centripetal forces toward producing a self-contained system. Every religious group has residual tribal impulses to unify itself around some central constellation of religious beliefs, practices, or forms of association. As Max Weber pointed out, "any aspect or cultural trait, no matter how superficial, can serve as a starting point for the familiar tendency to monopolistic closure."[43] This monopoly on truth has social consequences. It tends to encourage a closed religiopolitical system based on a tribal affinity among those people who adhere to that one truth, and the tendency to discount people who adhere to other truths. Every religious tradition has an inherent disposition toward otherness, a central strategy for responding to the social fact that not everyone wishes to conform to the same regimen of truth. The Protestant, Catholic, and Jewish traditions all have scriptural reference points that encourage them to demonstrate love in their dealings with both neighbors and strangers. They are encouraged to acknowledge the inherent human value of others. But at the same time, there are the centripetal forces that hold each tradition together as a unique, particular, and even tribal religious group. These forces define the terms of exclusion and inclusion in the relations between the *one* faith and the *many* others who live outside its field of power.

For Protestants there has been *one* biblical salvation through faith in Christ; for Catholics there has been *one* true church, outside of which there is no salvation; and for Jews there has been *one* people with a special covenant relationship with God and a unique destiny in human history. Each of these traditions has made one absolute truth claim that excludes the many. The traditional strategies of inclusion, however, set the specific terms under which others may convert and enter into the one community. Particularly for Christianity the missionizing impulse has been a moral imperative. The exclusive logic of only one possible salvation has led many Christians to conclude that they are not being true to the demands of love by being tolerant of other religions.

Such monopolistic closures around religious truth set up tensions in a plural society. Rousseau was convinced that these absolute, exclusive, and closed religious communities were inconsistent with the requirements of an open democratic society. "Anyone who dares to say," he asserted, "'Outside the Church there can be no salvation,' should be banished from the State . . . Such a dogma is good only where the government is theocratic. In any other it is pernicious."[44] A theocratic religiopolitical system would be able to harmonize the inner and outer demands of a single, absolute truth. It would conform the outer public relations of society to the internal private convictions of religious principle. This would bring the entire society into a single closure around religion. But an open, plural society resists all such religiopolitical closures. It eliminates the possibility that a single religious truth will determine the public order. And it demands of each particular group a minimum degree of public toleration of otherness in order for each to exist in the same civil space.

This plural arrangement may diffuse tensions between particular religious groups in the public arena, but it creates within each group a tension between its private commitment to a single truth and its public acceptance of the many. The tensions of pluralism—the one and the many, the open and the closed, the public and the private—become internalized in the self-understanding of each particular tradition. This split between absolute religious theory and plural social practice has presented a challenge to every American religious tradition. Some religious thinkers have tried to reconcile the absolute demands of their faith with the religious pluralism of American society. The Protestant theologian Reinhold Niebuhr affirmed the ideal of pluralism in the relations between Christians and Jews when he declared in 1958 that there was no need for Christians to try to convert the Jews.[45] He claimed that Christianity and Judaism were two religions with a common center in the prophetic revelations of the Hebrew Bible. In affirming the religious, ethnic, and cultural integrity of Judaism, Niebuhr called for a "genuine tolerance" that would accept, both in theory and in practice, religious pluralism in American society.

The Catholic theologian, John Courtney Murray, tried to work out a solution to the American question in the Catholic tradition by affirming the separation of church and state as a doctrine of peace—though it may not be accepted as a doctrine of Catholic faith. The division between church and state (and the religious pluralism it engenders) may be accepted in the interests of maintaining peaceful coexistence within a common civil space. "Religious pluralism is against the will of God," Murray observed in 1959. "But it is the human condition, it is written into the script of history. It will not somehow marvelously cease to trouble the city."[46] Murray's compromise on the issue of church and state sought to accommodate traditional Catholic theology to that condition of religious pluralism. Finally, the Reform movement in Judaism has represented an ongoing attempt to modify the distinctive ethnic and cultural features of an ancient religious tradition to the plural conditions of the modern world.[47] In each of these instances, part of the ancient tribal force of religion has been sacrificed in the interest of mutual coexistence as citizens of a common state.

But what are those duties of a citizen that define the shared rights and responsibilities of individuals within the state? The immigrant to America encounters at least three powerful social processes that represent cultural rites of passage into American society. The first is the naturalization process by which one becomes a citizen of the United States. Naturalization represents a transfer of national allegiance from the individual's country of origin to the United States. Beginning with the Naturalization Act of 1906, it was required that the applicant declare under oath that he or she would "support and defend the Constitution and laws of the United States against all enemies, foreign and domestic, and bear true faith and allegiance to the same."[48] This not only meant that people from different religious nationalities must sacrifice any political implications of their allegiances to symbolic sacred centers outside the territorial boundaries of the United States—whether Rome, Jerusalem, Mecca, or elsewhere—but they must be willing to make the supreme sacrifice in defense of their new faith and allegiance to the United States of America. That requirement suggests that the state has the power to demand this ultimate sacrifice of its citizens. Compulsory military service demonstrates the supreme power of the state over its citizens, and is presented in the Naturalization Act as the highest duty they owe to the state. Of course there are some religious groups who are traditionally opposed to military service, as well as individuals who assert the independent claims of moral conscience. These were officially accommodated in the Naturalization Act when it was changed in 1952 to allow for conscientious objection to military service on religious grounds. But this did not diminish the unifying force of the naturalization process to join all American citizens in a common allegiance to the power of the state.

The second cultural rite of passage is education. The founders of the American republic saw education as a means of preventing political power turning into tyranny by maintaining an educated, informed, and enlightened public. Jefferson held an ideal of an aristocracy of the enlightened who could be educated to protect the rights of the public. In advocating a state-supported elementary school system for Virginia, he proposed that "those persons, whom nature hath endowed with genius and virtue, should be rendered by liberal education worthy to receive, and able to guard the sacred deposit of the rights and liberties of their fellow citizens, and that they should be called to that charge without regard to wealth, birth or other accidental condition or circumstance."[49] Soon this notion of an educated elite was democratized, and the public school movement in the 1830s called for universal education as the best insurance for the preservation of democratic institutions. One appeal for public schools declared that while education was once the privilege of a social elite, which determined the destinies of society, "now this principle of universal mental cultivation destroys this usurping, tyrannizing system. It takes from the few the power of holding and disposing of the rights of the many, giving to the many the same mental superiority and knowledge. The promotion and the general well-being of society by a cultivation of the heart and the intellect is impliedly required of Americans, from the nature and structure of our government."[50]

The common school was viewed as an essential institution to preserve and foster the sacred values of democracy. From the beginning it was intended as a kind of established church of American civil religion. In 1837 the state of Massachusetts created the first state superintendent of schools in Horace Mann, who supervised the opening of the first state normal school in 1839. He proclaimed the sacred civil trust embodied in the school system: "If we do not prepare children to become good citizens," Mann declared, "if we do not develop their capacities, if we do not enrich their minds with knowledge, imbue their hearts with the love of truth and duty, and a reverence for all things sacred and holy, then our republic must go down to destruction, as others have gone before it."[51] It was no accident that this public school movement took shape at the same time that America had begun to experience the impact of immigration. The public school provided the children of immigrants with an initiation into the sacred beliefs and rituals of the American civic faith, and was seen as a sacred force in creating citizens who could participate in American institutions.

The religious aura in which public education emerged in American society raised the question of the relation between this civil institution and the particular, traditional religious faiths within American society. Some saw public education serving the interests of a homogeneous Protestant America. Lyman Beecher, for example, supported specifically Protestant political goals in his vision of education. The integrity of the United States, according to Beecher, depended upon a unified, homogeneous American character that would bind the people together. Education should produce a "sameness of views, and feelings, and interests, which would lay the foundation of our empire upon a rock."[52] And while there may be different political interests among its citizens, religion must supply the central force that holds the republic together. The Protestant bias in American education during the nineteenth century, including the use of the Protestant translation of the Bible, the encouragement of Protestant spirituality through prayers in school, and the tendency of textbooks to reflect a Protestant version of religious history, made alternative religious communities uncomfortable with the prospect of compulsory public education. This led to the coexistence between the public school system and private alternative schools, where the children of Catholics, Jews, and other religious groups could be educated in an environment that supported the particular faith of their communities.

During the controversy over the Protestant bias of the public schools in New York in 1840, Governor Seward observed the need to recognize alternative educational institutions. "The children of foreigners," he noted, "are too often deprived of the advantages of our system of public education, in consequence of prejudices arising from difference of language or religion."[53] He proposed to extend state support for the formation of schools where children could be instructed by teachers who professed the same faith. While such schools have flourished in America, they did not solve the problem of religious bias for students who did not identify with the Protestant denominations. The public school system was required to recognize the plural religious composition of its students. In order not to prejudice the system of education toward one religion, or religion itself for that matter, it was required to remove prayer, Bible reading, and religious instruction from the curriculum.

The third civil rite of passage is the immigrant's entry into the complex system of economic exchange that comprises the market economy of American society. The citizen participates in a shared public life by becoming immersed in the selling of labor and the buying of commodities. In a market economy, supply and demand determine the value of goods and services, and the same pricing mechanism also sets the value of individuals. The American citizen is an economic animal whose value can be measured by his or her contribution to the gross national product. But for each citizen there are the powerful personal motivations for achievement, success, and prosperity within an open economic system. America is an open money society where social mobility is in principle available equally to all citizens. The American dream of personal success through hard work, exploitation of human and natural resources, and the accumulation of wealth is the powerful myth that sustains the civic rituals of economic exchange.

Probably nothing has done more to dissolve traditional bonds of particular ethnic and religious heritages than the free market economy of American society. The vast impersonal network of economic interchange factors out all the traditional values which have been ascribed to a person by kinship, locality, class, or religion in order to reduce the value of the individual to a single economic indicator. The traditional vestiges of *ascribed* status fall away. And what remains is only the *achieved* status that the individual acquires through active participation in the market economy. This ideal of utilitarian individualism defines an ethical obligation to which each citizen must be committed in order to have a legitimate place in American society.

The expansion of the railroad in the nineteenth century provided a powerful American symbol of a unified nation. Not only was the continent bridged by tracks of steel, but the centralizing influence of the city was extended by railroad to disseminate urban values throughout the country. It contributed to the revolutionary process of integrating the countryside into the social orbit of the city. Richard Hofstadter has said that "America was born in the country and moved to the city."[54] And urban centers, with mass communication, industrial development, and the system of wage labor, became unifying forces in American society as those values began to dominate American public life.

But the railroad also symbolized the terms under which immigrant labor was incorporated into the American economic system. The tracks were laid by migrant workers of foreign origin in the service of American industry. The cheap labor of immigrants was simply another resource to be exploited in American industrial expansion. The first transcontinental line was completed in 1869. Central Pacific moving from the West had used Chinese labor; Union Pacific coming from the East had relied on European immigrants. When they joined together to drive in the final nail at Promontory Point, a symbolic drama was enacted to demonstrate America's appropriation of foreign labor in its national expansion. As 1,500 people, including guests of honor, gathered to watch the historic event, a reporter observed the significance of this drama.

> One fact . . . forcibly impressed me at the laying of the last nail. Two lengths of rails, fifty-six feet had been omitted. The Union Pacific people brought up their pair of rails, and the work of placing them was done by Europeans. The Central Pacific people then laid their pair of rails, the labor being performed by Mongolians. The foremen, in both cases, were Americans. Here, near the center of the American Continent, were the united efforts of representatives of the continents of Europe, Asia, and America—America directing and controlling.[55]

American industrial and economic power was symbolized by the control of foreign immigrant labor within American society, and this power was extended in the twentieth century to include foreign labor, lands, and resources outside of the territorial boundaries of the United States.

Nevertheless, the image of America as an unlimited land of economic opportunity provided a powerful attraction for immigrants, and a powerful motive for abandoning many of the distinctive characteristics of their traditions in the interest of a greater social mobility in America. Philip Schaff, the nineteenth-century Protestant historian, saw America as the grave of all foreign nationalities; but, he added, it was "a Phoenix grave, from which they shall rise to new life and new destiny."[56] A cultural truism about American immigrants has been suggested in Hansen's law: What the son wants to forget, the grandson wants to remember.[57] The sons of immigrants may have wanted to forget their traditional heritages—the distinctive features of race, culture, ethnicity, and religion—but the next generation may show an increased interest in learning about those traditions. Perhaps as part of a larger cultural response to the disruptions of American society during the sixties, many ethnic groups reasserted traditional identities in American society. Daniel Patrick Moynihan observed that "a powerful quest for specific community is emerging in the form of ever more intensive assertions of racial and ethnic identities."[58] In American religion we also find the reassertion of the more particularist forms of religious community. This trend not only appeared in the reemergence of conservative fundamentalist Protestantism, but also in such varied attempts to achieve a sense of community as the emergence of Catholic charismatic renewal, the resurgence of Orthodox Judaism, and the enthusiasm for Zionism within different strands of American Judaism.

Not all Americans find the primary locus of their identity in the civic rituals of American citizenship. Many derive a stronger sense of community, a more profound sense of meaning, and a more vital sense of power, in association with religion. Religions provide unique senses of place in American society, and if that larger society is to be truly open it must accommodate those alternative identities. Perhaps the most powerful alternative religious allegiances in recent years have been found in two areas: the emergence of new, strange, and exotic religious movements and the growth of conservative Protestantism. Both of these developments tested the limits of pluralism in American society. In the next section we will explore the legal structure of pluralism in American religion precisely at those points where religion challenges the political power invested in American society.

NOTES

1. ROLAND ROBERTSON, *The Sociological Interpretation of Religion* (Oxford: Basil Blackwell, 1970): 123; John Wilson, *Religion in American Society: The Effective Presence* (Englewood Cliffs, New Jersey: Prentice-Hall, 1978): 137-68; see H. Richard Niebuhr, *The Social Sources of Denominationalism* (New York: Meridian Books, 1957).
2. WILBUR G. KATZ and HAROLD P. SUTHERLAND, "Religious Pluralism and the Supreme Court," in *Religion in America*, eds., William G. McLoughlin and Robert N. Bellah (Boston: Beacon Press, 1968): 269.
3. ISRAEL ZANGWILL, *The Melting-Pot* (New York: Macmillan, 1909): 37; see R. Laurence Moore, *Religious Outsiders and the Making of Americans* (New York: Oxford University Press, 1986).
4. J. MILTON YINGER, *Sociology Looks at Religion* (New York: Macmillan, 1963): 105.
5. *Ibid.*: 107.
6. WILL HERBERG, *Protestant, Catholic, Jew: An Essay in American Religious Sociology* (Garden City, New York: Doubleday, 1955): 77.
7. SIDNEY AHLSTROM, *A Religious History of the American People* (Garden City, New York: Doubleday, 1975): I: 404; See James Hennesey, *American Catholics* (New York: Oxford University Press, 1981); and Jay P. Dolan, *The American Catholic Experience: A History from Colonial Times to the Present* (Garden City, New York: Doubleday, 1985).
8. WILLIAM CLEBSCH, "A New Historiography of American Religion," *Historical Magazine of the Protestant Episcopal Church* 32 (1963): 225-58; cited in David O'Brien, "American Catholicism and American Religion," in *Religion in American History: Interpretive Essays*, eds., John M. Mulder and John F. Wilson (Englewood Cliffs, New Jersey: Prentice-Hall, 1978): 400.
9. JOHN TRACY ELLIS, ed., *Documents of American Catholic History* (Milwaukee: Bruce Publishing Co., 1956): 100-01.
10. Maryland Archives, *Proceedings and Acts of the General Assembly*, 1: 244-47, cited in Ahlstrom, *A Religious History of the American People*, I: 407-8.
11. ANNABELLE M. MELVILLE, *John Carroll of Baltimore: Founder of the American Catholic Hierarchy* (New York: Charles Scribner's Sons, 1955): 55.
12. PETER GUILDAY, *The National Pastorals of the American Hierarchy 1790-1919*, (1923; Westminster, Maryland: The Newman Press, 1954): 78.
13. See Aaron I. Abell, ed., *American Catholic Thought on Social Questions* (Indianapolis: Bobbs-Merrill, 1968).

14. JAMES H. MOYNIHAN, *The Life of Archbishop John Ireland* (New York: Harper and Row, 1953): 33-4.
15. POPE LEO XIII, *Encyclical Longinqua Oceani* (January 6, 1895); in Ellis, ed., *Documents of American Catholic History*: 495; 498.
16. *Ibid.*: 504.
17. POPE LEO XIII, *Testem benevolentiae* (January 22, 1899); in *Ibid*: 542.
18. Cited in David Philipson, *The Reform Movement in Modern Judaism* (New York: Macmillan, 1931): 347.
19. ISAAC MAYER WISE, *Reminiscences* (Cincinnati, 1874).
20. NATHAN GLAZER, *American Judaism* (Chicago: University of Chicago Press, 1957): 151-2.
21. SOLOMON SCHECHTER, *Seminary Addresses and Other Papers* (1915; New York: Arno Press, 1969): 85-6; see Marshall Sklare, *Conservative Judaism: An American Religious Movement* (New York: Free Press, 1955).
22. WILL HERBERG, *Protestant, Catholic, Jew*: 35.
23. RALPH GABRIEL, *The Course of American Democratic Thought*, 2nd ed. (New York: Wiley, 1956): 154.
24. JAMES STUART OLSON, *The Ethnic Dimension in American History* (New York: St. Martin's, 1979): 80-1.
25. RAY ALLEN BILLINGTON, *The Protestant Crusade, 1800-1860: A Study in the Origins of American Nativism* (New York: Macmillan, 1938): 313.
26. Cited in Ray Allen Billington, *The Origins of Nativism in the United States, 1800-1844* (New York: Arno Press, 1974): 359.
27. Cited in Alice Felt Tyler, *Freedom's Ferment* (New York: Harper and Row, 1944): 383.
28. JOSIAH STRONG, *Our Country. Its Possible Future and Its Present Crisis*, ed., Jurgan Herbst (Cambridge: Harvard University Press, 1963).
29. JOSIAH STRONG, *The New Era; or, The Coming Kingdom* (New York, 1893): 79-80.
30. DONALD L. KINZER, *An Episode in Anti-Catholicism. The American Protective Association* (Seattle: University of Washington Press, 1964): 37.
31. *Ibid*: 41.
32. *Ibid*: 52.
33. *Ibid*: 222.
34. CARDINAL GIBBONS, "The Church and the Republic," *North American Review* 189 (March, 1909); reprinted in *A Retrospect of Fifty Years* (Baltimore: John Murphy and Co., 1916): I: 210.
35. JOHN HIGHAM, "American Antisemitism Historically Reconsidered," in *Antisemitism in the United States*, ed., Leonard Dinnerstein (New York: Holt, Rinehart and Winston, 1971): 66.
36. Cited in Arthur Gilbert, *A Jew in Christian America* (New York: Sheed and Ward, 1966).
37. DONALD S. STRONG, *Organized Anti-Semitism in America: The Rise of Group Prejudice During the Decade 1930-40* (Washington, D.C.: American Council on Public Affairs, 1941): 29.
38. *Ibid.*: 29.
39. *Ibid.*: 46.
40. For historical studies of anti-Semitism in the United States, see John Higham, "Anti-Semitism in the Gilded Age: A Reinterpretation," *Mississippi Valley Historical Review*, 43 (1957): 559-78; and "Social Discrimination Against the Jews in America, 1830-1930," *Publications of the American Jewish Historical Society* 47 (1957-58): 1-33; Oscar and Mary Handlin, *Danger in Discord: Origins of Anti-Semitism in the United States* (New York: Anti-Defamation League of B'nai B'rith, 1948); Carey McWilliams, *A Mask for Privilege: Anti-Semitism in America* (Boston: Little, Brown, 1948; Westport, CT: Greenwood Press, 1979); Lee Joseph Levinger, *Anti-Semitism in the United States: Its History and Causes* (1925; Westport, CT: Greenwood Press, 1972); For a discussion of Christian anti-Semitism, see Charles Y. Glock and Rodney Stark, *Christian Beliefs and Anti-Semitism* (New York: Harper and Row, 1966; Westport, CT: Greenwood Press, 1979).
41. JOHN HIGHAM, "American Antisemitism Historically Reconsidered": 65.
42. JEAN-JACQUES ROUSSEAU, *The Social Contract*, Chapter 8, Book 4; in *Social Contract: Essays by Locke, Hume and Rousseau*, ed., Ernest Barker (New York: Oxford University Press, 1962): 307.
43. MAX WEBER, "Ethnic Groups," in *Theories of Society*, eds., Talcott Parsons, et al. (Glencoe, Ill.: Free Press, 1961): I:305.
44. Cited in Barker, ed., *Social Contract*: 307.

45. JUNE BINGHAM, *Courage to Change: An Introduction to the Life and Thought of Reinhold Niebuhr* (New York: Scribner's, 1961): 363; The implications of Niebuhr's tolerance for American pluralism are discussed in John Murray Cuddihy, *No Offense: Civil Religion and Protestant Taste* (New York: Seabury Press, 1978): 31-47.

46. John Courtney Murray, *We Hold These Truths: Catholic Reflections on the American Proposition* (New York: Sheed and Ward, 1960): 28; see Cuddihy, *No Offense*: 64-100.

47. See Stephen Steinberg, "Reform Judaism: The Origin and Evolution of a 'Church Movement,'" in *Religion in Sociological Perspective*, ed., Charles Y. Glock (Belmont, California: Wadsworth Publishing Co., 1973): 221-34; and Stephen Isaacs, *Jews and American Politics* (Garden City, New York: Doubleday, 1974).

48. Naturalization Act of 29 June 1906, Ch. 3592, 34 Stat. 596, 598 (1906); cited in Robert T. Miller and Ronald B. Flowers, eds., *Toward Benevolent Neutrality: Church, State and the Supreme Court* (Waco, Texas: Markham Press Fund, 1977): 147.

49. Cited in Tyler, *Freedom's Ferment*: 230.

50. *Southern Literary Messenger* (May 1, 1836); cited in Tyler, *Freedom's Ferment*: 233; on nineteenth century public education, see Colin Green, *The Great School Legend: A Revisionist Interpretation of Public Education* (New York: Basic Books, 1972); and Ruth Miller Elson, *Guardians of Tradition: American School-books of the Nineteenth Century* (Lincoln: University of Nebraska Press, 1964).

51. MARY PEABODY MANN, *The Life of Horace Mann* (Boston: W. Small, 1888; Miami, Florida: Mnemosyne Publishing, 1969): III: 417.

52. LYMAN BEECHER, *Address of the Charitable Society for the Education of Indigent Pious Young Men for the Ministry of the Gospel* (Concord, Mass.: 1820): 20.

53. Cited in Tyler, *Freedom's Ferment*: 378.

54. RICHARD HOFSTADTER, *The Age of Reform* (New York: Vintage Books, 1960): 23.

55. RONALD T. TAKAKI, *Iron Cages: Race and Culture in Nineteenth-Century America* (New York: Alfred A. Knopf, 1979): 231.

56. PHILIP SCHAFF, *America: A Sketch of Its Political, Social, and Religious Character* (1855; Cambridge: Harvard University Press, 1961): 51.

57. MARCUS L. HANSEN, *The Problem of the Third Generation Immigrant* (Rock Island, Ill.: Augustana Historical Society, 1930): see the development of this idea in Herberg, *Protestant, Catholic, Jew*: 186.

58. Cited in Martin E. Marty, *A Nation of Behavers* (Chicago: University of Chicago Press, 1976): 177; on the relation between ethnicity and religion in America, see Martin E. Marty, "Ethnicity: The Skeleton of Religion in America," *Church History* 41 (1972): 5-21; Harry S. Stout, "Ethnicity: The Vital Center of Religion in America," *Ethnicity* 2 (1975): 204-224; Harold J. Abramson, "The Religioethnic Factor and the American Experience: Another Look at the Three-Generation Hypothesis," *Ethnicity* 2 (1975): 163-177; and on the relation between ethnic identities and politics, see Michael Novak, *The Rise of the Unmeltable Ethnics: The New Political Force of the Seventies* (New York: Macmillan, 1972); and Harold R. Isaacs, *Idols of the Tribe: Group Identity and Political Change* (New York: Harper and Row, 1975).

PART 3   FIELDS OF FORCE
Law, Political Order, and Religion

CHAPTER SEVEN
THE TRIAL OF RELIGION

Warfare is a uniquely human form of behavior. Other animals may fight, but they do not conduct wars. They do not plan strategies, develop and employ weapons, nor do they systematically destroy members of their species in the way that human beings do. Warfare may be significant in the evolution of the human species, and therefore a significant genetic inheritance of humanity. Sociobiologist Robert Ardrey even claimed that "man has emerged from the anthropoid background for one reason only: because he was a killer." Through the development of sophisticated technologies of killing, humans were able to dominate other species. Success in developing weapons had a major impact on the survival of the fittest among the human species. Those who did not become skilled in the arts of war, from this purely biological perspective, did not survive in order to pass on their genetic traits to future generations. From the beginning survival depended on specific skills in using specialized tools of violence. "And if all human history from that date," Ardrey concluded, "has turned on the development of superior weapons, then it is for a very sound reason. It is a genetic necessity. We design and compete with our weapons as birds build distinctive nests."[1]

Technologies of warfare may in this sense be viewed as adaptive strategies: as the instinctive means by which human beings have adapted to the challenges of a hostile environment, and have insured their survival by destroying all competition. In the battle for the survival of the fittest, warfare appears to have been an important biological mechanism for weeding out those who were too weak to survive and causing the more aggressive and violent human characteristics to proliferate in the human gene pool.

But warfare is a uniquely human form of behavior for another important reason—it is a social fact. It is a culturally conditioned social expression of the violence upon which human societies are based. Violence is built into the structure of human societies. The nation-state, in particular, could be described as the organized exercise of violence over a territory. A society controls the behavior of individuals within its boundaries through the implicit threat of violence. Laws are not simply social customs; they necessarily involve, in the words of Robert Redfield, "the systematic and formal application of force by the state in support of explicit rules of conduct."[2] Behind every law is the implicit threat of punishment. And all laws are coercive to the extent that they are reinforced by the inherent power of the state to exercise its privilege to use violence upon individuals who depart from the norms it has enshrined in codes of law. Punishment may take the form of fines, beatings, torture, imprisonment, or death. But, in all cases, the prerogative to exercise violence over individuals is reserved to the institutions of the state. The scaffold becomes a central symbol of the centripetal force of the state, in which punishment demonstrates the state's awesome binding power over its citizens. The institutions of internal power represent social strategies for using (as well as for limiting) the exercise of violence within the territorial boundaries of the state.

On the scaffold the state reinforces its power over its citizens; but on the battlefield it reinforces its power in relation to other states. Military institutions exert the centrifugal force by which the state extends its power, authority, and interests outside its territorial boundaries. But the rituals of war also mobilize the interests, enthusiasms, and efforts of citizens within the state. The power of martial rituals forces individuals and groups to transcend their differences in a coordinated effort against a common enemy. War performs an important social function in directing aggression that might be internally divisive outside the territorial boundaries of a community. In the words of René Girard, "the basic function of foreign wars, and of the more or less spectacular rites that generally accompany them, is to avert the threat of internal dissension by adopting a form of violence that can be openly endorsed and fervently acted upon by all."[3] The collective ceremonies of uniforms and banners, military marches and parades, battle drills, patriotic speeches and songs, and the glorification of sacrificial death all unify the community in the common goal of directing violence outside of its boundaries. These rituals are reinforced by powerful collective myths of national identity, goals, and destiny. The cult of patriotism has been one of the dominant religious orientations in the modern world. The American statesman Daniel Webster declared that patriotism produced "an elevation of soul" which lifted men "above the rank of ordinary men. Above fear, above danger [the true patriot] feels that the last end which can happen to any man never comes too soon if he falls in defense of the laws and liberties of his country."[4] Sacrificial death is the final ritual act of the patriot. His devotion to religious nationalism is measured by his willingness to make this supreme sacrifice in defense of the sacred ideals embodied in that national identity.

Legislation that requires compulsory military service makes the state's most powerful claim upon the lives of its citizens. Through mandatory military service the state exercises its supreme authority over individuals. Modern states have periodically instituted laws of conscription by which individuals are required to enter into military enlistment, training, and action. In these laws, the two modes of state violence come together: the military violence directed against foreign states and the legal violence exercised over citizens. In American history, government resorted to conscripting citizens into military service during the Revolution, the Civil War, and World Wars I and II. Between 1945 and 1973, a military draft was enforced in the United States even though there was no declared war. The draft has been a controversial political practice in American history; it will be important to look at some of the religious responses to such practices as conscription, mandatory service, and universal military training in that history.

Religion enters into the rituals of military power, into these ceremonies of violence, in one of four basic ways. In two of these ways, religion may present a *resistant* force; in the other two, religion provides a *cooperative* force in the military exercises of power.

Pacifism presents a resistant religious force to military violence. Certain Christian churches in America, most prominently the Quakers, Mennonites, Brethren, and Jehovah's Witnesses, have resisted military power based on a commitment to Christian ideals of nonviolence. These peace churches have denied the authority of the state to involve all its citizens in acts of war. And particularly the Quaker churches have been active in trying to offer nonviolent mediation in order to avoid international disputes turning into violence. But these pacifist churches have not been the only religious source of resistance to military action. Many Christians have felt a higher obligation to follow the religious conviction—"Thou shalt not kill"—and the example of Jesus in the political realm. An ethic of love would not permit violence. To use violence in order to defend or advance a truly Christian community, according to this perspective, would destroy that community from within. So, the central question for Christian pacifists is not whether they would be willing to die for their country; but, would they be willing to kill? For committed pacifists such an act of violence would not be consistent with the religious obligation of love in the Christian tradition.[5]

Just War Theory provides a second resistant force to military power. It consists in a set of criteria, developed during the Middle Ages by a series of Catholic theologians, that limits legitimate uses of violence for political purposes. The theory attempts to define ethical grounds for entering into war and an ethical basis for conducting war that would be consistent with Christian principles. For a state to legitimately enter into a war it must be declared by a legitimate ruler, initiated as a last resort after peaceful means of reconciliation have been exhausted, called in defense of a just cause, and embarked upon in the interest of restoring peace. Once war has been declared it must be conducted according to two basic principles of justice: There must be careful discrimination between combatants and noncombatants so that innocent civilians are not harmed, and there must be a sense of proportionality so that the conduct of the war will guarantee that more good will result than harm. These ideals of the just war have represented an accommodation of Christian principles over the centuries to the political necessities of state power; but in theory they are designed to serve as Christian principles of restraint upon the unlimited uses of violence by states in times of war. Although this line of theological reflection on war has played a limited role in American history, issues of justice in the causes and conduct of American war have been an important part of military history in the United States.[6]

The *Separation of Kingdoms* in much Protestant religious thought has provided a cooperative force in the exercise of military power. Martin Luther set the tone for this approach when he condoned the use of violence by the German princes in crushing a rebellion of peasants in 1525. The separation of religion from the political sphere assumes that political life in the world could never be ordered around the religious principle of love, and that therefore the use of violence is legitimate in maintaining political order in the state.[7] The mainstream conventional churches in America have traditionally been concerned with saving souls and allowing the bodies of citizens to be sacrificed to the military aims of the country. The role of chaplains in the armed forces indicates this division of interests: Without influencing the military policy of the armies in which they serve, they can tend to the spiritual needs of soldiers. The churches provide a cooperative force for military power by withdrawing from the public arena in which military decisions are made and carried out, thereby limiting the political power of religion to the purely spiritual interests of their congregations. This separation of kingdoms allows for a split personality in American military experience: Christian citizens in America can pray for peace and prepare for war.

Religious nationalism generates the most powerful cooperative force in furthering the interests of American military power. American churches have been quick to support national interests in times of war. As George Marsden observed, "the nation has set the agenda and Christians have supplied the flags and crosses."[8] Religious support for national military purposes has resulted in some curious alliances. During the Civil War churches were split between North and South, marshaling the same kinds of religious commitment, enthusiasm, and rhetoric for opposed military objectives. The Episcopal church, for example, was thus divided so that one Episcopal bishop led his troops into battle as a Confederate major general, while another exhorted his parishioners in the North by declaring that "the Lord of hosts is on our side."[9] During the First World War preachers rallied to the American cause and one of the more popular revivalists, Billy Sunday, proclaimed in his inimitable style that military service was a supreme Christian duty: "The man who breaks all the rules but at last dies fighting in the trenches is better than you Godforsaken mutts who won't enlist."[10] Similar Christian sentiments helped mobilize Americans for enlistment in World War II. But religious nationalism ultimately transcends Christianity itself as the source of deepest commitment and most profound sacrifice. It comes close to Baron d'Holbach's image of a nationalism in the service of "a God of armies, a jealous God, an avenging God, a destroying God, a God, who is pleased with carnage, and whom his worshippers, as a duty, serve to his taste. Lambs, bulls, children, men, heretics, infidels, kings, whole nations are sacrificed to him."[11] For American religious nationalism all wars appear to be holy wars with the American people identified with cosmic forces of justice, goodness, and light. Through such religious imagery, America has sustained a self-image, in the words of Reinhold Niebuhr, as "the most innocent nation on earth."[12]

Some individuals firmly believed they could not maintain their innocence by participating in military service. The United States has allowed for legal recognition of conscientious objection. It has recognized the special status of an individual conscience informed by deeply held religious beliefs, and has allowed for such individuals to be exempt from direct participation in the military. Originally those exemptions were allowed for members of the peace churches whose religious belief and training precluded their involvement in acts of violence in any form. Gradually the criteria for exemption have been expanded, so that by the twentieth century the Selective Service Acts, and the rulings of the Supreme Court, began to accept a wider range of religious objection to military service. Particularly in the Supreme Court during the twentieth century the trend has moved away from seeing conscience as something that is formed by a religious group, to seeing religion itself as an expression of a deeply held set of moral principles that make up the individual's conscience. This has raised important questions about the legal status of religious conscience when it is put to the supreme test in times of war.

A number of important rulings emerged out of the period of America's involvement in the Vietnam War. This time of national trial was an intense test of American conscience. The cases concerning conscientious objection heard by the Supreme Court during this period were part of a larger pattern of social conflict, which included opposition to the war, resistance to the draft, and important questions about America's military role in the world. The agonizing self-reflection involved in this conflict raised fundamental religious and political issues about American identity, and the Supreme Court decisions made important contributions to redefining the role of conscience in American society.

CONSCRIPTION

In the thirteen American colonies, military service was generally considered the duty of all citizens. The conscription of citizens into that service was asserted as a right by the colonies. Since colonization was—among other things—a military expedition of a foreign power into the New World, citizens were expected to participate actively in the defense of the settlements. But the statutes requiring universal military training were gradually relaxed. In Virginia the original requirement of daily military drills was reduced in 1632 to once a week; by 1642 to once a month; and by 1674 to three meetings a year. In Massachusetts, compulsory military exercises followed a similar pattern: reduced to one meeting a month in 1632, eight a year in 1638, and four days of military drills per year by 1679.[13] Colonial defense was based on these local militias. They were concerned with local defense; so any larger military operations relied upon a voluntary militia that spent more time in training and was prepared for more extended periods of military service. On several occasions, when volunteers did not provide an adequate military force, there were attempts to institute a draft. The military operations against the French in the Ohio valley, under the leadership of George Washington in 1755, required more soldiers than were willing to volunteer. Draft laws were enacted in Virginia to enlist a larger number of men, but they were very unpopular and resulted in public resentment, desertions, and a riot in Fredericksburg when angry citizens stormed the city jail to release draft resisters and deserters.[14] There was opposition to the inequalities in such draft laws, where wealthy colonists were given preferential treatment; but there was also a popular conviction that such involuntary conscription violated the principle of individualism which was becoming established in America.

One of the biggest problems faced by the Continental Congress during the Revolutionary War was recruiting sufficient manpower for the concerted effort against the British military. By 1777 all the states had resorted to a draft to acquire the necessary quota of men. But exemption from compulsory military service could be obtained on a number of different grounds. An individual could avoid military service by paying a fine or, in some cases, submitting to double taxation. A second means of avoiding the draft was the option of providing a substitute. It was possible for a citizen to hire someone else to take his place when called for military service. And in one case, the entire town of Epping, New Hampshire, was able to avoid compulsory military service by hiring substitutes from other towns.[15] These measures clearly favored the wealthy who could afford to pay the fines or hire the substitutes, and reflected basic inequalities in the implementation of the draft. But a third basis for exemption from military service was religion. The Resolution of the Continental Congress, July 18, 1775, acknowledged that "As there are some people, who, from religious principles, cannot bear arms in any case, this Congress intends no violence to their consciences."[16] This provision was particularly directed toward the Quakers, who were an active religious minority in Pennsylvania, as well as separatist communities such as the Mennonites, Dunkers, and Schwenkfelders, who were committed to pacifist isolation from the world. The Congress exempted them from direct military service, but encouraged religious objectors to contribute to the cause in ways that would be consistent with their religious principles.

The new republic remained concerned about the religious consciences of those groups that objected to military service. George Washington recommended that they be treated "with great delicacy and tenderness" and that the laws of the United States should be "as extensively accommodated to them as the . . . essential interests of the nation may justify."[17] James Madison even went so far as to propose a constitutional amendment specifying that "no person religiously scrupulous of bearing arms shall be compelled to render military service in person."[18] And after the Revolutionary War no one who avoided the draft was punished. Imprisonment was reserved, however, for anyone who refused to pledge their allegiance to the new state governments.

The new nation was also concerned with maintaining an adequate military defense, and a committee appointed to study the issue resulted in a statement by George Washington in 1783 that affirmed military service as a duty of every citizen. This military obligation was to be understood as the first principle of citizenship. "It may be laid down as a primary position, and the basis of our system," Washington stated, "that every Citizen who enjoys the protection of a free Government owes . . . his personal services to the defense of it."[19] But the American people were wary of creating a permanent standing army. One of the long-standing sources of American political resentment had been the presence of the British standing army in the colonies. The new nation was apprehensive of creating a similar situation with a permanent federal army. So the system of militias under state control was adopted as the first line of peacetime military defense. The Militia Act of 1792 required that all able-bodied citizens, (with the exception of blacks) between the ages of 18 and 45 be enrolled in their local state militias. In effect, this was a system of registration for military service on the state level, and no punishments were suggested for anyone who refused to enroll. The militia system that developed was largely volunteer and it provided states with forces for their defense and for filling national military quotas in times of emergency.

One such national emergency was the War of 1812. When it seemed that an army of volunteers and recruits from state militias would be an inadequate military force, a proposal was made in Congress for a system of national conscription. James Monroe proposed a bill that would institute a national military draft. The proposal had considerable support in Congress, but the war ended before it could be passed. An eloquent opponent of the proposed measure was the congressman from Massachusetts, Daniel Webster. He saw the draft as a serious danger to the basic principles of American government. The draft appeared to him to have no constitutional basis. "Who will show me any constitutional injunction," he asked, "which makes it the duty of the American people to surrender everything valuable in life, and even life itself, not when the safety of their country and its liberties may demand the sacrifice, but whenever the purposes of an ambitious and mischievous Government may require it?"[20]

One issue was the limitation of the power of government. A free government, according to Webster, would call for the free and voluntary assent of its citizens to military service. It would evoke their patriotic enthusiasm, not demand their service. He even went so far as to call conscription a form of slavery. And a government dedicated to civil liberties could not violate them without losing its basic integrity. A second issue was the limits placed on military power. The Constitution specified that Congress had the power to raise armies "to repel invasion, suppress insurrection, or execute laws." But Webster feared that a conscripted army would be used for the purposes of national conquest, expansion, and conflicts that would not be supported by the American people. Rather than drawing upon the patriotic impulses of Americans to voluntarily rise to the defense of their country, such a conscription of soldiers would result in a mercenary force seeking military gains. This he felt was inconsistent with the role of the military specified in the Constitution.

Finally, there was the issue of violence. Conscription was a form of violence exerted by the government on its own citizens. And Webster was convinced that the American public would not accept such a system, if it was imposed on them, without resistance. He stated: "If the administration has found that it can not form an army without conscription, it will find, if it venture on these experiments, that it cannot enforce conscription without an army."[21] The irony of conscription, for Webster, was that in order for the government to increase its military power, it must first turn that power upon its own citizens. Daniel Webster declared that he was "anxious, above all things, to stand acquitted before God, and my own conscience," of any participation in such a plan that would commit the United States to increased violence at home and abroad.

The first federal conscription laws were not passed until the Civil

War. The Confederacy in the South enacted a law on April 16, 1862 which placed all state militias under the control of the central government, and the North followed shortly with the creation of a federal draft on March 3, 1863. For the first time citizens were drafted directly into a federal army. The Union divided its states into districts, which corresponded to congressional districts, and sent enrolling officers door-to-door to enlist eligible men. Many resisted by moving from one location to another, or deserting, and a large-scale draft riot broke out in New York City, from July 13 to 16, 1863, which resulted in nearly 500 deaths, millions of dollars of property damage, and required federal troops to be sent from Gettysburg to restore order.[22] Again, much of the resentment that caused draft riots was based on the inequalities in the methods of recruitment. A wealthy individual could be immune to the draft by paying a commutation fee of $300.00 or by hiring a substitute, and a similar exemption could be obtained from the Confederate army for $500.00. As a result, the poor and the powerless were the segment of society most vulnerable to conscription.

By the time the war was over, draft riots had occurred in almost every state in the Union, and one general criticizing the inefficiency of conscription wrote that "your ranks cannot be filled by the present draft. . . . It takes more soldiers to enforce than we get by it."[23] Nevertheless, conscription seemed to be a requirement for waging the kind of total war that the Civil War represented. It necessitated the universal obligation for military service. And as the scope of American military power increased, this principle was not forgotten. As Russell Weigley observed, "Federal conscription would be the principal legacy of the Civil War experience to future American armies."[24]

The federal draft during the Civil War did not make any special provision for conscientious objectors. They could avoid military service through the standard means: paying the fine or hiring a substitute. But some religious objectors were unable to afford this kind of exemption, or refused to participate, and were inducted into the military. The experience of Henry D. Swift, a member of the Society of Friends, was characteristic of many Quakers who were in conflict with the military because of their religious convictions. Swift refused to take part in military drills. And although he willingly helped with the care of the wounded in a military hospital, he was told by his officers that he would be shot for refusing to obey orders. They even tried to get him to change his convictions by forcing him to watch an execution, and warning him that he would soon suffer the same fate if he persisted. Eventually, he was tried and sentenced to be shot. It was only through the intercession of influential Quakers with President Lincoln that Henry Swift's execution was prevented and he was put on parole.[25] The War Department adopted a policy of putting objectors on parole, and then in February 1864 amended the Draft Act to assign conscientious objectors to noncombatant status in hospitals. The special consideration given to religious objectors was evident in that by July 1864 they were the only ones who were still allowed exemption from military service by paying a fine.

World War I represented another total war effort that called for the enforced conscription of civilians into the armed services. But where the draft during the Civil War accounted for only about 6 percent of the total forces, the draft during the World War I called up almost 3 million men, amounting to approximately two-thirds of the total military force of the United States. The Draft Act made a provision for conscientious objection, but limited the classification to members of those religious groups that had historically been opposed to war. The Draft Act of 1917 stated:

> Nothing in this Act contained shall be construed to require or compel any person to serve in any of the forces herein provided for who is found to be a member of any well-recognized religious sect or organization at present organized or existing and whose creed or principles forbid its members to participate in war in any form and whose religious convictions are against war or participation therein in accordance with the creed or principles of said religious organizations.[26]

The Act specifically singled out the peace churches, such as the Quakers, which had historically been opposed to participation in war. The Act also stipulated that such objectors were not exempt from all forms of service, but would be required to serve in some noncombatant capacity. A total of 20,873 conscientious objectors were inducted into the army to serve in such noncombatant roles. Those religious objectors who were not members of the recognized peace churches, yet still found military service a violation of conscience, were acknowledged by an executive order of President Woodrow Wilson in March of 1918. Those who objected to war on account of "conscientious scruples" could serve in the same kinds of noncombatant assignments. Approximately 4,000 conscientious objectors claimed exemption on this basis, and out of that group some were assigned to noncombatant status in the military, while others were assigned to farm or industrial labor under civilian authority. There were about 500 objectors who refused any participation in the military, and out of these 450 were convicted in military courts to serve prison sentences ranging for the most part between 10 and 30 years; 142 received life sentences; and 17 were sentenced to death, although their death sentences were finally commuted.[27]

The treatment of these prisoners was sometimes harsh: many reportedly chained to the bars of their cells for eight hours a day. Roger Baldwin, founder of the National Civil Liberties Bureau, was willing to face such punishment rather than perform any services that would aid the war effort. He felt he had no moral obligation to comply with the draft, and was prosecuted for failing to respond. Baldwin declared that conscription was "a flat contradiction of all our cherished ideals of individual freedom, democratic liberty, and Christian teaching."[28] He was willing to undergo punishment for violating the law, rather than violate moral principles of conscience that he held sacred. Norman Thomas observed, regarding the trial of Roger Baldwin and other objectors, that these moral absolutists performed an important role in American society. "The example of the conscientious objectors in war time," he suggested, "ought also to strengthen a wholesome iconoclasm in peace time directed against that extraordinary idol, the political state, which in Lord Acton's words 'suffers neither limit nor equality, and is bound by no duty to nations or to men, that thrives on destruction, and sanctifies whatever things contribute to increase of power.' "[29]

The religious objectors provided a resistant force against this deification of the modern state, and presented the possibility of higher moral standards to which the political actions of the state could aspire. Those aspirations were embodied in the *Manifesto for the Universal Abolition of Conscription,* which was signed in 1926 by such international personalities as Albert Einstein, Mahatma Gandhi, H.G. Wells, and Bertrand Russell. It cited Wilson's proposal that the League of Nations agree to make conscription illegal in all member countries, and it expressed the hope that the end of conscription would make a positive contribution to stopping the expansion of militarism in the modern world.[30]

That militarism continued to be an important feature of American identity was reflected in the requirement of new citizens to declare their commitment to "support and defend the Constitution and laws of the United States against all enemies, foreign and domestic, and bear true faith and allegiance to the same."[31] To become a naturalized citizen was to assume the responsibility for military service. And the implication followed that anyone who would not be willing to take up arms in defense of the country could not become a citizen. This assumption was tested in two cases that came before the Supreme Court between the world wars. The first was the case in 1929 of a Hungarian-born writer, Rosika Schwimmer, who was well known for her pacifist commitments. She was asked: "If necessary, are you willing to take up arms in defense of this country?" Schwimmer responded that as a pacifist she could not promise to do that and remain consistent with her moral principles. The Naturalization Service denied her application for citizenship. The Supreme Court upheld the denial of citizenship to those who were not willing to perform this supreme obligation, and it suggested that the country would be in danger if it permitted people to become citizens who would not carry out this moral duty. Madame Schwimmer, however, represented a conflicting sense of moral duty in her commitment to pacifism. And the dissenting opinion in this case maintained that although Rosika Schwimmer's convictions were not based on religion, they were nevertheless consistent with a strand of American religious belief, exemplified by the Quakers, that has played an important role in American history. Justice Holmes defended pacifists in America, suggesting that "I had not supposed hitherto that we regretted our inability to expel them because they believe more than some of us do in the teachings of the Sermon on the Mount."[32] Nevertheless, the majority ruling of the Court was that such pacifists should be excluded.

The second case involved a Canadian-born Baptist minister and professor of religion, Douglas Macintosh, who was denied United States citizenship because he would not pledge to fight in any war into which the country should enter. Macintosh refused to pledge such an unconditional allegiance to a nation—an allegiance he felt should only be pledged to God. The Court in 1931 also upheld this denial of citizenship. In this case religious conscience was directly involved but the majority decision of the Court insisted that it carried no weight in the matter. The exemption from military service was a privilege granted under special circumstances by Congress, and not a right that was protected by the First Amendment freedom of religion. Commitment to serve in the military remained a condition for anyone who wanted to become a naturalized citizen of the United States.[33]

It was not until 1946 that the Supreme Court reconsidered this position. In the case of a Seventh Day Adventist (*Girouard v. United States*), who stated that he could not bear arms on religious grounds, the Court reversed its previous decisions and maintained that willingness to perform military service was not a condition of citizenship. The Court observed that during times of national emergency, citizens can serve their country in a number of important ways that do not involve direct military action. The Congress did not intend a willingness to bear arms to be a precondition for becoming a citizen. On this basis, the Court reversed its earlier rulings. Although this attention to the meaning of the Naturalization Act did not directly involve constitutional issues, the majority opinion submitted by Justice Douglas reflected a concern for preserving the freedom of religious conscience in American society. He concluded:

> The struggle for religious liberty has through the centuries been an effort to accommodate the demands of the state to the conscience of the individual. The victory for freedom of thought recorded in our Bill of Rights recognizes that in the domain of conscience there is a moral power higher than the state.[34]

Revisions in the Naturalization Act of 1952 brought the requirements for citizenship into line with this ruling of the Supreme Court. An applicant who objected to military service could still become a citizen if he or she could prove "by clear and convincing evidence to the satisfaction of the naturalization court that he is opposed to the bearing of arms in the Armed Forces of the United States by reason of religious training and belief."[35] This was an important step toward extending the liberty of individual conscience. It represented a greater acceptance of the legitimacy of religious conscience in American society. New citizens who professed such moral convictions did not represent a threat to the United States, as they did in the earlier rulings of the 1920s, and they were allowed to participate as citizens without committing themselves to military actions that would be inconsistent with their consciences.

The experience of World War II completely altered American attitudes toward compulsory military service. The preparations for another total war required vast numbers of Americans to be mobilized for military service. The first step in this mobilization was the Draft Act of 1940. By the time the war was over a network of approximately 6,500 local draft boards had registered almost 50 million men and drafted about 15 million into military service.[36] The machinery of military conscription was supported by a dramatic change in American public opinion about compulsory military training and service. Beginning in 1940 political leaders in Congress worked to adapt American opinion to the demands of war. As one congressman, Sol Bloom, observed, it was necessary to bring about "the installation of an attitude in the American people that would cause them to accept the possibility, and, gradually, the likelihood, of their direct participation in the war."[37]

This new acceptance of the necessity of military service was reflected in a series of public opinion polls taken by George Gallup. At the end of 1938 he reported that only 37 percent of the American public were in favor of mandatory military service for all young men twenty years of age; by the end of the war as many as 75 percent of Americans supported a program of universal military training and service.[38] This change in public support for conscription was certainly one factor in the decision to continue the draft after the end of the war. Prior to 1941, the armed forces of the United States never employed more than 1 percent of the adult male population, and this figure was only reached in times of war. Since 1941 the percentage of adult males in the armed services has always been over 3 percent; while since the Korean War the figure has been over 5 percent.[39]

President Harry Truman supported a program of Universal Military Training for all young men in America. Insisting that America's safety, peace, and prosperity depended on a strong military force, he advocated that all young men be trained in some area of military skills and specialization. This was not a form of conscription, he claimed, because they would not be inducted into the armed forces. Rather, they would be trained in military camps in order to be prepared for induction in case of a national emergency. Besides the military benefits, however, Truman seemed to have a vision of the spiritual power that could be mobilized through the Universal Military Training of American youth. He declared that this training would serve "to develop skills that could be used in civilian life, to raise the physical standards of the nation's manpower, to lower the illiteracy rate, to develop citizenship responsibilities, and to foster the moral and spiritual welfare of our young people."[40] Universal Military Training was to be a kind of social engineering that would mold the moral and spiritual character of American citizens. The Congress rejected Truman's proposal, but compromised by extending the Selective Service Act to require that all young men register for a draft. The idea of Universal Military Training reappeared from time to time. Periodically, politicians argued that training would be a kind of socialization producing acceptable, disciplined, and homogeneous young American citizens. This notion was reflected in one of Dwight Eisenhower's arguments for Universal Military Training (UMT) as recently as 1966: "I deplore the beatnik dress, the long, unkempt hair, the dirty necks and fingernails now affected by a minority of our boys. If UMT accomplished nothing more than to produce cleanliness and decent grooming, it might be worth the price tag."[41] Military discipline was a prescription for physical, as well as spiritual purity, and a regimen that would produce more uniformly socialized behavior in American society.

The Draft Act of 1940 allowed exemption from military service for conscientious objectors, and even permitted them to serve in a nonmilitary capacity in alternative civilian occupations. The definition of religious grounds for objection to military service was significantly broadened over the language of the Selective Service and Training Act of 1917. Where exemption was specified in 1917 for members of pacifist churches, the 1940 Draft Act allowed exemption for all those who could convince their local draft boards that they sincerely held religious beliefs opposed to their involvement in war. No person would be required to undergo military training or service "who, by reason of religious training and belief, is conscientiously opposed to participation in war in any form."[42] About 12,000 conscientious objectors were granted exemptions during World War II in order to serve in Civilian Public Service Camps. But another 6,000, the vast majority of whom were Jehovah's Witnesses, refused even this accommodation with the military and were sentenced to prison for violations of the Draft Act.

Although the language of the Draft Act expanded the definition of religion under which objectors to military service could claim exemption, the reference to religious training and belief involved certain ambiguities about precisely what would count as legitimate religious belief under the law. Congress tried to clarify the legal definition of religious training and belief in an amendment to the Draft Act in 1948 by defining it as "an individual's belief in a relation to a Supreme Being involving duties superior to those arising from any human relation, but [not including] essentially political, sociological, or philosophical views or a merely personal moral code."[43] This reaffirmed the basic assumption that there are moral demands derived from a higher source than human interests. And religion was defined as that area of individual belief (as opposed to individual beliefs based on a review of history, a consideration of social issues, or a pragmatic concern with political factors) that had access to this higher moral authority.

Such religious concern was assumed to be different from the secular concerns of philosophy, history, or politics; but what was religion in and of itself? The assumptions about religion embodied in the Draft Act included three fundamental propositions. First, religion was theistic. The assertion that religious belief necessarily involved the notion of a human being's relation to a Supreme Being suggested that the only forms of religion that could be recognized under the law would be traditional monotheisms—Judaism, Christianity, and Islam. This called into question the status of those systems of religious belief that do not revolve around a single Supreme Being. Buddhism is a primary example of such a religion, but many other traditions do not hold the belief in a relation between humans and a Supreme Being as a central doctrine. The Draft Act seemed to show a preference for traditional forms of western theism in its definition of religious belief.

Second, religion was organized. In excluding an individual's private and personal moral code from the definition of religion, the Draft Act showed a preference for religious beliefs that are held by conventional, organized religious groups. This was partly a persistence of the special status given to the peace churches. But it was also the assumption that legitimate religious beliefs are formed through a process of training and indoctrination within organized religious groups. This of course challenged the status of personal religious convictions based on private reflection or influenced by more general sources of religious inspiration which could preclude an individual from serving in the military.

Third, religion was *either* a resistant force *or* a cooperative force in relation to war. Either a system of religious training and belief was opposed to war or it was not. This absolute either/or status of religion in relation to war required religious conviction to be opposed to all wars in order for it to qualify the individual for exemption. This of course challenged systems of religious belief that require individuals to evaluate each particular war against religious principles of justice. The just war tradition in Christian thought, which requires a selective opposition to some wars and a reluctant approval of others based on whether or not they conform to the standards of justice, would be ruled out by the assumption of the Draft Act that the religious objector must be opposed to "war in any form." The law assumed that religious training and belief could justify opposition to all wars, but could not justify selective opposition to some wars. These three assumptions about religion—that religion is necessarily theistic, conventionally organized, and nonselective when it opposes warfare—were all tested in important Supreme Court cases during the sixties. These cases contributed toward redefining the role of religion in American society and the relation between religious conscience and military power.

RELIGION AND CONSCIENCE

The intention of the First Amendment seemed to be to separate out an area of personal thought and expression that would be protected from the coercive influences of government. Personal opinion, belief, and speech are under ordinary circumstances immune from any direct control by political power. Religious belief and moral conscience reside in this protected area; but there is a certain ambiguity regarding their relation to each other. In James Madison's original draft of the Bill of Rights he distinguished religion and conscience as two different human rights needing protection by the Constitution:

> The civil rights of none shall be abridged on account of religious belief or worship, nor shall any national religion be established, nor shall the full and equal rights of conscience be in any manner, or on any pretext, infringed.[44]

There were two dimensions to the freedom guaranteed in this version: The public dimension represented the liberty of religion allowed by the absence of a single national religion; the private dimension was the liberty of moral conscience. The public and private were fused, however, in the language that was finally adopted for the First Amendment. And the same word—religion—was used for both of these freedoms.

Yet the ambiguity remained. What was the relation between religion and conscience? For rationalists like Franklin, Jefferson, and Madison, conscience was the essence of religion. Enlightened religion was heightened moral conscience; everything else was considered unnecessary superstition. But religion could also be described on several different levels. The influential Baptist leader, John Leland, maintained that religion was made up of three parts: "Internal religion is a right exercise of the soul towards God and man. By practical religion, I mean those righteous external actions, which men as individuals perform towards God and their fellow creatures. Social religion includes the various duties of religious society."[45] Religion thus could be described in three dimensions: a theoretical level of religious *beliefs*; a practical level of religious *practices*; and a social level of religious *association*.

The 1917 Selective Service Act recognized exemptions from military service for those affiliated with religious groups prohibiting involvement in war. This gave priority to the dimension of religious association in deciding on matters of conscience. It was assumed that conscience was determined by an individual's association with a specific group. But the history of conscientious objection to military service in the twentieth century reveals a basic trend in the Supreme Court toward broadening the definition of religion, so that it was not necessary for an individual to belong to a pacifist religious group in order to object to war based on religious training and belief. The Court began to recognize that personal conscience could be informed by religious beliefs outside of the context of organized religion.

The conscientious objection cases decided by the Court in the sixties revealed a change of perspective in the conceptual relationship between religion and conscience. As Douglas Sturm put it: "The change has been from understanding conscience as a function of religion to interpretation of religion as a function of conscience."[46] In one sense, this represented a return to the priority of conscience in the protection of religious freedom. But the Court also developed a new approach to the definition of religion itself: It shifted from a concern with the *content* of religion to a consideration of its *function*. Religion was not defined by its content; it did not consist of a prescribed set of necessary beliefs. Rather, religion came to be defined by the central role beliefs play in the life of an individual. If those beliefs performed a function that was analogous, parallel, or equivalent to the role of conventional religious beliefs, then they could qualify the individual for exemption from military service based on a conscience informed by religious training and belief.

The important cases of *Seeger* in 1965 and *Welsh* in 1970 broadened the definition of religion in the Court by introducing this test of functional equivalence. In *Seeger* the Court ruled that a given belief would qualify as religious if it was sincerely held and occupied a meaningful place in the life of its possessor that was parallel to the place occupied by more orthodox, conventional, and easily recognized forms of religious belief. The decision in *Welsh* carried this reasoning further by ruling that even if the registrant did not describe his own belief as "religious" it could be considered religious if it functioned in the individual's life in a way that was equivalent to traditional religious beliefs.

This new concern with a functional definition of religion conflicted with the language about religion in the Selective Service Act and in earlier Supreme Court decisions. The Court had defined religion, in the opinion of Justice Hughes in *Macintosh* (1931), as "belief in a relation to God involving duties superior to those arising from any human relation." This definition gave specific content to the Court's notion of religion: It was necessarily based on belief in God. The Selective Service Act incorporated this language when it was amended in 1948; but it substituted the term "Supreme Being" in place of the term "God" in its clarification of what would count as recognized religious belief under the law. Yet even if Congress intended to broaden the range of acceptable beliefs that would be included, it still presented a definition of religion based on content. The essence of religion was determined to be a specific kind of belief—personal theism—and therefore would exclude systems of religious belief that held different kinds of content. *United States v. Seeger* (1965) confronted this issue directly.[47] The applicant for conscientious objection on religious grounds stated that he wanted to leave open the question of whether or not a Supreme Being existed, and therefore his religious convictions were not based on the specific content required by the law—belief in a Supreme Being. But, Seeger continued in his application, his "skepticism or disbelief in the existence of God" did "not necessarily mean lack of faith in anything whatsoever." He claimed to have a vital religious faith in goodness, virtue, and a purely ethical creed. Seeger was convicted in a federal district court for refusing to submit for induction into military service.

In the unanimous decision of the Court the religious basis of Seeger's conscientious objection was upheld. Justice Clark stated that it was not the intention of Congress to restrict the exemption only to those who believed in a traditional God. He pointed out that Congress had changed the language of the Selective Service Act to "Supreme Being" for this very reason, and by that term it intended to embrace all religions. The test must simply be whether or not the belief in question "occupies a place in the life of its possessor parallel to that filled by the orthodox belief in God of one who clearly qualifies for the exemption." The functional equivalence test would allow for a wide variety in the actual *content* of religious belief, so long as its *function* in the life of the believer was religious. This functional approach to religion was similar to definitions that have been proposed in the academic study of religion. Robert Bellah, for example, has defined religion as "symbolic forms and acts that relate man to the ultimate conditions of his existence."[48] This definition says nothing about the specific content of those symbolic forms, but only that they play a central role in relating human beings to their ultimate life concerns.

Certainly the mainstream of American religion has symbolized those ultimate concerns in relation to the image of a transcendent God. *Macintosh* (1931) attempted to enshrine this majority opinion as the standard for all religion. Justice Sutherland stated, "We are a Christian people." He even went so far as to venture a theological statement of faith in maintaining that "unqualified allegiance to the nation and submission and obedience to the laws of the land, as well those made for war as those for peace, are not inconsistent with the will of God." Whether or not all religious people would agree on this interpretation of the will of God, the Court in *Macintosh* assumed that in order to count as religious, they must at least believe in such a God. But personal theism is only one way to symbolize a sense of religious obligation that transcends ordinary human relations. And the Court in the case of *Seeger* (1965) took important steps toward expanding the interpretation of the Selective Service Act to accommodate nontheistic religious beliefs.

Justice Clark asked whether the term "Supreme Being" referred only to the orthodox concept of God. Or did it carry the broader meaning of a power, faith, or value to which all else is subordinate and upon which all else is ultimately dependent? For guidance in this matter, Justice Clark referred to the work of the Protestant theologian Paul Tillich as an alternative to traditional Christian theism. In his *Systematic Theology,* Tillich had said "I have written of the God above the God of theism . . . the 'God above God,' the power of being, which works through those who have no name for it, not even the name God." Religion, for Tillich, was the ultimate concern. The word "God" was not important: "And if the word has not much meaning for you," Tillich recommended, "translate it, and speak of the depths of your life, of the source of your being, of your ultimate concern, of what you take seriously without any reservation. Perhaps, in order to do so, you must forget everything traditional that you have learned about God." Justice Clark also turned to the theological reflections of John A. T. Robinson, whose book *Honest to God* (1963) had been an important influence in the formation of the Death of God movement. Robinson had suggested that religious commitment could still be meaningful even when it had outgrown the literal belief in a God "out there." These references to the work of Tillich and Robinson demonstrated the Court's willingness to take seriously contemporary developments in religious thought in forming its functional definition of religion.

But a second consideration was the actual variety of religious traditions, groups, and movements in American society. Justice Clark observed that there were over 250 different religious groups in the United States, and not all of them believed in a purely personal God. Some were American experiments that thought of religion as a way of life directed toward an ultimate goal of human understanding or peace. One such group that Clark considered was the Ethical Culture Movement. The founder of this group, David Saville Muzzey, stated in his book *Ethics as a Religion* (1951) that, "instead of positing a personal God, whose existence man can neither prove nor disprove, the ethical concept is founded on human experience . . . Thus the 'God' that we love is not the figure on the great white throne, but the perfect pattern, envisioned by faith, of humanity as it should be, purged of the evil elements which retard its progress toward the knowledge, love and practice of the right."

While this American religious group was clearly not based on a traditional theism, there were other, more ancient, traditions flourishing in American society that held no belief in a personal God. The most obvious example was Buddhism. Justice Clark observed that Buddhists do not necessarily believe in a personal God, but "strive for a state of lasting rest through self-denial and inner purification." In a supporting opinion, Justice Douglas went into greater detail to argue for the legal status of Buddhism as a system of religious belief. He cited the work of the Buddhalogist Edward Conze to support the contention that Buddhism is a religion even though it is not based on an essential belief in a God as the personal creator of the universe. Justice Douglas noted that when the present Selective Service Act was adopted, with its definition of religion as belief in a Supreme Being, "we were a nation of Buddhists, Confucianists, and Taoists, as well as Christians." Buddhism in fact was the major faith of the Hawaiian territory, as well as having many adherents in the western part of the United States. To define religion exclusively as a belief in a traditional concept of a personal God would be to exclude this large segment of the American population. Therefore, Douglas concluded, the Court could not assume so narrow and parochial an interpretation of the phrase "Supreme Being," but must interpret broadly in order to be consistent with the actual religious composition of American society.

The ruling in *Seeger* followed such an interpretation of the language of the Selective Service Act. It did not raise the constitutional issues of the freedom of religion, but rather interpreted the terminology of religious exemption so that it could clarify the standards used by local draft boards in determining whether or not an applicant's objection to war was based upon religion. Justice Clark instructed local draft boards that "their task is to decide whether the beliefs professed by a registrant are sincerely held and whether they are, in his own scheme of things, religious." The definition of religion which the Court provided to local draft boards was descriptive rather than normative. It did not prescribe essential beliefs that must be held in order for the claim for conscientious objection to be described as religious. If a registrant described his own beliefs as religious, his claim had to be taken seriously. And it had to be considered even if those beliefs did not conform to orthodox, traditional, or conventional expectations about the content of religious belief.

The case of *Welsh* (1970) expanded the religious basis for conscientious objection even further.[49] The applicant had signed the required Selective Service Form to request exemption from military service for reasons of conscientious objection. The form stated: "I am, by reason of my religious training and belief, conscientiously opposed to participation in war in any form." Welsh signed this form; but only after crossing out the words "my religious training and." He denied that his objection to war was based on religious belief. He was convicted by a United States District Court for refusing to submit to induction and sentenced to three years in prison. The Court of Appeals recognized the sincerity of Welsh's commitments, and it noted that his "beliefs are held with the strength of more traditional religious convictions." But, his beliefs were insufficiently religious to qualify for the exemption. The Appeal Board and the Department of Justice "could find no religious basis for the registrant's beliefs, opinions, and convictions." And so the conviction was upheld.

The majority opinion of the Supreme Court was delivered by Justice Black. He noted that Welsh was more insistent than Seeger in denying that his beliefs were religious. Where Seeger had put quotation marks around the word "religious," Welsh had crossed it out entirely. Welsh had "denied that his objection to war was premised on religious belief." But Justice Black felt that the Court should not place too much emphasis on the applicant's description of his own beliefs. The Court had decided that an applicant's description of his beliefs as religious should be given great weight; but this did not imply that if he characterized his beliefs as nonreligious the description should be treated as binding. Few registrants were aware of the broad scope that the Court had given to the word "religious" in the Selective Service Act, and, therefore, the registrant's description of his beliefs as nonreligious was not a reliable criterion for what should count as religious for the purpose of exemption.

After his initial hearing, Welsh had written a long letter to the Appeal Board, in which he declared that his beliefs were "certainly religious in the ethical sense of the word." There had been some confusion in his original responses, because he assumed that the government was using the term *religion* to mean conventional, organized religious groups. Welsh said that he had assumed that the Department of Justice hearing officer "was using the word 'religious' in the conventional sense, and, in order to be perfectly honest did not characterize my belief as 'religious.' " The Court ruled here that it was the responsibility of government officials to use the test of functional equivalence developed in *Seeger*, and not simply rely on the registrant's self-description. The Court held that because Welsh's beliefs had the strength of more traditional religious convictions, they were functionally equivalent to religious beliefs. Therefore, he should be eligible for exemption from military service.

The other problem with Welsh's case, however, was that his beliefs were based *in part* on considerations of world politics. The Selective Service Act ruled out beliefs that "were essentially political, sociological, or philosophical views." In other words, it tried to distinguish a genuinely religious conscience from convictions based on a secular point of view. But Justice Black insisted that once the registrant had determined that the applicant's conscience was sincerely based on moral, ethical, or religious principles, and not simply on pragmatic considerations of policy, then the applicant's opinions on domestic and foreign affairs could not change his status as a religious objector. The law, according to Justice Black, intended only to eliminate those whose beliefs were not sincerely held and those whose beliefs were only based on purely political considerations. As soon as the grounds for religious objection were established, then it could not be said that the applicant's beliefs were *essentially* of a political nature.

The assessment of religious and political beliefs was an important issue in the struggles of Muhammad Ali to obtain exemption from military service. As a minister in the Black Muslim faith he claimed conscientious objector status on religious grounds in 1966. But the Justice Department decided that Muhammad Ali's objection was based on "grounds which primarily are political and racial" and did not fulfill the requirements for religious objection. It is possible that the Justice Department was giving in to the temptation to discount the legitimacy of an unconventional religious movement by claiming that it was really a base for political action to establish black power in America. It came close to suggesting, however, that any religious groups that the government finds objectionable may be denied its status as a religion. After protracted legal battles, the Supreme Court finally ruled on Ali's case in 1971. The Court declared that the Justice Department "was simply wrong as a matter of law in advising that the petitioner's beliefs were not religiously based and were not sincerely held."[50]

This ruling was consistent with the 1970 decision in *Welsh*. Holding political opinions in opposition to the prevailing government did not negate the seriousness, nor the compelling nature, of an applicant's religious convictions. All that needed to be determined was whether or not the applicant had a sincere religious basis for objection. Justice Black concluded for the Court in *Welsh* that the Selective Service Act should be interpreted as exempting from military service "all those whose consciences, spurred by deeply held moral, ethical, or religious beliefs, would give them no rest or peace if they allowed themselves to become a part of an instrument of war." Equating morality, ethics, and religion in this way broadened the basis for religious exemption. In a concurring opinion, Justice Harlan agreed that Welsh's religious objection to war should qualify him for exemption from military service. But he felt that both the *Seeger* and *Welsh* decisions had stretched the language of the Selective Service Act beyond the original intention of the Congress. As he read the act, it seemed to imply the very exclusive definition of religion—as theistic, conventional, and organized—which the recent Court decisions had expanded. The Court had made important judicial repairs by interpreting the Selective Service Act in a more expansive way; but there was still the need for a closer examination of the constitutional issues involved.

The question of whether conscientious objection may be protected under the First Amendment guarantee of free exercise of religion is an issue that the Supreme Court has avoided. It has suggested that religious exemption from military service is not a right guaranteed by the Constitution, but a privilege granted by Congress. The Court then has proceeded to concern itself with the scope of that privilege within the terms mandated by Congressional legislation. But it may be argued that exemption from military service when it would violate deeply held religious convictions is protected under the free exercise clause of the First Amendment. Douglas Sturm, for example, has maintained that "the free exercise clause may be and should be construed as exempting from compulsory military service those who have conscientious scruples against participation in war, whether all wars or particular wars."[51] But the Court has been reluctant to extend the constitutional guarantee of free exercise of religion to include the right to religious exemption from war. Conscientious objection has remained an act of grace legislated by Congress out of a longstanding tradition of respect for the power of religious conscience. But even in its most expansive mood the Court has not allowed the power of religious conscience to include the right to pick and choose which wars to support. This was particularly an important issue during the Vietnam era, in which the United States was involved in a war that was abhorrent to the moral consciences of many Americans. The experience of that war at home represented a trial of American conscience.

VIETNAM AND RELIGIOUS CONSCIENCE

The sixties were certainly one of the most eventful and tumultuous decades in American history. The tone for the decade was set in the inaugural address of President John F. Kennedy. He concluded his speech by invoking the sacrificial imagery of religious nationalism. "Since this country was founded," he recalled, "each generation of Americans has been summoned to give its testimony to its national loyalty. The graves of young Americans who answered the call to service surround the globe."[52] But, now Kennedy was calling the country to embark upon a crusade of social action against serious problems in American society.

> Now the trumpet summons us again—not as a call to bear arms, though arms we need—not as a call to battle, though embattled we are—but a call to bear the burden of a long twilight struggle . . . against the common enemies of man: tyranny, poverty, disease and war itself . . . . And so, my fellow Americans: Ask not what your country can do for you—ask what you can do for your country.[53]

The sacrificial devotion to national ideals that American youth had demonstrated on the battlefield was to be directed against social forces that threatened the freedom, health, and prosperity of all humanity. This was a call for a new commitment to conscience and a greater sense of responsibility for advancing the cause of human well-being. One group that responded to this call was the Students for a Democratic Society. When the SDS was founded in 1962 its original statement pledged to take up "the torch which had been passed."[54] But soon this commitment to the moral equivalent of war was confronted by American involvement in a real war in Asia. And by 1965 the SDS had turned its efforts to opposing the war in Vietnam. Student demonstrations, protest marches, and "sit-ins" were organized on college campuses to express that opposition.

Draft resistance began to be organized as a movement. Young men burned their draft cards, refused to report for induction, and denied the moral power of the government over personal conscience. One declaration of opposition to the war read:

We Refuse to Serve. The war in Vietnam is criminal and we must act together, at great individual risk, to stop it. Those involved must lead the American people, by their example, to understand the enormity of what their government is doing . . . . The government cannot be allowed to continue with its daily crimes.[55]

Draft resisters not only refused to serve. Many would not acknowledge that the government had any moral authority to compel them to participate in a system that was carrying on what they considered to be an immoral war. Many refused to take student deferments, or to apply for conscientious objector status, and the result was often a choice between prison, exile, or living underground. Some of the resistance was mobilized by traditional religious groups. A number of Catholic leaders were actively involved in the antiwar movement.[56] In a prominent case, Reverend Sloan Coffin, along with Doctor Spock, was convicted of conspiracy to counsel draft evasion. But for the most part mainstream American religious groups were reluctant to openly oppose the war. The religious conscience most often involved in draft resistance fit the more expansive definition that emerged in the Supreme Court decisions beginning with *Seeger* (1965). Its convictions were often eclectic, drawn from a number of sources of religious inspiration, often including forms of eastern spirituality; it was a conscience that was often primarily humanist in its religious concerns. And yet this conscience which was awakening in many young Americans in response to a war they perceived as evil was often not opposed to war in all forms. It was particularly mobilized against this war. And therefore it did not qualify its possessor for exemption from military service according to the Selective Service Act.

The status of selective objection to war was tested in Supreme Court cases decided in 1971 involving a rock musician from New York and a Roman Catholic gardener from California.[57] Both had applied for conscientious objector status out of deeply held religious convictions. They had also both specified that they were not necessarily opposed to all wars, but could not in good conscience participate in this particular war which they held to be immoral. The first applicant, Gillette, based his religious convictions on a personal faith he called Humanism. The Court did not doubt the sincerity of his religious beliefs; the issue was that they were specifically directed against the war in Vietnam, which Gillette characterized as unjust.

The second applicant, Negre, came from a Roman Catholic background. The tradition of just war theory in Catholic thought requires that each individual must be reponsible for assessing if a war is just or unjust. To be consistent with the demands of religious conscience, he must not serve in an unjust war. Negre stated that before making any decision he wanted to hear the army's own explanation for the violence in

Vietnam. He completed advanced infantry training. But he was not sat-isfied with the military's justification for the war. Negre concluded, "I knew that if I would permit myself to go to Vietnam, I would be violating my own concepts of natural law and would be going against all that I had been taught in my religious training." Both Gillette and Negre were de-nied conscientious objector status not because they did not have religious scruples against participation, but because they did not object to war in all forms. Their cases tested the status of selective conscientious objection.

The majority opinion of the Court, submitted by Justice Marshall, upheld the denial of conscientious objector status for selective objectors. He began with an interpretation of the language of the Selective Service Act, which required the applicant to be "conscientiously opposed to par-ticipation in war in any form." This could only be read, he stated, to mean that conscientious objection to military service must amount to op-position to participating personally in any war and all war. In this act the Congress had recognized the value of conscientious action for a demo-cratic community and had acknowledged that under some circumstances individual conscience and religious duty may override the demands of the secular state. But Congress had specified objection to war as such, and had excluded objectors who refuse to participate in particular wars. The only previous case which had confronted this issue was *Sicurella v. United States*, where the applicant, a Jehovah's Witness, claimed to object on reli-gious grounds to all wars, except for a "theocratic war" commanded by Jehovah. The Court had allowed Sicurella exemption from military serv-ice because such a spiritual war between the forces of good and evil was a highly abstract concept, and as Justice Marshall summarized the decision, "no such war had occurred since biblical times, and none was contem-plated." Congress, on the other hand, had in mind "real shooting wars." Both Gillette and Negre wanted to make ethical distinctions based on reli-gious conscience between such "real shooting wars." And this was denied to them under the requirements for conscientious objection in the Selec-tive Service Act.

Both petitioners argued that this violated their First Amendment protection of religious freedom. On the one hand it seemed to violate the *establishment* clause of the First Amendment by giving preference to a par-ticular theological orientation, which opposed war in all forms, and disad-vantaging other theological beliefs that required discrimination between wars. On the other hand, it seemed to violate the *exercise* clause by forcing them to participate in military actions prohibited by their religious con-sciences. Both of these issues were considered by Justice Marshall in his majority opinion. With regard to the establishment clause, the Court as-serted that by restricting the exemption to those opposed to all wars Con-gress had reduced the involvement of government in religion. It was not necessary for the government to evaluate the religious merits of applicant claims concerning each particular war, and the Court did not have to rule on the relative merits of individual claims about just and unjust wars. Marshall asserted that "the relevant individual belief is simply objection to all war, not adherence to any extraneous theological viewpoint." To say that something like just war theory, the essence of conscientious reflection on war within one religious tradition, is an extraneous theological viewpoint is questionable. And Justice Douglas, in the only dissent to the Court's opinion, observed that Catholics are required by their tradition to evaluate the justice of any particular war. "No one can tell a Catholic," Douglas stated, "that this or that war is either just or unjust. This is a personal decision that an individual must make on the basis of his own conscience after studying the facts." The requirement that the individual must oppose all wars does seem to discriminate against this religious commitment to the responsible assessment of each war. The Court, however, ruled that the interests of the law were secular and neutral with regard to matters of religious opinion, and therefore it did not intend to establish or give preference to one religion.

Concerning the free exercise of religion, the Court ruled that the government had compelling secular interests in raising an army. To allow religious pacifists exemption from military service was consistent with those interests. But to allow individuals, even on the grounds of religious conscience, to pick and choose which wars they would support would frustrate the government's efforts to maintain a fair system for determining "who serves when not all serve." Justice Marshall claimed that opposition to a particular war is more likely to be based on political considerations rather than on purely religious conscience. And since political conditions may change, be reversed, or even be inadequately understood, this becomes an unreliable basis for granting exemption. The Court concluded that the government had compelling interests in raising an army and administrating a fair and workable system of conscription that were sufficient to justify overriding First Amendment protection of religion for those applicants who objected to particular wars. The law's intention was not to burden the free exercise of religion; but where such burdens were felt—as with those who objected to particular wars on religious grounds—they were justified by the compelling interests of the state.

The Court noted that Congress would not have been acting irrationally or unreasonably if it had specified in the Selective Service Act that conscientious objectors to particular wars should be granted exemption. It simply did not do that. The fact that someone feels compelled by religious conscience to make distinctions between wars that are just and unjust may demonstrate an even more sensitive moral conscience than one who is simply opposed to all war. Justice Holmes, in his dissenting opinion in *Macintosh* (1931), expressed his support for those who conscientiously objected to wars of aggression or wars that were otherwise unjustified, and stated that "there would seem to be no reason why a reservation of religious or conscientious objection to participation in wars believed to be unjust should constitute such a disqualification." This has been a minority opinion in the Court. And yet the constitutional question still remains open, and many have argued for the constitutional right to exemption from military service on the grounds of the free exercise of religion. This right could extend to exemption from participation in particular wars, as well as from war in any form.

The argument in favor of this constitutional right notes the difference between *prohibiting* an action that is consistent with religious faith, and *commanding* an action that is inconsistent with religious faith. In commanding someone to perform actions against his or her conscience, the state is placing a heavy burden upon the individual. It may be an even greater disadvantage to the free exercise of religion than laws which prohibit certain religious practices. Since military service commands the ultimate sacrifice of the individual, it is the supreme test of the personal power of religious conscience in relation to the state. Those who argue for selective religious objection insist that the First Amendment guarantees the freedom of religious conscience from state coercion, especially from the heavy burden placed on conscience by any military involvement inconsistent with religious faith.

The Court has responded to this challenge by claiming that the government has compelling national interests in the case of religious objections to particular wars that override the demands of individual religious conscience. As long as the government's intention is primarily secular and neutral it is not violating the prohibition against an establishment of religion; and as long as it can demonstrate compelling state interests in preserving the public welfare, it is not violating the free exercise of religion protected by the First Amendment. These tests of First Amendment freedoms, balancing the interests of religion and state, emerged from a series of court cases involving the religious practices of unconventional, marginal, or alternative religious groups in American society. Groups like the Mormons, the Jehovah's Witnesses, and a host of smaller religious groups have come into conflict with the government over the issue of the free exercise of religion. We will turn to these issues in the next chapter.

NOTES

1. ROBERT ARDREY, *African Genesis* (London: Collins, 1967): 30.
2. ROBERT REDFIELD, "Primitive Law," in *Law and Warfare: Studies in the Anthropology of Conflict*, ed., Paul Bohannen (Garden City, New York: The Natural History Press, 1967): 4-5.
3. RENÉ GIRARD, *Violence and the Sacred*, trans. Patrick Gregory (Baltimore. John Hopkins, 1973): 280.
4. Cited in Boyd Shafer, *Nationalism: Myth and Reality* (New York: Harcourt, Brace and World, 1955): 180−81.
5. For recent, influential statements of Christian pacifism, see Jacques Ellul, *Violence: Reflections from a Christian Perspective* (New York: Seabury, 1969); and John Howard Yoder,

The Politics of Jesus (Grand Rapids, Michigan: Eerdmans, 1972); also see Peter Brock, *Pacifism in the United States: From the Colonial Era to the First World War* (Princeton: Princeton University Press, 1968); and Charles Chatfield, *For Peace and Justice: Pacifism in America, 1914-1941* (Knoxville: The University of Tennessee Press, 1971), for the role of pacifism in American history.

6. For discussions of just war theory from a historical perspective, see Frederick H. Russell, *The Just War in the Middle Ages* (Cambridge: Cambridge University Press, 1975); Michael Walzer, *Just and Unjust Wars: A Moral Argument with Historical Illustrations* (New York: Basic Books, 1977); and Leroy Walters, "Historical Applications of the Just War Theory," in *Love and Society*, eds., J. T. Johnson and D. H. Smith (Missoula, Montanta: Scholars Press, 1974).

7. See Heinrich Bornkamm, *Luther's Doctrine of the Two Kingdoms* (Philadelphia: Fortress Press, 1966); and Hubert Kirchner, *Luther and the Peasants' War* (Philadelphia: Fortress Press, 1972).

8. GEORGE MARSDEN, in *The Wars of America: Christian Views,* ed., Ronald A. Wells (Grand Rapids, Michigan: Eerdmans, 1981): 12.

9. *Ibid.*: 80.

10. *Ibid.*: 143.

11. Cited in Frank Manuel, ed., *The Enlightenment* (Englewood Cliffs, New Jersey: Prentice-Hall, 1965): 59.

12. Cited by Augustus Cerillo, Jr., in *The Wars of America*: 95.

13. HERBERT L. OSGOOD, *The American Colonies in the Seventeenth Century* (New York: Columbia University Press, 1904): I:506.

14. JAMES THOMAS FLEXNER, *George Washington: The Forge of Experience* (Boston: Little, Brown and Co., 1965): 138.

15. DON HIGGINBOTHAM, *The War of American Independence* (New York: Macmillan, 1972): 393.

16. Cited in John O'Sullivan and Alan M. Meckler, eds., *The Draft and Its Enemies: A Documentary History* (Urbana: University of Illinois Press, 1974): 12–13.

17. W.H. HARBAUGH, *Lawyer's Lawyer: The Life of John W. Davis* (New York: Oxford University Press, 1973): 281.

18. LILLIAN SCHLISSEL, ed., *Conscience in America: A Documentary History of Conscientious Objection in America, 1757-1967* (New York: E.P. Dutton, 1968): 35–6.

19. JOHN C. FITZPATRICK, ed. *The Writings of George Washington from the Original Manuscript Sources, 1745-1799* (Washington, D.C.: U.S. Government Printing Office, 1931-44): XXVI:374-91; cited in O'Sullivan and Meckler, eds., *The Draft and Its Enemies*: 27.

20. C.H. VAN TYNE, ed., *The Letters of Daniel Webster* (1902; New York: Greenwood Press, 1968): 56-68; cited in O'Sullivan and Meckler, eds., *The Draft and Its Enemies*: 47.

21. *Ibid.*: 50.

22. JAMES F. RICHARDSON, *The New York Police: Colonial Times to 1901* (New York· Oxford University Press, 1970): 145.

23. JIM DAN HILL, *The Minute Man in Peace and War: A History of the National Guard* (Harrisburg, Pennsylvania: Stackpole Co., 1964): 71; for histories of the draft during the Civil War, see Eugene C. Murdock, *One Million Men: The Civil War Draft in the North* (Madison: The State Historical Society of Wisconsin, 1971); and Albert Burton Moore, *Conscription and Conflict in the Confederacy* (New York: Macmillan, 1924).

24. RUSSELL F. WEIGLEY, *History of the United States Army* (New York: Macmillan, 1967): 216.

25. EDWARD N. WRIGHT, *Conscientious Objectors in the Civil War* (Philadelphia: University of Pennsylvania Press, 1931): 124–5.

26. Cited in O'Sullivan and Meckler, eds., *The Draft and Its Enemies*: 124–5.

27. *Ibid*: 106.

28. CHARLES W. LOMAS, ed., *The Agitator in American Society* (Englewood Cliffs, New Jersey: Prentice Hall, 1968): 114–19.

29. NORMAN THOMAS, *The Conscientious Objector in America* (New York: B. W. Huebsch, 1923): 284–92.

30. Cited in O'Sullivan and Meckler, eds., *The Draft and Its Enemies*: 153–55.

31. Act of 29 June 1906, Ch. 3592, 34 Stat. 596, 598 (1906).

32. *United States v. Schwimmer*, 279 U.S. 644 (1929).

33. *United States v. Macintosh*, 283 U.S. 605 (1931).

34. *Girouard v. United States*, 328 U.S. 61 (1946).

35. 54 Stat 885, 889 (1940); cited in Robert T. Miller and Ronald B. Flowers, eds., *Toward Benevolent Neutrality: Church, State and the Supreme Court* (Waco, Texas: Markham Press Fund, 1977): 150.

36. U.S., Bureau of the Budget, *The United States at War* (Washington, D.C.: Government Printing Office, 1946): 462.

37. SOL BLOOM, *The Autobiography of Sol Bloom* (New York: G.P. Putnam's Sons, 1948): 246.

38. ROBERT DAVID WARD, "The Movement for Universal Military Training in the United States, 1942–52," (Ph.D. diss., University of North Carolina, 1958): 40; cited in O'Sullivan and Meckler, eds., *The Draft and Its Enemies*: 162.

39. BRUCE M. RUSSETT, *What Price Vigilance? The Burdens of National Defense* (New Haven: Yale University Press, 1970): 2.

40. HARRY S. TRUMAN, *Memoirs* (Garden City, New York: Doubleday, 1955): I:511.

41. Cited in O'Sullivan and Meckler, eds. *The Draft and Its Enemies*, 219.

42. 54 Stat. 885, 889 (1940); cited in Miller and Flowers, eds., *Toward Benevolent Neutrality*: 150.

43. Selective Service Act of 1948, 62 Stat. 604, 613 (1948).

44. ANSON PHELPS-STOKES and LEO PFEFFER, *Church and State in the United States* (New York: Harper and Row, 1964): 1.

45. JOHN LELAND, "A Blow at the Root," (1801); in *Writings of Elder John Leland,* ed., L.F. Greene (New York, 1845): 248; cited in Elwyn A. Smith, *Religious Liberty in the United States: The Development of Church-State Thought Since the Revolutionary Era* (Philadelphia: Fortress Press, 1972): 64.

46. DOUGLAS STURM, "Constitutionalism and Conscientiousness: The Dignity of Objection to Military Service, *Journal of Law and Religion* 1 (1983): 267–8.

47. *United States v. Seeger*, 380 U.S. 163 (1965).

48. ROBERT N. BELLAH, *Beyond Belief: Essays on Religion in a Post-Traditional World* (New York: Harper and Row, 1970): 21.

49. *Welsh v. United States*, 398 U.S. 333 (1970).

50. See John Richard Burkholder, " 'The Law Knows No Heresy': Marginal Religious Movements and the Courts," in *Religious Movements in Contemporary America*, eds., Irving I. Zaretsky and Mark P. Leone (Princeton: Princeton University Press, 1974): 42.

51. STURM, "Constitutionalism and Conscientiousness," 266.

52. Cited in Ronald Lora, *America in the Sixties: Cultural Authorities in Transition* (New York: Wiley, 1974): 33.

53. *Ibid*: 34; see David Halberstam, *The Best and the Brightest* (New York: Random House 1972).

54. MASSINO TEODORI, ed., *The New Left: A Documentary History* (Indianapolis: Bobbs-Merrill, 1969) 163–72; see Edward J. Bacciocco, *The New Left in America: Reform to Revolution, 1956–70* (Stanford, CA: Hoover Institution, 1974); and Stanley Rothman and S. Robert Lichter, *The Roots of Radicalism: Jews, Christians, and the New Left* (New York: Oxford University Press, 1982).

55. TEODORI, ed., *The New Left*: 297; see Michael Ferber and Staughton Lynd, *The Resistance* (Boston: Beacon Press, 1971).

56. See Francine Du Plessix Gray, *Divine Disobedience: Profiles in Catholic Radicalism* (New York: Knopf, 1970).

57. *Gillette v. United States, Negre v. Larsen*, 401 U.S. 437 (1971).

CHAPTER EIGHT
THE EXERCISE
OF RELIGION

The constitutional guarantee of religious freedom was intended to protect individuals from government interference in their religious lives. It allowed for an exercise of religion free from the coercive power of the state. For Jefferson, Madison, and others influenced by the Enlightenment, religion was essentially a matter of opinion. And to arrive at opinions individuals must be able to participate in a free and open arena of enquiry. Differences of religious opinion were not a concern of the state. The government was not concerned with deciding what might be orthodox or heretical religious beliefs. The notion of heresy, from the Greek word *hairesis*, meaning "to choose", was beyond the reach of law. In fact, the affirmation of religious freedom involved what has been called a *heretical imperative*.[1] Individuals could choose to believe in anything they wished; or not to believe at all. To create an atmosphere of informed choice, the free exercise of reason and persuasion must be allowed to flourish and, as Jefferson insisted, "to make way for these, free enquiry must be indulged." Religious belief was not an issue in which the state had any interest; and it was certainly beyond the boundaries of legislation. No religious belief could be a crime. "It does me no injury," Jefferson observed, "for my neighbor to say there are twenty gods, or no god. It neither picks my pocket nor breaks my leg."[2] The protection of religious belief, therefore, allowed for a variety of religious opinions to be held and to be expressed without any intervention on the part of the government.

But where the protection of religious belief has been absolute, the free exercise of certain forms of religious practice and association have created conflicts between the interests of the state and the freedom of religion. Supreme Court interpretations of the First Amendment protection of religion have faced the conflict of interest between certain religious practices and the interests of the state in protecting public health, order, and morals. It is easy to see that a *belief* in human sacrifice might be tolerated; but carrying that belief into *practice* may create conflict with the state's interest in protecting the lives of its citizens. The Supreme Court has gone through two stages in applying the free exercise clause of the First Amendment to religious practices: (1) Separating belief and practice so that belief is always immune from government intervention, but practice is always under the jurisdiction of civil law. This approach to the issue is found in those court cases involving the Mormons (Church of Jesus Christ of Latter-day Saints), whose practice of polygamy was prohibited and punished by law even though it was based on religious belief. (2) Balancing the competing interests of religious practice and the interests of the state. This approach was initiated in *Sherbert* (1963) and represented the Court's concern that restrictions should be placed on religious practice only when the state has compelling interests in protecting the health and well-being of individuals and the order and security of the state. Limits on religious practice should be a last resort, and the state should only intervene when it can find no alternative way to achieve its interests. It will be important to examine some of these cases against religious practices that have come into conflict with state interests—cases involving Mormons, Jehovah's Witnesses, and the I AM movement of Guy Ballard—in which the Supreme Court has interpreted the extent of First Amendment protection extended to the free exercise of religious practices.

The freedom of religious association also comes under First Amendment protection. Madison, for example, was convinced that religious freedom could only be guaranteed if many different religious groups were allowed to flourish. "This freedom arises," he observed, "from the multiplicity of sects, which pervades America, and which is the best and only security for religious liberty in any country."[3] By allowing for a variety of different religious associations, the government would insure that the individual remained free from the coercion of a single established religion. And in this freedom, the individual would not only be free to exercise religious opinion, but to affiliate with the religious group of his or her choice. Madison could speak of the multiplicity of sects however, fairly confident that the groups which pervaded America would all be different varieties of Christianity, and that these groups would contribute to a mainstream American consensus on the social role of religion.

Throughout America history there has been a general mainstream of American religious associations, beginning with the major Protestant denominations, and then eventually including Catholicism and Judaism into what Will Herberg called America's tri-faith system. This is mainstream American religious life. And such mainline religious groups tend to be very comfortable in American society. They easily accommodate themselves to their social environment; identify with national identity, purposes, and goals; and adopt civil religious values into their basic systems of belief. But at the same time, there have been religious groups which might be called marginal or alternative, that resist the influences of their social environment. They embody alternative ideals of religious and political authority, and therefore, they often conflict with mainstream American society. The structure of authority within such alternative religious movements may be based on a charismatic leadership, exclusive requirements for membership, demands for total commitment, rigorous discipline, and the attempt to separate the group from its social environment.[4]

There have always been alternative religious movements in American society. The separatism of the Amish, the Shakers, and a variety of utopian experiments have provided important forms of social and religious power on the periphery of American society. Such marginal religious groups provide two important functions in society: First, they represent the boundary against which the mainstream of American society defines itself. By calling basic mainstream values into question, these marginal groups provide an opportunity for the main body of the society to reaffirm its most cherished values. Marginal groups are held up as examples of *abnormal* religious beliefs, practices, and associations, against which the *normal* can be defined, clarified, and reaffirmed. This function of marginal groups may be so important that if they did not exist, the mainstream popular imagination might have to invent them. Second, these groups demonstrate a willingness to experiment, a total involvement, and an intense enthusiasm that injects a new vitality into American religion. They may revitalize the power of religion in the larger society by infusing new energy into the system.

Beginning in the mid-sixties there has been a proliferation of new religious movements—exotic foreign imports from the East, indigenous experiments, alternative spiritualities, or sometimes combinations of foreign and domestic elements—which have created tensions between the center and periphery of American society. Some movements were essentially *therapeutic* in their intentions. They provided alternative techniques for the health and well-being of body, mind, and spirit. Transcendental Meditation, for example, introduced the ancient meditation technique of chanting a mantra, and claimed that this would achieve beneficial therapeutic results in lowering stress, creating peace of mind, and increasing happiness. Scientology also provided an alternative form of psychotherapy in developing techniques designed to "clear" the individual of inhibiting psychological patterns that block the full realization of human potential.

While alternative therapeutic practices pervaded all the alternative religious movements that have emerged since the sixties, there were a number of groups that specifically sought to create a *totalistic* life style. A group like the Children of God is a good example of a movement that tried to create a total religious way of life. Growing out of the Jesus Movement in the late sixties, the Children of God was led by David Berg (Moses David), who organized the group as a separatist community around a millennial vision of the end of the world that was expected soon. In 1985 the world entered the period of tribulation; and when Jesus returns in 1993, according to Moses David, "the children of God shall rule and reign with Him."[5] The Children of God therefore, represented an alternative political structure, a total pattern of authority, which would survive the coming catastrophe to rule under divine authority. This alternative structure of political power, embodied in a religious vision which placed the Children of God at the center of human history, brought the group into conflict with American society. And Moses fled the United States to continue his work in exile. But many other groups remained, and simply their presence in American society resulted in a series of legal and social conflicts between competing systems of religiopolitical power. We will look at some of the conflicts surrounding three groups in America: The International Society for Krishna Consciousness (ISKCON), the Unification Church, and the movement founded by Bhagvan Rajneesh. Each case raised important issues of political power and authority in relation to the free exercise of religion in American society.

There has been an ongoing attempt to exclude alternative religious movements from American society. Those who have a vested interest in preserving the authority of mainstream social values have experienced these groups as a danger to the American way of life. A coalition of lawyers, mental health professionals, mainline religious leaders, and families of members, has come together to form an anticult movement to combat this perceived danger.[6] But first the anticultists had to get around the First Amendment protection of religious freedom extended to all religious groups. Their basic strategy was to argue that these new religious movements, or cults, were not *really* religious.

One of the earliest and most active figures in the anticult movement was Ted Patrick. He undertook a personal crusade against such movements as the Children of God, ISKCON, and the Unification Church of Reverend Sun Myung Moon. Patrick's basic justification for attacking these groups was that they were not legitimate religions and therefore did not deserve First Amendment protection as religions.

First, these so-called cults were lucrative businesses, according to Patrick, exploiting young people in order to increase the wealth and power of devious leaders. Regarding the leader of the Unification Church, Patrick declared: "Moon doesn't have anything to do with religion. It's a big business operation, plain and simple."[7] A second argument against these groups was that they were really political movements. Again with reference to Reverend Moon, Patrick insisted that his interests were primarily in political power: "He's said over and over again that he wants to rule the world."[8] A third reason given to discount the legitimacy of these groups was the claim that they violated the voluntary principle of American religious denominations. Patrick, and other anticult leaders, claimed that these groups practiced coercive techniques of brainwashing, coercive persuasion, or mind control in order to recruit members. For all these reasons, the anticult movement felt justified in attacking alternative religious movements. Anticultists even tried to justify the practice of kidnapping members of these groups, forcibly restraining them, and submitting them to a process of reindoctrination that would convince them to give up their beliefs and repudiate their association with the alternative religious group.

Beneath this conflict over the status of alternative religious movements is the deeper question of what counts as a legitimate social role. Those individuals who are not seen to be fulfilling a legitimate role tend to be excluded from society. There are two major categories of exclusion in American society: *crazy* and *criminal*. And those individuals who fall into one (or both) of these categories are excluded from society through institutionalized confinement in asylum or prison. These categories of crazy and criminal were also employed in the anticult movement in its efforts to exclude alternative religious movements from legal recognition and protection under the First Amendment guarantee of religious freedom.

The stereotype of "cult madness" was a common feature in literature about new religious movements. Eli Shapiro, M.D., went so far as to diagnose "cultism" as a disease, "which makes its victims ill both physically and emotionally."[9] Membership in an alternative religious movement became in and of itself a symptom of mental illness and, as Harvey Cox observed, "it is thought that no sane person could belong to a movement 'like this' and therefore the participant must be there involuntarily."[10]

The medical diagnosis that members of alternative religious movements were suffering from brainwashing, mind control, or destructive cultism was joined with the legal argument that young people were coerced into such movements to be enslaved and exploited against their wills. This argument was suggested by Richard Delgado to encourage government actions against these groups on the grounds that they violated the Thirteenth Amendment prohibition of slavery.[11] The stereotype of "cult criminality" also appeared in the recent study of Gallup and Poling, based upon their statistical researches into the character of religion in America today, which titled one of its subsections: "The Crimes of the Cults." But rather than documenting specific criminal activities perpetrated by members of new religious movements—and certainly some illegal activities could be documented—the authors devoted this section almost exclusively to a series of recommendations that would help main-stream Christian churches to hold the interest, attention, and enthusiasm of young people in America[12] At this point we have to ask: Is it crime or heresy? Cult controversies certainly involved a conflict of religious world-views that were embodied in mainstream and marginal religious groups. Claims that alternative religious groups practiced brainwashing, which had to be countered with kidnapping, physical restraint, and deprogram-ming, intensified the issues surrounding the free exercise of religion in American society.

THE LIMITS OF RELIGIOUS PRACTICE

As a matter of personal belief, conviction, or conscience, religion is be-yond the scope of government action. This principle was embodied in the First Amendment, and has been affirmed in numerous Supreme Court cases which have sought to interpret it and apply it in specific cases. One of the earliest tests of this limitation of governmental intervention in mat-ters of religious belief came before the Supreme Court in the 1870s. The Presbyterian Church had split in 1861 over the issue of slavery, and the Court was asked to decide whether the northern or the southern division of the Church represented the true Presbyterian faith. The Court ruled that it could not enter into what it perceived as an essentially theological dispute within Presbyterianism. The government could not intervene to determine which side was orthodox and which was heretical. In its deci-sion, the Supreme Court insisted that, "The law knows no heresey, and is committed to the support of no dogma, the establishment of no sect." To decide which position on slavery was legitimate within the Presbyterian Church would be to engage in an internal theological and ecclesiastical dispute, and this the Court refused to do. There was the deeper principle of the freedom of religious belief from government intervention. And the Court upheld this standard of religious freedom by insisting that "In this country the full and free right to entertain any religious belief, to practice any religious principle, and to teach any religious doctrine which does not violate the laws of morality and property, and which does not infringe personal rights, is conceded to all."[13] This ruling reaffirmed the limits on government involvement in questions of religious belief; but it also raised the possibility that the government may have some interest in prohibiting certain forms of religion that violate morality, property, and personal rights. Just six years later the Supreme Court was involved in another case in which a religious movement affirmed, taught, and practiced a form of behavior that was perceived by the government as a threat to common moral values in American society.

　　The Church of Jesus Christ of Latter-day Saints began in upstate New York when its prophet, Joseph Smith (1805-1844) received a new sacred text, the *Book of Mormon*, and gathered a band of followers around its new message of the appearance of Christ in America after his resurrection and the promise of a New Jerusalem in America. Smith was a peculiarly American prophet. Not only did he see America as the center stage of God's drama in history, but he even ran for president of the United States when his group was in Illinois. After Smith's death, the Mormons were led by Brigham Young out of the United States and into the Utah territory. There they established a theocracy where Mormon revelation carried the authority of civil law. Many of the alternative religious movements of the nineteenth century experimented with new patterns of sexuality. Creating a new community also meant working out alternative patterns of human relationship. The Shaker community of Mother Ann Lee, for example, practiced celibacy; while the Oneida community of John Humphrey Noyes experimented with "complex marriages," in which everyone in the community was theoretically married to everyone else.[14] The Mormons also instituted an alternative marriage relationship in the practice of polygamy, in which a man would have more than one wife. This was a marriage pattern encouraged by the example of Joseph Smith, who at one point had almost fifty wives. In the theocratic society of the Mormon Utah territory, such polygamous marriages became a common practice. But this raised the issue of whether or not such a practice, based as it was on religious conviction, should be tolerated by the United States government.

The first test of the Mormon practice of polygamy came before the Supreme Court in 1878. An act of Congress had made it illegal to practice polygamy in the territories of the United States. The Court had to decide if the practice could be permitted if it was based on religious grounds. In the case of *Reynolds v. United States* (1879) the Court upheld the government's authority over polygamy, and denied that a Mormon could be protected against conviction for polygamous marriage under the First Amendment. In passing judgment, the Court insisted on a clear distinction between religious belief and religious action. Beliefs were protected under the free exercise clause of the First Amendment; but actions came under the jurisdiction of the civil law. According to the Court's ruling, "Laws are made for the government of actions, and while they cannot interfere with mere religious belief and opinions, they may with practices." The Court insisted that actions can never be immune from legal restraint simply because they are based on religious beliefs. Religious practices such as human sacrifice, or the religious obligation of wives in some forms of Hinduism to join their deceased husbands on the funeral pyre, would clearly come under the jurisdiction of civil law. The state has a responsibility to protect its citizens against actions that endanger themselves and others, even if those actions are motivated by religion. But what danger is there in polygamous marriage? The Court in *Reynolds* insisted that the family is the moral foundation of civil government, and, therefore, the state has an interest in preserving the institution of the American family.

> Marriage, while from its very nature a sacred obligation, is nevertheless, in most civilized nations, a civil contract and regulated by law. Upon it, society may be said to be built, and out of its fruits spring social relations and social obligations and duties, with which government is necessarily required to deal.[15]

Although Mormons may have seen marriage as a sacred obligation that required a polygamous arrangement, the state insisted on seeing it as a civil contract to be regulated by law. And since marriage was of such consequence to the entire fabric of society, the government had an interest in maintaining the marriage arrangement and nuclear family pattern upheld by common tradition in America. In this decision the Court ruled that the integrity of the monogamous American family was the important civil issue at stake, and the theological concerns of Mormons were irrelevant in the decision to uphold the legal punishment of anyone practicing polygamy.

Of course many Mormons continued to practice the marriage arrangement that had been given to them by their prophet, and a second case came before the Supreme Court in 1890. In *Davis v. Beason* (1890) the Court upheld a law in the territory of Idaho, where many Mormons lived, which required that anyone who wanted to register to vote swear that he was not a member of "any order, organization or association which teaches, advises, counsels, or encourages its members, devotees, or any other person to commit the crime of bigamy or polygamy." The irony of this law was that Davis, the defendant, was not punished for practicing polygamy, but simply for being a member of a group that advocated its practice. The Court in *Davis* dismissed Mormonism as a legitimate religion, and declared that, "to call [its] advocacy [of polygamy] a tenet of religion is to offend the common sense of mankind."[16] The government's attack against the Mormon Church was complete when Congress enacted a law later in 1890 which dissolved the charter of the Church and confiscated its property. The Mormons at this point capitulated and changed their official marriage practices in order to submit to federal law. There was a certain reluctance; and in their declaration of the change the Mormons placed the responsibility on the force of national laws, which they felt had unconstitutionally restricted their freedom of religion. But clearly the Court had determined that the free exercise of religion was not an issue by insisting on a distinction between belief and practice. Belief was free, but practice was regulated by the laws of the land.

The Supreme Court dealt with only six or seven cases involving the First Amendment protection of the free exercise of religion before 1940.

Since that time there has been an increased sensitivity to conflicts between the exercise of personal religious freedom and the law. The group that has appeared most often in such cases has been the Jehovah's Witnesses. They were a millennial group, expecting the imminent second coming of Christ, who embarked on an aggressive campaign to spread their message. They passed out literature door-to-door, stopped people in the streets, and held public rallies. Hostile communities in the 1930s tried to stop the Witnesses by passing ordinances that prohibited such practices. The Witnesses ignored these laws and were arrested in large numbers. The convictions of Jehovah's Witnesses were usually upheld when they were appealed because the Court held to the distinction between belief and action. The active proselytizing by Witnesses could be restricted by civil laws. Even in the case of *Cantwell v. Connecticut* (1940), where the Court reversed the conviction of a Jehovah's Witness for creating a public nuisance through his preaching on the street, the decision still invoked the distinction between religious belief and action. "Thus the Amendment embraces two concepts," observed Justice Roberts, "freedom to believe and freedom to act. The first is absolute but, in the nature of things, the second cannot be. Conduct remains subject to regulation for the protection of society."[17] The turning point for the Jehovah's Witnesses came in the Supreme Court decision in *Murdock v. Pennsylvania* (1943), in which the Court recognized the religious force behind the Witnesses' obligation to spread their message through public proselytizing.

> The hand distribution of religious tracts ... occupies the same high estate under the First Amendment as do worship in the churches and preaching from the pulpits. It has the same claim to protection as the more orthodox and conventional exercise of religion.[18]

The Court suggested that for the Witnesses the streets were their church, and the religious practices of passing out pamphlets, soliciting door-to-door, and preaching in public were essential features of their religious worship. As long as these activities presented no obvious danger to the public welfare, they should be protected under the First Amendment. This decision was not only an important breakthrough for the Jehovah's Witnesses, but it was an important development in the interpretation of the free exercise clause by the Supreme Court. For the first time the Court indicated that religious actions, as well as beliefs, should be seriously considered for protection under the First Amendment.

At the same time, the Jehovah's Witnesses were engaged in legal battles on another front. As a millennial movement, they looked forward to the imminent return of Christ, the end of the world, and the establishment of God's kingdom on earth. Their worldview was essentially theocratic, and they felt compelled to live by divine law in the present in order to prepare themselves for living under God's rule in the immediate future. From this perspective, rituals of nationalism such as the oath of allegiance and flag salute were exercises in idolatry. They violated divine commandments against worshiping other gods and making graven images. So when the children of Jehovah's Witnesses refused to participate in the daily pledge of allegiance to the flag in public schools, they conflicted with the state's interest in reinforcing a shared national identity through that ritual. Many Witness children were expelled from school. The constitutionality of these expulsions was upheld in the case of *Minersville School District v. Gobitis* (1940). The majority opinion written by Justice Felix Frankfurter insisted that the flag represented shared patriotic sentiments that transcended internal differences within the country. He asserted the unifying power of this symbol:

> The ultimate foundation of a free society is the binding tie of cohesive sentiment. Such a sentiment is fostered by all those agencies of the mind and spirit which may serve to gather up the traditions of a people, transmit them from generation to generation, and thereby create that continuity of a treasured common life which constitutes a civilization. We live by symbols. The flag is the symbol of our national unity, transcending all internal differences, however large, within the framework of the Constitution.[19]

The Witnesses who refused to salute the flag or to allow their children to participate in such civil ceremonies of national unity were perceived as a danger to American society. That danger, however, was clearly symbolic. The very alternative to American nationalism that the Witnesses represented seemed to challenge deeply shared national sentiments. And the physical violence against Witnesses, including disruption of their meetings and destruction of their meeting places, during the two years after the *Gobitis* decision was an indication of how the flag salute issue outraged public opinion.

But with the entry of the United States into war against Germany and Japan, the violence against Witnesses seemed to dissipate, as hostilities became directed against foreign enemies. It was perhaps for this reason, as well as a change in the composition of the Supreme Court, that the decision of *Gobitis* was reversed in 1943. It may have been that by this time a small group of school children refusing to salute the flag did not seem such a serious danger to American civilization. In *West Virginia State Board of Education v. Barnette* (1943) the Jehovah's Witnesses finally achieved a victory over the compulsory flag salute that violated their religious conscience. Justice Jackson maintained that the Witnesses should be exempt from a public ceremony that they perceived as idolatrous. They should be exempted from such a practice that placed a burden on the free exercise of their religious faith. Again First Amendment protection was extended to matters of practice. In the words of Justice Jackson, "If there is any fixed star in our constitutional constellation, it is that no official, high or petty, can prescribe what shall be orthodox in politics, nationalism, religion, or other matters of opinion or force citizens to confess by word or act their faith therein." The Court insisted that the government could only intervene in matters of religious faith where religious practices would directly, and not just symbolically, endanger the public. The freedom guaranteed by the First Amendment was "susceptible of restriction only to prevent grave and immediate danger to interests which the state may lawfully protect."[20] There was an important difference between the polygamy cases and the flag salute cases. In the first instance, individuals were being *prohibited* from practices that were felt to endanger the public order; in the flag salute cases, however, individuals were being *commanded* to perform actions that were contrary to their religious beliefs. As in the conscientious objection cases, the government's compulsion of individuals to perform actions in violation of their religious consciences placed a heavy burden on their free exercise of religion.

Another group that tested the limits of religious practice was the I AM movement. Its founder, Guy Ballard, a student of spiritualism, the occult, and esoteric wisdom, claimed that while he was hiking near Mt. Shasta, California, in 1930, he was visited by the spiritual messenger, St. Germain. Germain was an "ascended master," who had overcome the cycle of death and rebirth to assume his place in the heavenly hierarchy. Ballard emerged from this initial meeting convinced that he, as well as his wife and son, were to be representatives of the ascended masters on earth. They would channel, transmit, and publicize the teachings of the masters and reveal the "Mighty I AM Presence" to the world. Ballard published *Unveiled Mysteries* in 1934, and soon thousands of followers were subscribing to books, pamphlets, and letters containing the secret teachings of the spiritual masters. A large mail-order operation resulted. When Ballard died in 1939, his wife and son assumed leadership of the movement. Edna and her son Donald ran into trouble, however, when a Federal Grand Jury indicted them for mail fraud. They were accused of using the mail to deceive the public regarding the fraudulent teachings of the masters, and what is more, they were accused of knowingly publishing false statements of spiritual visions, instructions, and promises of healing to make money for their own use. The Ballards were convicted on these charges.

The case finally came before the Supreme Court in *United States v. Ballard* (1944).[21] The trial judge had originally instructed the jury that they should not try to decide if the beliefs of the Ballards were literally true. They were not to pass judgment on whether Jesus actually shook hands with Guy Ballard, whether Jesus sat for a portrait by the artist Charles Sindelar, or whether there actually was a spiritual hierarchy transmitting messages to the Ballards. They were only to decide if the Ballards themselves actually believed these things. The majority of the Supreme Court upheld the conviction of the Ballards on these grounds. The Court specified that it was beyond the competence of the government to rule as to whether certain religious beliefs were true or whether certain religious experiences actually occurred. As Justice Douglas spoke for the Court: "Heresy trials are foreign to our Constitution. Men may believe what they cannot prove." He noted that religious beliefs, practices, and experiences that may be as real as life to some are incomprehensible to others. These matters of religious belief could not be tested in a court of law. The New Testament also contained accounts of miracles, the divinity of Christ, and the promise of life after death. How could such beliefs be proven in court? "If one could be sent to jail," Douglas insisted, "because a jury in a hostile environment found those teachings false, little indeed would be left of religious freedom." On the other hand, if the *truth* of the belief could not be decided, the Court ruled its *sincerity* could. If a jury was convinced that such beliefs were not in fact genuinely held by the defendants, then they could be convicted for raising money under false pretenses.

The Court was split in its response to this issue, indicating the difficulty of the questions of sincerity and truth. Dissenting opinions presented strong arguments for different rulings. The dissent of Justice Stone argued that some of the claims, such as the statement in the Ballards' literature that they had cured hundreds of people of disease through their spiritual powers, could be put to the test of evidence. In this case, according to Justice Stone, the *truth* of religious statements (and not merely the sincerity with which they may be believed) could be put to the test. An entirely different position was argued in the dissent of Justice Jackson. He stated that the prosecution should never have been undertaken because no jury could be expected to find that the Ballards sincerely believed in something that the jury itself found unbelievable. He personally found "nothing but humbug" in the teachings of the I AM movement; but, nevertheless, the question of their truth, value, or desirability was beyond the power of the government to decide. "That is precisely the thing," Jackson asserted, "the Constitution put beyond the reach of the prosecutor, for the price of freedom of religion or of speech or of the press is that we must put up with, and even pay for, a good deal of rubbish." Jackson concluded that he would dismiss the indictment and put an end to judicial examinations of other people's faiths.

The I AM movement came up before the Supreme Court again in 1946; but this time the Court threw out the indictment on a procedural issue. The Court concluded, as Leo Pfeffer noted, "with what appears to be a broad hint that it would be wise for the California authorities to forget the whole thing."[22] And this they did. But there were at least two issues that emerged from the *Ballard* (1944) case that had consequences for the legal status of future alternative religious movements. One was the clear statement that the *truth* of religious beliefs cannot be subject to trial by law. People may believe what they cannot prove, and the government cannot interfere in matters of belief. But a second issue emerged in the position taken by Justice Jackson—that the *sincerity* of religious beliefs cannot be tried by the Court. Putting sincerity on trial places alternative religious movements in an impossible position by demanding that their leaders prove they sincerely hold beliefs that mainstream society finds unbelievable. The issue of sincerity would be further complicated if the leaders of a group were insincere, yet hundreds of followers sincerely held beliefs revolving around that group. Would the insincerity of the leaders make the religious beliefs of their followers less valid in a court of law? The opinion of Justice Jackson in *Ballard* (1944) was that neither the truth nor the sincerity of religious beliefs should become legal issues. The free exercise of religion requires that they be beyond the control of law.

A major turning point in the Supreme Court's interpretation of free exercise came in *Sherbert v. Verner* (1963). Adell Sherbert was a Seventh Day Adventist who was fired from her job because she refused to work on Saturday for religious reasons. The observance of Saturday as a Sabbath day of rest was an important belief of Seventh Day Adventists, and Adele Sherbert refused to sacrifice this religious principle by accepting employment that would require her to work on Saturday. When she applied for unemployment benefits from the state of South Carolina she was denied those benefits because of the requirement of the state's Unemployment Compensation Act which specified that "a claimant is not eligible for benefits if he has failed without good cause to accept suitable work when offered him." Sherbert had refused to accept jobs that required working on Saturday; and she was denied benefits. When she argued before the South Carolina Supreme Court that her First Amendment right to free exercise of religion was being violated, the Court ruled that her religious beliefs were a personal matter and did not affect her employment. It was decided that her beliefs did not represent a sufficient cause for refusing employment, and her request for employment benefits was denied.

The Supreme Court reversed this ruling in a decision that clarified the legal application of the free exercise clause to many issues of conflict between religious beliefs and the interests of the state. The Court determined that the state of South Carolina had forced Adell Sherbert into a choice between abandoning her religious principles or remaining unemployed, and it suggested that this placed "the same kind of burden upon the free exercise of religion as would a fine imposed against appellant for her Saturday worship."[23] This was unacceptable under the protection of the First Amendment. And so the state was instructed to revise its legislation to remove this burden on the free exercise of religion. Although the question of unemployment compensation may seem to be a minor political issue, the formula worked out in *Sherbert* (1963) had important implications for all future cases involving the free exercise of religion. It developed what was essentially a two part test: (1) Does the legislation in question place any substantial burden upon the individual's free exercise of religion? If it can be determined that a law interferes with an individual carrying out practices or observing principles that are central to his or her religious belief, then a second question must be asked. (2) Does the legislation in question represent a compelling state interest that would justify the infringement of religious freedom? The state's interests must be demonstrated to be highly serious to justify placing a burden on the free exercise of religion. "Only the gravest abuses," the Court concluded, "endangering paramount interests, give occasion for permissible limitation." The burden of proof was transferred from the religious believer to the state. The state must demonstrate not only that it has compelling interests in protecting public safety, but also that it has no other ways of legislating those interests that do not place such an infringement on the free exercise of religion. The state can only regulate activities that are related to the free exercise of religion if that regulation is the least restrictive means available for achieving some compelling state interest.

Subsequent court cases involving alternative religious practices have involved this balancing act developed in *Sherbert* (1963). There have been cases involving the use of illegal drugs in religious practice that have tried to balance the free exercise of religion against the state's interest in controlling those substances. The Native American Church, formed in 1918, made use of peyote in religious ceremonies. A group of Navajos were arrested in 1962 and convicted in California for the possession and use of a controlled substance. The California Supreme Court, however, reversed that conviction in *People v. Woody* (1964). It was determined that the use of peyote in the context of an all-night ritual was an integral component, the "theological heart," of the Native American Church. To prohibit its use would place a serious burden on the free exercise of religion. On the other hand, the state could not demonstrate that the ritual use of peyote represented a danger to public safety. There was no evidence that its use had a negative effect on the Native American community; nor was there a convincing argument that its use in this specific ritual context would endanger the larger public. Justice Tobriner illustrated the balancing test:

> We have weighed the competing values represented in the case on the symbolic scale of constitutionality. On the one side we have placed the weight of freedom of religion as protected by the First Amendment: on the other, the weight of the state's 'compelling interest.' Since the use of peyote incorporates the essence of the religious expression, the first weight is heavy. Yet the use of peyote presents only slight danger to the state and to the enforcement of its laws; the second weight is relatively light. The scale tips in favor of the constitutional protection.[24]

The ritual of peyote in the Native American Church therefore came under the protection of the First Amendment. One concern expressed by the state was that this would encourage the formation of religious movements dedicated to the use of illicit drugs and demanding constitutional protection. Those attempts have been unsuccessful. One example is the Neo-American Church, which was registered as a church in California in 1965. Its founder was known as Chief Boo Hoo; its central teaching was that marijuana and LSD were the true sacraments; its church symbol was a three-eyed toad, its official songs were "Puff the Magic Dragon" and "Row, Row, Row Your Boat," and its church motto was "Victory over Horseshit!" When the Neo-American Church came before the U.S. District Court for the District of Columbia in 1968, Judge Gesell suggested that all these features of the church might lead the court to be skeptical about the sincerity of the group's religious beliefs. But, even if the church's sincerity were granted, the state would still have a compelling interest in controlling the use of the illegal drugs that would override the claim for a religious exemption.[25]

Another free exercise issue has arisen in cases where individuals have refused medical treatment for religious reasons. The state claims a compelling interest in protecting public health. But what about the health of individuals who refuse blood transfusions, vaccinations, or medical care because it would violate their religious principles? Christian Scientists convinced that accepting medical treatment is a denial of the healing power of prayer have been exempt in some cases from certain mandatory public health measures. On the other hand, Jehovah's Witnesses—believing that blood transfusions are forbidden by the Bible—have run into conflict with the government. When a minor child is involved, the courts have tended to override the wishes of the parents in providing medical care.

In most cases involving adult Jehovah's Witnesses, the court has authorized blood transfusions against the wishes of the individual in the interest of the state's compelling obligation to protect human life. But one exception was a case heard by the Illinois Supreme Court, which ruled that the religious belief regarding blood transfusion as a violation of divine law must be respected. Even if such a belief seems "unwise, foolish or ridiculous, in the absence of overriding danger to society we may not permit interference."[26] Again, the decision regarding free exercise of religion involved a careful balancing of the competing interests of the believer and the state. Only the most compelling concerns for protecting public safety could warrant the restriction or compulsion of actions that would result in an infringement of the individual's right to put his or her religion into practice.

These compelling state interests represent the heart of what we might call mainstream social values in America. In the free exercise cases that have come before the Supreme Court, those compelling interests have been the institution of the *family*; the support and encouragement of *nationalism*; and the maintenance of *public health.* Mainstream religious groups in America have not conflicted with these compelling interests because they tend to accept these interests as their own. They are mainstream religious groups because they have adapted the interests of the church to the social interests of the state. But alternative religious movements represent different sets of values, and these alternative value systems have often conflicted with state interests. The religious movements that emerged in American society in the late sixties came into conflict with mainstream public interests in three major areas:

Family. New religious movements were experienced as a threat to the nuclear family in America. Members of some groups repudiated the materialism of their parents and adopted communal life styles to achieve a total religious way of life. Like the Mormons, some of the new religious movements experimented with alternative patterns of marriage and sexuality. In the International Society for Krishna Consciousness, marriage was considered a sacred obligation for the purpose of producing children for Krishna. Sexuality within marriage was regulated so that a couple could have sexual relations once a month, only after performing fifty rounds of chanting, and only for the purpose of procreation. The Unification Church performed a mass wedding of 2,000 couples in Madison Square Garden in 1982. Husbands and wives had been matched by the Reverend Moon himself. The marriage relationship was considered sacred within the church. And Reverend Moon and his wife stood as the true parents of the Unification family. These and other alternative images of family relationships have been perceived as a highly charged threat to the mainstream American family.

Nationalism. New religious movements provided alternative definitions of political power. The Mormons, Jehovah's Witnesses, and the I AM movement were all (to one degree or another) theocratic movements, relying on a highly specific vision of divine revelation to determine their relation to law, government, and national identity. Many new religious movements were also essentially theocratic in their political orientation. The Children of God, for example, expected the second coming of Christ to abolish all national governments. Those forms of political power would be replaced by small-scale, self-sufficient communities. According to Moses David, "God's government is going to be based on the small village plan . . . Each village will be virtually completely self-controlled and self-sufficient unto itself, like one big happy family or local tribe, just the way God started man out in the beginning. His ideal economy, society and government based on His own created productive land for man's simple necessities."[27] ISKCON, the Unification Church, and a number of other groups also had alternative political visions for America's future. And when they put these visions into practice by creating alternative community structures they often came into conflict with the state's interest in reinforcing a unified national identity.

Public Health. Perhaps the most intense controversy regarding new religious movements has involved the state's interest in protecting mental health. Anticult activists claimed that alternative religious movements used recruiting and indoctrination practices that endangered the mental health of individuals and therefore presented a larger danger to the public welfare. Some states have attempted to introduce amendments to their mental health statutes to restrict the expansion of new religious movements. And many court cases have involved the testimony of expert witnesses from the mental health professions, claiming that alternative religious movements brainwash their members. As we will see, this was a useful strategy for trying to circumvent the First Amendment protection of the exercise of religion. But it was also an indication that these alternative religious worldviews, life styles, and organizations were experienced as threats to mainstream values.

These issues represent some of the public interests at stake in the conflict between mainstream and marginal groups throughout American history. In cases dealing with the free exercise of religion, the Supreme Court has been increasingly sensitive to the need to make special legislative accommodations for minority groups. The legal separation of religion and politics has not required the political system to ignore religion; rather, it has given government the responsibility to be aware of the power of religious beliefs and practices and to refrain from placing any unnecessary restrictions on their exercise.

NEW RELIGIOUS MOVEMENTS

The appearance of new religious movements in modern western societies has been subjected to different interpretations. Bryan Wilson has understood them to be products of a larger process of secularization in the modern world. They appear as random anticultural statements against the prevailing trends toward rationalization, technological efficiency, and institutionalized control of human behavior that dominate modern industrialized societies. Cults are gestures of defiance against the progress of secularization, but they are largely irrelevant. They have, according to Wilson, "little impact on the inexorable cost efficiency processes of modern economics and technology."[28] Such new religious movements themselves can be seen as an open market making a variety of techniques for salvation available to the religious consumer. While few members of new religious movements have adopted a totally different communal life style devoted to serving the goals of their religious organization, most members have a *client* relationship with the group. They continue in their ordinary occupations, family relationships, and life styles; but they purchase goods and services from alternative religious movements designed to aid them in realizing their human potential, expanding their awareness, or working out their salvation.[29] In this sense, Wilson has suggested, "they have no real consequences for the other social institutions, for political power structures, for technological constraints and controls. They add nothing to any prospective reintegration of society, and contribute nothing towards the culture by which a society might live."[30]

It is possible, however, that on a deeper level these new religious movements are indicators of a crisis in modernity. They may represent a set of alternative responses to the dominant religiopolitical system in America which emerged during a period when that dominant system was being questioned. Dick Anthony and Thomas Robbins have suggested that new religions are "survivors of the crisis of meaning that characterized the sixties."[31] They are systematic countercultural responses to the crisis in civil religion during the sixties, a period identified by Robert Bellah as a crucial test of American civil religion. If civil religion emerged from the sixties, as Bellah has suggested, an empty and broken shell, then these new religious movements represented attempts to create new patterns of religious and political order in the vacuum that was left. Anthony and Robbins have tried to view new religions as strategies for coping with the decline of civil religion, as "public theologies attempting to formulate new approaches to civil religion and the meaning of America."[32] They have distinguished between two basic kinds of religious groups: *monistic/privatistic mystical religions*, which "implicitly reject the insertion of nationalistic or political themes in spiritual life"; and *dualistic/civil religious sects*, which put forward a "revitalized synthesis of political and religious themes," and strive toward a "restoration of a national covenant and the recreation of a virtuous public."[33] The first type of new religious group tries to withdraw from the national political arena to cultivate a private spirituality, while the second type announces a new vision for a theocratic national order. It is difficult to neatly classify all new religious groups along these lines, but there does seem to be an important difference between those groups which primarily focus on *therapeutic* interests and those which try to create a *totalistic* pattern of life. One may be primarily concerned with private self-realization. The other begins with a new vision for the public order. Both, however, involve important religious and political issues.

Scientology is a religious movement whose original aims were clearly therapeutic. Its founder, L. Ron Hubbard, had achieved some success as a science fiction writer before he wrote *Dianetics: The Modern Science of Mental Health* in 1950. This book outlined his theory of *engrams*, which were understood to be psychological scars left in the unconscious mind by past traumatic experiences, and which inhibit a person from realizing his or her full potential. Two years later Hubbard introduced Scientology as a set of techniques for clearing the unconscious mind of engrams and achieving greater psychological freedom. The primary technique was called auditing. The individual held tin cans which were connected to an electronic meter, while the auditor evoked images, words, or phrases that would bring memory patterns to consciousness. If the person had a negative reaction to those memories, it would register on the meter. The goal was to become clear of those negative reactions. In 1955 Hubbard established the Founding Church of Scientology to emphasize the spiritual dimension of mental health and to maintain that auditing was essentially a religious practice.

In 1963 the Federal Food and Drug Administration raided Hubbard's church, confiscated a number of E-meters, and accused Scientology of making false and misleading claims about the ability of these machines to cure disease. The Scientologists appealed this judgment because, as they insisted, they were a religious movement protected by the First Amendment. Their appeal was evaluated in the case of *Founding Church of Scientology of Washington, D.C. v. United States* in 1969. Judge Wright acknowledged that claims of religious healings were generally exempt from FDA regulation, but it was necessary to determine whether or not Scientology was a legitimate religion. Observing that Scientology was incorporated as a church, that it ordained ministers, and that it involved a system of beliefs comparable in scope (if not in content) to recognized religions, the Judge concluded that "the Founding Church of Scientology has made out a *prima facie* case that it is a *bona fide* religion."[34] Therefore, the religious use of E-meters would not be subject to Federal Food and Drug regulations for proper labeling.

This decision was supported in another case involving Scientology later that year when Judge Moore acknowledged the legitimate religious context in which the E-meters were used. "It is not for us to prejudge," he stated, "the benefits, or lack thereof, which may come to members of the Church from being audited while holding in their hands two tin soup cans linked by an electrical apparatus."[35] The final judicial statement on the matter came in a decision in 1971 in which the United States District Court specified that "E-meter auditing will be permitted only in a religious setting subject to placing explicit warning disclaimers on the meter itself and all labeling."[36] These cases reflected the government's obvious uneasiness with Scientology's alternative therapeutic techniques. On the other hand, they were part of a larger struggle that Scientology conducted in America to be recognized as a religion. It not only fought court battles to establish its auditing technique as a religious ritual, but also to achieve tax exemption for its churches and conscientious objector status for its members. The movement may have had some larger political intentions, in addition to its initial therapeutic goals. Roy Wallis noted that Scientology ultimately wanted to "bring the whole world under the Org board, i.e., to run the whole world on Scientology lines."[37] But if this was a long-term political goal, it is clear from the legal history of the movement that its first challenge was to establish itself as a recognized religious group.

The Transcendental Meditation movement of the Guru Maharishi

Mahesh Yogi has taken an entirely opposite trajectory in its development. TM began as a clearly religious movement based on ancient traditions of Hindu spirituality, and centered on a basic eastern religious practice of chanting a sacred tone, word, or phrase. The ritual of chanting a *mantra* was the basic technique that the Maharishi brought to America, and the movement was a loosely organized network of individuals who had been initiated into this practice. The movement gained notoriety during the sixties when celebrities like the Beatles traveled to India to receive initiation in TM from the Guru. But a shift occurred around 1970 when the movement dropped its associations with Hindu spirituality and began to promote its meditation as a practical, scientific technique for stress reduction. Research was done to document the psychological benefits and therapeutic results of Transcendental Meditation in purely secular terms. It has been suggested that TM denied its religious status for public relations reasons. Charles Lutes, a leading figure in the movement, was quoted as saying that "the popularization of the movement in nonspiritual terms was strictly for the purpose of gaining the attention of people who wouldn't have paid the movement much mind if it had been put in spiritual terms."[38] TM was confronted with just the opposite problem that troubled Scientology: It did not want to be recognized as a religion. And it even tried to establish in a court in New Jersey that it was not a religion so that its meditation technique could be taught in public schools. But the court determined that TM was a religion, and therefore its religious practices could not be propagated in the secular school system.

In recent years TM has expanded its original therapeutic interests to include a new political dimension. The organization began taking out advertisements in international magazines that proclaimed a new Age of Enlightenment that would result from the application of Maharishi's unified-field theories of consciousness. The governments of the world were invited to apply to the Transcendental Movement for consultation in putting these principles into effect. The Maharishi's theory was based on the claim that if the square root of 1 percent of the world's population, which would amount to about 7,000 people, would chant their mantras together in one place, then crime, accidents, sickness, and natural disasters would fall off sharply. The Maharishi Effect had supposedly been demonstrated in 1974 at Maharishi International University, in Fairfield, Iowa, where the efforts of 7,000 chanters were claimed to produce a brief lull in world crises. "The Maharishi Effect on a global scale," the advertisements promised, "results in ideal societies everywhere and invincibility for every nation."[39] One nation that apparently did apply was the dictatorship of Philippines President Ferdinand Marcos. In July of 1984, 1,200 meditators began arriving in the Philippines. They were welcomed by Marcos, who was declared the "founding Father of the Age of Enlightenment in the Philippines." They hoped to have the necessary meditators assembled by the end of the year to put the Maharishi Effect into action. But *Newsweek*, in reporting this event, was skeptical:

> Since the transcendentalists have arrived, Manila has been racked by violent street protests. The Mayon volcano erupted unexpectedly, two strong earthquakes have shaken the country (including Marcos's home town), and a chain of hotel fires has killed several dozen people—and injured some of the Maharishi's own followers.[40]

One of the appeals of TM's redefinition of political power may have been that the new "Governors of the Age of Enlightenment" could achieve significant changes in the world around them without leaving their hotel rooms. But it also indicated the tendency of new religious groups to move at some point into the political arena, even if their original intentions had been essentially therapeutic.

Other groups, however, seem from their beginnings to have been interested in alternative political structures. These *totalistic* groups began as countercultural social arrangements, in tension with the prevailing society. As total, all-inclusive life styles, they presented different visions of social order. The International Society for Krishna Consciousness (ISKCON) was started by a former businessman in an Indian pharmaceutical firm, A.C. Bhaktivedanta Swami Prabhupada. Prabhupada renounced the world in 1959 to devote his life to the service of Krishna. In the Hindu tradition, Krishna was one of the incarnations, or *avatars*, of the god, Vishnu, and there was a long tradition of devotional worship in India directed toward this god in human form. Prabhupada arrived in New York in 1965, at age 69, and attracted a small group of followers. But when he moved to San Francisco two years later he found tremendous interest in eastern spirituality within the counterculture. He directed his religious message toward young people who had been experimenting with mind altering drugs, and he promised that through chanting the names and praises of Krishna, and adopting a life style centered on the service of God, the devotee could "Stay high all the time and discover eternal bliss."

The orange robes, shaved heads, and public chanting, singing, and dancing the praises of Krishna to the sounds of bells and chimes distinguished the devotees of Krishna from their social environment. They were encouraged to withdraw from the materialism, sensory gratification, and corruptions of the world in order to devote their lives to God. And to accomplish this, many lived in communal arrangements in one of the fifty temples that had spread throughout the United States by the mid-seventies. To support the organization, members engaged in street solicitation for funds. They sold literature, incense, and flowers in public places, and like the Jehovah's Witnesses, the street was their place of worship. Street solicitation was a natural source of revenue for an alternative religious movement that began without a capital base. It allowed members to combine

proselytizing with fundraising for a more efficient use of time. Once sufficient funds were raised, however, groups tended to invest in various business ventures—publishing, real estate, marketing vegetarian food, and so
on—that would provide a stable economic foundation for the movement.

By the time Prabhupada died in 1977, ISKCON had stabilized at
about 4,000 members in the United States.[41] The leadership of the organization was passed to a Governing Body Commission, which divided the
world into twelve zones. The swamis responsible for each zone had a certain degree of independence in their regions. One of the more independent regional leaders was Hansadutta Swami, who was based in the Berkeley area and was responsible for administering a zone that included
Northwest America, Southeast Asia, and China. Although he may not be
considered as speaking for the entire movement, Hansadutta Swami gave
some indication of the kinds of political interests represented by one of its
leaders. In a sermon recorded in 1980, Hansadutta Swami responded to
questions regarding automatic weapons that had been reported to be in
the possession of Krishna devotees. He answered by affirming that the
right to bear arms was a basic American value. "America was won by the
gun," the swami declared, "and it's maintained by the gun." He assured
his audience that the Hare Krishnas were not violent, nor did they plan to
overthrow the country; rather, they saw themselves as America's only
hope to be saved from the evil influences of communists and homosexuals. Regarding communism, Hansadutta Swami evoked a theme basic to
American Cold War, civil religiosity: "We are appealing to American
youth," he pleaded. "Become a hero and save your country . . . Make the
whole world God-conscious. Destroy communism . . . because it's godless."
And with regard to homosexuals, the swami openly declared his intolerance: "There are some things that are forbidden to human beings. If this
can't be understood, you can't have a nation like America much
longer."[42]

Hansadutta Swami was clearly invoking traditional civil religious imagery of a unique American covenant with God; the novel innovation, of
course, was the substitution of Krishna in the role of Supreme Being. But
this emphasis on American themes and concerns reflected a growing interest among new religious movements to establish a place within American society by appropriating the symbols of civil religion. Other examples
could be cited: The Healthy-Happy-Holy Organization (3HO), an off-
shoot of Sikhism, with a mixture of kundalini yoga, which was started by
Yogi Bhajan in Los Angeles in 1967, represented a similar appropriation
of American civil religious symbols. They reportedly "raise the American
flag and sing 'God Bless America,' for this is a way to claim a new space
within the American culture, a space delimited by the founding myths
taken as literal exemplars."[43] Even an alternative Buddhist movement,
such as the Nichiren Shoshu movement in America, could claim American civil religious symbols and sentiments. The American flag flew over

all Nichiren Shoshu of America (NSA) buildings in the United States, and in fact, the flags at the Denver and Seattle headquarters were certified as having flown over the Capitol in Washington, D.C. The General Director of the organization, speaking as an American, asserted that "only Nichiren Shoshu can actualize our forefathers' dream of a perfect democracy."[44] All these examples suggest that new religious movements can develop alternative visions of a unique religious covenant for American society. These alternative religiopolitical orientations may seem subversive to mainstream social groups. So the use of civil religious rhetoric is one way that these groups can try to establish themselves in the shared civil space of American society.

Probably no new religious movement has been more active in making use of civil religious symbols than the Unification Church of Reverend Sun Myung Moon, and no group has met more resistance. The movement began in Korea when Moon, a charismatic Christian evangelist who had been imprisoned by the North Koreans, founded the Holy Spirit Association for the Unification of World Christianity. The group sent its first missionaries to America in 1959, but had little success until the late sixties. Moon's teachings were contained in the *Divine Principle*. This sacred text of the Unification Church described how God's original plan for Adam and Eve was to create a perfect family pattern centered on God. But Eve's adultery with Satan destroyed this pattern. Jesus (the second Adam) was intended to restore this pattern, but he failed. He was crucified before he could marry and restore the perfect family pattern. In this era, according to the *Divine Principle*, a Lord of the Second Advent (the third Adam) was expected to appear. He was expected to come from Korea (based on Rev. 7:2-4). His task was to achieve the material and spiritual salvation of humanity. Moon was this potential Messiah, but he also could fail. Therefore, the members of the Unification Church had to commit their lives to creating the material and spiritual foundations for this messianic age.

America had a central role in Unification theology. The focus of the movement shifted to America by 1971; and in 1973 Reverend Moon became a permanent resident. His American tours during the bicentennial year featured his picture set against an American flag on posters. And Moon insisted that the United States was "God's Nation." America was the second Israel; but of course Korea, in replacing Israel as the land of the Messiah, was the "Third Israel." The United States, in Moon's view, must play a decisive role in the battle against communism, or what he referred to as "satanic socialism." Moon declared that "America must be God's champion. I know clearly that the will of God is centered on America."[45] God's plan for human history revolved around America. Reverend Moon observed that America was hidden from the world by God in order to play this central role in the battle against the forces of evil. "After all," Moon remarked, "America belonged to God first, and only after that to the Indians."[46] Like America's own Puritans, Moon imagined a theocratic covenant between God and America. But America seemed to be forsaking God and retreating from its role in sacred history. It was possible that America would not accept the theocratic vision of the Lord of the Second Advent, and the divine plan could again fail. Moon spoke in prophetic tones of the dangers in failing to follow the divine plan. "Unless this nation," he warned, "unless the leadership of the nation, lives up to the mission ordered by God, many troubles will plague you. God is beginning to leave America. This is God's warning."[47] By invoking civil religious symbols of the theocratic covenant between God and America, Moon may have tried to revitalize, restore, and renew those civil religious sentiments that seemed to dissolve in the sixties. This may have been part of the Unification Church's appeal to American converts. But Moon's appropriation of these symbols may also reflect a strategy of identifying his alternative religiopolitical movement with American civil religion in order subversive and to establish a place in America.

The recent case in which Moon was tried and convicted for tax evasion illustrates some of the problems he and his organization encountered in trying to establish themselves in America.[48] Moon was indicted in December of 1981 on three counts of filing false tax returns, and one count of conspiracy to cover up tax evasion, produce fraudulent records, and obstruct the Internal Revenue Investigation. It was held that during the period 1973-75 he had knowingly filed false returns. In 1973 Moon had applied for permanent residence the same day his wife had been granted hers. The government submitted that Mrs. Moon claimed to have a job as cook for the Korean Angels singing group, making $7,000 a year; and that this would be sufficient income to support her husband and twelve children. The government also claimed that Moon filled out a form where he said he would not be looking for a job. That same year, however, it was established that he opened an account in the Chase Manhattan Bank that between 1973 and 1975 apparently exceeded $1.7 million. His income tax return of 1973 declared an income of around $14,000. The government insisted that this bank account, as well as $50,000 in stock which was also in Moon's name, were beneficially owned by him and interest on these holdings was liable for taxation.

Moon's defense never denied that these funds were in his name, but it insisted that he was in a unique position as the living embodiment of the Unification faith, holding these financial resources in trust to advance the religion. The trial jury, however, was not allowed to consider what at one point was called the "Messiah defense." They were instructed to decide if the amounts were held by him personally, used according to his personal discretion, and involved in transactions for his personal gain. The jury was required to decide in what capacity Moon was acting in the interests of religion and in what circumstances he was engaged in personal business ventures. And they concluded that Moon was using these funds, in buying real estate, investing in a mining company, and making personal loans, in ways that indicated that he owned them. He was convicted on all counts. On appeal, Moon's defense insisted that there was an important First Amendment issue involved: The government can not interfere with the internal organization of a religious group. In order to uphold the full protection of the free exercise of religion, the state must accept the religious organization's *own* definition of what counts as religious. In this case, because Moon was regarded by his church as the personal embodiment of the faith and the potential Messiah, anything he did with these funds should be considered as working to advance religious purposes. Simply because the funds were in his name and used at his discretion did not mean that they were not held in religious trust for the Unification movement. But the Second Circuit Court of Appeals did not accept this line of argument, and Moon's conviction of eighteen months in jail and a $25,000.00 fine was upheld.

A second First Amendment issue was raised regarding the weight of religious prejudice directed against Moon that made a fair trial by jury impossible. After his indictment in December 1981, Moon had made a speech, which was later reprinted as a paid advertisement in the *New York Times*, in which he stated:

> I would not be standing here today if my skin were white and my religion were Presbyterian. I am here today only because my skin is yellow and my religion is Unification Church. The ugliest things in this beautiful country of America are religious bigotry and racism . . . Why are we singled out? Simply because our name is Unification Church and the founder happens to be a Korean, a yellow man.

Apparently to show that the trial was not a form of judicial inquisition, the state responded to Moon's complaint by insisting on a jury trial rather than a trial before a judge. Moon's defense wanted to avoid a jury trial, because they felt the jurors would be prejudiced against Moon and his religion. Their application was denied; but apparently the fears of religious prejudice had some basis because ten out of the twelve jurors who finally served commented about Moon in the pretrial review, indicating that they had very negative impressions of him. Many of the jurors seemed convinced from the beginning that Moon brainwashed young people and exploited them for his own financial gain. Moon's defense insisted that these impressions of him and his movement made it difficult for him to get a fair trial by jury. But the court decided that since Moon's religion was not an issue, the jury would be able to decide simply on the question of tax liability. Moon's defense, however, insisted that religion was very much involved in the case: First, the court could not understand the internal financial arrangements of the church unless it acknowledged the role of Moon as embodiment of the faith. Second, it was impossible to convince a jury of the religious basis, and therefore First Amendment protection, of these financial transactions if the jury members did not accept the religion itself as legitimate.

Certainly one of the political issues involving new religious movements has been the tremendous economic power that some of them have been able to generate. Reverend Moon's Unification Church presents an example of the discomfort many Americans feel when a religious leader accumulates large sums of money; a similar anxiety is not necessarily felt in relation to athletes or entertainment figures. But religion is one of the biggest businesses in America, and many new religious movements have successfully built strong financial bases for their alternative visions of society.

One group that created considerable controversy was the movement started by Bhagvan Rajneesh.[49] A former philosophy professor in India, Rajneesh began teaching a combination of spiritual techniques that drew upon the psychotherapeutic resources in eastern forms of meditation and western forms of encounter-group therapy. The original intent of the group that formed around his headquarters in Poona, India, was essentially *therapeutic*. But in 1981 he moved to the United States and in July of that year purchased the 100 square mile Big Muddy Ranch in Antelope, Oregon, about 19 miles southeast of Portland. He also leased another 25 square miles of adjoining land from the U.S. Bureau of Land Management. A group of about 550 disciples set out to create a utopian agricultural community, and the new city of Rajneeshpuram was the result. Citizens of the small neighboring town of Antelope were outraged by this development. In language reminiscent of nineteenth-century fears of the political power of the Catholic Church, a spokesman for the Citizens for Constitutional Cities said, "We don't want any Vatican Cities in the United States." Rajneeshpuram was accused of being an unconstitutional union of church and state. Another community group, the Friends of Oregon, tried to insist that the land could only be used for agricultural purposes, not for the creation of a new city.

Rajneeshpuram was incorporated as a city in May, 1982. As a city it had its own police force and court system, it collected taxes, and it was eligible for state and federal revenue-sharing funds. The city's mayor dismissed the fears of this new religious city by saying that "Most American towns started as religious cities." He cited the example of Salt Lake City, Utah, founded by Mormons, and observed, "This is just happening in the present." There is no constitutional provision that everyone in a town cannot belong to the same religion; but if the city council of Rajneeshpuram enacted laws that required everyone to worship in a certain way, or that denied people the right to buy property or vote in the community who were not members of the religion, then conflicts between church and state would be involved. The new city seemed to function primarily as a conference center and retreat for Rajneesh's 250,000 followers worldwide. Most of his followers had a client relationship with the organization—buying literature and paying for meditation instruction, retreats, and workshops. But, there was a sense in which the original therapeutic intentions were becoming more *totalistic* simply by virtue of incorporating the organization into a city. In order to protect its new communal interests in America, the group even brought transients up from the streets of Los Angeles by bus to increase their voting strength in a local election. County officials suspected that 4,000 homeless were brought in to sway a county court election, and required that all new voters be interviewed. The transients were then apparently dropped off by the Rajneeshis in nearby towns.

By 1984 there were around 1,200 followers of Rajneesh living in Rajneeshpuram. They sought to create a total life style where work, in any of the forty communal businesses, was experienced as a form of worship. Everyday, Rajneesh would drive through the city in one of numerous Rolls Royces, and receive the worshipful greetings of his followers lined along the roads. As much as $110 million was reportedly invested in the development of Rajneeshpuram. In order to sustain a more totalistic communal organization, Rajneesh drew upon powerful symbolic imagery of purity and danger. The world inside was pure. The world outside was dangerous. The guru-therapist became a prophet. He predicted that two-thirds of the world's population would die of AIDS; and that a nuclear holocaust would occur within the next ten to fifteen years. The imagery of such dangers outside produced a powerful centripetal force that helped to hold the community together as pure, self-contained religiopolitical system. And although the group probably posed no tangible threat, the fearful reactions of its neighbors in Oregon indicated how such a group, by trying to retreat from the dangers of the world, could itself be perceived as dangerous by people who occupy the mainstream social environment around it. Finally, in 1985 Rajneesh was arrested for immigration violations and agreed to be deported rather than face trial. The city of Rajneeshpuram was dissolved.

THE BRAINWASHING-DEPROGRAMMING CONTROVERSY

New religious movements have been part of a larger conflict of religious worldviews in American society. Cult and anticult movements have carried this conflict into the courts. While most of the new religious movements have successfully achieved legal recognition as religious organizations, their status as legitimate religions has been attacked by a coalition of psychologists, lawyers, politicians, religious leaders, and family members who have insisted that cults are deceptive covers for powerful charismatic leaders to prey on young people and to exploit them for the purposes of expanding their personal economic power. The primary explanation offered for the success of such groups in recruiting members was brainwashing.

The basic concept of brainwashing was developed by the psychologist, Robert Jay Lifton, to explain the process of "thought reform" by which prisoners of war in Chinese prison camps were coerced into accepting communist ideology. The captors employed coercive techniques of indoctrination. The prisoners were physically restrained, confined in a totally controlled environment, and subjected to a barrage of propaganda. The result was what Lifton called "ego destruction." Prior thought patterns were dissolved, and a new allegiance to the captors was born out of this process.[50] William Sargent, in his *Battle for the Mind*, was probably the first to try to make the connection between such coercive thought reform and religious conversion. He suggested that religious evangelists developed similar techniques to break down the individual's defenses, soften willpower, and produce a dramatic change in thoughts and feelings.[51] When it appeared that many people in America were going through such dramatic changes in their conversions to alternative religious movements, the brainwashing explanation captivated the public media and the popular imagination. As one critic of the new religions put it, "An uncomfortable reality has at last come home to the American public: brainwashing, which seemed exclusively a communist technique, is alive in America and used by cults."[52] The frightening image of an alien, evil, and coercive power turning Americans into robots seemed the stuff of science fiction. And it certainly seemed to crystallize mainstream public apprehensions of alternative religious movements. But the brainwashing explanation was given further credence by the support it received from representatives of the mental health professions. There was a widespread attempt to "medicalize" the language used to understand alternative religious groups. Religious beliefs, practices, and associations became transposed into medical terminology.

> A religion becomes a cult; proselytizing becomes brainwashing; persuasion becomes propaganda; missionaries become subversive agents; retreats, monasteries and convents become prisons; holy ritual becomes bizarre conduct; religious observances become aberrant behavior; devotion and meditation become psychopathic trances.[53]

As we have seen, there has always been a feeling within the mainstream of American society that alternative religious movements present a threat. They have been perceived to endanger mainstream values such as the family, nationalism, and public health. The perceived danger of religious movements that have emerged since the mid-sixties has been defined predominantly in medical terms. The dangerous influence of alternative religious movements has been identified as the "mental illness" of brainwashing. But, as Thomas Szasz has observed, "We do not call all types of personal psychological influences 'brainwashing.' We reserve this term for influences of which we disapprove."[54] Disapproval of new religions has been cast in these psychomedical terms. Psychological medical discourse has allowed opponents of these groups to disguise an underlying religious conflict as an issue of public health.

One problem with the brainwashing explanation is that there is no evidence that new religious movements used physical violence to restrain and confine their recruits in order to subject them to a discipline of coercive indoctrination. Members of the anticult movement, however, argued that mental coercion placed an even more powerful control over individuals than physical restraints. Brainwashing destroyed willpower and therefore converts, having lost their wills, were forced to remain in these groups involuntarily. But recent studies have shown a substantial rate of voluntary defections from new religious movements. Members become dissatisfied, they change their minds, or simply get bored, and leave. A recent study of forty-five former members of new religious movements, including defectors from the Unification Church, Hare Krishna, and Children of God, called the brainwashing explanation into question. All had left voluntarily; but forty-one out of the forty-five said that their entire participation in the movements had been on a voluntary basis and that they had benefited from their experiences in these groups. They did not say they had been brainwashed. Apparently, the only ones who used that language had come into contact with anticult literature and had been influenced by it sufficiently to reconceptualize their experience.[55]

In the controversy over new religious movements the anticult movement has argued that members suffer from a variety of mental illnesses created by the coercive manipulation and thought control of cults. But serious psychological analysis of current and former members of new religious groups has revealed no evidence of mental illness.[56] Researchers have not been able to diagnose the conventional symptoms that would indicate a pathological condition. It seems therefore that for the anticult movement, membership in an alternative religious movement was the only symptom necessary to declare an individual mentally incompetent. But it is hard to avoid the assumption that some forms of religious association were exempted from the brainwashing explanation. Conversions to mainstream religious denominations were rarely regarded as the result of mental manipulation, and yet, as Stillson Judah has observed, there was no great difference "between conversion of a youth attending a Unification weekend workshop and one converting to a mainline Christian church after spending a weekend in the Young Life group or after attending a denominational summer camp."[57] Perhaps there was a difference in the degree of commitment and the intensity of enthusiasm which many new religious movements seemed to awaken in their converts. But, as Robert Shapiro insisted, converts to these groups "should not find the intensity of their faith being used as proof of their incompetence."[58]

Yet this seemed to be the assumption on the part of deprogrammers, like Ted Patrick, who insisted that converts to cults had lost both their reason and their free will. Patrick would tell the parents of a young man who had joined a new religious movement, "You're not dealing with your son at this point. You're dealing with a zombie. You have to do whatever is necessary to get him back."[59] And the solution that Patrick proposed was to become the major tactical strategy of the anticult movement: deprogramming. It began with kidnapping. As Patrick told concerned families, "What I concluded we had to do was bodily abduct the children from the communes and colonies they were living in."[60] The cult member then would be taken into isolation, physically restrained, and confined under the close scrutiny of the deprogrammers. Under their guidance he or she would be subjected to a rigorous process of reindoctrination. Patrick described deprogramming as simply "reasoning" with the individual. Margaret Singer, a psychologist who has been very active in promoting the aims of the anticult movement, called it "nothing more than an intense period of information giving."[61] But even the accounts of these sessions given by the deprogrammers themselves told of subjecting the prisoner to shouting and verbal abuse, deprivation of sleep, and constant attacks on his or her religious beliefs. One example from Ted Patrick's *Let Our Children Go* seems to be characteristic. Patrick recalled the deprogramming of a Hare Krishna devotee: "I had a picture of Prabhupada and I tore it up in front of him and said, 'There's the no-good son of a bitch you worship. And you call him God!'[62] Members of the Unification Church would be forced in their confinement to listen to Patrick reading passages from the Bible and trying to argue that the cult had misinterpreted them. Deprogrammers insisted that all this was necessary to restore to the individual the power to choose that had been taken away by the cult. But it is clear from these direct attacks on the content of religious beliefs that the deprogrammer was asking the person to reinterpret his or her experience in the religious movement. And those who were successfully deprogrammed almost always reinterpreted their cult experience as brainwashing. A large percentage converted to some form of evangelical Christianity, became active in the anticult movement, or both.[63] This suggested that the conflict was basically a kind of small-scale religious warfare, and that deprogramming was the "new exorcism" for eliminating deviant religious worldviews.

Of course one immediate problem for deprogrammers was that kidnapping is illegal. This made the case for brainwashing all that much more crucial. If the opponents of the cults could establish that a member had lost the use of reason and the power of will, then they could argue that the person should be declared legally incompetent. At that point it might be possible to obtain a conservatorship with which a relative would be given custody as a legal guardian. During the seventies such conservatorships were advocated.[64] And in numerous cases they were granted for the purpose of legal deprogramming. In each case the arguments for brainwashing, mind control, and coercive persuasion were presented to justify the parents of adult children taking control over their lives. But two court cases changed this trend and helped clarify the First Amendment issues that were at stake in the controversy over cults.[65]

The first case involved two members of the International Society for Krishna Consciousness. Both were college-age adults who had joined the Hare Krishna movement. Merylee Kreshour had been a member for about two years when her mother arranged for deprogrammers to kidnap her off the street in Queens County, New York, and to subject her to a four-day forced treatment. The mother claimed that such treatment was necessary to restore her daughter's free will, which had been destroyed when she became a victim of "mental kidnapping" by Hare Krishna. Ed Shapiro had joined the movement after a trip to India. His father, a physician, was disturbed by his son's religious conversion and he hired Ted Patrick to perform the deprogramming while Ed was held against his will in his parents' home. Both deprogrammings were "failures." And the two devotees of Krishna returned to their movement. Merylee Kreshour then tried to bring a suit against her deprogrammers for illegal kidnapping and imprisonment. But when her case was put before the Grand Jury, not only did the Jury reject her plea, but it issued an indictment against the International Society for Krishna Consciousness. The essence of the indictment was that the Hare Krishnas, and their local leader, Angus Murphy, imprisoned members like Merylee Kreshour and Ed Shapiro through brainwashing. The Grand Jury's indictment, as summarized by Judge John Leahy, was that members of this group

> were deceived or inveigled into submitting themselves 'unknowingly to techniques intended to subject their will to that of the defendants . . .' and that the same resulted in 'an evil consequence . . .' The entire argument propounded by the People is that through 'mind control,' 'brainwashing,' and/or 'manipulation of mental processes' the defendants destroyed the free will of the alleged victims, obtaining over them mind control to the point of absolute dominion and thereby coming within the purview of the issue of unlawful imprisonment.[66]

In *People of the State of New York v. Angus Murphy* (1976), expert testimony was presented by mental health professionals to establish that Hare Krishna members were brainwashed. The psychiatrist John G. Clark, who apparently had only examined Ed Shapiro by watching him talk to his parents from across a room, told the court that Ed was "incompetent as a result of mind control."[67] Ed Shapiro was forced to enter a mental hospital for further diagnosis. Dr. Clark diagnosed him as "paranoid schizophrenic." But the doctors at the hospital after two weeks could find no evidence of any mental disorder. In court Dr. Clark changed his diagnosis to "borderline personality." But the prosecution continued to insist on the argument of mind control to establish that members had been illegally imprisoned by Angus Murphy and the Hare Krishna. An ironic note was given to the trial by the fact that Angus Murphy, who was being accused of orchestrating the mental manipulation of Ed Shapiro, was a year younger than Ed, a high school friend, and apparently had been introduced to Hare Krishna by *him*.[68]

Judge Leahy finally dismissed the indictment against Hare Krishna for using mind control over its members. In his court memorandum he stated "as to the premise posed by the People that the religious rituals, daily activities and teaching of the Hare Krishna religion constitute a form of intimidation to maintain restraint over the two alleged victims, the court finds no legal foundation or precedent."[69] But he was concerned that the Grand Jury's indictment had ignored the constitutional right to the free exercise of religion. The Jury had failed to protect the freedom of religion. Judge Leahy found the Grand Jury's approach to this case to be "brought with danger in its potential for utilization in the suppression—if not outright destruction—of our citizens' right to pursue, join and practice the religion of their choice."[70] But the Grand Jury had not simply ignored the First Amendment protection of free exercise. With the brainwashing argument, it had tried to establish that the free exercise of religion was not even an issue. Not only was Hare Krishna not considered a legitimate religion, but the converts were portrayed as having no free will to exercise. In this case, however, the brainwashing explanation, as a strategy for circumventing the free exercise clause of the First Amendment, was not accepted by the court.

A second case involved five adult members of the Unification Church in California. Their parents joined forces to request court-ordered, temporary conservatorships for thirty days in order to submit their children to deprogramming therapy. They intended to send the Moonists to the rehabilitation center provided by one of the most active anticult organizations, the Freedom of Thought Foundation in Tucson, Arizona. During 1976, dozens of such conservatorship orders had been issued by California courts. They were justified under a California state law which permitted conservatorships that could designate a legal guardian over another if that person was disabled through age, illness, injury, mental weakness, intemperance, addiction to drugs, or "likely to be deceived or imposed upon by artful and designing persons."[71] This last phrase (which has since been removed from the California law) seemed to apply to new religious movements in these cases and to warrant granting conservatorships.

The parents argued that all five Unification members were suffering from mental illness and in need of immediate counseling and therapy. Again, the accusation was made that they were not participating in this group of their own free will, but were subject to the mental manipulation of "artful and designing persons." Expert testimony was given by Dr.

Samuel Benson, who claimed that the five must leave the Church in order to receive psychiatric treatment and restore their mental health; and by Dr. Margaret Singer, who claimed the ability to diagnose the symptoms of brainwashing and recommended "reality therapy" at the Freedom of Thought Foundation. Judge Lee Vavuris, however, seemed less concerned with the brainwashing explanations than with what he perceived to be the sanctity of the family relations at stake. Even though the five Unificationists were all adults, Judge Vavuris said, "We're talking about the essence of life here, mother, father, children." As in the Mormon polygamy cases, the compelling state interest in preserving the institution of the American family was invoked to override any consideration for the protection of religious freedom.

Conservatorships were granted on March 25, 1977; but they were postponed three days later by an appeals court. When the decision of the appeals court was finally delivered, in *Katz v. Superior Court* (1977), the judges found no basis to establish that the members of the Unification Church were suffering from substantial inabilities that would warrant conservatorships. The appeals court found that "there is no real showing here that the conservatees are physically unhealthy, or actually deprived of, or unable to secure food, clothing, and shelter." So there did not seem to be any immediate physical danger to the five that would merit the intervention of legal guardians. The court was not convinced that a case had been made for the mental impairment of the Unificationists. But if such a case were made, it would have to be consistent with protection of civil liberties. "To do less," the court stated, "is to license kidnapping for the purpose of thought control." The accusation of thought control was deflected back onto the parents. But the court took the argument a step further. How could a court determine whether a religious commitment was based on faith or mind control without questioning the legitimacy of that commitment? The judges pointed out that "evidence was introduced of the actions of the proposed conservatees changing their life styles. When the court is asked to determine whether that change was induced by faith or by coercive persuasion is it not in turn investigating and questioning the validity of that faith?" At this point the court looked back to *Ballard* (1944) to suggest that the fundamental question regarding the *truth* of a set of religious beliefs was beyond the reach of prosecution. One of the fundamental principles of the free exercise clause of the First Amendment, as it had been interpreted in *Ballard*, was that the government was not in a position to decide what is a true religion. And therefore, the state does not have the power to rule that a religion is false and to allow parents the authority to remove their adult children from that religion against their will.

The decision in *Katz*, although not binding in other states, set a precedent which discouraged granting conservatorships to the parents of cult members. Perhaps for this reason, anticult activists put their efforts into drafting new legislation that would control new religious movements. One bill, which was introduced in New York by Assemblyman Howard Lasher in 1980, passed through the New York state legislature, but finally vetoed by Governor Carey, would have legalized conservatorships.[72] Significantly, the bill was an amendment to the state's mental hygiene law. It was another attempt to translate religious beliefs, practices, and experiences into medical terms. The law would have applied to religious groups that kept members isolated from their families. Anyone who associated with such a group and went through "a sudden and radical change in behavior, life style, habits, and attitudes" could be placed in the custody of a conservator. In most cases this would be the parents. Again, the goal was to preserve the institution of the family at the expense of the free choice of alternative religious life styles. The period of custody would last forty-five days; but could be renewed for another period of forty-five days. Police could use any reasonable force to remove the person from the religious group and bring him or her into custody. Once under the control of the conservator, the person could be ordered by the court to submit to psychological or psychiatric treatment. This bill was not passed into law; but many other states have considered similar measures. The law proposed in the state of Oregon, for example, would permit temporary guardianship for anyone who had "undergone a sudden and radical change of behavior, life style, habits and attitudes," whose "judgment has become impaired to the extent that the person is unable to understand the need for such care." This kind of legislation puts members of alternative religious movements in a peculiar double bind. If they do not feel the need for mental health treatment, then that proves their judgment is impaired. The only way to show that their judgment has been restored would be to renounce the religious group and submit for treatment. These proposed laws place a very heavy burden upon the free exercise of religion. If their constitutionality is to be upheld, the states must submit more compelling arguments that these religions are so dangerous to the mental health of the community that they do not deserve the protection of free exercise extended to all faiths in America.

NOTES

1. PETER L. BERGER, *The Heretical Imperative: Contemporary Possibilities of Religious Affirmation* (London: Collins, 1980).
2. THOMAS JEFFERSON, *Notes on the State of Virginia*, ed., William Peden (Chapel Hill: University of North Carolina Press, 1954): 159; see Dean Kelley, ed. *Government Intervention in Religious Affairs*, 2 vols. (New York: Pilgrim Press, 1982; 1986).
3. SAUL K. PADOVER, ed., *The Complete Madison* (New York: Harper, 1953): 306.
4. Church has been defined as "a religious group that accepts the social environment in which it exists"; a sect is "a religious group that rejects the social environment in which it exists." Benton Johnson, "On Church and Sect," *American Sociological Review* 28 (1963): 542; see J. Milton Yinger, *Religion, Society and the Individual: An Introduction to*

the Sociology of Religion (New York: Macmillan, 1952); and Rodney Stark and William Sims Bainbridge, *The Future of Religion: Secularization, Revival, and Cult Formation* (Berkeley: University of California Press, 1985): 19-37.

5. MOSES DAVID, "Daniel 7," May, 1975; cited in Roy Wallis, *The Elementary Forms of the New Religious Life* (London: Routledge and Kegan Paul, 1984): 12.

6. DAVID G. BROMLEY and ANSON D. SHUPE, *The New Vigilantes: Deprogrammers, Anti-Cultists and the New Religions* (Beverly Hills, California: Sage, 1980); see also Bromley and Shupe, "The Moonies and the Anti-cultists: Movement and Counter-movement in Conflict," *Sociological Analysis* 40 (1979): 325-334. Legal aspects of the cult controversies are covered in William Shepherd, *To Secure the Blessings of Liberty: American Constitutional Law and the New Religious Movements* (Chico, CA: Scholars Press, 1985); and Thomas Robbins, William Shepherd, and James McBride, eds., *Cults, Culture and the Law: Perspectives on New Religious Movements* (Chico, CA: Scholars Press, 1985).

7. TED PATRICK (with Tom Dulack), *Let Our Children Go* (New York: Dutton, 1976): 242.

8. *Ibid.*: 238.

9. ELI SHAPIRO, "Destructive Cultism," *American Family Physician* 15 (1977): 80-83.

10. HARVEY COX, "Deep Structures in the Study of New Religions," in *Understanding the New Religions*, eds. Jacob Needleman and George Baker (New York: Seabury, 1978): 127.

11. RICHARD DELGADO, "Religious Totalism as Slavery," *Review of Law and Social Change* 9 (1979-80): 51-68.

12. GEORGE GULLAP, JR. and DAVID POLING, *The Search for America's Faith* (Nashville: Abingdon, 1980): 29-39.

13. *Watson v. Jones*, 13 Wallace 679 (1872). On the legal implications of marginal religious movements in American history, see Leo Pfeffer, "Legitimation of Marginal Religions in the United States," in *Religious Movements in Contemporary America*, eds., Irving I. Zaretsky and Mark P. Leone (Princeton: Princeton University Press, 1974): 9-26; and John Richard Burkholder, "The Law Knows No Heresy": Marginal Religious Movements and the Supreme Court," in *Ibid.*: 27-50.

14. See Lawrence Foster, *Religion and Sexuality: The Shakers, the Mormons, and the Oneida Community* (Urbana: University of Illinois Press, 1984). On nineteenth-century alternative religions, see Ira L. Mandelker, *Religion, Society, and Utopia in Nineteenth-Century America* (Amherst: University of Massachusetts Press, 1984).

15. *Reynolds v. United States*, 98 U.S. 1545 (1879); see Klaus J. Hansen, *Mormonism and the American Experience* (Chicago: University of Chicago Press, 1981); and Richard Bushman, *Joseph Smith and the Beginnings of Mormonism* (Urbana: University of Illinois Press, 1985).

16. *Davis v. Beacon*, 133 U.S. 333 (1890).

17. *Cantwell v. Connecticut*, 310 U.S. 296 (1940).

18. *Murdock v. Pennsylvania*, 319 U.S. 105 (1943).

19. *Minersville School District v. Gobitis*, 310 U.S. 586 (1940).

20. *West Virginia State Board of Education v. Barnette*, 319 U.S. 586 (1943); see David R. Manwaring, *Render unto Caesar: The Flag Salute Controversy* (Chicago: University of Chicago Press, 1962).

21. *United States v. Ballard*, 332 U.S. 78 (1944).

22. PFEFFER, "Legitimation of Marginal Religions in the United States," in *Religious Movements in Contemporary America*: 23.

23. *Sherbert v. Verner*, 374 U.S. 398 (1963).

24. *People v. Woody*, 394 p.2d 813 (1964).

25. See Burkholder, "The Law Knows No Heresy," in *Religious Movements in Contemporary America*: 40; For discussions of drug cults, see the entire issue of *California Law Review* (January, 1968); and "Drug Crime Defense-Religious Freedom," 35 *American Law Review* 3d 939.

26. *In re Brooks*, 205 N.E. 2d 435 (1965).

27. MOSES DAVID, "Heavenly Homes," (October, 1974); cited in Wallis, *The Elementary Forms of the New Religious Life*: 10; see Rex Davis and James T. Richardson, "The Organization and Functioning of the Children of God," *Sociological Analysis* 37 (1976): 320-41.

28. BRYAN R. WILSON, "The New Religions: Some Preliminary Considerations," in *New Religious Movements: A Perspective for Understanding Society*, ed. Eileen Barker (New York and Toronto: Edwin Mellen Press, 1982): 16-32.

29. On the client relationship to new religious movements, see William Sims Bainbridge and Rodney Stark, "Cult Formation: Three Compatible Models," in *Religion and Religiosity in America*, eds., Jeffrey K. Hadden and Theodore E. Long (New York: Crossroad, 1983): 41-6.

30. BRYAN R. WILSON, *Religion in Sociological Perspective* (London: Oxford University Press, 1982): 96.

31. DICK ANTHONY and THOMAS ROBBINS, "Spiritual Innovation and the Crisis of American Civil Religion," *Daedelus* 111 (1982): 217.

32. DICK ANTHONY and THOMAS ROBBINS, "Culture Crisis and Contemporary Religion," in *In Gods We Trust*, eds., Thomas Robbins and Dick Anthony (New Brunswick, New Jersey: Transaction, 1981): 10.

33. *Ibid.*: 17.

34. *Founding Church of Scientology of Washington, D.C. v. United States*, 409 F.2d 1146 (1969).

35. *Barr v. Weise*, 412 F.2d 338 (1969).

36. *United States v. Article or Device . . . Hubbard Electrometer*, 333 F. Supp. 357 (1971).

37. WALLIS, *The Elementary Forms of the New Religious Life*: 65; On Scientology, see Robert Kaufman, *Inside Scientology: How I Joined Scientology and Became Superhuman* (New York: Olympia Press, 1972); Roy Wallis, "Scientology: Therapeutic Cult to Religious Sect," *Sociology* (1975): 89-100; and Wallis, *The Road to Total Freedom: A Sociological Analysis of Scientology* (London: Heinemann, 1976).

38. Cited in R.D. Scott, *Transcendental Misconceptions* (San Diego: Beta Books, 1978): 217; also see Eric Woodrum, "The Development of the Transcendental Meditation Movement," *The Zetetic* 1 (1977): 38-48.

39. Cited in Wallis, *The Elementary Forms of the New Religious Life*: 25.

40. *Newsweek* (Jan. 2, 1984).

41. This may be an inflated figure. Marcia Rudin estimates an American membership of 1,500 at this time. See Rudin, "The New Religious Cults and the Jewish Community," *Religious Education* 73 (1978): 351-3; on the International Society for Krishna Consciousness see J. Stillson Judah, *Hare Krishna and the Counterculture* (New York: Wiley, 1974); Francine Jeanne Daner, *The American Children of Krishna: A Study of the Hare Krishna Movement* (New York: Holt, Rinehart and Winston, 1976); Gregory Johnson, "The Hare Krishna in San Franciso," in *The New Religious Consciousness*, eds., Charles Y. Glock and Robert N. Bellah (Berkeley: University of California Press, 1976): 31-51; and E. Burke Rochford, Jr., "Recruitment Strategies, Ideology and Organization in the Hare Krishna Movement," *Social Problems* 29 (1982): 399-410.

42. Cited in Carol Brydolf, "Krishna Guru: 'Americans Should Bear Arms'," *Oakland Tribune*, May 25, 1980.

43. ALAN TOBEY, "The Summer Solstice of the Healthy-Happy-Holy Organization," in *The New Religious Consciousness*, 29.

44. EMMA McCLOY LAYMAN, *Buddhism in America* (Chicago: Nelson-Hall, 1976): 134.

45. Cited in Thomas Robbins, Dick Anthony, Madeline Doucas, and Thomas Curtis, "The Last Civil Religion: Reverend Moon and the Unification Church," in *Science, Sin and Scholarship: The Politics of Reverend Moon and the Unification Church*, ed., Irving L. Horowitz (Cambridge: MIT Press, 1978): 52.

46. *Ibid.*: 61

47. *Ibid.*: 61

48. Information on the Moon tax evasion case has been gathered from the transcript of the appeal, the Reply Brief for Appellant Sun-Myung Moon and *Amicus Curiae* of the National Council of Churches and the American Civil Liberties Union; for a good introduction to the Unification Church, see David G. Bromley and Anson D. Shupe, *"Moonies" in America* (Beverly Hills, California: Sage, 1979); for an earlier sociological study of the early movement, see John Lofland, *Doomsday Cult* (Englewood Cliffs, New Jersey: Prentice-Hall, 1966; enlarged edition, New York: Irvington Publishers, 1977); for a more recent study, see Eileen Barker, *The Making of a Moonie: Choice or Brainwashing?* (Oxford: Basil Blackwell, 1984).

49. Information on the movement of Bhagvan Sri Rajneesh was gathered from the articles in the *San Francisco Examiner*, October 14, 1982; and *Newsweek*, December 3, 1984.

50. ROBERT JAY LIFTON, *Thought Reform and the Psychology of Totalism* (New York: Norton, 1961). The notion of communist brainwashing was popularized in the 1950s by Edward

Hunter, who apparently was working as a journalist undercover for the CIA. See Edward Hunter, *Brainwashing* (New York: Pyramid Books, 1958). On the CIA connection, see Alan Scheflin and Edward Opton, *The Mind Manipulators* (New York: Paddington Press, 1978): 226-28.

51. WILLIAM SARGENT, *Battle for the Mind: A Physiology of Conversion and Brainwashing* (London: Heineman, 1957); see also Sargent, *The Mind Possessed: A Physiology of Possession, Mysticism and Faith Healing* (New York: Penguin , 1975). Perhaps a more sophisticated approach to mental coercion is found in Edgar H. Schein, et al. *Coercive Persuasion* (New York: Norton, 1961); and a recent attempt to expose cultic mind control, based on communication theory, is found in Flo Conway and Jim Siegelman, *Snapping: America's Epidemic of Sudden Personality Change* (New York: Lippincott, 1978).

52. P.A. VERDIER, *Brainwashing and the Cults* (Hollywood, California: Institute of Behavioral Conditioning, 1977): 11.

53. JEREMIAH GUTMAN, "Constitutional and Legal Aspects of Deprogramming," in *Deprogramming: Documenting the Issue* (New York: American Civil Liberties Union, 1977): 210-11.

54. THOMAS SZASZ, "Some Call it Brainwashing," *New Republic* (March 9, 1976): 10.

55. STUART A. WRIGHT, "Defection from New Religious Movements: A Test of Some Theoretical Propositions," in *The Brainwashing/Deprogramming Controversy: Sociological, Psychological, Legal, and Historical Perspectives*, eds., David Bromley and James Richardson (New York: Edwin Mellen Press, 1983).

56. J. THOMAS UNGERLEIDER and DAVID WELLISCH, "Coercive Persuasion (Brainwashing), Religious Cults and Deprogramming," *American Journal of Psychiatry* 136 (1979): 279-82.

57. J. STILLSON JUDAH, "New Religions and Religious Liberty," in *Understanding the New Religions*: 204.

58. ROBERT N. SHAPIRO, " 'Mind Control' or Intensity of Faith: The Constitutional Protection of Religious Beliefs," *Harvard Civil Rights—Civil Liberties Law Review* 13 (1978): 795; also see Shapiro, "On Persons, Robots and the Constitutional Protection of Religious Beliefs," *Southern California Law Review* 56 (1983): 1277-1318.

59. PATRICK, *Let Our Children Go*: 11

60. *Ibid.*: 58; see Anson Shupe, Roger Spielmann, and Sam Stigall, "Deprogramming: The New Exorcism," in *Conversion Careers*, ed., James Richardson (Beverly Hills: Sage 1978): 145-60.

61. Cited in Thomas Robbins, "Constructing Cultist 'Mind Control,' " *Sociological Analysis* 45 (1984): 245.

62. PATRICK, *Let Our Children Go*: 189.

63. TRUDY SOLOMON, "Integrating the Moonie Experience," in *In Gods We Trust*: 275-94.

64. RICHARD DELGADO, "Religious Totalism: Gentle and Ungentle Persuasion," *Southern California Law Review* 51 (1977): 1-99.

65. These cases are reviewed in John LeMoult, "Deprogramming Members of Religious Sects," *Fordham Law Review* 46 (1978): 599-640.

66. Reprinted in Herbert Richardson, ed., *New Religions and Mental Health: Understanding the Issues* (New York and Toronto: Edwin Mellen Press, 1980): 86.

67. Affidavit of September 29, 1976, submitted to Supreme Court of New York in *People v. Angus Murphy*; cited in Lee Colman, *Psychiatry, the Faithbreaker* (Sacramento, California: Printing Dynamics, 1982): 7.

68. Cited in Richardson, ed., *New Religions and Mental Health*: xxxii.

69. *Ibid.*: 86.

70. *Ibid.*: 86.

71. See the discussion of *Katz* in William C. Shepherd, "The Prosecutor's Reach: Legal Issues Stemming from the New Religious Movements," *Journal of the American Academy of Religion* 50 (1982): 187-214.

72. Reprinted in Richardson, ed., *New Religions and Mental Health*: 20-30.

CHAPTER NINE
THE ESTABLISHMENT
OF RELIGION

The First Amendment prohibition of the establishment of religion broke with the customary practice of the colonies, which was to set aside tax monies to support selected churches. By 1833 all of the states had come into line with the principle of disestablishment. Government was not in the business of religion, and this separation of religion from government was considered healthy for both church and state. Thomas Jefferson wrote to a group of Baptists in Danbury, Connecticut, praising this separation between religion and the state. "I contemplate with sovereign reverence," he wrote, "the act of the whole American people, which declared that their legislature should 'make no law respecting an establishment of religion or prohibiting the free exercise thereof, *thus* building a wall of separation between church and state."[1] This particular phrase—separation of church and state—was, of course, not contained in the First Amendment. But it captured something of Jefferson's understanding of its implications: Religion and government should operate independently. The wall of separation became such an influential metaphor for church-state relations in America, that, by the Mormon polygamy case in 1879, the Supreme Court referred to it "almost as an authoritative declaration of the scope and effect of the amendment."[2]

We have seen how the wall of separation between religion and the state was applied in cases involving the free exercise of religion. The government may never interfere in matters of religious belief, and may only restrict religious practices that present a clear and present danger to society. Religion is protected by a wall of separation from government intervention. But this wall has also been used to prohibit an establishment of religion. First, the government is clearly prohibited from enacting laws that would establish a single national religion. The authors of the First Amendment wanted to avoid any use of government coercion in matters of religious belief, practice, and association. So the formation of a state church that required the allegiance of all Americans was prohibited.

Second, the government may not finance, subsidize, or support religious groups. James Madison, while President, vetoed a U.S. land grant to a Baptist church in Mississippi because, as he wrote, "the bill in reserving a certain parcel of land of the United States for the use of said Baptist church comprises a principle and precedent for the appropriation of funds of the United States for the use and support of religious societies, contrary to the article of the Constitution which declares that, 'Congress shall make no law respecting a religious establishment.'"[3] The state cannot subsidize religious officials or places of worship with public funds. States have, however, traditionally exempted religious property from taxation. Some people have argued that the special exemption of religious groups from property taxes does contribute to their financial support in such a way that it violates the principle that government should not establish religion. The issue of religious tax exemptions did not come before the Supreme Court until 1970. It will be useful to take a brief look at the case of *Walz v. Tax Commission* to see how this question was resolved.

Third, the wall of separation not only prohibits the government from supporting one religion over the many, but it also prohibits the government from putting the weight of its support behind religion in any form. The government is not only restricted from establishing a single religion, but it is prohibited from financing, supporting, or subsidizing religion in general. This issue of government support for religion, as opposed to non-religion, was behind the Supreme Court cases that ruled on the status of prayer in the public schools. State mandated religious practices in public schools, such as devotional Bible reading and prayer, have been interpreted by the Supreme Court as violations of the First Amendment prohibition of religious establishments. These decisions have produced intense emotional reactions on the part of parents who want religion to be a part of the public school experience of their children. It will be important to examine the constitutional logic behind the exclusion of religious practices from the public school.

The most vocal opponents of these Supreme Court decisions have been conservative Protestants. Many evangelical and fundamentalist Protestants have insisted that by excluding devotional religious practices from the public schools the United States has abandoned its most important religious commitment to being "one nation under God." By eliminating religious practices from the classroom, they have argued, the state has actually established the "religion of secular humanism." And this nonreligious worldview has been blamed for what they see as the moral decay of modern American society. Getting prayer back into the public schools has been one of the most important issues on the political agenda of those conservative religious groups that make up what has been called the New Religious Right. By the late seventies, they had attracted considerable attention to their conservative religiopolitical causes through television and radio ministries, sophisticated mass-mailing techniques, and aggressive political action committees. They were demonstrating that the separation of church and state in America did not mean that religion could not exert an influence on the political process. And their influence even extended to the Presidency. As Ronald Reagan sought the support of the Religious Right in an address to the Convention of National Religious Broadcasters, in October 1980, he advocated the return of prayer to the public schools. He declared, "I don't think we should ever have expelled God from the classroom."[4] This resurgence of conservative Protestantism in the public arena has had important implications for the relation between religion and politics in American society.

Fundamentalism grew out of the tradition of evangelical revivalism that dominated the mainline Protestant denominations throughout the nineteenth century. But it was a particular reaction to certain modernizing trends, such as biblical criticism, the influence of science, and the Social Gospel movement that came to be identified as liberal Protestantism. The historian George Marsden has defined fundamentalism as a "twentieth century movement closely tied to the revivalist tradition of mainstream evangelical Protestantism that militantly opposed modernist theology and the cultural change associated with it."[5] fundamentalists solidified their doctrinal position in the first two decades of the twentieth century, and proceeded to wage a war against liberalism in both religion and society. But after a series of setbacks they retreated from the public arena to create separate institutions in the form of fundamentalist private schools, universities, publishing houses, and churches. In response to the social disruption of the sixties, however, fundamentalists have reemerged, as the religious historian Martin Marty has put it, "with a vengeance."[6] Against the pluralism and permissiveness of modern American society, Fundamentalists have asserted a claim to being the authentic American conservative tradition. In attempting to appropriate and revitalize American civil religious values, they have demanded a restoration of a theocratic vision of America grounded in Protestant fundamentalism. As Walter Capps observed, "the New Right has captured the prominent positive national symbols: nationalistic feeling, patriotism, the family, motherhood, virtue and moral rectitude."[7]

The fundamentalist vision of a Christian America raises important

issues regarding the establishment of religion in America. Fundamentalists may uphold the separation of church and state; but they have nevertheless insisted that American public life and institutions must be infused
with their private vision of Christian morality. Their reform programs
hae been directed toward three basic areas of American life: family, community, and nation. In each area they have demanded that Christian morality be inserted into matters of public policy. As Jerry Falwell, director
of the Moral Majority, expressed it, "When we as a country again acknowledge God as our Creator and Jesus Christ as the savior of mankind,
we will be able to turn this nation around economically as well as in every
other way."[8] But how can a country committed to religious pluralism and
the separation of church and state, dedicate itself to this one particular
faith? Reverend Moon and Hansadutta Swami, as we saw in the last chapter, also insisted that their religious visions held out the promise for the
salvation of America. Why should Falwell's promise of Christian salvation
be given a special public status over the salvation offered by Moon or
Krishna?

This is the first issue of the establishment of religion: The United
States cannot legally adopt a single national religion. It cannot constitu-
tionally declare itself a Christian nation. In this sense, the prohibition of
establishment protects the free exercise of religious diversity in American
society. This is linked to the second issue: The United States cannot place
its legal, financial, or coercive support behind particular religious groups.
But what about supporting religion in general? Here the third issue is
raised: The United States cannot place the weight of its authority behind
religious as opposed to nonreligious concerns. There are some Americans who believe that economic policy should be the result of the careful
consideration of social interests, and not based on the acknowledgment
of God as Creator, Jesus as Savior, and the Bible as the only legitimate
authority. Economics is seen as a secular concern. But in fundamentalist
politics all secular concerns are infused with religious significance. And to
deny the religious basis of the family, the community, and the nation is to
fall into the dangerous error of secular humanism. This, they are convinced, the Supreme Court has done in removing religious instruction,
devotional Bible reading, and prayer from the public schools. It will be
useful to review the Supreme Court's interpretation of the establishment
clause in the First Amendment, in order to clarify its understanding of
the separation of church and state, before examining the public policy
issues raised by the New Religious Right.

THE SEPARATION OF CHURCH AND STATE

The Supreme Court dealt with the issue of the taxation of religious
groups in the 1940s by invoking the free exercise clause of the First

Amendment. In a case involving the Jehovah's Witnesses in the state of Pennsylvania, a state law which required licensing fees for religious groups came before the Court. In *Murdock v. Pennsylvania* (1943), the Court considered whether or not states could require religious groups to pay regular fees in order to be licensed within the state as recognized organizations.[9] The Court responded by prohibiting all such licensing fees. Justice Douglas summarized the free exercise issue at stake. First Amendment freedoms must remain beyond government control; but, "the power to tax the exercise of a privilege," Justice Douglas insisted, "is the power to control or suppress its enjoyment." A state may not impose a charge, fee, or tax upon First Amendment freedoms that are guaranteed by the Constitution. Therefore, the exercise of religion must be free from government control through taxation. It was not considered necessary to prove that a particular tax or license fee was actually used to suppress particular groups; it was sufficient to recognize that such taxation could repress the free exercise of religion in order to prohibit any taxation of religion in principle.

In a related case, *Jones v. Opelika* (1942), Chief Justice Stone strongly opposed any form of religious taxation.[10] The First Amendment did not simply protect the freedom of speech and the freedom of religion from government attempts to restrict or eliminate their exercise; it placed these freedoms in a preferred position. The principle of the free exercise of religion extended "to every form of taxation which, because it is a condition of the exercise of the privilege, is capable of being used to control or suppress it." Therefore, the requirement of fees and taxes placed conditions on the unconditional right to the free exercise of religion. State constitutions have traditionally included provisions which exempted religious groups from taxation of property used exclusively for religious purposes. In *Murdock* (1943) and *Jones* (1942), the Supreme Court indicated that these customary exemptions were consistent with the constitutional provision for the free exercise of religion.

But in 1970 a group of complainants in New York maintained that the exemption of religious property from taxation contradicted the establishment clause of the First Amendment. To exempt religious groups from taxation, they argued, was to provide an indirect form of financial support to religion. Not only did it place a greater tax burden on property owners, but it appeared to give a special financial advantage to the support of religion. In their appeal to the Supreme Court they claimed that the state exemption of religious property "indirectly requires the appellant to make a contribution to religious bodies and thereby violates the provisions prohibiting establishment of religion."[11] For the first time the traditional practice of tax exemption for religious property was challenged on the grounds that it violated the First Amendment prohibition of the establishment of religion.

Although the case of *Walz v. Tax Commission* (1970) was raised as an establishment issue, it was resolved by the Supreme Court as a question of free exercise. As in the earlier cases, taxation was interpreted as an undue burden on the free exercise of a First Amendment right. The majority opinion of the Court described the taxation of religious property as an inhibition of religious freedom, and went on to observe that the taxation of religious property would put religious groups at risk of losing their religious freedom for nonpayment of taxes. The Court noted that "grants of exemption historically reflect the concern of authors of constitutions and statutes as to the latent dangers inherent in the imposition of property taxes; exemption constitutes a reasonable and balanced attempt to guard against those dangers."

The majority opinion in *Walz* (1970) also recognized the importance of religious groups in American public life within a broader classification of nonprofit corporations that operate in the public interest. Such nonprofit organizations provide beneficial public welfare services that the government might otherwise have to provide. It would be reasonable for states to support such beneficial and stabilizing enterprises by relieving them of the burden of taxation. But religion involves a unique consideration that would not be relevant to other charitable nonprofit organizations. The government is committed to minimizing entanglements with religion by the prohibition of religious establishments. And the Court ruled that tax exemptions reduce the involvement of the state in the affairs of religious groups. To require taxation of religious groups would lead to an excessive entanglement of church and state. A direct financial subsidy, the Court insisted, is different from tax exemption. A direct subsidy would assign income from general revenues to religious groups, but, as Justice Brennan later explained, in "the case of an exemption, the state merely refrains from diverting to its own uses income independently generated by churches through voluntary contribution.[12]

Therefore, three basic reasons were presented by the Court in *Walz* (1970) to maintain that tax exemption of religious property or income was not an establishment of religion. First, such exemptions fell under the larger category of exemptions for nonprofit organizations operating in the public interest. But this alone cannot be the criterion for religious exemption, because it could involve the government in setting up standards to evaluate whether or not religious groups are actually providing social benefits. So the second justification of tax exemptions was based on the principle of the separation of church and state. Exemptions minimize the entanglements of government in the business of religion, and it was maintained that the involvement of the state in church affairs would only be increased through taxation. Finally, the Court maintained that exemptions are different from direct subsidies. A subsidy would require the state to support the church; but an exemption simply relieves religious groups from the obligation of supporting the state by turning over revenues that were raised through voluntary contributions to religion.

But if the indirect financial assistance provided to religion through tax exemptions does not represent an establishment of religion, what does? The Court's response to the issue of establishment has been worked out over a series of cases involving the status of religion in the public schools. These cases involved situations in which government institutions of public education directly supported religious instruction, prescribed prayers, and required devotional readings of the Bible. Defenders of these activities insisted that they were essential to the free exercise of their religious commitments. Opponents, however, argued that such practices, reinforced by the authority of the state, violated the prohibition against the establishment of religion. Religious freedom was the central issue; but there were conflicting interests on each side of the controversy. Defenders of religion in the public schools demanded freedom *for* religious exercise, while opponents of state mandated religious practices demanded freedom *from* religious coercion. When the public school institutes programs of religious instruction or devotion, they argued, it places the weight of the state's authority behind the promotion of religion. The public school cases tried to clarify the separation of church and state in mandatory public education.

The first two cases involved religious instruction. Illinois state schools had created a system of religious education, in which students were released from their regular classes once a week for an hour of religious instruction on school premises. Religious training took place in school buildings on school property, with the pupils separated by their respective religious faiths. School officials supervised the selection of religious teachers and administered the program. This arrangement was challenged by a parent, who claimed that it involved "segregation and embarrassment to those not participating which amounts to interference with their religious freedom." This case came before the Supreme Court in *McCollum v. State of Illinois Board of Education* (1948). The Court ruled that the Illinois public school program for religious instruction used state authority in the interests of religion in a way that amounted to the religious coercion of pupils. Justice Black wrote for the majority of the Court by observing that "Here not only are the state's tax-supported school buildings used for the dissemination of religious doctrines. The state also affords sectarian groups an invaluable aid in that it helps to provide pupils for their religious classes through use of the state's compulsory public school machinery. This is not separation of Church and State." The Court insisted on a strict wall of separation in *McCollum* (1948). But Justice Reed, in his dissent, questioned the holes in that wall. He pointed to the numerous instances of close association between church and state, and noted that the Court had approved the use of tax revenues to reimburse parents for textbooks and transportation for their children attending church-related parochial schools. "The prohibition of enactments respecting the establishment of religion," he wrote, "do not bar every friendly gesture between church and state."[13]

This line of reasoning seemed to hold in the next case involving religious instruction. In *Zorach v. Clauson* (1952), students in New York City were released from their classes one hour each week so that they might leave school and go to religious centers for instruction or worship. Again, parents complained that in this program "the weight and influence of the school is behind a program of religious instruction."[14] In this case, however, the Supreme Court upheld the practice of release time for religious instruction. It ruled that the school authorities were neutral, and not coercive, in their cooperation with this program. Justice Douglas affirmed the basic principle of separation. "Government," he insisted, "may not finance religious groups nor undertake religious instruction nor blend secular and sectarian education or use secular institutions to force one or some religion on any person." While maintaining the prohibition of religious instruction on public school property established in *McCollum*, the Court nevertheless ruled that the New York City "release time" program was different. In Illinois the public school system gave religion its space; but in New York the schools simply gave religion some time. There is nothing in the First Amendment, the Court ruled, that prohibited the public school from suspending its operations in order to allow students to go to their houses of worship for religious instruction. Justice Douglas wrote that separation of church and state does not imply that "public institutions can make no adjustment of their schedules to accommodate the religious needs of the people." Such strict separation, the Court argued, would be evidence of government hostility toward religion, rather than neutrality.

McCollum (1948) and *Zorach* (1952) may have left some ambiguity about the strict separation between church and state. But while *Zorach* allowed for a greater cooperation with the religious needs of parents and students, it did not deny the compelling force of the decision in *McCollum* that religious instruction should not be supported by state funds, introduced into the curriculum, nor permitted on public school premises. The reminder provided by Justice Douglas, that state institutions should not be used to force one, or even some, religion on public school pupils, reinforced the state's interest in protecting nonbelievers from an establishment of religion in the public schools. The controversial school prayer cases in the early sixties asserted the rights of nonbelievers to be free from the imposition of religious beliefs and practices by the authority of the state.

In *Engel v. Vitale* (1962), the Supreme Court ruled that official prayer in the public schools violated the prohibition against religious establishments.[15] The Regents of the New York State public school system had drafted a prayer that was to be recited daily by school children. The prayer was short and simple: "Almighty God, we acknowledge our dependence upon Thee, and we beg Thy blessings upon us, our parents, our teachers, and our country." The defenders of the prayer argued that it reflected a broadly based national religious heritage, and exposure to this cultural tradition should be a regular part of public school education. They claimed that "the intent of the First Amendment was to prohibit the establishment of a state religion; it was not intended to prohibit the growth and development of a religious state." The Regents' school prayer was defended as an effective means of nurturing an appreciation of the nation's religious heritage among students in the public schools.

In prohibiting the New York school prayer, the Supreme Court reinforced its interpretation of the separation of church and state in the public schools which it had outlined in *McCollum* (1948). First, the Court established that it was not appropriate for public schools to use religious means in order to achieve civil ends. Informing students about America's religious heritage is a legitimate educational objective; but indoctrinating them into religious practices is not. There is a difference between teaching *about* religion, and the teaching *of* religion, which is important to the Court's interpretation of the role of religion in the public schools. It may be one thing for public school teachers to explain the importance of religion in American history; but it would be a different matter for instructors to initiate their students into the religious practices of prayer, worship, or other rituals. For the defenders of the school prayer to insist that these practices have important civil benefits is not sufficient to justify introducing religious practices into the public school.

Second, the Court reminded the state of New York that the First Amendment did not simply protect the many religious groups in America from being dominated by a single state religion; it also protected those who have chosen no religion. The freedom of religion, conscience, and speech insures the right to dissent, and this protects dissenting minorities from the tyranny of the majority even in matters of religion. Even if the Regents' prayer did reflect the sentiments of a Judeo-Christian majority in American society, it would still come into conflict with the plural composition of the public schools. Finally, the Court denied that the state had any constitutional justification for composing prayers and requiring that they be recited in the public schools. "The constitutional prohibition against laws respecting an establishment of religion," read the majority opinion, "must at least mean that in this country it is no part of the business of government to compose official prayers for any group of the people as part of a religious program carried on by the government." This answered the narrower question that was at issue in *Engel* (1962). The Court did not rule that students could not pray in school; it simply prohibited the state from writing prayers and requiring them to be recited. But there was a larger issue at stake: the constitutional right of parents who dissented from the religion expressed by the public school. This right of parents and children to be protected from religious coercion in the schools—the freedom *from* religion—was acknowledged in *Engel* and reinforced in the Supreme Court rulings on prayer and devotional Bible reading in the public schools the following year.

The case of *School District of Abington Township, Pa. v. Schempp* (1963) considered a Pennsylvania state law which required daily Bible reading.[16] Teachers were required by law to read, or cause to be read at the opening of every school day, ten verses from the Bible without comment. The law specified that teachers who refused to conduct this daily Bible reading would be discharged. Each school day began with a reading by a student of ten verses from the Bible. Next, students were to stand and recite together the Lord's Prayer. And finally they would repeat the Pledge of Allegiance to the flag. Prayer and devotional Bible reading were, therefore, part of a regular ritual practice in the classroom. The Schempp family brought suit against the state for violating its First Amendment protection from religious coercion by government. Pennsylvania responded by including a provision in the law that would excuse students from the exercises upon written request of their parents or guardians. But, Mr. Schempp insisted, this was not sufficient. Children would still suffer coercion under peer pressure. The Pennsylvania school system was ignoring the Supreme Court ruling, in *Everson* (1947), that the government cannot force a person "to profess a belief or disbelief in any religion."[17] The practice of prayer in the public schools, even with the provision that some students could be excused, still violated the First Amendment.

The Supreme Court in *Schempp* (1963) agreed with this assessment. The majority upheld the ruling of the District Court of Eastern Pennsylvania, which had determined that religious coercion was not avoided by allowing students the option of being excused from the religious ceremony. They agreed with Judge Biggs of the lower court when he observed that this "ignores reality and the force of social suasion." Students were forced into a situation in which they were compelled to make a public profession of belief or disbelief; and this the state was forbidden to require. The very fact of mandatory school attendance, Judge Biggs noted, places students "in the path of compulsion."

The Supreme Court in *Schempp* (1963) also reaffirmed the distinction between the *devotional* and the *academic* role of religion in the public classroom. They agreed with the lower court of Pennsylvania, when it observed that the Bible could be studied as an academic subject: "If study of the Bible as an artistic work, a treasury of moral truth, or historical text can be separated from the espousal of doctrinal matters and religiousness, we should find no objection." But the daily readings from the Bible, joined as they were with the recitation of the Lord's Prayer, clearly indicated a devotional use. The Pennsylvania court concluded that such a practice was designed to "inculcate or promote the inculcation of various religious doctrines in childish minds." The Supreme Court in *Schempp* strongly supported the academic study of religion. "One's education is not complete," said the Court, "without a study of comparative religion or the history of religion and its relationship to the advancement of civilization." Nothing in the First Amendment would prohibit such a course of study in the public schools. This leaves open a third option for the place of religion in state schools. The public school must be neither friendly to religion by promoting religious beliefs and practices, nor hostile to religion by excluding it from all consideration. The third position supported by the Court is one of neutrality. Therefore, the test proposed by *Schempp* for evaluating the status of religion in the public schools begins by identifying its primary effect. If the primary effect of Bible reading, or the study of religious teachings, is to inculcate religion, then these practices involve an inappropriate use of the coercive power of the state to establish religion.

These Supreme Court cases relating to the establishment clause in the First Amendment have struggled to work out an interpretation of the separation of church and state based on a "benevolent neutrality." The basic assumption has been that both church and state prosper when they operate as much as possible in separate spheres. The tax exemption cases established that religious groups do not support the state; and the school prayer cases have ruled that the state does not support religion. The reimbursement of parents who send their children to private religious schools for books and bus transportation, as well as the accommodation of school schedules to release students for religious observances, indicate that the Court does not understand the neutrality of government in matters of religion to be hostility. On the other hand, the limitations on religious instruction and devotional practices in the public schools indicate that the government is not in the business of promoting religion. In these establishment cases, as in the issues relating to free exercise, the Court has evolved a neutral approach that attempts to balance competing secular and religious interests.

The school prayer cases, however, generated an intensely emotional controversy in American society. Many interpreted the Supreme Court decisions as a direct attack on religion. With God "expelled from the classroom" they felt that America's school system would be surrendered to atheists and secular humanists. The destruction of the moral fabric of American society would surely follow. Senator Everett Dirksen, a Republican from Illinois, had considerable grassroots support for his prayer amendment, which stated that nothing in the Constitution could be interpreted to prohibit public schools from "providing for or permitting the voluntary participation by students or others in prayer." But he failed in two attempts to get this bill through the Senate. It clearly would have contradicted the Court's interpretation of the First Amendment as protecting religious (and non-religious) minorities from any form of coercion in matters of religious conscience.

The issue of prayer in the public schools has been one of many public policy issues on the agenda of religious groups that make up the New Religious Right. These groups have recently renewed the controversy over the role of religion in public life. They have claimed to be a religious majority that has been persecuted by the small elite of nonbelievers, atheists, and secular humanists who have excluded religion from American society. The New Religious Right wanted to restore a religious foundation for the family, the community, and the nation. But that foundation was not a general, diffused civil religious *ethos*; it was a particular form of fundamentalist Christianity which has resurfaced in the public awareness and reasserted itself in the political process.

FUNDAMENTALIST POLITICS

Protestant fundamentalism emerged in the twentieth century from the mainstream evangelicalism that had characterized the major Protestant denominations throughout the nineteenth century. Evangelical revivals of the nineteenth century, particularly in the 1830s and 1840s, were linked with social reform movements. Evangelical Christians were actively involved in a number of social and political causes. Many evangelicals were concerned with transforming their personal conversion experiences into a positive influence upon public morals, social relations, and politics. There were moral reform movements, such as the New York Female Moral Reform Society, which could list the causes of immorality as, "Impure imagination, Dress of females, Slavery, Public opinion licenses the evil, Females receiving visits of gentlemen protracted to a late hour, Low prices of labor in cities, Voluptuousness, Balls, Parties, Theaters, Novel reading, Classics, Prints and Books."[18] This appears to be a fairly complete, if somewhat eclectic, list of the immoral influences that were believed to threaten Christian moral decency.

There were also social reform movements. Evangelical Christians were very active in the abolition societies and the temperance crusades that fought to eliminate social evils. Revivalistic enthusiasm often inspired evangelical Christians to active participation in these voluntary societies for social reform. And there was a concern for the political influence that could be exerted by evangelical Christians. The evangelical leaders of Oberlin College in the mid-eighteenth century, for example, were convinced that Christians should not stop at moral persuasion; but they should commit themselves to the political process. As evangelical Christians, they declared, "we have Christian duties toward our government; we feel bound to use our best endeavors to promote the election of good rulers . . . We aim and endeavor to throw the power of our elevated and earnest Christianity into the domain of politics."[19]

But the Social Gospel movement of the late nineteenth century, in seeking to make Protestant Christianity relevant to the social problems of modern, industrial society, embraced modern culture in ways that made many conservative evangelicals very uncomfortable. The liberal theologians of the Social Gospel movement tried to derive from the Christian message a motive for social reforms in the factories, tenement slums, and streets of urban America. Christianity was to become relevant to the problems of the modern world by forming a base for social action by which the social welfare, living conditions, and employment prospects of all people in America might be improved. And in order to respond effectively to these human needs, Christian theology would have to adapt to the new demands of modern culture. Walter Rauschenbusch, the leading theologian of the Social Gospel, insisted that "if theology stops growing, or is unable to adjust to its modern environment, it will die."[20] But, to many conservative, evangelical Protestants, this modern culture appeared as a threatening conspiracy between secular science and secular society. Fundamentalism emerged as a reaction against these modernizing trends in American society.

The rise of modern science to a position of prestige and power in American intellectual life was represented by the influence of Darwin's theory of evolution. The publication of Charles Darwin's *Descent of Man* (1871), which applied the theory of natural selection to the human species, generated an intense theological controversy. The theologian Charles Hodge of Princeton Theological Seminary, attacked evolutionary theory as if it were a rival religious doctrine to Christianity. In assuming that the natural world was the result of the "blind unconscious laws of nature," Hodge insisted, evolution denied that God created the world according to an intentional design.[21] To deny this creative design in the universe was to deny the existence of God, and for Hodge and other opponents of evolution, Darwin's theory (even though Darwin himself was not an atheist) was a form of atheism.

Liberal theologians tried to adapt modern scientific theory to religious doctrine. Lyman Abbott, for example, in his *Theology on an Evolutionist* (1897), felt that evolutionary theory was compatible with the Bible. "The objection that evolution could not be reconciled with Genesis gave me no concern," Abbott observed, "for I had long decided that the Bible is no authority on scientific questions."[22] The liberal response, therefore, was to separate religion and science so that the authority of the Bible extended only over the inner spiritual life of the Christian. But for many conservative Christians this attack on the factual authority of the Bible threatened the authority of the Bible as a whole. One of the most popular defenders of the authority of the Bible was William Jennings Bryan. He had been a Congressman, Secretary of State, and presidential candidate; but Bryan once said, "I am interested in the science of government, but I am more interested in religion."[23] Toward the end of his life he became the public defender of biblical authority in the battle against the modern science of evolution. He objected to Darwinism, not only because he felt there was nothing in the Bible to support it, but because it undermined the absolute authority of the Bible. The Bible, for Bryan, must be the ultimate standard in both religion and science. When a liberal theologian like Henry Emerson Fosdick suggested that the Bible was a text of faith, not science, Bryan responded by saying that this was like saying a cello would make a good dinner table. The Bible was authoritative in matters of both faith and knowledge, and to question this authority was to attack the fundamental basis of a Christian society.

The trial of John Scopes, a high school biology teacher in Dayton, Tennessee, brought this battle between conservative and liberal approaches to biblical authority to national attention in 1925. Scopes was charged for violating a state law that prohibited teachers from introducing in the classroom "any theory which denies the divine creation of man as taught by the Bible, and to teach instead that man has descended from a lower order of animals." John Scopes tested this law on the grounds of academic freedom. After a controversial twelve-day trial, in which Clarence Darrow took the evolutionary cause against William Jennings Bryan, Scopes was convicted and fined for violating the law. But although the liberal forces lost this battle, they seemed to win the war for public opinion.[24] After the Scopes Monkey Trial, the American public increasingly accepted the independence of scientific authority, and the conservative opponents of modern science gradually retreated from public confrontations. But out of these controversies emerged the basic conservative Protestant doctrine of the literal inerrancy of the Bible. Throughout the Christian tradition the Bible has been a sacred authority; but now, in response to modern science, it became an alternative scientific textbook.

Liberal theologians not only adapted Protestant Christianity to modern science, but also to modern secular society. Henry Emerson Fosdick, the liberal pastor of a Presbyterian church in New York City, spoke on behalf of "the cause of magnanimity and liberality and tolerance of spirit."[25] His liberal openness, expansiveness, and toleration were defended as attitudes that Christians must develop in order to adapt their message to the modern world. The liberals were open to the social changes within secular society. But conservative Protestants saw this secularization as a dangerous decline in the religious power of Christianity in the world. The evils of secular society could be fought in two basic ways: first, through evangelism; and second, through the development of dispensationalism. The urban evangelism of Dwight Moody, toward the end of the nineteenth century, introduced effective techniques of advance publicity, mobilization of local churches, religious services with choirs and counselors, and a simple, straightforward evangelical appeal in his revival crusades. He pressed his audience to make their decision for Christ and be saved. The central question was "Have I been born again?" Moody was pessimistic about secular society. He described it as a sinking ship, a "wrecked vessel," from which he was endeavoring to save as many souls as possible in the lifeboat of the gospel. The mass evangelism of Moody and other evangelical crusaders was directed toward winning souls for Christ out of the wreckage of modern secular society.[26]

This pessimism regarding the larger society was connected with a second line of attack against secularism that developed a view of sacred history in which this modern age was seen as the last days before the end. The hope, expectation, and anticipation of Christ's return was an important ingredient in evangelical faith. Some were *postmillennial* in their expectation of this second coming. Jonathan Edwards, who had played such an important role in the Protestant revival of the eighteenth-century Great Awakening, was convinced that the world had already moved into the millennial period in the spiritual unfolding of God's kingdom on earth. The stirrings of religious enthusiasm were interpreted as signs that Christ's thousand-year reign had already begun, and that He would return at the end of this period of gradual improvement in the religious character of church and society. There was a spirit of optimism in this postmillennial interpretation of history that found it easy to identify the emergence of the kingdom of God with the destiny of America. A form of civil millennialism developed which witnessed the American experience as a progressive unfolding of God's kingdom on earth.[27] Liberal Protestants around the turn of this century shared this postmillennial optimism, and they saw the emerging millennial influence of Christ in modern social progress.

Many evangelical Christians, however, have been *premillennial* in their understanding of sacred history. They expected things to worsen before Christ suddenly appeared to institute his thousand-year reign on earth. This return was to be expected at any moment. As Lyman Beecher, an evangelical leader of the early nineteenth century, declared, "The millennium is at the door."[28] But premillennialists were also eager to identify specific signs in current events that indicated that the end was close at hand. These signs would be various trials, tribulations, and natural disasters; but they could also take the form of specific international events which could be interpreted as fulfillment of biblical prophecy. When the Pope was driven from Rome in 1798 by French troops many premillennialists saw this as a sign of the last days foretold in the Book of Revelation.[29] One of the largest millennial movements of the nineteenth century was started in the 1830s by William Miller. Based on mathematical calculations, applied to a passage in the Book of Daniel (8:14), Miller determined that Christ would return sometime in 1843. When Jesus did not appear, the calculations were corrected, and October 22, 1844 was set as the date of the end. Miller attracted a large and enthusiastic following. Many people quit their jobs, sold their houses, and put on ascension robes, in anticipation of being carried into heaven on that last day. Although the Millerite movement dissolved after the great disappointment of 1844, other millennial, or adventist, groups soon emerged to take its place.[30]

Toward the end of the nineteenth century, premillennial thought became standardized in the theory of dispensations developed by John Nelson Darby. In this dispensational system Christ was expected to return after two dramatic events: the rapture of the saints, in which believing Christians would be carried miraculously into heaven; and the period of tribulations, in which the world would suffer turmoil through the appearance of the antichrist. Dispensationalism had a number of important political implications for conservative Protestants. First, on the level of political theory, it represented a symbolic inversion of the present political order. The secular leadership of modern society would be destroyed and it would be replaced by the kingdom of Christ. Conservative Protestants who felt impotent in the face of the modernization and secularization of American society could anticipate the imminent restructuring of power relations at the second coming. They took seriously the biblical promise that "the first shall be last, and the last shall be first." Second, this expectation of the imminent reversal of the social order motivated conservative Protestants to separate themselves from this larger society that was destined for destruction. They felt compelled to maintain a strict separation from all the corrupting influences of modern society in order to prepare for the end. Third, in order to facilitate this separation, conservative Protestants created separate institutional structures (such as separatist churches, denominations, universities, and publishing houses) and produced a large network of interrelated conservative Protestant institutions.

The theological position supporting these separate institutions was solidified in 1909 with the publication of twelve pamphlets, financed by two executives of Union Oil, Lyman and Milton Stewart, entitled *The Fundamentals: A Testimony of Truth*. At the heart of the fundamentalist doctrine embodied in these publications were five points which came to be accepted, according to the historian Norman Furniss, as the "*sine qua non* of Fundamentalism."[31] These five fundamentals were (1) the literal inerrancy of the Bible; (2) the virgin birth of Christ; (3) the saving death, or substitutionary atonement, of Christ; (4) the resurrection of Christ; and (5) the expectation of Christ's imminent return. These fundamentals, therefore, reinforced conservative Protestant commitments in the battle against modernism. They affirmed the unquestionable, literal, and factual authority of the Bible in reaction to the threat posed by modern science, and they affirmed the premillennial dispensationalism that promised an imminent reversal of the social order in response to the increasing, pervasive power of modern secular society. Fundamentalism, therefore, was a modern religious movement, in the sense that it developed in the twentieth century out of mainsteam evangelical Protestantism. But it was also an antimodern religious movement, reacting against the rising power of science and secularism in modern society.

Separatist fundamentalists actively formed new churches, denominations, and fellowships, and after the 1930s they were particularly dedicated to creating schools, institutes, and universities for the promotion of education based on fundamentalist Christian principles. These fundamentalist institutions sought to maintain a strict separation from mainstream, modern American society. But, when they did become involved in the public arena, fundamentalist leaders organized dramatic crusades against the evils of the modern world.

Carl McIntire was a prominent fundamentalist crusader who broke with the Presbyterian Church and formed his own Bible Presbyterian Churches as a coalition of separatist fundamentalist groups. From this platform he launched attacks against the ecumenical movement, represented by the World Council of Churches and the National Council of Churches, for their deviation from fundamentalist principles. But the primary targets of his attacks were communists and Catholics. He identified God's government with capitalism, free enterprise, and individualism, and opposed the satanic influences of communism. The battle against communism was perceived as a sacred war against the forces of evil. McIntire, as well as many other leaders among right wing fundamentalists, opposed any form of collectivism, and this included the Social Gospel, the New Deal, and any forms of social welfare in America. These were seen as forerunners of communism. McIntire also represented a revival of Protestant nativism, and at one point, in 1945, he stated that Catholics in America posed an even greater threat than communism. McIntire's crusades against ecumenicalism, communism, and Catholicism—supported by books, pamphlets, and regular radio broadcasts—represented one attempt by a separatist fundamentalist to take political action against what were perceived as great spiritual evils.[32]

A similar fundamentalist movement was started in 1947 by Billy James Hargis, who, at age twenty-two, began his Christian Crusade. The Crusade was dedicated to the battle against communism, based on a simple creed which combined fundamentalism, Americanism, and the values of free enterprise. Through publications and radio broadcasts, Hargis also reached a wide audience with his conservative religious, moral, and political message. Hargis insisted on the importance of preserving moral virtues in reaction against a permissive modern society. His best-selling book in 1968, *Is the Little Red School House the Proper Place to Teach Raw Sex?*, was an attack on sex education in the public schools. But his primary concern was to promote conservative political causes. Hargis suggested that there was a natural link between fundamentalist Christianity and conservative politics. "Christ is the heart of the conservative cause," Hargis once said. "We are fighting for God and country."[33] Any born-again fundamentalist, according to Hargis, must be politically conservative. The Christian Crusade ran into difficulties in 1966 when it lost its tax-exempt status due to its political activities. And then in 1974 Hargis confessed to allegations that he had had sexual relations with five students—four of them men—at his American Christian College in Tulsa. In a curious invocation of the authority of science he blamed his behavior on "genes and chromosomes."[34]

A third example of a separatist fundamentalist movement was the Christian Anti-Communism Crusade founded in 1953 by Frederick C. Schwarz. He dedicated himself to informing Americans about the dangers of communism; but his political concerns were animated by a fundamentalist religious commitment. "I am not ashamed," Schwarz declared, "to say that I am a narrow-minded, Bible-believing Baptist. On that basis I built my crusade."[35] He achieved a certain national prominence in 1957 by appearing before the House Un-American Activities Committee and aligning his fundamentalist crusade with the general Cold-war Fear of international communism that pervaded the postwar American imagination. His testimony on the dangers of communism was later published in a book entitled *You Can Trust the Communists (To Be Communists)*, which sold nearly a million copies. Throughout the sixties Schwarz conducted programs around the country to educate Americans about the atheistic conspiracy threatening to destroy Christian civilization.

These fundamentalist crusades, as well as other organizations that emerged during this period, were dedicated to a conservative political vision of America. But the pattern of American political life they defended (which would preserve the values of individualism, free enterprise, and military strength) was grounded in separatist fundamentalism. The result was a distinctive Christian Americanism. Bob Jones III, whose grandfather had founded the influential fundamentalist Bob Jones University, declared: "We hold with old-fashioned Christian Americanism. We think it made this country great, we think it serves freedom, and we think it serves God."[36] Billy James Hargis even insisted that America is a Christian nation. He stated:

> Patriotism and Christianity are very close to each other. It is impossible to be a true Christian and not be a true patriot. One who loves God also loves his country. Our forefathers believed in Jesus Christ and his atoning blood . . . America is and always has been a Christian nation.[37]

This notion of a Christian America, however, involved these fundamentalist crusaders in two major conflicts regarding the relationship between religion and society. First, they generated a conflict within fundamentalism itself. The political crusaders of the religious right combined a *premillennial* separatism in theology with a *postmillennial* religiopolitical vision of God's kingdom unfolding in America. Many separatist fundamentalists felt that a Christian nation was a contradiction in terms, and they held to a premillennial pessimism regarding the larger society. And second, by insisting that America was a Christian nation, these crusaders created some confusion about the constitutional relationship between religion and politics in American society. They invoked the memories of the founding fathers of America in defense of their particular understanding of an American covenant; but they neglected those founders' concern to create a social contract guaranteeing the freedom of conscience and prohibiting the establishment of religion. The United States was not founded as a Christian nation, but rather as a religiopolitical system that encouraged religious pluralism. To invoke its founding fathers as fundamentalists before the fact was a distortion of the historical record.

Yet this mixture of fundamental Christianity and patriotic Americanism had an increasingly persuasive appeal for many Americans. A large part of the public enthusiasm for conservative Christianity was mobilized by the effective use of the new electronic media. Christian crusaders, fundamentalist preachers, and evangelical revivalists attracted large national followings through regular radio broadcasts. In the early 1940s the single most popular radio program in America was the "Old-Fashioned Revival Hour" of Charles E. Fuller. And in the fifties, the evangelist Billy Graham began a regular radio ministry to supplement his successful revival crusades called *Hour of Decision*. Graham came from a fundamentalist background; but by accepting support from liberal Protestant denominations on his revival tours throughout the country he alienated the fundamentalists. Nevertheless, he appealed to the sentiments of Christian Americanism through his radio broadcasts. In one sermon he told his audience: "Unless America at this tragic hour is willing to turn to Jesus Christ and be cleansed by the blood of Christ and know the regenerating power of the Holy Spirit, Christ will never save the nation." And how will America be saved? "When you make your decision for Jesus Christ," Graham declared, "it is America making her decision through you."[38]

The real revolution, however, in the relationship between fundamentalists and the electronic media came with the explosion of opportunities for religious programming on television. The Electronic Church was born as fundamentalist preachers began to dominate the airwaves with their simple, straightforward, soul-saving messages; their promotion of Christian Americanism; and their persistent appeals for voluntary donations from the viewing audience. The Federal Communications Commission had ruled in the 1970s that it would consider paid religious broadcasts as satisfying its requirement that stations provide regular public service programming. Religious broadcasters could purchase regular blocks of air time, and these programs were sought by television stations because they not only fulfilled the need for public service programming, but also provided a regular income. Paid religious broadcasting soon forced most mainline, noncommercial religious programs off the air. Mainline Protestants, Catholics, or Jews who had been involved in presenting religious television programs were not willing, for the most part, to pay for air time or solicit funds on television. But the fundamentalists were willing to do both, and religious broadcasting soon became a very lucrative business for these conservative Protestant ministries of the air. During fiscal year 1979, for example, it reportedly cost Jerry Falwell, of the "Old-Time Gospel Hour," around $9 million to broadcast weekly television programs and daily radio shows. From these efforts he took in over $50 million in contributions. Other religious broadcasters were also financially successful during this period. A survey of the most popular ministries in 1980 revealed large incomes: Oral Roberts ($60 million); Rex Humbard ($25 million); Jimmy Swaggert ($20 million); Pat Robertson ($58 million); and Jim Bakker ($51 million). By 1985, Falwell, Robertson, Bakker, and Swaggert were each taking in over $100 million a year; the following year, they were grossing around $130 million each.[39] The tremendous incomes generated by viewer contributions to these programs indicated the ability of the Electronic Church to amass power through television. This inspired Jeremy Rifkin to observe that "a close look at the evangelical communications network . . . should convince even the skeptic that it is now the single most important cultural force in American life."[40]

Some of these electronic evangelists have been involved in religious broadcasting for a long time. Oral Roberts was a tent show evangelist and faith healer in the fifties, but soon switched to a television ministry. His programs emanated from Tulsa, Oklahoma, where in the early sixties he established Oral Roberts University. In 1977 he began construction of the $120 million City of Faith hospital; but when he encountered financial difficulties he came on television to relate his vision of a 900-foot Christ who had appeared to him to assure the project's success. He claimed an audience of 50 million viewers by 1976, and their donations helped support this larger Oral Roberts empire. In 1987 Oral Roberts created controversy when he claimed that unless viewers contributed $8 million by the end of March, God would "call him home." Rex Humbard has also had a long history of religious broadcasting, with around 50 years on radio and over 30 years of television. He hosted his programs with his wife Maude, and presented a straightforward appeal for soul-winning salvation. The Oral Roberts and Rex Humbard broadcasts basically transferred the traditional revival meeting to television. It was a simple religious message, well-suited to the short attention span produced by the television medium.

Television broadcasting, by its very nature, involves certain technical events—quick cutting between camera angles, the camera zooms in and zooms out, the camera pans across a room—which are constantly shifting the viewer's attention. Television involves techniques which artificially change the viewer's perspective, and these technical events happen so rapidly—perhaps every ten to twenty seconds—that they often go unnoticed. The fundamentalist, or evangelical, religious message was particularly well-suited for this medium because it usually consisted of a brief, persuasive, emotional appeal that was quick enough to get through to the audience in between the technical events. Oral Roberts declared: "Something good is going to happen to you"; Rex Humbard simply assured his audience: "You are loved." In the Electronic Church, theology tended to be reduced to slogan. It is difficult to imagine a more complex religious discourse, let alone ritual, being so easily transmitted. Yet in fundamentalist religious broadcasting there was a perfect match between a direct, emotionally charged message and the short attention span induced by the technology of the medium.[41]

This did not restrain electronic ministers, however, from attacking the medium that supported them. Jimmy Swaggert, for example, created a successful television ministry through his country and gospel music and his camp-meeting style of dramatic preaching. Stomping, shouting, and waving the Bible he preached against the evils of the age. Of course, one of the most serious evils was television. In one sermon he attacked the immorality, profanity, and indecency of television as a symptom of the evils that pervaded American society in the modern world:

> Now we're living in a dirty, filthy age. I mean it's *dirty*! Twenty years ago, you turned on television, you would not have heard the profanity! . . . Now you turn on television and it's one curse word after another. Besides that the—I want to say *ladies*—but, the women are so indecently dressed that it's so vulgar that it defies desciption. It's inane! It's absurd! It is a ludicrosity! It is stupid![42]

This invective revealed something of the ambivalent relationship between the electronic ministers and television. They were effective in exploiting this modern technology, and yet they used it to build a fundamentalist, antimodern, power base.

A new format for religious broadcasting was created by the ex-marine and former lawyer, Pat Robertson, with the formation of the 700 Club in 1963. This Christian talk and variety show featured music and conversation, special guests from the entertainment industry, and an elaborate supporting system of prayer counselors, who took phone calls and pledges for donations from the viewers. A similar program was created in 1972 by Robertson's associate Jim Bakker. Bakker's PTL Club ("Praise the Lord"), which he hosted with his wife Tammy, quickly expanded to include a large network of broadcast and cable stations. Both programs financed expanding religious empires: Robertson started the Christian Broadcasting Network (CBN) to make a wide range of Christian programming available through cable television; and Bakker founded a large recreational, entertainment, and educational complex in Charlotte, North Carolina, which he called Heritage, U.S.A. Toward the end of the seventies, both began to recognize the potential political impact they could mobilize through their religious broadcasting. Pat Robertson observed that "We have enough votes to run the country."[43] And Bakker declared: "Our goal is to influence all viable [presidential] candidates on issues important to the church. We want answers. We want appointments in government."[44] By 1986, Robertson had even declared himself to be a viable candidate for the presidency.

The electronic minister who most effectively capitalized on this latent political power in religious broadcasting was Jerry Falwell. He attributed his own religious conversion to the influence of Charles Fuller's "Old-Fashioned Revival Hour" on radio. During the sixties he was the pastor of Liberty Baptist Church in Lynchburg, Virginia. In the midst of the social disturbances of the decade, he advocated the traditional fundamentalist separation from political involvement. His 1965 sermon— "Ministers and Marchers"—chastised religious leaders for their political involvement in the civil rights movement. "Believing the Bible as I do," Falwell declared, "I would find it impossible to stop preaching the pure saving gospel of Jesus Christ, and begin doing anything else—including fighting communism, or participating in civil rights reforms . . . . Preachers are not called to be politicians, but to be soul winners."[45] Falwell was later to repudiate this separation from political involvement, as he began to use his television ministry, the "Old-Time Gospel Hour," to promote a program of social reforms. There was a militant tone in his exhortations as he encouraged his fundamentalist following to declare war against the moral, social, and political evils of modern society. His Old-Time Gospel Hour issued a "Declaration of War."

> Be it known to all that The Old-Time Gospel Hour hereby declares war against the evils threatening America during the 1980s.
> Furthermore, this shall be a Holy War, not a war with guns and bullets, but a war fought with the Bible, prayer and Christian involvement.
> The Old-Time Gospel Hour hereby dedicates itself to spearhead the battle and lead an army of Christian soldiers into the war against evil.[46]

The text of this dramatic declaration identified those evils: abortion, pornography, homosexuality, socialism, and the deterioration of the home and family. In this crusade against social evils, Falwell described the role of the church as that of a "disciplined, charging army. Christians, like slaves and soldiers, ask no questions."[47] And the crusade against moral, social, and political evils was conceived as a military operation. This disciplined, charging, Christian army would engage all Americans, "bring them under submission to the Gospel of Christ, move them into the household of God, put up the flag and call it secured."[48]

The popular appeal of the Electronic Church coincided in the late seventies with the rise of a politically active New Right. This conservative political coalition attacked liberalism as a model of society "based on state regulation, supervision and coercion."[49] And the New Right promoted free-market capitalism, military strength, and a wide ranging list of conservative causes, including opposition to abortion, gun control, and the Panama Canal treaty. These causes were financially supported by a sophisticated mass-mailing network. Richard Viguerie, for example, marshaled computerized mass-mailing lists of 25 million names to make direct-mail appeals for donations. In his book, *The New Right: We're Ready to Lead*, Viguerie attributed the increasing power of the conservative movement to this mass-mailing, fund-raising technology. "The conservative movement," he said, "is where it is today because of direct mail. Without direct mail, there would be no effective counterforce to liberalism, and certainly there would be no New Right."[50] This sophisticated fund-raising technology became the primary medium of the New Right, and it raised funds to finance various conservative political action committees: The National Conservative Political Action Committee; the Conservative Caucus; and the Committee for the Survival of a Free Congress.

The founder of the Conservative Caucus, Ed McAter, who had been lobbying for conservative interests through this organization since 1974, started Christian Voice in 1979. It was a political platform for Christian Americanism. Christian Voice had a bill introduced in Congress that would declare the United States a "Christian Nation"; and it issued "Moral Report Cards" which rated congressmen on their political positions regarding abortion, prayer in schools, support for Taiwan, and other conservative issues. The director of the Committee for the Survival of a Free Congress, Paul Weyrich, was also aware of the potential for mobilizing evangelicals and fundamentalists as a large voting bloc in support of conservative causes. Weyrich and Viguerie joined forces with Jerry Falwell in the formation of a new political organization in 1980—the Moral Majority. In the Electronic Church, Viguerie observed, conservatives had their "own ready made network;" and he described Jerry Falwell as the New Right's "most important asset."[51] The New Religious Right, which took shape in organizations such as Christian Voice and the Moral Majority, tried to harness conservative political causes to the energy of religious revivalism. Viguerie was quoted as saying: "We believe we should be in politics as a way of improving the world from a religious concept."[52] And Weyrich addressed the National Affairs Briefing of the Religious Roundtable, a gathering of the stars of the Electronic Church in Dallas, 1980, by exhorting conservative Protestant preachers to renew their commitment to Christian Americanism. Weyrich declared: "You are the pastors who have been chosen by God Almighty to lead; we are talking about Christianizing America."[53]

Jerry Falwell emerged as the primary spokesperson for this New Religious Right. His Moral Majority presented itself as a broadly based conservative political organization which intended to promote moral virtue in American public life. Its political agenda was dedicated to furthering conservative goals in four areas: pro-life, pro-family, pro-moral, and pro-American. Falwell insisted that his political activities in the Moral Majority were different from his religious efforts in Christian preaching at Liberty Baptist Church and Christian education at Liberty Baptist College. Moral Majority was presented to the American public as a political, not a religious, organization. Yet one observer who attended a Moral Majority meeting in fall, 1980, described his experience:

> Falwell stated that they were meeting on a political—not a religious—platform, but then they prayed. He stated again that it was not a religious meeting, but then they read the Scripture. Again, he reiterated that it was not a religious meeting, but then he preached for 40 minutes."[54]

It was often difficult to tell when Falwell was speaking from his Christian fundamentalist pulpit and when he was speaking from his political platform. And when he stated that "a politician, as a minister of God, is a revenger to execute wrath upon those who do evil," it was even more difficult to see how he understood this separation between religion and politics.[55]

Perhaps he felt that Moral Majority was not a religious movement because it was not exclusively comprised of Christian fundamentalists. The organization claimed active support from politically conservative Jews, Catholics, and Mormons, as well as Protestants. But there was some ambivalence about the role of non-Christians in the New Religious Right. Reverend Bailey Smith, president of the Southern Baptist Convention, stirred up a considerable controversy when he told the Religious Roundtable National Affairs Briefing in 1980 that, "God Almighty does not hear the prayer of a Jew." He later tried to clarify this statement by saying "I am pro-Jew. I believe they are God's special people, but without Jesus Christ, they are lost."[56] Jerry Falwell actively encouraged Jewish participation in the Moral Majority; he formed coalitions with some politically conservative rabbis, addressed Jewish audiences, and emphasized the importance of America's support for Israel. Yet he described the Jews as a people "spiritually blind and desperately in need of their Messiah and Savior."[57] When asked whether God hears the prayers of Jews, Falwell responded by reaffirming the fundamentalist conviction that all people are in need of Christian redemption. "I believe that God answers the prayers of any redeemed Jew or Gentile, and I do not believe that God answers the prayer of any unredeemed Gentile or Jew."[58] These responses gave some indication that the New Religious Right had abandoned the liberal Protestant compromise with religious pluralism in America. When Reinhold Niebuhr, in 1959, declared that it was not necessary to convert the Jews, he was embracing this liberal ideal of religious tolerance in the public arena. But in 1979 Jerry Falwell wanted "to turn this into a Christian nation."

In his book, *Listen America!*, Jerry Falwell the preacher insisted that everyone needed the fundamentalist "new birth" experience. He called for a religious revival of American society. "We must," he declared, "from the highest office in the land right down to the shoeshine boy in the airport, have a return to biblical basics." Falwell posed an absolute choice between national conversion or destruction: "Will it be revival or ruin? There can be no other way." And this religious revival must include the political leadership of the United States, because "only by godly leadership can America be put back on a divine course."[59] Falwell's Christian Americanism drew opposition from three different Protestant positions.

First, the mainline Protestant churches objected because Falwell's pronouncements seemed too intolerant. A public statement issued by thirteen mainline Protestant denominations attacked Falwell for violating the liberal consensus on the inherent value of American pluralism:

> There is no place in a Christian manner of political life for arrogance, manipulation, subterfuge or holding others' sin in contempt. There is no justification in a pluralistic and democratic society for demands for conformity along religious or ideological lines.[60]

Second, Falwell was attacked by the separatist fundamentalists for being too tolerant. George Dollar, a historian of the fundamentalist movement, criticized Falwell for his political affiliations with nonfundamentalists. "Falwell has become," he said, "the leading TV bishop of Compromise, Inc."[61] The Fundamental Baptist Fellowship made a public statement which castigated anyone "who has an unscriptural belief in national conversion by repentance and faith in our Lord Jesus Christ"; and it called on all "Bible-believing churches to reject pseudo-fundamental activities as those of the Jerry Falwell ministries."[62]

A third criticism of the Christian Americanism of the New Religious Right was voiced by the evangelist Billy Graham. Graham had preached his own version of Christian nationalism, and had served as an unofficial White House chaplain during the Eisenhower, Johnson, and Nixon presidencies. He had been particularly close to Nixon. Graham apparently urged Nixon, after they had read the Bible together and prayed, to run for president in 1967, and in 1971 told a gathering in Charlotte, North Carolina, that he had always looked to Nixon for "moral inspiration." After the Watergate scandal, Graham seemed to retreat from direct political involvements. Perhaps from hard experience, he stated that it was an "error to identify the Gospel with any one particular system or culture. This has been my own danger. When I go to preach the Gospel, I go as an ambassador for the Kingdom of God—not America."[63]

Beginning in 1980, Jerry Falwell responded to these criticisms by insisting that he was not proposing that the United States establish itself as a Christian nation. He was quoted in the *New Yorker* as saying: "I am not one of those who use the phrase 'Christianizing America.'"[64] And in an interview with *Christianity Today*, Falwell stated: "I think America is great, but not because it is a Christian nation: it is not a Christian nation, it has never been a Christian nation, it is never going to be a Christian nation."[65] Occasionally he seemed to lapse back into Christian Americanism, as when he was quoted as saying that America has violated "the principle of divine establishments." But what about other religions? An associate of Falwell tried to clarify his position on the establishment of religion: "He's realistic. He knows that this will not happen until the Messiah returns."[66] This was partly an attempt to correct a negative public image. When critics claimed the Moral Majority was fighting a holy war, Falwell complained, "it looks like we're coming on like religious crusaders of the Dark Ages, rule or ruin."[67] But Falwell moderated his religious rhetoric as he worked to adapt his moral message to a plural American society. The theologian Richard Neuhaus observed that the central problem of the New Religious Right was that it wanted "to enter the political arena making public claims on the basis of private truths."[68] But the pluralism of the American public arena resists any such private religious imperialism. Falwell may have adapted to this situation by keeping his private fundamentalist faith at Liberty Baptist Church, and trying to project his Moral Majority as a purely political movement for moral reform.

The New Religious Right has claimed a tremendous impact on recent American elections, and the popular media has given considerable attention to its apparent influence. Richard Viguerie even took credit for the Reagan election in 1980. "Ronald Reagan won his stunning victory last week," Viguerie declared, "not because the country as a whole went conservative, but because the conservatives—particularly the white moral majority—gave him such massive support."[69] He may have been right that there was little evidence to suggest that the entire country turned conservative. Only 26 percent of the adult population actually voted for Reagan, and this was almost the same percentage that voted for Carter in 1976. But if he was suggesting that the Moral Majority, and other New Religious Right organizations, successfully mobilized this national political power, then empirical studies call that conclusion into question. A Gallup poll in November, 1980, revealed that only 40 percent of the nation had even heard of the Moral Majority. And only 8 percent of the public expressed approval of its political objectives.[70] Public opinion surveys suggested that the influence of the New Religious Right was dramatically overestimated by the popular media. Nevertheless, the activities of the New Religious Right raised important issues about the relation between religion and politics in American society. Clearly, the prohibition of the establishment of religion in the First Amendment ruled out any legislation that would declare the United States a Christian nation. But that did not prohibit the proponents of Christian Americanism from inserting their private moral faith into the political process through lobbying for legislation and promoting specific issues of public policy.

PUBLIC POLICY ISSUES
OF THE NEW RELIGIOUS RIGHT

The policy issues supported by the New Religious Right involved basic fundamentalist moral commitments to the family, community, and nation. But they also promoted specific legislation that would have a direct impact in these areas of personal, social, and national life. So on the one hand, these policy issues represented a program for moral reform; but on the other, they constituted specific proposals for reshaping the American government in order that it might conform to the moral (and religious) demands of the New Religious Right.

Family Issues

Jerry Falwell maintained that there were three separate institutions ordained by God in the Bible: government, church, and family. Ignoring the polygamy of the biblical patriarchs, or the celibacy recommended by the Apostle Paul, Falwell insisted that the monogamous nuclear family was the ideal pattern established by God. The family was seen as the fundamental building block of society. The health of the community and the nation depended upon the health of the family. The second half of the twentieth century had seen major changes in the nature of American family life, and the New Religious Right viewed those changes as dangerous threats to this primary institution. The most dangerous enemy in the war against the family, Falwell maintained, was the "cult of the playboy." He argued that "men are satisfying their lustful desires at the expense of the family."[71] But, there were other dangers that directly involved public policy which were taken up by the New Religious Right.

Abortion. The question of legal abortion became the single most important religiopolitical issue in the 1980s. Americans were deeply divided on the basic definition of the issue: Is abortion the "murder of an unborn child" or the "termination of a woman's pregnancy"? The opposing sides in the controversy—prolife and prochoice—both agreed that abortion involved questions of human rights. But there was no agreement as to which rights should be given legal priority, the right of every fetus to be born or the right of every woman to self-determination over her own body. The Supreme Court in *Roe v. Wade* (1973) determined that a fetus does not have full legal personhood. When scientific experts are unable to provide conclusive evidence as to the beginning of human life, Justice Blackmun said for the 7 to 2 majority, "the judiciary, at this point in the development of man's knowledge, is not in a position to speculate as to the answer."[72] But to deny the constitutional right of abortion would violate a woman's right to make private decisions about her own reproductive process. So the right to terminate pregnancy, until its last three months when the fetus could in most cases live outside the womb, was upheld by the Supreme Court. This compromise worked out in *Roe v. Wade* was an attempt to balance carefully the rights of women with the interests of the state in protecting viable human life.

The Right to Life movement in America became a highly charged illustration of single-issue politics. Following the National Conference of Catholic Bishops Pastoral Plan for Pro-Life Activities, conservative Catholics formed coalitions with conservative Protestants of the New Religious Right to attack the *Roe v. Wade* decision. By 1980, nine versions of a Right to Life Amendment, which would make abortion illegal, had been proposed by anti-abortion groups.[73] And prolife organizations conducted educational campaigns, exerted pressure on legislators, and even in some extreme cases launched violent attacks on medical clinics that performed abortions. Jerry Falwell, and other leaders of the New Religious Right, insisted that human life begins at conception and must be protected from "biological genocide." But when Falwell noted in his book *Listen America!* that one-third of all abortions are obtained by teenagers, and three-fourths by unmarried women, he seemed equally upset by this evidence of sexuality outside of marriage.[74]

Public opinion polls have revealed that approximately two-thirds of the American public oppose making abortion a criminal offense. And mainline religious groups, recognizing that abortion involves a highly personal moral decision, have made public statements against the criminalization of abortion. The Religious Coalition for Abortion Rights (RCAR) has collected and issued the public statements on abortion by mainline religious denominations.[75] But the New Religious Right, which in other cases opposed government regulation, advocated the legislation of morality in the case of abortion.

Homosexuality. The Moral Majority listed homosexuality as one of its primary targets. It was perceived as a major threat to the institution of the family. "Today thousands of men and women in America," Falwell declared, "flaunt their sin openly, the entire homosexual movement is an indictment against America and is contributing to its ultimate downfall."[76] He invoked the image of Sodom and Gomorrah, and the biblical account of their destruction by God, to warn America that it too would be destroyed by the wrath of God if it permitted homosexuality to become an acceptable alternative life style. "We must not allow homosexuality to be presented to our nation as an alternative or acceptable life style," stated Falwell. "It will only serve as a corrupting influence upon our next generation and will bring down the wrath of God upon America."[77] His Moral Majority combated any legislation—such as the "Gay Rights Bill"—that would recognize homosexuals as a *bona fide* minority in America with rights to be protected, and it opposed any extension of the Civil Rights Act to protect homosexuals from discrimination in employment or housing. The Moral Majority attempted to defend the monogamous nuclear family against what it perceived as a threatening alternative pattern of sexual relations. But these strident attacks on homosexuals prompted one gay author to write a book, which, among other things, made claims about the homosexuality of some of the leaders of the New Right, entitled *God's Bullies.*[78]

Women's Rights. When they invoked the authority of America's founding fathers, the New Religious Right tended to neglect the political concerns of its founding mothers. Abigail Adams, the wife of John Adams, wrote to her husband in 1776, while he was at the Continental Congress:

> In the new code of laws which I suppose it will be necessary for you to make, I desire you would remember the ladies, and be more generous and favorable to them than your ancestors. Do not put such unlimited power into the hands of their husbands.[79]

Her son, John Quincy Adams, who also served as President of the United States, expressed a similar concern for the political rights of women when he said that "women are not only justified but exhibit the most exalted virtue, when they do depart from the domestic circle, and enter upon the concerns of their country, of humanity and their God."[80] Evangelical leaders throughout the nineteenth century were active in promoting the rights of women for full participation in American religion and politics.[81]

But the most successful political campaign of the New Religious Right was its effort to defeat the Equal Rights Amendment. This proposed amendment to the Constitution was a simple statement that a woman's equal civil rights could not be denied on the basis of gender. But, in opposing the Equal Rights Amendment, Jerry Falwell claimed that it would lead to such social disasters as homosexual marriages, unisex bathrooms, and mandatory drafting of women for military combat.[82] Behind the opposition to the ERA was the fundamentalist ideal of the Christian family. Edward Hinson, the family guidance pastor at Falwell's Liberty Baptist Church, outlined the different male and female roles in his book, *The Total Family.* "The Bible clearly states," he insisted, "that the wife is to submit to her husband and help him fulfill God's will for his life."[83] The woman's role was to be subservient to her husband within the Christian family unit. This definition of the female role informed the policy positions of the New Religious Right regarding the rights of women in American society.

Community Issues

The New Religious Right tried to identify and combat the immoral influences that seemed to threaten the moral fabric of American society. It crusaded against drugs and pornography; but these were seen as symptoms of a dangerous moral permissiveness in America. "Against the growing tide of permissiveness and moral decay that is crushing our society," Jerry Falwell said, "we must make a sacred commitment to God Almighty to turn this nation around immediately."[84] The image of "turning America around" appeared frequently in the rhetoric of the New Religious Right; it evoked a powerful nostalgia for a simpler American society with stable families and small town communities based on Protestant civic virtues. The school was viewed as the community institution responsible for cultivating those virtues. Although Falwell stated that the private Christian school was the movement of the future, the New Religious Right, nevertheless, was concerned with promoting certain public policy issues in the public school system.

Prayer in School. Jerry Falwell stated that "we support the return of voluntary prayer to public schools and strongly oppose the teaching of the 'religion' of secular humanism in the classroom."[85] The Supreme Court, as we have seen, had already determined that even voluntary programs of school prayer, which allowed students to be excused from participation, involved an illicit use of state coercion in matters of religion. Even a voluntary program in the classroom would force students into a position where they would have to make a public statement of their religious belief or disbelief, and this the Court has not allowed. But the New Religious Right claimed that these Court decisions had established the "religion" of secular humanism in the public schools. And this secular humanism was the primary enemy of the New Religious Right.

The basic sourcebook for their understanding of secular humanism was Tim LaHaye's *The Battle for the Mind.* Founder of Christian Heritage College in San Diego, LaHaye defined secular humanism as the attempt to solve human problems independently of God. He saw this humanism as the world's greatest evil, "destroying our culture, families, country—and one day, the entire world."[86] The five basic tenets of humanism were defined as (1) atheism, (2) evolution, (3) amorality, (4) autonomy of man, and (5) one-world socialism. These were the humanistic values currently being taught in the public schools, LaHaye contended, and they were responsible for a wide range of social evils. "Today's wave of crime and violence in the streets, promiscuity, divorce, shattered dreams and broken hearts," he asserted, "can be laid right at the door of secular humanism."[87]

Since the first Supreme Court decision dealing with religion in the public schools there has been an attempt by public school educators to identify the values that may be taught in the classroom. The National Educational Association in 1951 even produced a list of these values:

1. Human personality as the basic value
2. Moral responsibility
3. Institutions as the servants of men
4. Common consent
5. Devotion to truth
6. Respect for excellence
7. Moral equality
8. Brotherhood
9. The pursuit of happiness
10. Spiritual enrichment[88]

But for the New Religious Right, any moral values were inadequate unless they were based on specific religious principles, the authority of the Bible, and faith in God. The religious foundation of moral values, they argued, must be supported by the faithful practice of prayer in the public schools. But, it must also be supported through textbooks and a public school curriculum that reflect religious values. Jerry Falwell praised the work of Mel and Norma Gabler in their organization, Educational Research Analysts, for their reviews of school textbooks that were seen to attack Christian values.[89] After identifying the offensive "humanist" passages in these texts, they attempted to pressure local school boards and textbook publishers to have these texts changed. As recently as 1987, U.S. District Judge W. Brevard Hand banned several dozen textbooks from Alabama schools on the grounds that they promoted "the religion of secular humanism."

Creation Science.   The most controversial curricular issue in public school education from the perspective of the New Religious Right remained the scientific theory of evolution. Jerry Falwell revived the fundamentalist opposition to the teaching of evolution in the public schools. He asserted that the only acceptable philosophy of education in this area "rests upon our belief in the Bible as the authentic and reliable guide and authority for all areas of life."[90] But the New Religious Right carried the debate over evolution a step further than the Scopes Monkey Trial. In recent years institutes of "Creation Science" or "Scientific Creationism" have emerged to marshal scientific arguments in defense of the biblical story of creation.[91] These organizations have tried to put creationism on an equal scientific footing with evolution.

Again, the debate over evolution entered the courtroom. The state of California, under Governor Ronald Reagan in 1969, was the first state to declare creationism a valid alternative to evolutionism in public schools. But the equal time provisions for evolution and creationism, as two rival scientific theories, was tested in a number of recent court cases. The "two model approach" was supported in Georgia in 1981, where Judge Braswell Dean exclaimed that "this monkey mythology of Darwin is the cause of permissiveness, promiscuity, pills, prophylactics, perversion, pregnancies, abortions, pornography, pollution, poisoning and proliferation of crimes of all types."[92] But in a decisive case in Arkansas in 1982, a Federal Court overturned a state law that required equal time for evolution and creationism. Judge William Overton ruled that "since creation science is not science, the conclusion is inescapable that the only real effect of [the law] is the advance of religion. It was simply and purely an effort to introduce the biblical version of creation into the public school curricula."[93] The Federal Court therefore ruled that the requirement that creation science be taught in the public schools was a violation of the First Amendment prohibition of the establishment of religion. Nevertheless, leaders in the New Religious Right, supported by some Christians in the academic community, continued to argue that evolutionary science was a myth, and that the biblical story of creation was the basis for a science.

Sex Education.   Programs of sex education in the public schools also continued to be a moral issue in the New Religious Right. Jerry Falwell, for example, made dramatic claims about the corrupting influence sex education represented in the community. Referring to sex education as academic pornography and pornographic brainwashing, Falwell blamed it for the immoral permissiveness in sexuality which he saw pervading American communities. "The materials used," he claimed, "include wholesale endorsements of masturbation, premarital sex, extramarital sex, and homosexuality. They even include allusions to the acceptability of sex with animals!"[94] Although this may have misrepresented the public school curriculum in the area of sex education, it nevertheless revealed the New Religious Right's fear that public schools were contributing to the moral decay of American society.

National Issues

The New Religious Right championed the conservative cause in both domestic and foreign policy. But fundamentalists insisted that conservative positions on economic and military issues were derived from the authority of the Bible. A local leader of the Moral Majority chapter in New York even went so far as to declare, "God is an ultra-conservative."[95] Jerry Falwell claimed that "millions are fed up with the fruits of liberalism, both in politics and religion." And the major problem with liberalism in both religion and politics, according to Falwell, was that liberals assumed the "inherent goodness of mankind."[96] They assumed that human beings have the inherent ability to create social contracts that would protect innate human rights, and that these social arrangements would respond to the challenges of social, economic, and political life. But the conservatives of the New Religious Right insisted, on the contrary, that humans could only *become* good by conforming their actions to the divine covenant represented by the Bible. And so, for the New Religious Right, authentic domestic and foreign policies always had to refer back to the authority of the Bible. The Bible was not only the fundamentalist's guide for salvation, but also a political charter for economic policy and the exercise of military power. These religious and political functions could be combined, however, as they were in a statement by William H. Marshner appearing in a publication by the Committee for the Survival of a Free Congress: "Speaking directly to the issue of saving the souls of the liberals themselves, I am firmly convinced that removing them from power is the first prerequisite."[97]

Economic Policy.   The conservatives of the New Religious Right confidently proclaimed that capitalism was the only economic system justified by the Bible. The capitalist free-market economy was therefore understood to be ordained by God. As Jerry Falwell put it:

> The free-enterprise system is clearly outlined in the Book of Proverbs in the Bible. Jesus Christ made it clear that the work ethic was a part of His plan for man. Ownership of property is biblical. Competition in business is biblical. Ambitious and successful business management is clearly outlined as a part of God's plan for His people.[98]

This tribute to free-market capitalism as God's divine economic system ignored the precedent of the earliest Christian community, who, according to the Book of Acts, "held all things in common" (Acts 4:34−5). But it enshrined traditional conservative values of individualism, private property, and entrepreneurial free enterprise. These economic practices were believed to be derived from the Bible, rather than from the rise of modern capitalism since the Industrial Revolution.

The New Religious Right differed from evangelical reform movements of the nineteenth century by not actively addressing the problem of poverty. Jerry Falwell commented that for internal organizational reasons "we could never bring the issue of the poor into Moral Majority . . . we just have to stay away from helping the poor."[99] He noted that addressing the issue of poverty would involve the Moral Majority in trying to identify who was poor, deciding who should receive assistance, and determining who should provide that assistance. So the Moral Majority refrained from demonstrating a direct concern with poverty as a social issue. But behind this reluctance to address the problem of poverty was a general conservative aversion to social welfare programs. They tended to see these programs as the first step toward socialism, and as liberal interventions by government that inhibited individual initiative, industry, and hard work. In his book *America Can Be Saved*, Falwell proposed an argument against social welfare programs in the form of a parable about two spoiled dogs who were accustomed to living on a diet of meat. When they were given into Falwell's care he insisted on feeding them dry dog food, and after four days the dogs finally gave in and ate the food. He suggested that the same kind of treatment was indicated for "that lazy, trifling bunch lined up in unemployment offices who would not work in a pieshop eating the holes out of donuts."[100] This parable seemed to suggest that unemployment, poverty, and hunger were not real problems in American society; all people needed was the discipline of the Protestant work ethic.

A more extreme system of biblical economics was developed by organizations in what has been described as the Christian Far Right. Chalcedon in California and the Institute for Christian Economics in Texas cooperated to develop economic principles for public policy based exclusively on the authority of the Bible.[101] Rousas John Rushdoony, Gary North, and other Christian economists tried to disseminate these principles in a number of publications. They began with the proposition that the solution to every question was in the Bible. They proceeded to analyze the Bible in order to distill a system of economic laws. There was one test for any economic policy: Is it specifically mandated in the Bible? If the policy *is not* found in the Bible, then it is forbidden. They claimed to have found no biblical support for such policies as unemployment compensation, product safety standards, and environmental protection laws. If the policy *is* found in the Bible, then the biblical precedent must be followed exactly. Taxation of income, for example, has a biblical precedent in the tithe; but since the tithe was a 10 percent flat-rate tax, the Bible was interpreted as forbidding the progressive income tax. Property tax was also forbidden. Since God, according to Rushdoony, ultimately owns all the land on the earth, "a tax on land . . . is a tax against God: this is not lawful."[102]

It was not sufficient, however, to simply discern the economic laws inherent in the Bible; it was necessary to recognize that these laws were part of a larger covenant system backed up by the force of God's rewards and punishments. The divine economy was "a covenantal law-order which has built in sanctions."[103] God rewards those who follow these economic laws, but will punish here and hereafter those who disobey. Built-in blessings and curses were believed to operate in this Christian economic covenant. As one Christian economist put it, "God physically blesses the nation that obeys Him." However, He curses those who disobey. Poverty was interpreted as a sign of God's wrath. The Christian economist continued: "God works to overthrow the ungodly, and increasingly the world will come under the domination of Christians—not by military aggression, but by godly labor, saving, investment, and orientation toward the future."[104]

This vision of international economics produced some curious interpretations: The Japanese have been rewarded by God because they have *acted* like good Protestants; but the inhabitants of the Third World have been punished with poverty, famine, and hunger, because they followed false gods. These interpretations served to enshrine the profit motive as a fundamental religious value based on the authority of the Bible.

Military Policy.   The New Religious Right placed a great emphasis on the importance of military strength. A strong military posture was seen as consistent with the example of Christ. As Jerry Falwell declared: "Jesus was not a pacifist. He was not a sissy."[105] A strong American military presence in the world was justified as a means of maintaining peace, law, and order, so that Christians could spread their gospel throughout the world. To support this objective, the New Religious Right consistently promoted a basic public policy that would cut welfare spending at home and, in the words of Jerry Falwell, increase "our defense budget to whatever it takes to put us solidly back to No. 1 for good."[106]

That dominant position in international military power, according to the New Religious Right, had recently been taken by the Soviet Union. The military competition between the two superpowers was consistently symbolized as a cosmic battle between the forces of good and the forces of evil. "The Soviets are liars and cheaters," according to Falwell, "and they are determined to conquer our free country and to infiltrate the American people with godless communism."[107] President Ronald Reagan echoed those sentiments at an annual convention of the National Association of Evangelicals in 1983, when he called on Americans to pray for the Soviets. "Let us pray," he exhorted, "for the salvation of all those who live in that totalitarian darkness—pray they will discover the joy of knowing God. But until they do, let us be aware they are the focus of evil in the world." The conviction that the godless communists represented this absolute focus of evil in the world was not in the least diminished when Leonid Brezhnev, in his last summit meeting on nuclear arms control, declared: "God will not forgive us if we fail."[108] The United States did have genuine differences and real conflicts with the Soviet Union; but the millennial militarism of the New Religious Right framed those conflicts in the apocalyptic imagery of the final battle between God and the demonic forces of evil.

True to the apocalyptic imagery of the Book of Revelation, fundamentalist politicians tended to see Israel as the center of the final battle between good and evil. The battle of Armageddon between the forces of light and darkness was to be fought in Israel. Therefore, the land of Israel played an important role in their premillennial understanding of world history. But in addition to this, Jerry Falwell took literally the biblical promise that God would bless those who blessed Israel, and would curse those who cursed Israel (Gen 12.1–3). He maintained that this biblical passage should determine American foreign policy toward the modern state of Israel. "To stand against Israel," Falwell often repeated, "is to stand against God."[109] The fundamentalist interpretation of the Bible, therefore, was not simply a guide for personal salvation and moral communities; it was the first and last authority for all domestic and foreign political policies.

A Liberal Response

In 1983 the senior Senator from Massachusetts, Edward Kennedy, received a membership card in the Moral Majority, which was mailed to him by mistake. As a liberal leader in the Democratic party, Kennedy had once been called by Jerry Falwell, "the most dangerous American today." A computer error had apparently made him a member in good standing of the Moral Majority. Kennedy called the Moral Majority spokesman, Cal Thomas, to ask if the membership card should be returned. Thomas responded: "No, we don't believe anyone is beyond redemption." Out of the conversation that ensued Ted Kennedy accepted an invitation to speak at Jerry Falwell's Liberty Baptist College. In October, 1983, he spoke to an audience of several thousand evangelicals and fundamentalists on the topic: "Tolerance and Truth in America."[110] This speech represented one liberal response to the challenge posed by the New Religious Right, and it briefly set out one version of the liberal principles defining the relation between religion and politics in American society.

Kennedy began by reaffirming the basic liberal value of toleration in the quest for truth in both religion and politics. There may be such a thing as truth; but who would claim to have a monopoly on it? Jerry Falwell himself had been the victim of the narrow prejudice of those separatist fundamentalists, who accused him of committing a grave sin when he associated in the Moral Majority with nonfundamentalists. Toleration of diversity in religious commitments to truth was the first principle of a liberal, democratic, and pluralistic society. Americans have traditionally been wary of a single religious power exercising undue influence in political matters. This was an issue in the presidential campaign of John F. Kennedy, who worked hard to assure the voters that his primary responsibility as president would be to the American public, and not to a single religious community. Addressing a meeting of evangelicals during his presidential campaign, John F. Kennedy said, "I believe in an America where there is no [religious] bloc voting" Twenty years later presidential candidate Ronald Reagan appealed to an evangelical meeting of the Religious Roundtable as a religious voting bloc. "I know that you can't endorse me," Reagan said, "I want you to know that I endorse you and what you are doing." For many Americans this solicitation of a particular religious constituency in electoral politics represented a breakdown in the separation between church and state.

Religion, according to Ted Kennedy, did have an important role to play in the political process. Moral and religious concerns have a legitimate and important place in the public arena. But he distinguished between private moral questions and public moral questions. In matters of personal morality and private conscience, a religious group may be tempted to use the power of government to impose a moral value which they have been unable to persuade others to accept. "The real transgression," Kennedy claimed, "occurs when religion wants government to tell citizens how to live uniquely personal parts of their lives." The failure of the constitutional prohibition of alcoholic beverages, which had largely been supported by religious temperance societies, was an illustration of the problems that arise when government tries to legislate personal morality. Abortion, Kennedy suggested, was another area of private moral concern that involved intensely personal moral decisions. In such matters of private moral conscience, "the proper role of religion is to appeal to the conscience of the individual, not the coercive power of the state."

Other policy issues, however, involved public moral questions. Some issues, such as the threat of nuclear war, were inherently public in nature. Nuclear policy was an issue of moral concern; but it would be decided by government, not individuals in the privacy of their own lives. In such areas people with religious and moral commitments must speak directly about public policy. Kennedy recalled the efforts of evangelicals in the abolition societies, the opposition to the war in Vietnam by Reverend Sloan Coffin, and the civil rights movement of Martin Luther King. Those religious leaders, Kennedy claimed, were active in awakening the national conscience, not advocating legal coercion. John F. Kennedy had said that "no religious body should seek to impose its will"; but religious people should be engaged in the ethical debates concerning public policy.

Ted Kennedy proposed four tests of toleration in the relation between religion and politics:

(1) *The respect for the integrity of religion.* "Religious values cannot be excluded from every public issue," he noted, "but not every public issue involves religious values." Some policy matters involved purely secular considerations, and should not be used as a test of faith. God has no position on the Department of Education, Kennedy insisted, and the Federal Budget "is a matter for economic analysis, not heavenly appeals."

(2) *The respect for independent judgments of conscience.* The Moral Majority seemed to imply that only one set of public policies was moral, and public officials who arrived at different judgments on these issues automatically had their religious faith called into question. This posed a danger to the freedom of religious conscience, Kennedy noted, "when we re-establish, directly or indirectly, a religious test for public office."

(3) *The respect for the public debate.* In the debate over public policy issues, private faith was no substitute for facts that could be publicly analyzed and verified. By introducing religious faith as the primary condition of public decisions, Kennedy observed, "it does not advance the debate to contend that the arms race is more divine punishment than human problem—or that in any event, the final days are near."

(4) *The respect for the motives of those who exercise their right to disagree.* The New Religious Right engaged in rhetorical invective that called into question the integrity, morality, and religious faith of any who disagreed. But those who supported the Equal Rights Amendment were not thereby necessarily "antifamily" or "blasphemers" or launching an "attack on the Bible." Kennedy noted that his mother, who had supported the Equal Rights Amendment, would be surprised to learn that she was "antifamily."

Kennedy's speech concluded with a liberal vision of the relation between religion and politics in America. It was a vision of an America dedicated to religious toleration, where no one would be considered a greater or lesser American because of religious doubt (or belief); where no modern religious inquisition would create fear, coercion, or division; and where the liberal ideal of civility in religion and politics would be upheld, making the nation safe for democracy and diversity. He reaffirmed the liberal commitment to toleration as the principle of peaceful coexistence in religion and politics by recalling a passage from a speech given by John F. Kennedy in November, 1963, before the Protestant Council of New York City:

> The family of man is not limited to a single race or religion, to a single city or three billion strong. Most of its members are not white—and most of them are not Christian . . . the members of this family should be at peace with one another.

The New Religious Right has attempted to re-establish the powerful religiopolitical symbol of divine covenant in American public life. Groups like the Moral Majority have tried to align that covenant with specific conservative positions on matters of public policy. In his liberal response, Senator Kennedy attempted to outline the religiopolitical conditions of the democratic social contract. The conditions of entry into the democratic arena were described as liberal values of respect, civility, and mutual toleration. After his address to Liberty Baptist College, Kennedy and Falwell apparently developed a close personal friendship. When they appeared together two years later at the National Religious Broadcasters Convention in Washington, D.C., each was asked what he would change about the other. Kennedy said that since Jerry Falwell was working too hard he should take a year off during the presidential election of 1988. Falwell responded, "I'd like the senator to become a great, great Republican Baptist."[111] It seemed more likely, however, that Jerry Falwell would continue to moderate his particularist theo-politics in order to participate more effectively in the pluralistic public arena. That public political arena may sustain the ongoing influence of religious values; but it cannot tolerate the establishment of a particular religious faith through the coercive power of government. To tolerate such an establishment of religion would be a denial of toleration.

NOTES

1. JULIAN BOYD, *The Papers of Thomas Jefferson* (Princeton: Princeton University Press, 1950): XVI: 281 ff.
2. *Reynolds v. United States*, 98 U.S. 145 (1879); on the separation of church and state, see Mark D. Howe, *The Garden and the Wilderness: Religion and Government in American Constitutional History* (Chicago: University of Chicago Press, 1965); Francis Sorauf, *The Wall of Separation: The Constitutional Politics of Church and State* (Princeton: Princeton University Press, 1976); Norman De Jong and Jack Van Der Silk, *Separation of Church and State: The Myth Revisited* (Jordan Station, Ontario: Paideia Press, 1985); and Leonard W. Levy, *The Establishment Clause: Religion and the First Amendment* (New York: Macmillan, 1986).
3. IRVING BRANT, *James Madison: The Virginia Revolutionist* (Indianapolis: Bobbs-Merrill, 1941–61): III:271ff.
4. DAVID R. SHEPHERD, *Ronald Reagan: In God I Trust* (Wheaton, Illinois: Tyndale House Publishers, 1984): 72.
5. GEORGE MARSDEN, "Fundamentalism as an American Phenomenon: A Comparison with English Evangelism," *Church History* 46 (1977): 215; see Marsden, *Fundamentalism and American Culture* (New York: Oxford University Press, 1981); Some have contested the assumption that fundamentalism was a *reaction* in response to the stimulus of modernism. See Grant Wacker, "Uneasy in Zion: Evangelicals in Postmodern Society," in *Evangelicalism in Modern America*, ed., George Marsden (Grand Rapids, Michigan: Eerdmans, 1984): 17–28. But, in the same volume, Martin Marty argues that "the movement makes no sense except as a very modern reaction to modernism." Marty, "Fundamentalism as a Social Phenomenon," *Ibid.*: 58.
6. MARTIN MARTY, "Fundamentalism Reborn: Faith and Fanaticism" *Saturday Review* (May, 1980): 37–42; For additional sociological discussion and analysis of the New Religious Right, see John L. Kater, Jr., *Christians on the Right: The Moral Majority in Perspective* (New York: Seabury Press, 1982); Samuel S. Hill and Dennis E. Owen, *The New Religious Political Right in America* (Nashville: Abingdon, 1982); Robert C. Liebman and Robert Wuthnow, eds., *The New Christian Right: Mobilization and Legitimation* (New York: Aldine Press, 1983); and David G. Bromley and Anson D. Shupe, eds., *New Christian Politics* (Macon, Georgia: Mercer University Press, 1984).
7. WALTER CAPPS *The Unfinished War: Vietnam and the American Conscience* (Boston: Beacon Press, 1982): 134.
8. JERRY FALWELL, *Listen America!* (Garden City, New York: Doubleday, 1980): 81.
9. *Murdock v. The Commonwealth of Pennsylvania*, 319 U.S. 105 (1943).
10. *Jones v. City of Opelika*, 316 U.S. 585 (1942).
11. *Walz v. Tax Commission*, 397 U.S. 664 (1970).
12. Cited in ELWYN A. SMITH, *Religious Liberty in the United States* (Philadelphia: Fortress Press, 1972): 295.
13. *Illinois ex rel. McCollum v. Board of Education*, 333 U.S. 203 (1948); for discussions of religion in the public schools, see Sam Duker, *The Public Schools and Religion* (New York: Harper and Row, 1966); and Robert S. Michaelsen, *Piety in the Public School* (New York: Macmillan, 1970).

14. *Zorach v. Clauson*, 343 U.S. 306 (1952).
15. *Engel v. Vitale*, 370 U.S. 421 (1952).
16. *School District of Abington Township, Pa., et al. v. Schempp, and Murray v. Curlett*, 374 U.S. 203 (1963).
17. *Everson v. Board of Education*, 330 U.S. 1 (1947).
18. Cited in Robert S. Fletcher, *A History of Oberlin College* (Oberlin, Ohio: Oberlin College, 1943): I:305; see Donald W. Dayton, "Some Perspectives on 'The New Christian Right,'" *Fides et Historia* 15 (1982): 57.
19. Cited in Charles C. Cole, Jr., *The Social Ideas of the Northern Evangelists, 1826–1860* (New York: Columbia University Press, 1954): 133; see Arthur M. Schlesinger, *The American as Reformer* (Cambridge: Harvard University Press, 1950); Timothy L. Smith, *Revivalism and Social Reform: American Protestantism on the Eve of the Civil War* (Baltimore: John Hopkins Press, 1980); James Brewer Stewart, *Holy Warriors: The Abolitionists and American Slavery* (New York: Hill and Wang, 1976); and David O. Moberg, *The Great Reversal: Evangelism and Social Concern* (Philadelphia: Lippincott, 1977).
20. Cited in William R. Hutchison, *The Modern Impulse in American Protestantism* (Cambridge: Harvard University Press, 1976): 170; see Ronald C. White, Jr. and C. Howard Hopkins, *The Social Gospel: Religion and Reform in Changing America* (Philadelphia: Temple University Press, 1976).
21. CHARLES HODGE, *What is Darwinism?* (New York: Scribner, Armstrong & Co., 1874).
22. LYMAN ABBOTT, *Reminiscences* (Boston: Houghton Mifflin & Co., 1923): 459.
23. PAUL W. GLAD, ed., *William Jennings Bryan: A Profile* (New York: Hill and Wang, 1968): 39; see Lawrence W. Levine, *Defender of the Faith, William Jennings Bryan: The Last Decade, 1915–1925* (New York: Harper and Brothers, 1938).
24. On the Scopes Trial, and the surrounding controversy, see Gail Kennedy, *Evolution and Religion* (Boston: D.C. Heath, 1957); and L. Sprague de Camp, *The Great Monkey Trial* (New York: Doubleday, 1968).
25. HENRY EMERSON FOSDICK, "Shall the Fundamentalists Win?" in *American Protestant Thought: The Liberal Era*, ed. William R. Hutchison (New York: Harper and Row, 1968): 173.
26. For a discussion of Moody in the context of American revivalism, see James F. Findlay, *Dwight L. Moody, American Evangelist, 1837–1899* (Chicago: University of Chicago Press, 1969).
27. On civil millennialism, see Ernest Tuveson, *Redeemer Nation: The Idea of America's Millennial Role* (Chicago: University of Chicago Press, 1968); and Nathan O. Hatch, *The Sacred Cause of Liberty: Republican Thought and the Millennium in Revolutionary New England* (New Haven: Yale University Press, 1977).
28. For an interpretation of fundamentalism arguing that it grew out of this type of nineteenth-century premillennialism, see Ernest R. Sandeen, *The Roots of Fundamentalism: British and American Millenarianism, 1800–1930* (Chicago: University of Chicago Press, 1970).
29. See Timothy P. Weber, *Living in the Shadow of the Second Coming: American Pre-Millennialism, 1875–1925* (New York: Oxford University Press, 1979): 15 ff.
30. See Erwin S. Gaustad, *The Rise of Adventism* (New York: Harper and Row, 1974); and David Rowe, *Thunder and Trumpets: Millerites and Dissenting Religion in Upstate New York, 1800–1850* (Macon, GA: Scholars Press, 1985).
31. NORMAN F. FURNISS, *The Fundamentalist Controversy, 1918–1931* (Hamden, Connecticut: Yale University Press, 1954): 12–13.
32. See Richard V. Pierard, *The Unequal Yoke: Evangelical Christianity and Political Conservatism* (Philadelphia: Lippincott, 1970): 64–66; and Erling Jorstad, *The Politics of Doomsday: Fundamentalists on the Far Right* (Nashville: Abingdon, 1970).
33. Cited in John H. Redekop, *The American Far Right: A Case Study of Billy James Hargis and the Christian Crusade* (Grand Rapids, Michigan: Eerdmans, 1968): 43.
34. *Time* (February 16, 1976): 32.
35. Cited in Mark Sherwin, *The Extremists* (New York: St. Martin's Press, 1963): 119; see Pierard, *The Unequal Yoke*: 53–5.
36. Cited in Larry L. King, "Bob Jones University: The Buckle of the Bible Belt," *Harpers* (June, 1966): 58.

37. BILLY JAMES HARGIS, *Communist America . . . Must it Be?* (Tulsa, Oklahoma: Christian Crusade, 1960): 35.
38. BILLY GRAHAM, *Changing the Tide of History* (Minneapolis: Billy Graham Evangelical Association, 1966): 3; cited in Pierard, *The Unequal Yoke*: 108.
39. T. BISSET, "Religious Broadcasting: Assessing the State of the Art," *Christianity Today* (December 12, 1980): 28−31; see Ben Armstrong, *The Electronic Church* (Nashville: Thomas Nelson, 1979); and Jeffrey K. Hadden and Charles E. Swann, *Prime-Time Preachers: The Rising Power of Televangelism* (Reading, Massachusetts: Addison-Wesley, 1981).
40. JEREMY RIFKIN, *The Emerging Order* (New York: G.P. Putnam's Sons, 1979): 105.
41. See Jerry Mander, *Four Arguments for the Elimination of Television* (Morrow: Quil, 1978).
42. Cited in Flo Conway and Jim Siegelman, *Holy Terror: The Fundamentalist War on America's Freedoms in Religion, Politics and our Private Lives* (Garden City, New York: Doubleday, 1982): 48.
43. Cited in Frances Fitzgerald, "Reporter at Large: A Disciplined, Charging Army," *New Yorker* 57 (May, 18, 1981): 60.
44. *Ibid.*: 60.
45. Cited in William R. Goodman, Jr. and James J.H. Price, *Jerry Falwell: An Unauthorized Profile* (Lynchburg, Virginia: Educational Services, 1981): 91.
46. "Declaration of War," obtained by mail from "The Old Time Gospel Hour."
47. FITZGERALD, "A Disciplined, Charging Army": 106.
48. *Ibid.*: 108.
49. RICHARD A. VIGUERIE, *The New Right: We're Ready to Lead*, rev ed. (Falls Church, Virginia: Caroline House, 1981): 91.
50. *Ibid.*: 90−1; see Alan Crawford, *Thunder on the Right: The 'New Right' and the Politics of Resentment* (New York: Pantheon, 1980); and Gillian Peele, *Revival and Reaction: The Right in Contemporary America* (New York: Oxford University Press, 1984).
51. VIGUERIE, *The New Right*: 6−8.
52. Cited in Thomas J. McIntyre, with John C. Obert, *The Fear Brokers: Peddling the Hate Politics of the New Right* (Boston: Beacon Press, 1979): 99.
53. Cited in Conway and Siegleman, *Holy Terror*: 93−4: see Robert T. Handy, *A Christian America: Protestant Hopes and Historical Realities*, 2nd ed. (New York: Oxford University Press, 1984).
54. FRANK BUMPERS, "Guidelines for Political Involvement," *Faith for the Family* 8 (1980): 5; cited in Jeffrey K. Hadden, "Televangelism and the New Christian Right," in *Religion and Religiosity in America*, eds. Jeffrey K. Hadden and Theodore E. Long (New York: Crossroad, 1983): 114.
55. FALWELL, *Listen America!*: 98.
56. *New York Times* (September 18, 1980).
57. FALWELL, *Listen America!*: 107.
58. Cited in Fitzgerald, "A Disciplined, Charging Army": 133.
59. FALWELL, *Listen America!*: 63; 18; 24; 17.
60. *New York Times* (October 21, 1980).
61. DAVID SPROUL, *An Open Letter to Jerry Falwell* (Tempe, Arizona: Fundamental Baptist Press, 1979): 28.
62. *Ibid.*: 31−2.
63. BILLY GRAHAM, "Why Lausanne?," *Christianity Today* 18 (September 13, 1974): 7.
64. Cited in Fitzgerald, "A Disciplined, Charging Army": 133.
65. "An Interview with the Lone Ranger of Fundamentalism," *Christianity Today* 25 (September 4, 1981): 24.
66. *Newsweek* (September 21, 1981).
67. FITZGERALD, "A Disciplined, Charging Army": 135.
68. RICHARD JOHN NEUHAUS, *The Naked Public Square: Religion and Democracy in America* (Grand Rapids, Michigan: Eerdmans, 1984): 36.
69. VIGUERIE, *The New Right*: 128.
70. "Public Views on the Moral Majority," *PRRC Emerging Trends* 3 (January, 1981): 1; see Anson Shupe and William A. Stacey, *Born Again Politics and the Moral Majority: What Social Surveys Really Show* (New York: Edwin Mellen Press, 1982).

71. JERRY FALWELL, "Future Word: An Agenda for the Eighties," in *The Fundamentalist Phenomenon: The Resurgence of Conservative Christianity*, eds., Ed Dobson and Ed Hinson (Garden City, New York: Doubleday, 1981): 205.
72. *Roe v. Wade*, 410 U.S. 113 (1973); see Eva R. Rubin, *Abortion, Politics, and the Courts: Roe v. Wade and its Aftermath* (Westport, CT: Greenwood Press, 1982).
73. *New York Times* (March 30, 1980).
74. FALWELL, "Future-Word," in *The Fundamentalist Phenomenon*: 195.
75. For a survey of public statements by mainline religious groups on the issue of abortion, see Arthur J. Dyck, "Religious Views," in *Population Policy and Ethics: The American Experience*, d. Robert M. Veatch (New York: Irvington Publishers, 1977): 277−323.
76. FALWELL, "Future-Word," in *The Fundamentalist Phenomenon*: 203.
77. *Ibid.*: 205.
78. PERRY DEANNE YOUNG, *God's Bullies: Power Politics and Religious Tyranny* (New York: Holt, Rinehart and Winston, 1982).
79. Cited in Anson Phelps Stokes, *Church and State in the United States*, 3 vols. (New York: Harper and Brothers, 1950): III:35.
80. Cited in Tyler, *Freedom's Ferment*: 429.
81. See Alice Rossi, ed., *The Feminist Papers* (New York: Columbia University Press, 1973).
82. FALWELL, "Future-Word," in *The Fundamentalist Phenomenon*: 190.
83. Cited in Fitzgerald, "A Disciplined, Charging Army": 74; see Pamela Johnston Conover and Virginia Gray, *Feminism and the New Right: Conflict over the American Family* (New York: Praeger, 1983).
84. FALWELL, *Listen America!*: 244.
85. FALWELL, "Future-Word," in *The Fundamentalist Phenomenon*, 194.
86. TIM LAHAYE, *The Battle for the Mind* (Old Tappan, New Jersey: Fleming H. Revell, 1980): 9.
87. *Ibid.*: 26; see Tim LaHaye, *The Battle for the Pubic Schools* (Old Tappan, New Jersey: Fleming H. Revell, 1982).
88. MICHAELSON, *Piety in the Public Schools*: 242.
89. FALWELL, "Future-Word," in *The Fundamentalist Phenomenon*: 199.
90. *Ibid.*: 219.
91. See Isaac Asimov, "The 'Threat' of Creationism," *New York Times Magazine* (June 14, 1981).
92. *Time* (March 16, 1981).
93. *New York Times* (January 6, 1982).
94. FALWELL, "Future-Word," in *The Fundamentalist Phenomenon*: 200.
95. DAN C. FIORE, cited in *New York* (May 18, 1981): 30.
96. FALWELL, "Future-Word" in *The Fundamentalist Phenomenon*: 187.
97. WILLIAM H. MARSHNER, *The New Creatures and the New Politics* (Washington, D.C.: Committee for the Survival of a Free Congress, 1981): 24.
98. FALWELL, *Listen America!*: 13.
99. FALWELL, "Interview with the Lone Ranger of Fundamentalism": 27; On nineteenth century evangelical concerns for poverty as a social issue, see Clifford S. Griffin, *Their Brother's Keeper: Moral Stewardship in the United States, 1800−1865* (New Brunswick, New Jersey: Rutgers University Press, 1960); and Norris Magnuson, *Salvation in the Slums: Evangelical Social Work, 1865−1920* (Metuchen, New Jersey: Scarecrow Press, 1977).
100. JERRY FALWELL, *America Can be Saved* (Murfreesboro, Tennessee: Sword of the Lord Publishers, 1979): 35.
101. See Thomas E. Van Dahm, "The Christian Far Right and the Economic Role of the State," *Christian Scholar's Review* 12 (1982): 17−36.
102. ROUSAS JOHN RUSHDOONY, *Politics of Guilt and Pity* (Nutley, New Jersey: Craig Press, 1970): 335.
103. GARY NORTH, "Isaiah's Critique of Inflation," *The Journal of Christian Reconstruction* 7 (1980): 10−11.
104. DAVID CHILTON, *Productive Christians in an Age of Guilt Manipulation* (Tyler, Texas: Institute for Christian Economics, 1981): 78−9.
105. Cited in Crawford, *Thunder on the Right*: 195.
106. FALWELL, *America Can be Saved*: 141.

107. FALWELL, "Future-Word," in *The Fundamentalist Phenomenon*: 213.
108. These remarks by Reagan and Brezhnev are cited in *Time* (March 21, 1983): 40.
109. FALWELL, "Future-Word," in *The Fundamentalist Phenomenon*: 215.
110. EDWARD KENNEDY, "Tolerance and Truth in America," *Historical Magazine of the Protestant Episcopal Church* 53 (1984): 7–12.
111. Reported in *Christianity Today* (March 1, 1985): 33.

POSTSCRIPT

America's Statue of Liberty celebrated her 100th birthday on the Fourth of July in 1986. All America celebrated. I was not there. Far away from home, I watched some of the festivities on the South African Broadcasting Corporation's state owned and operated television network. Millions of Americans made their pilgrimage to that sacred site of American culture religion to bask in the radiant glow of national pride and patriotism. "We are the keepers of the flame of liberty," declared President Ronald Reagan. Like most Americans, I saw the pageantry of a national faith unfolding. America was one nation under God, indivisible, with liberty and justice for all, with its torch held high for the entire world to see and to be illuminated. American civil religion was alive and well. The birthday of the statue that Ronald Reagan called "everybody's gal" was a special opportunity to reaffirm and renew the bonds that unified all the many Americans within one national identity. This was a uniquely American religious and national event.

The civil religious rituals surrounding the Statue of Liberty represented a collective celebration of patriotism. But it should be noted that this was a patriotism of a very particular kind. It was a patriotism of power. In American history, the patriotism of power has resonated through the commitments to a divine covenant and a sacred destiny that have animated both the self-understanding and territorial expansion of a nation.

In South Africa as well, a patriotism of power has emerged in the religious and political self-understanding of a particular people. Afrikaner civil religion has its sacred history, its saints, its shrines, its rituals, its sacred calendar, and even a civil religious monument to its own language, the only sacred shrine devoted to a language in the world.[1] Most of the people in South Africa, however, speak other languages. The patriotic power generated by this mythic and ritual complex is extremely exclusive. The "whites only" signs that are gradually, grudgingly being removed from restaurants, beaches, trains, and public facilities symbolically are still in place in this South African patriotism of power. And the symbols of the patriotism of power are still mobilized to legitimize white, minority domination of the black majority of South Africa's population. These are symbols of a white, Christian, Afrikaner conquest of a nation.

In this situation, I have been made more aware than I otherwise might have been of a second kind of patriotism: a deep love of country that might be called the patriotism of pain. This is a patriotism often arising in the hearts of the defeated, dispossessed, and disenfranchised, and those identifying with their struggle as they work to articulate their political situation in the medium of religious symbols. The patriotism of pain is a patriotism of the land, but not of the alien architecture that has been constructed on the land. In the geography of the spirit, this is an "existential outsideness" in which people feel displaced even in the land of their birth.[2] The patriotism of power may be sustained by the accumulation of wealth, an ideology of progress, and unrestrained territorial expansion, but the patriotism of pain grows out of a shared sense of unredeemable loss.

The loss of land, the loss of cultural values, and the loss of human dignity, however, may not be entirely unredeemable. Religious redemption, metaphorically signifying an act of "buying back," may mobilize powerful resources for recovery. While the patriotism of power radiates from the military, political, and economic centers of power, the patriotism of pain may mobilize alternative resources on the periphery. As in the biblical narrative of ancient Israel's exodus from captivity in Egypt, religious redemption may be identified with political liberation from forces of oppression.[3] In American history, the Puritans of New England and the revolutionaries of 1776 mobilized precisely such religious symbols for a redemption from what they experienced as religiopolitical forces of persecution, oppression, and tyranny. Others, however, experienced these theocratic and democratic experiments themselves as religious and political systems of oppression, as Native Americans, Black Americans, Immigrant Americans, and all others were forced to negotiate new strategies of accommodation and redemption in relation to the political realities of America. In a preliminary fashion, this book has attempted to outline the basic patterns of power within which those negotiations have been carried out. At stake in those negotiations has been the very definition of what it is to be a human being in American culture.

Ultimately, both religion and politics are about being human and the mutual recognition of human beings in the ceremonies of power. In a recent ceremony of power in South Africa, the enthronement of Desmond Tutu as the first black Anglican Archbishop of Cape Town, the Nobel Laureate expressed a deep love of country and a vision of liberation from dehumanizing oppression which have grown out of what I am calling the patriotism of pain. "We have a wonderful country with truly magnificent people," Tutu observed, "if only we could be allowed to be human together, because we are all dehumanized by injustice and oppression." A religiopolitical system that dehumanizes certain people on the basis of race, ethnicity, gender, poverty, or religion, and excludes those people from the ceremonies of power, dehumanizes everyone within its territorial domain. "A person is a person," Tutu noted, "because he recognizes others as persons."[4] In this sense, those who fail to recognize others as human have failed in their own humanity.

Historically, religion has served the functions of both humanization and dehumanization. Religion has operated through powerful rituals of inclusion to objectify the symbolic terms and conditions for mutual recognition of human beings within a shared political environment. But religion has also provided justifications for exclusion. In America, religious patterns of inclusion and exclusion have been interwoven in the patriotism of power in the three basic, and sometimes overlapping, forms that we have considered: theocratic power, democratic power, and civil religious power. Each of these religiopolitical systems, as we have seen, has generated its distinctive ceremonies of power. These systems have dominated the centers of power in American society by establishing the rituals of inclusion through which certain persons might be recognized and empowered as fully human persons by virtue of their ability to participate fully in the network of social relations each system has engendered. It might be useful to briefly recall the rituals of inclusion into the ceremonies of power within American religiopolitical systems.

As we found it displayed among the Puritans of the Massachusetts Bay Colony, theocratic power was based on a shared commitment to a sacred covenant between God and a people. Religious conversion, mediated through and recognized by the church, was the ritual of inclusion into this system of power. Conversion symbolized inclusion into the covenant community. The church, therefore, stood as the central axis around which the systematic distribution of religiopolitical power revolved. The state, the economy, the entire network of social relations, as the Puritan divine John Cotton insisted, was to be fashioned around the frame of the church. The sacred covenant of the Puritan theocracy, therefore, was not simply based on a particular type of religious faith, but it was established within a very specific institutional arrangement that was at the same time religious and political.

Democratic power was based on the premise of a social contract freely entered into for the protection of certain inalienable, God-given rights, including the rights to life, liberty, and the pursuit of happiness. The primary symbol of this contract, indicating the basis by which one might be included in the ceremonies of power, was enfranchisement. Of course slaves, women, children, and the poor were excluded in the arrangement. The franchise represented a sharing of power by granting the vote originally to adult, property-holding males, and then gradually extending and broadening the franchise. Eventually, the voice of the people was transfigured into the voice of God. The people became the central, symbolic axis from which the systematic distribution of power emanated. As a symbol of sacred proportions in the American cultural imagination, the people came to represent the central symbol of religious and political empowerment in a new religiopolitical order.

Finally, civil religious power was based on a collective commitment to a shared divine destiny. Entry into this sacred destiny operated on at least three levels. First, the ceremonies of power in American civil religion have required a process of acculturation through which Americans, often from different cultural backgrounds, have entered into the same symbols, myths, and rituals of what we have called a common culture religion. Educational institutions have played a primary role in this acculturation process, allowing Americans to remember the same past in order to contemplate a common future. Second, civil religious ceremonies of power have required a commitment to territorial expansion. By embracing a divine, manifest destiny of territorial expansion, the United States conquered a continent and became a global force in international relations. Expansion was supported by that variety of civil religion we have called religious nationalism. And, third, the ceremonies of power in American civil religion have allowed for the accommodation of a certain degree of pluralism, allowing many different religious, social, and economic interests to coexist in America, under an overarching set of shared symbols and values that have assumed the form of a transcendent religion of America. In this sense, America has been regarded as one nation under God, indivisible in spite of the many diverse interests protected under its Constitution. In all three forms of American civil religion, however, the nation-state has been the central axis of religiopolitical power in American society.

The church, the people, the nation-state: These axial centers of American religiopolitical power, defining the conditions of possibility for inclusion, have also generated forces of exclusion. Dissenters, heretics, antinomians, Quakers, witches, Catholics, Jews, blacks, women, the poor, children, immigrants, Southerners, communists, socialists, conscientious objectors, alternative religious movements—all these, and others, have at some time in American history experienced the force of exclusion from full participation in the ceremonies of power. And throughout American history, Native Americans have been violently crushed by the full force of religious and political exclusion from a Christian civilization that defined them as *other*. This dynamic of inclusion and exclusion has represented the central dilemma in American religiopolitical systems. The dilemma persists. While America celebrated the birthday of "everybody's gal," and repeated the liturgy of inclusion inscribed at the Statue of Liberty's base, undocumented workers, illegal aliens, and political refugees at the southern borders of the United States were being denied entry into the ceremonies of power. Another patriotism of pain was in the process of being born.[5]

Most people seeking entry, however, probably do not come to bask in the glow of liberty's flame, but to participate in the American economy as a wage laborer or entrepreneur in a land of economic opportunity. This middle range of inclusion—not in power, but not quite disempowered—has probably been the characteristic experience of most Americans. Religiopolitical systems in America have also been economic systems. Economic power represented by wealth, gain, accumulation, profit, and the systematic utilization of natural resources and human labor, has been an integral force in American religiopolitical systems. This power has been justified, legitimated, and given a sacred aura in terms of two fundamental ethics of economic power: the ethics of custodial power and the ethics of developmental power.

The Puritan, patriarchal ethics of economic power, as John Winthrop expressed it in his sermon on charity, held that God had ordained that there should be rich and poor in the world so that people would have need of each other. The poor need the rich in order that they might develop the virtues of humility, patience, and obedience; the rich need the poor, however, not simply as a source of labor to exploit, but so that they might develop the virtues of magnanimity and charity in relation to those in need. On the one hand, this theocratic ethics of economic power certainly justified inequalities in the distribution of wealth. Wealth and poverty simply appeared to be God's plan for humanity. In another sense, however, theocratic economics enshrined the Puritan ideal of custodial economic power. The rich were divinely appointed custodians of wealth, but they were also entrusted with the responsibility of caring for those less fortunate through acts of charity. God was glorified, Winthrop argued, when His custodians of wealth redistributed some of their riches to the poor. Divorced from its theological basis, this economic ethics of custodial power has persisted throughout American history. Although custodial power has entrenched often vast inequalities in wealth and poverty, and has created networks of economic dependence, there is an important sense in which it has also diffused a religious and political ethics of custodial care and responsibility into American social relations.

The rise of democratic capitalism in America unleashed a developmental power with its inherent ethics of utilitarian individualism. This economic ethics also was invested with a sacred aura in American culture, as individuals were encouraged to utilize their talents, natural resources, and even the labor of others in order to realize their God-given rights to life, liberty, and the pursuit of happiness in the economic sphere. The pursuit of happiness was closely aligned with the pursuit of property. Individual ownership of property, as T.H. Crawford observed in the controversy over Indian lands in the 1830s, lies at the foundation of the entire American social system. Private ownership, free enterprise, and the expanding consumption of goods and services have been justified by an ethics of developmental power that has promised to develop human potential by developing American economic potential. The other side of developmental power, however, is what the political economist C.B. Macpherson has called "extractive power." The power to develop is also the power to extract and exploit natural resources, raw materials, and human labor. Just as the custodial ethics has resulted in vast disparities of wealth, religious justifications for economic privilege, and conditions of dependence, the economic ethics of developmental power has produced its own unexpected consequences in the depletion of natural resources and the exploitation of human labor.

The extractive power of the American economy now operates on a global scale. Americans consume over 50 percent of the world's resources and control vast economic empires that extract raw materials and cheap labor around the world. Custodial and developmental ethics coincide with America's confidence that it is both custodian of the world's wealth and developer of the world's undeveloped countries. The nation that Abraham Lincoln once called an "almost chosen people" has become an almost omnipresent people, not only in the international economic arena, and not only through an international military presence, but also through television, films, music, advertising, news, and information media which give the impression that America extends to every region of the globe and even to the moon and beyond. America has assumed cosmic proportions.

But has American civil religion, as the transcendent religion of America, dedicated to the moral architecture of the Declaration of Independence, Bill of Rights, Constitution, and other foundational documents, also become universal? Obviously, it has not. Certainly, American culture religion and religious nationalism resist exportation because they are grounded in a specific geographical territory and the historical experience of people occupying that territory. Other territories have different, indigenous forms of these types of civil religion.[6] However, the founding principles of the third variety of American civil religion, based on a commitment to equal human rights to life, liberty, and the pursuit of happiness, constituting what we have been calling the transcendent religion of

America, would seem to be ripe for export. Why has this form of American civil religion not received global acceptance?

This form of American civil religion has not found responsive, receptive audiences for at least two reasons. First, American civil religion has been too closely tied to the economics of custodial and developmental power to be attractive to countries—particularly to the so-called "underdeveloped countries"—that have only experienced the dependency and extractive exploitation which have resulted from American economic power.[7] American economic exploitation in Asia, South America, and Africa has often been carried out under the auspices of advancing democracy, promoting American values, or extending the "American way of life" to the rest of the world. These American sentiments, however, are perceived by much of the world with suspicion. They are seen as pious disguises for an American economic, political, and military expansion that is often referred to as neo-imperialism or neo-colonialism. Experiencing only its negative consequences, a large proportion of the world's population mistrusts the civil religious symbols that have justified this expansion.

Second, American civil religion has come up against powerful competing ideologies in the international arena that are based on different distributions of economic power. Varieties of Marxism and Islam have found different ways of unifying the symbolic and economic orders in the modern world. Both Marxism and Islam have supported religiopolitical systems based on what we called in the *Introduction* to this book an "organic model" that fuses religious and political functions within a single, unitary, and all-encompassing social structure. Marxism has functioned as if it were a religious system in the Soviet Union, China, Asia, Latin America, and Africa to lend a sacred aura to the redistribution of wealth.[8] Islam, as well, has represented a total way of life by fusing the religious, political, and economic spheres in the interest of an all-embracing traditional pattern of social justice.[9] Although the rich variety of Marxisms and Islams in the modern world is beyond the scope of this book, it is simply important to acknowledge that these religiopolitical systems present powerful alternatives to American civil religion on an international scale. The future of the American religiopolitical system may depend to a large extent on its ability to respond to and interact with these alternative systems.

Interaction with other religiopolitical systems will certainly be helped by a greater openness to learning about the worldviews of others. But, worldview analysis first requires a recognition of the humanity of other humans. If religion and politics are ultimately about ways of being human, then the challenge is to fashion religious and political relations that affirm the reciprocal recognition of human beings in patterns of power that allow them to be fully human.

NOTES

1. On Afrikaner civil religion, see T. Dunbar Moodie, *The Rise of Afrikanerdom: Power, Apartheid, and the Afrikaner Civil Religion* (Berkeley: University of California Press, 1975); and Leonard Thompson, *The Political Mythology of Apartheid* (New Haven: Yale University Press, 1985).
2. E.C. RELPH, *Place and Placeness* (London: Pion, 1976): 55.
3. See Michael Walzer, *Exodus and Revolution* (New York: Basic Books, 1985).
4. *Cape Times* (September 8, 1986): 6.
5. Perhaps this patriotism of pain already has a history. See Arnoldo DeLeon, *They Called Them Greasers: Anglo-Attitudes Toward Mexicans in Texas, 1820-1900* (Austin: University of Texas Press, 1983).
6. On the religious character of cultural and national identities, see Peter Merkl and Ninian Smart, eds., *Religion and Politics in the Contemporary World* (New York: New York University Press, 1983); on other civil religions, see Robert N. Bellah and Phillip E. Hammond, *Varieties of Civil Religion* (Berkeley: University of California Press, 1980); and Charles S. Liebman and Eliezar Don-Yehiya, *Civil Religion in Israel: Traditional Judaism and Political Culture in the Jewish State* (Berkeley: University of California Press, 1983).
7. See L.S. Stavrianos, *Global Rift* (New York: William Morrow and Co., 1981).
8. On Marxism as a worldview, see John McMurtry, *The Structure of Marx's Worldview* (Princeton: Princeton University Press, 1978); on Marxism as an organic religiopolitical system in the Soviet Union, see Christel Lane, *The Rites of Rulers: Ritual in Industrial Society—The Soviet Case* (Cambridge: Cambridge University Press, 1981); on Marxist Christianity, see José Miguèz Bonino, *Christians and Marxists: The Mutual Challenge to Revolution* (Grand Rapids, MI: Eerdmans, 1976).
9. On Islam and politics, see Hamid Enayet, *Modern Islamic Political Thought* (Austin: University of Texas Press, 1982); John L. Esposito, *Islam and Politics* (Syracuse: Syracuse University Press, 1984). James P. Piscatori, ed., *Islam in the Political Process* (Cambridge: Cambridge University Press, 1983); and Daniel Pipes, *In the Path of God: Islam and Political Power* (New York: Basic Books, 1983).

INDEX

309